A Dynamic Economic Theory of Heterogenous Households

Wei-Bin Zhang

A Dynamic Economic Theory of Heterogenous Households

Complexity of Income and Wealth Distribution

Springer

Wei-Bin Zhang
College of International Management
Ritsumeikan Asia Pacific University
Beppu-shi, Oita, Japan

ISBN 978-981-95-8917-3 ISBN 978-981-95-8918-0 (eBook)
https://doi.org/10.1007/978-981-95-8918-0

This Springer imprint is published by the registered company Springer Nature Singapore Pte Ltd.
The registered company address is: 152 Beach Road, #21-01/04 Gateway East, Singapore 189721, Singapore

Preface and Acknowledgements

> The simplicity of nature is not to be measured by that of our conceptions. Infinitely varied in its effects, nature is simple only in its causes, and its economy consists in producing a great number of phenomena, often very complicated, by means of a small number of general laws.
>
> Pierre-Simon Laplace

The distribution of income and wealth is a central concern in modern economics. A proper study of distributional issues and their dynamics undoubtedly requires a dynamic theory of the economy that incorporates heterogeneous households. However, one might be surprised at how poorly (mainstream) formal economic theory explains the complex dynamics of income and wealth distribution. This book, grounded in the author's general economic theory, uses a comprehensive microeconomic foundations framework to reveal this complexity in a unique way. It analyzes the dynamic interdependencies between economic growth, structural changes in the economy, and the distribution of income and wealth among heterogeneous households (interchangeably referred to in this book as groups, classes, and ethnic groups). Economic growth with heterogeneous households is an important topic, yet it has rarely been systematically studied. Karl Marx's famous two-class theory of economic growth is a simplistic approach to modern economic development, but from this book's perspective, it is theoretically misleading and empirically inapplicable. Contemporary analytical economics has largely ignored the dynamics of economies that include heterogeneous households.

This book offers an original approach that deals with endogenous wealth, knowledge growth, human capital accumulation, economic structure, and the dynamic interdependence between growth and heterogenous households, within a comprehensive economic framework based on microeconomics. This book is part of my economic theory that deals with endogenous population, capital, knowledge, preferences, gender, local and international economies, environmental change, tourism, institutions, economic structures, and exchange value across time and space (). My economic theory is based on modern nonlinear (synergetic, chaos) sciences (Zhang, 1991, 2005a, 2006b, 2023, 2024c). My theoretical work on complexity began with Synergetics, a theory developed by Hermann Haken (2027-2024). I have applied complexity theory and economic theory to explain economic development in America (Zhang, 2003a, 2001b), Japan (Zhang, 1998, 1999b), oversea Chinese societies (Zhang, 2002b, 2003b, 2006b), mainland China (Zhang, 2007a, 2011, 2021c) and to provide insights into ethics (Zhang, 2000, 2010, 2024b). I have tried to use as few concepts and methods as possible to explore the complexity of humans, society, and the environment. There are few compelling laws in socio-economic evolution. It would be very misleading to emphasize only one rule and ignore, downplay, or prejudice the other mechanisms. I have tried to reveal the complexity of wealth, power, and gender under different technologies, geographies, and institutions with mathematical equations and computers. This book presents multiple theoretical models within a unified framework that provide insights into differences in prosperity across households and nations. It summarizes the research results I have conducted on this topic since the late 1990s.

This book focuses on further developing theories of heterogenous households and economic development within a single comprehensive analytical framework with minimal numbers of assumptions. It deals with dynamic interdependence between capital accumulation, human capital accumulation and application, knowledge creation and utilization, economic growth, price structures, preference differences and changes, and gender division of labor and consumption under different market structures. The theory is constructed based on a few concepts within a compact framework. It advances economic dynamics with heterogenous households and growth by integrating various theories of modern economics into a comprehensive analytical framework. It comprises many models, each emphasizing interactions between races and some economic, technological, institutional, structural, or gender variables. Each model can be mathematically integrated with any other model in the book. The book provides a computational simulation procedure so anyone can see the system's dynamics with computers. It constructs a theoretical framework that permits further generalizations and points out alternative directions for exploring the complexity of economic evolution with genders.

I am very grateful to Editor Juno Kawakami and the anonymous referee for valuable comments, constructive suggestions, and effective cooperation. I would like to thank my wife, Gao Xiao, for her support over the years. This book is primarily based on my previous journal publications. I mention these journals when I refer to them, and I am deeply grateful to them. There are some quotes, almost all of which are from https://www.brainyquote.com, with a few exceptions. I am deeply gratitude to the website. I completed this book at Ritsumeikan Asia Pacific University. Over the last 25 years, I truly enjoyed and benefited from Japan's cultural and academic environment, nestled in the mountains near a small seaside tourist city of 100,000 residents and boasting over 1,000 hot springs and many good restaurants, which allowed me the freedom to focus on my research and produce fruitful results.

Beppu, Japan
Spring 2026

Wei-Bin Zhang

Contents

1 Economic Development with Heterogeneous Households 1

2 Growth and Structure with Income and Wealth Distribution 11
2.1 The Growth Model with Income and Wealth Distribution 14
2.2 The Dynamics and Its Properties 18
2.3 Group 1 Improving Human Capital 21
2.4 Group 3 Increasing the Propensity to Consume Agricultural Goods 23
2.5 Group 3's Population Increases 24
2.6 Group 1's Population Increases 25
2.7 Concluding Remarks 25
Appendix: Proving Lemma 2.1 27

3 Growth and Distribution with Endogenous Leisure Time 31
3.1 The Two-Sector Two-Group Model with Leisure Time 33
3.2 The Dynamics and Equilibrium of the Economic System 36
3.3 An Improvement in the Capital Goods Sector's Productivity 40
3.4 An Enhancement in Group 1's Human Capital 41
3.5 An Enhancement in Group 2's Propensity to Save 41
3.6 Concluding Remarks 43
Appendix: Proving Lemma 3.1 43

4 Income and Wealth Distribution with Endogenous Wealth and Human Capital 49
4.1 The Dynamic Model with Endogenous Wealth and Human Capital 51
4.2 The Dynamics and Its Properties 58
4.3 A Rise in the RC's Propensity to Obtain Education 60
4.4 A Rise in the RC's Propensity to Obtain Education 62
4.5 A Rise in the RC's Population 63

4.6 A Rise in the Total Factor Productivity 64
4.7 Concluding Remarks 64
Appendix: Proving Lemma 4.1 66

5 Growth, Trade, and Knowledge with National Research 69
5.1 The Multi-Country Trade Model with Capital and Knowledge 71
5.2 Behavior of Producers 72
5.3 Behavior of Consumers 73
5.4 Knowledge Creation 74
5.5 University Maximizing its Output With the Research Fund 76
5.6 Full Employment and the Demand and Supply Balance 77
5.7 The Economic Dynamics of the Global Economy 77
5.8 The DE'S Knowledge Utilization Efficiency Rises 82
5.9 The DE'S Tax Rate Is Enhanced 83
5.10 The UE'S Tax Rate Is Increased 85
5.11 The DE'S Propensity to Save Is Enhanced 85
5.12 Concluding Remarks 87
Appendix A1: Proving Lemma 5.1 88
Appendix A2: Examining the Dynamic Properties With Identical Preference 90

6 Group-Based Human Capital Externalities and Inequality 97
6.1 The Basic Model With Group-Based Human Capital Externalities and Inequality 98
6.2 The Dynamics and its Properties 103
6.3 Group 1 Strengthening Human Capital Externalities 107
6.4 Group 1's Population Being Increased 107
6.5 Group 1's Decreasing Returns to Scale in Human Capital Accumulation Being Strengthened 108
6.6 The Consumer Goods Sector's Total Factor Productivity Being Augmented 109
6.7 Group 1 Increasing its Propensity to Save 109
6.8 Concluding Remarks 111
Appendix: Proving Lemma 6.1 112

7 How Do the Richest 1% Own 50% of Wealth? 115
7.1 The Neoclassical Growth Model With Heterogeneous Households 116
7.2 Full Employment of Labor and Capital 117
7.3 Capital Goods Sector 117
7.4 Consumer Goods Sector 118
7.5 Consumer Behaviors and Wealth Dynamics 118
7.6 Change in Household Wealth 120
7.7 Dynamics of Human Capital 120
7.8 Demand for and Supply of Consumer Goods 121

7.9 Demand for and Supply of Capital Goods 122
7.10 The Dynamics and its Properties 122
7.11 The Rich Applying Human Capital more Effectively 125
7.12 The Rich's Propensity to Save Being Augmented 126
7.13 The Rich's Propensity to Consume Being Increased 127
7.14 The Rich's Propensity to Enjoy Leisure Being Increased 128
7.15 A Rise in the Total Factor Productivity of the Capital Goods Sector 129
7.16 The Rich's Learning through Consuming Being Strengthened 129
7.17 Concluding Remarks 130
Appendix: Proving Lemma 7.1 131

8 Discrimination, Growth, and Inequality 135
8.1 The Growth Model With Discrimination 137
8.2 The Dynamics and Its Properties 142
8.3 The Discrimination Rate on Wage Income Being Increased 145
8.4 The Discrimination Rate on Wealth Being Increased 146
8.5 The Discrimination Rate on Consumption Being Increased 146
8.6 Strengthened Discrimination Associated With Positive Reaction of the Discriminated 147
8.7 Concluding Remarks 149
Appendix: Proving Lemma 8.1 150

9 Growth and Gender With Time Distribution 155
9.1 The Growth Model with Endogenous Time Distribution 156
9.2 The 3-Group Dynamic Economy 161
9.3 A Rise in Human Capital of the Women in Group 1 164
9.4 A Rise Group 1's Female Propensity to Stay at Home 166
9.5 A Rise in Group 1's Propensity to Save 166
9.6 Concluding Remarks 167
Appendix: Proving Lemma 9.1 168

10 An Economic Growth Model with Endogenous Birth and Mortality Rates 171
10.1 The Multi-Race Growth Model With Endogenous Time 172
10.2 The Dynamics and Its Properties 177
10.3 Human Capital of Race 1's Woman Being Improved 180
10.4 Race 1's Mother Spending More Time on Per Child Fostering 182
10.5 A Rise in the Total Factor Productivity 182
10.6 A Fall in the Propensity to Have Children 183
10.7 Race 1's Income Having Stronger Impact on the Mortality Rate 184

10.8 A Rise in Woman's Propensity to Pursue Leisure Activities ... 185
10.9 The Impact of Race 1's Propensity to Save ... 185
10.10 Concluding Remarks ... 187
Appendix: Proving Lemma 10.1 ... 187

11 Economic Growth with Social Status and Inequality ... 191
11.1 The Basic Model with Social Status and Inequality ... 192
11.2 The Dynamics and Its Properties ... 197
11.3 Group 1's Spirit of Capitalism Rises ... 200
11.4 The Total Productivity of the Capital Goods Sector Rises ... 200
11.5 Group 1's Social Status More Strongly Affecting Its Propensity to Save ... 202
11.6 Group 3's Population Being Increased ... 202
11.7 The Depreciation Rate of Physical Capital Rises ... 203
11.8 Group 3's Human Capital Rises ... 204
11.9 A Rise in the Output Elasticity of Capital of the Capital Goods Sector ... 205
11.10 Concluding Remarks ... 205
Appendix: Proving Lemma 11.1 ... 206

12 Income and Wealth Distribution in a Monetary Growth Model ... 211
12.1 The Monetary Growth Model with Multiple Groups ... 212
12.2 The Equilibrium Structure of the Dynamic Economy ... 217
12.3 A Rise in the Inflation Policy ... 218
12.4 Group 1 Increases the Propensity to Hold Money ... 219
12.5 Group 3's Human Capital Is Enhanced ... 220
12.6 Group 3's Population Enlarged ... 221
12.7 Group 3's Propensity to Save Increases ... 221
12.8 Group 3's Propensity to Use Leisure Time Is Increased ... 222
12.9 The Consumer Good Sector's Total Productivity Is Enhanced ... 223
12.10 Concluding Remarks ... 223
Appendix: Proving Lemma 12.1 ... 224

13 Global Trade and Business Cycles with Endogenous Human Capital ... 229
13.1 The Multi-Country Growth Model with Exogenous Shocks ... 231
13.2 The Dynamics and Its Properties ... 235
13.3 Exogenous Oscillations in the Efficiency of Applying Human Capital by Country 1's Rich Group ... 239
13.4 Fluctuations in Country 1's Total Factor Productivity ... 240
13.5 The Propensity to Save of Country 1's Group1 Periodically Oscillating ... 240
13.6 Fluctuations in the Return to Scale in Human Capital Accumulation ... 242

13.7 Fluctuations in Country 1's Depreciation of Physical Capital 242
13.8 Fluctuations in the Depreciation of Human Capital of Country 1's Group 1 243
13.9 Concluding Remarks 243
Appendix: Proving Lemma 13.1 244

14 Growth and Inequality in an Economy with Perfect and Monopolistic Competition 249
14.1 Modeling Returns to Scale and Growth with Heterogenous Households 251
14.2 The Dynamic Properties of the Model 259
14.3 The Elasticity of Substitution Between Two Varieties Rises 261
14.4 The Fixed Labor Cost of the Middle Goods Firm Is Increased 262
14.5 A Rise in Variety of Middle Goods 262
14.6 The Total Factor Productivity of the Final Goods Sector Is Increased 263
14.7 Group 1's Propensity to Consume Middle Goods Is Enhanced 264
14.8 Group 1's Propensity to Save Is Enhanced 265
14.9 Group 3 Enhances Human Capital 265
14.10 Group 3's Population Is Increased 267
14.11 The Profit Distribution Is Shifted 267
14.12 Concluding Remarks 268
Appendix: Proving Lemma 14.1 269

15 Further Issues 273

References 275

About the Author

Wei-Bin Zhang, Ph.D. (Umeå, Sweden) has been a Professor at APU since 2000. He graduated in 1982 from Beijing University. He got a master's degree and completed the Ph.D. course at the Department of Civil Engineering, Kyoto University, in September 1987. He completed his dissertation on economic growth theory in Sweden by April 1989. Since then, he researched at the Swedish Institute for Futures Studies in Stockholm for 10 years. His main research fields are complexity theory in economics (nonlinear economic dynamics, chaos theory, synergetic economics), ancient Chinese thought, American civilization, and the economic development and modernization of Chinese societies and Japan. He single-authorized 490 academic articles (240 in international peer-reviewed journals), 39 academic books in English by well-known international academic publishing houses.

About the Authors

List of Figures

Fig. 2.1	The motion of the economic system	20
Fig. 2.2	A rise in group 1's propensity to save	22
Fig. 2.3	A rise in group 1's human capital	23
Fig. 2.4	A rise in group 3's propensity to consume agricultural goods	24
Fig. 2.5	A rise in group 3's population	25
Fig. 2.6	A rise in group 1's population	26
Fig. 3.1	The motion of the economic system	37
Fig. 3.2	A unique meaningful solution of Eq. (3.22)	39
Fig. 3.3	An improvement in the capital goods sector's technology	41
Fig. 3.4	An enhancement in group 1's human capital	42
Fig. 3.5	Group 2's propensity to save being enhanced	42
Fig. 4.1	The motion of some variables	61
Fig. 4.2	A rise in the rich class's propensity to receive education	62
Fig. 4.3	A rise in the rich class's propensity to save	63
Fig. 4.4	A rise in the rich class's population	64
Fig. 4.5	A rise in the education sector's total productivity	65
Fig. 5.1	The motion of the system	79
Fig. 5.2	Confirming the uniqueness of equilibrium	81
Fig. 5.3	The DE's knowledge utilization efficiency being enhanced	84
Fig. 5.4	The DE's tax rate being enhanced	84
Fig. 5.5	The UE's tax rate being enhanced	86
Fig. 5.6	The DE's propensity to save being enhanced	86
Fig. 6.1	The motion of the economic system	105
Fig. 6.2	Group 1 strengthens its human capital externalities	105
Fig. 6.3	A rise in group 1's population	106
Fig. 6.4	Group 1's decreasing returns to scale being strengthened	109
Fig. 6.5	The consumer goods sector's total factor productivity being augmented	110
Fig. 6.6	Group 1 increasing its propensity to save	110
Fig. 7.1	The motion of the economic system	124

Fig. 7.2 The rich applying human capital more effectively 126
Fig. 7.3 The rich's propensity to save being augmented 127
Fig. 7.4 The rich's propensity to consume being increased 128
Fig. 7.5 The rich's propensity to enjoy leisure being increased 128
Fig. 7.6 A rise in the total productivity of the capital goods sector 130
Fig. 7.7 The rich's learning through consuming being strengthened 130
Fig. 8.1 The motion of the economic system 144
Fig. 8.2 A rise in the discrimination rate on wage income 146
Fig. 8.3 A rise in the discrimination rate on wealth 147
Fig. 8.4 A rise in the discrimination rate on consumption 147
Fig. 8.5 Strengthened discrimination and positive reaction from the discriminated 148
Fig. 9.1 The existence of a unique equilibrium point 164
Fig. 9.2 The motion of the system 165
Fig. 9.3 The dynamic effects of a rise in human capital of group 1's wife 166
Fig. 9.4 The dynamic effects of a rise in the wife's propensity to use leisure 167
Fig. 9.5 The dynamic effects of a rise in group 1's propensity to save . . 168
Fig. 10.1 The motion of the economic system 180
Fig. 10.2 Human capital of race 1's woman being improved 181
Fig. 10.3 Race 1's mother spending more time on per child fostering . . . 182
Fig. 10.4 A rise in the total productivity 183
Fig. 10.5 A fall in race 1's propensity to have children 184
Fig. 10.6 Race 1's disposable income having stronger impact on the mortality rate 185
Fig. 10.7 A rise in woman's propensity to pursue leisure activities 186
Fig. 10.8 The impact of race 1's propensity to save 187
Fig. 11.1 The motion of the economic system 199
Fig. 11.2 Group 1's spirit of capitalism rises 201
Fig. 11.3 The total productivity of the capital goods sector being enhanced 201
Fig. 11.4 Group 1's social status more strongly affecting its propensity to save 202
Fig. 11.5 Group 3's population being increased 203
Fig. 11.6 The depreciation rate of physical capital rises 204
Fig. 11.7 Group 3's human capital rises 205
Fig. 11.8 A rise in the output elasticity of capital of the capital goods sector 206
Fig. 13.1 Global and national wealth distributions over time 238
Fig. 13.2 The motion of the economic system 238
Fig. 13.3 Fluctuations in the efficiency of applying human capital by country 1's rich group 240
Fig. 13.4 Fluctuations in country 1's total factor productivity 241

Fig. 13.5 The propensity to save of country 1's group1 periodically oscillating ... 241
Fig. 13.6 Fluctuations in the return to scale in human capital accumulation ... 242
Fig. 13.7 Fluctuations in country 1's depreciation of physical capital ... 243
Fig. 13.8 Fluctuations in country 1's depreciation of human capital ... 244
Fig. 14.1 The motion of the economic system ... 260
Fig. 14.2 The elasticity of substitution between two varieties rises ... 261
Fig. 14.3 Fixed labor cost of the middle goods firm is increased ... 262
Fig. 14.4 A rise in variety of middle goods ... 263
Fig. 14.5 The total productivity of the final goods sector rises ... 264
Fig. 14.6 Group 1's propensity to consume middle goods falls ... 265
Fig. 14.7 Group 1's propensity to save is enhanced ... 266
Fig. 14.8 Group 3 enhances human capital ... 266
Fig. 14.9 Group 3's population is increased ... 267
Fig. 14.10 The profit distribution is shifted ... 268

Chapter 1
Economic Development with Heterogeneous Households

> A model is a good model if first it interprets a wide range of observations in terms of a simple and elegant model, and second if the model makes definite predictions that can be tested, and possibly falsified, by observation.
>
> Stephen Hawking

The economic, political, social, cultural, historical, and behavioral differences between heterogeneous groups have been widely discussed, but few adequate mathematical models exist to explain them. This book aims to systematically explore the issue of economic growth across—for instance, racial and ethnic—groups within a unified analytical framework, based on minimal assumptions. I integrate various economic theoretical approaches into a single analytical framework. This theoretical construction process began in the early 1990s. In *The General Economic Theory* (Zhang, 2020b), I integrate economic theory into a comprehensive framework. This book is part of my broader approach to unraveling economic complexity. It explores the complexity of multi-group economic growth. The book contains different mathematical models. Each model explores some of the issues related to economic growth with heterogeneous households. Each model can be integrated with any model(s) in this book. An economy's population is divided into groups based on preferences, human capital, occupation, ethnic origin, social status, and so on. These models are applicable to economies with any number of groups. For illustration of their dynamic behavior, the models are simulated by computer. Most of these simulations are made for the economies with three groups. The book contains 15 chapters.

Chapter 2 builds an economic growth model with economic structure and heterogeneous households. The model determines land distribution and value. The model is based on three core theories in economics—Walrasian general equilibrium theory, Ricardian theory of distribution, and neoclassical growth theory. The Walrasian general equilibrium theory of pure exchange and production economies has played an important role in the development of contemporary general equilibrium theory. The general equilibrium theory is essential for understanding economic mechanisms of

W. Zhang, *A Dynamic Economic Theory of Heterogenous Households*,
https://doi.org/10.1007/978-981-95-8918-0_1

production, consumption, and exchanges with heterogeneous industries and households. Nevertheless, this theory has not been further developed to explain modern economic phenomena. For instance, endogenous wealth has not been successfully introduced into the general equilibrium theory. Ricardo dealt with income distribution. He tried to explain how a shift in this distribution could affect accumulation. His *On the Principles of Political Economy and Taxation* of 1817 made a very valuable contribution to economics. Ricardo considered three different production factors: labor, capital, and land. He provided a theory to determine the functional income shares of labor share, the capital, and the land rent in the total income. Neither the Walrasian theory nor the Ricardian theory provides a profound microeconomic mechanism of wealth accumulation. The neoclassical growth theory explicitly deals with endogenous wealth accumulation with microeconomic foundation. This chapter synthesizes the neoclassical growth theory, the Walrasian general equilibrium theory, and the Ricardian theory of distribution into a single compact analytical framework. The rest of the chapter is structured as follows. Section 2.1 shows the growth model of income and wealth distribution with heterogeneous households. Section 2.2 studies the dynamics and the properties of the economic system. Section 2.3 shows how a rise in group 1's propensity to save affects the motion of the economic system. Section 2.4 studies how a rise in group 1's human capital impacts the dynamics of economic structure and income and wealth distribution between heterogeneous households. Section 2.5 examines the effects of a rise in group 3's propensity to consume agricultural goods on the economic system. Section 2.6 shows the effects of a rise in group 3's population on the system. Section 2.7 analyzes the effects of a rise in group 1's population on the economic system. Section 2.8 concludes the chapter. The appendix proves Lemma 2.1.

Chapter 3 examines the dynamic interdependence between economic growth and economic structural change with endogenous time distribution and durable consumer goods. It is well known that the traditional neoclassical growth theory has not adequately modeled economic structural change with heterogeneous capital on the basis of microeconomic foundation. This chapter builds a two-sector two-group growth model to examine dynamics of wealth and income distribution with capital accumulation as the main engine of economic growth. The approach is influenced by the neoclassical growth theory as well as by the post-Keynesian theory of growth and distribution. The chapter is organized as follows. Section 3.1 develops the two-sector two-group model with endogenous wealth accumulation and time distribution between work and leisure. Section 3.2 shows the dynamics and equilibrium of the economic system. Section 3.3 examines how an improvement in the capital goods sector's productivity affects the motion of the economic system. Section 3.4 analyzes the impact of a rise in group 1's human capital on the economic system. Section 3.5 shows how an enhancement in group 2's propensity to save affects the wealth distribution and time distribution. Section 3.6 concludes the chapter. The appendix proves Lemma 3.1.

Chapter 4 is concerned with a dynamic interdependence between economic growth and human capital. The literature on endogenous knowledge and economic growth has increasingly expanded in recent decades. Nevertheless, in the Uzawa-Lucas model and many of their extensions and generalizations, it implicitly assumes that all skills and human capital are formed due to formal schooling. Nevertheless, much of human capital may be accumulated in family and many other social and economic activities. This chapter introduces other sources of learning into the Uzawa-Lucas two-sector growth model. Different households have different propensities to save and to receive education and have different abilities in absorbing knowledge and increasing human capital through education, learning by doing, and learning by consuming. Most extensions and generalizations of the Uzawa-Lucas model are limited to a single representative household. Heterogeneous households make investments in schooling quantity and quality. The main deviation of my approach from the previous models is that I derive demand for education in an alternative approach to the typical Ramsey approach. The model is built on the three main growth models—Solow's one-sector growth model, Arrow's learning by doing model, and Uzawa-Lucas's growth model with education—in the growth literature. The chapter is organized as follows. Section 4.1 constructs the dynamic model with endogenous wealth and human capital. Section 4.2 shows the dynamics of the economic system and its properties. Section 4.3 studies how a rise in the RC's propensity to obtain education affects the motion of the economic system. Section 4.4 studies the impact of a rise in the RC's propensity to save on the income and wealth distribution between the groups of the population. Section 4.5 analyzes the effects of a rise in the RC's population on the system. Section 4.6 follows the changes in the path of the system as the total factor productivity rises. Section 4.7 concludes the chapter. The appendix proves Lemma 4.1

Chapter 5 studies the effects of trade upon income distribution among nations in a globalizing world economy. Many studies demonstrate that productivity differences explain much of the variation in incomes across countries, and technology plays a key role in determining productivity. The purpose of this chapter is to study inequalities among nations with endogenous wealth accumulation and knowledge dynamics. This chapter deals with the effects of free trade and national governments' research policies on global growth and inequalities among nations. This chapter follows the neoclassical growth trade model, particularly the Oniki-Uzawa model. It is organized as follows. Section 5.1 defines the multi-country model with capital accumulation and knowledge creation. Section 5.2 shows that the dynamics of the world economy with J countries can be described by $(J + 1)$ differential equations. Section 5.3 shows how the economic system is affected when the DE's knowledge utilization efficiency rises. Section 5.4 shows the effects of a rise in the DE's tax rate on the motion of the economic system. Section 5.5 analyzes what happens in the system where the UE's tax rate is increased. Section 5.6 analyzes the impact of a rise in the DE's propensity to save. Section 5.7 concludes the chapter. The analytical results in Sect. 5.2 are confirmed in Appendix A1. Appendix A2 examines the case when all the countries have the same preference.

Chapter 6 is concerned with relationships between growth and groups. For instance, there are great differences in living conditions and income among different ethnic groups in the USA. Irrespective of numerous publications on growth and ethnics based on empirical research, there are only a few theoretical growth models which formally deal with interactions of ethnic human capital externalities, income, and wealth distribution among groups and economic growth in a comprehensive framework. The chapter is to introduce group-based human capital externalities into an integrated Walrasian general equilibrium and neoclassical growth theory. The economy consists of any number of groups. The production side is neoclassical. The way that human capital externalities are introduced is influenced by how production externalities are introduced in the literature of economic growth and spatial agglomeration. The chapter is organized as follows. Section 6.1 proposes the basic model with group-based human capital externalities and inequality. Section 6.2 shows the dynamics and their properties. Section 6.3 shows how the system reacts to a rise in group 1's human capital externalities. Section 6.4 shows the effects of a rise in group 1's population on the economic system. Section 6.5 studies the impact of a rise in group 1's decreasing returns to scale in human capital accumulation. Section 6.6 shows how the system reacts to a rise in the consumer goods sector's total productivity. Section 6.7 studies how a rise in group 1's propensity to save affects the system. Section 6.8 concludes the chapter. The appendix confirms Lemma 6.1.

Chapter 7 shows a theoretical possibility for the fact that the richest 1% of the world's population owns almost half of the world's wealth. It does seem that inequality be enlarged in the near future in tandem with rapid economic globalization. There is a need-to-know determinants of inequality and dynamics of inequality. Surprisingly, theoretical economics still has little to say about determinants and dynamics of economic growth and inequality. The mainstream of modern theoretical economics has failed in providing a proper analytical framework to analyze relations between growth and inequality. Without a proper analytical framework, economics can hardly analyze the complicated dynamic issues with nonlinear interactions among many variables over time. The chapter is especially interested in the phenomenon of contemporary free-market economies where the richest 1% of the population own more than half of wealth. By comparative dynamic analysis it is demonstrated that inequalities will not be shrunk but will be enlarged in free-market economies with rapid technological changes and connected markets. In order to analyze these issues, this chapter introduces endogenous human capital and human capital externalities into the general equilibrium theory with heterogeneous households and endogenous wealth. This chapter is organized as follows. Section 7.1 develops the neoclassical growth model with heterogeneous households. Section 7.2 examines the dynamics of the economic system and its properties. Section 7.3 illustrates what happens to the economic system when the rich apply human capital more effectively. Section 7.4 shows the effects of a rise in the rich's propensity to save. Section 7.5 shows the impact of an increase in the rich's propensity to consume. Section 7.6 studies the change in the path of economic development when the rich's propensity to enjoy leisure rises. Section 7.7 shows how the inequality of income and wealth is affected when the total productivity of the capital goods sector rises. Section 7.8 analyzes the effects of a rise in the rich's learning through consumption. Section 7.9 concludes the chapter. The appendix proves Lemma 7.1.

Chapter 8 studies the dynamic interdependence between growth, distribution, and discrimination. Discrimination is conducted against different people in different forms over human history in different parts of the world. For instance, discrimination in the form of slavery had a long history in the United States. After the end of slavery, discrimination under the embracement of US legal system was continued for a long time in the form of stated-sponsored racial segregation in schools, transportation, and public accommodations. In modern times racial and gender discrimination is still conducted in different parts of the world. Arrow (1998) states the significance of economic study on discrimination as follows: "Racial discrimination pervades every aspect of a society in which it is found. It is found above all in attitudes of both groups, but also in social relations, in intermarriage, in residential location, and, frequently, in legal barriers. It is also found in levels of economic accomplishment; that is, income, wages, prices paid, and credit extended. This economic dimension hardly appears in general treatments of economics, outside of the specialized literature devoted to it." Although there are some studies about discrimination in economics, it is argued that there are only a few formal economic models which explicitly deal with economic growth and distribution in income and wealth with discrimination. This chapter focuses on the role of discrimination in interdependence between growth and dynamics of inequality in income and wealth. This chapter is organized as follows. Section 8.1 introduces the basic model with wealth and income distribution with discrimination. Section 8.2 examines the dynamic properties of the model and simulates the model with three groups. Section 8.3 shows how the system changes its development path when there is a rise in the discrimination rate on wage income. Section 8.4 follows the changes in a rise in the discrimination rate on wealth. Section 8.5 studies how a rise in the discrimination rate on consumption affects the system. Section 8.6 examines the effects of a rise in discrimination associated with positive reactions of the discriminated against on economic growth and the distribution. Section 8.7 concludes the chapter. The appendix proves Lemma 8. 1.

Chapter 9 models the gender division of labor in a framework of growth with heterogeneous households. There are many empirical studies on issues related to labor market and economic development with gender. On the demand side, firms have become more willing to hire women due to factors such as the rise of service sectors, anti-discrimination policy measures, the increase of higher education among women, and the development of new technologies (which allow firms to substitute male for female workers). On the supply side, for instance, women tend to work more in labor markets as a consequence of lower fertility rates, the availability of new household technologies, and the emergence of flexible-time work. It is significant to study how time distribution and economic growth interact with each other. This chapter is organized as follows. Section 9.1 defines the one-sector growth model with gender, leisure time, and heterogeneous groups. Section 9.2 analyzes the dynamic behavior of the three-group model. Section 9.3 shows how a rise in human capital of the women in group 1 affects the motion of the economic system. Section 9.4 follows what happens in the economic system when there is a rise group 1's female propensity to stay at home. Section 9.5 studies the impact of a rise in group 1's propensity to save on the time distribution and economic growth. Section 9.6 concludes the chapter. The appendix confirms Lemma 9.1.

Chapter 10 considers an economic dynamics with co-existence of multiple races. Different races have different habits, customs, and attitudes to family and having children. Even if a society was fair and there was no racial discrimination, it is reasonable to consider that the cultural differences may result in differences in wealth, income, and population. In order to explain consequences of racial differences in values and human capital, this chapter deals with dynamic interdependence between different races' birth rates, mortality rates, populations, wealth accumulation, and time distributions between work, leisure, and children caring. It emphasizes the role of human capital, technological and preference changes on the birth and mortality rates and time distributions. The basic economic structure is based on the Walrasian general equilibrium theory, and wealth accumulation is based on the Solow growth model. The wealth and income inequality are due to heterogeneity in households' preferences and human capital levels as well as the households' initial wealth. I also model gender differences in human capital, the propensity to use leisure time, and children caring efficiency. This chapter is organized as follows. Section 10.1 introduces the basic model with wealth accumulation and population dynamics. Section 10.2 examines the dynamics of the system and its properties. Section 10.3 shows how the system reacts to a rise in the human capital of race 1's women. Section 10.4 shows the effects of a rise in race 1's mother spending time on per child fostering. Section 10.5 shows how a rise in the total factor productivity changes the dynamics of income and wealth distribution between the races. Section 10.6 shows how a fall in the propensity to have children shifts the path of economic development. Section 10.7 analyzes what happens in the system when race 1's income has a stronger impact on the mortality rate. Section 10.8 examines the impact of a rise in woman's propensity to pursue leisure activities on the economic system. Section 10.9 studies the impact of a rise in race 1's propensity to save. Section 10.10 concludes the chapter. The appendix proves Lemma 10.1.

Chapter 11 is concerned with the economic consequences of conspicuous consumption and social status. According to Veblen, people are interested in pursuing conspicuous consumption as it signals wealth and social status. Duesenberry held that people may try to improve social status by imitating the consumption standard of the social or classes above them. The purpose of this study is to introduce social status into a growth economic theory with heterogeneous households. It is argued that people are concerned with social status because it serves as a signal of non-observable abilities. Introduction of social status makes traditional growth models more robust in explaining economic growth processes. This study is concerned with social status and growth with inequalities in income and wealth. The way that social status is integrated into the growth model is influenced by the literature that studies the macroeconomic effects of consumers' wealth-induced preferences for social status. In this literature social status is considered as functions of private wealth within neoclassical growth models. This chapter deals with social status within an integrated framework of the Walrasian general equilibrium and neoclassical growth theories. This chapter is organized as follows. Section 11.1 develops the growth model of wealth and income distribution among heterogeneous households with endogenous social status. Section 11.2 examines dynamic properties of the model and simulates the model with three groups. Section 11.3 analyzes how the system reacts to a rise in group 1's spirit of capitalism. Section 11.4 shows the effects of a rise in the total productivity of the capital goods sector on the income and wealth distribution. Section 11.5 demonstrates what happens in the economic dynamics when group 1's social status more strongly affects its propensity to save. Section 11.6 follows the shifts in the motion of the economic system when group 3's population rises. Section 11.7 analyzes the impact of a rise in the depreciation rate of physical capital. Section 11.8 shows the changes in social status and inequality when group 3's human capital rises. Section 11.9 shows what happens to the system when there is a rise in the output elasticity of capital of the capital goods sector. Section 11.10 concludes the chapter. The appendix proving Lemma 11.1.

Chapter 12 studies the relationship between money and economic growth. From empirical as well as theoretical literatures on money and growth, it is known that the relationships are ambiguous in the sense that they can be positive, independent, negative, or situation-dependent, depending on countries or periods within the same country or analytical frameworks. This chapter readdresses issues related to the interdependence between economic growth and money. But different from the most formal models in the literature of money and growth, I study the relationship between money and distribution between heterogeneous households. If money is not neutral, inflation policy affects economic growth. As households have various preferences for consumption and saving and varied levels of human capital, it is reasonable to expect that inflation policy should have different effects on income and wealth distribution between heterogeneous households. This chapter is an integration of the core ideas in Walrasian general equilibrium theory, neoclassical growth theory, and monetary growth theory. This chapter is organized as follows. Section 12.1 develops the monetary growth model with endogenous wealth and capital with income and wealth distribution between heterogeneous households. Section 12.2 analyzes properties of the model and identifies the existence of an equilibrium point. Section 12.3 shows the impact of a rise in the inflation policy on the economic equilibrium structure. Section 12.4 shows how a rise in household 1's propensity to hold money changes the economic equilibrium. Section 12.5 analyzes the impact of a rise in household 3's human capital. Section 12.6 shows how a rise in group 3's population changes each group's economic conditions in the long term. Section 12.7 studies the effects of a rise household 3's propensity to save. Section 12.8 analyzes the long-run economic structural change when household 3's propensity to use leisure time is increased. Section 12.9 analyzes the impact of a rise in the consumer good sector's total factor productivity. Section 12.10 concludes the chapter. The appendix proves Lemma 12.1.

Chapter 13 deals with business cycles in a multi-country growth model with endogenous wealth and human capital accumulation. There are different ideas and theories to explain well-observed business cycles and economic oscillations. The two contemporary theories of business cycles are the Keynesian economics and the real business-cycle theory. The Keynesian economic business-cycle theory considers demand changes as the main sources of business cycles. The real business-cycle theory explains business-cycle fluctuations by real shocks. The purpose of this chapter is to demonstrate the existence of business cycles in the dynamic growth model of heterogeneous households. It shows how fluctuations in one country cause business cycles not only in the national economy but also in all the countries in the global economy with free trade. This chapter is organized as follows. Section 13.1 defines the neoclassical growth model of a multi-country economy with capital accumulation and human capital accumulation. Section 13.2 shows that the dynamics of the economy can be described by a set of dimensional differential equations. Section 13.3 studies how exogenous oscillations in the efficiency of applying human capital by country 1's rich group affect the global economic structure and income and wealth distribution. Section 13.4 shows the processes that fluctuations in country 1's total factor productivity affect the dynamic system. Section 13.5 shows the effects that the propensity to save of country 1's group 1 periodically oscillates. Section 13.6 follows the changes in the system when the return to scale in human capital accumulation of country 1's group 1 periodically oscillates. Section 13.7 analyzes the impact on the dynamics when there are exogenous fluctuations in country 1's depreciation of physical capital. Section 13.8 plots what happens in the system when there are fluctuations in the depreciation of human capital of country 1's group 1. Section 13.9 concludes the chapter. The appendix proves Lemma 13.1.

Chapter 14 is concerned with economic growth and income and wealth distribution in an economy characterized by co-existence of markets with perfect competition and monopoly. In modern growth theory, there are two main approaches with (proper) microeconomic foundations. Traditional neoclassical growth theory is mostly concerned with capital accumulation with economic structure but a homogeneous population (which implies no insight into income and wealth distribution among households). New dynamic economic theory is mainly concerned with perfect and monopolistic competition and knowledge creation and utilization without a proper mechanism for dealing with wealth accumulation. The two approaches failed to deal with economic growth with heterogeneous households. The unique contribution to the literature of economic growth of this chapter is integrating the basic economic mechanisms in the Walrasian general equilibrium model, the Solow one-sector growth model, and the Dixit-Stiglitz model. This chapter is organized as follows. Section 14.1 constructs the growth model of heterogeneous households under perfect competition and monopolistic competition. Section 14.2 analyzes the properties of the economy and simulates the economic system. Section 14.3 shows how the economic system reacts to a rise in the elasticity of substitution between two varieties. Section 14.4 shows the effects of a rise in the fixed labor cost of the middle goods firm on the income and wealth distribution and economic growth. Section 14.5 follows the dynamics of the changes caused by a rise in the variety of middle goods. Section 14.6 studies the impact of a rise in the total productivity of the final goods sector on the motion of the economic system. Section 14.7 studies how the income and wealth distribution and national growth are affected owing to a rise group 1's propensity to consume middle goods. Section 14.8 follows the changes caused by a rise group 1's propensity to save. Section 14.9 studies how the system is affected then there is a rise in group 3's human capital. Section 14.10 examines the effects of a rise in group 3's population. Section 14.11 shows how a shift in the profit distribution affects the growth, income, and wealth distribution. Section 14.12 concludes the chapter. The appendix proves Lemma 14.1. Chapter 15 discusses some further issues about the topics examined in this book.

Chapter 2
Growth and Structure with Income and Wealth Distribution

> To be a poor man is hard, but to be a poor race in a land of dollars is the very bottom of hardships.
>
> W. E. B. Du Bois (1868–1963)

Various economic theories have been proposed to study economic phenomena in different economic systems. Traditionally, a distinction is made between micro (behavior of households and enterprises) and macro (national or globally aggregated models). There are also intermediate stages, such as the interaction of the agricultural and industrial sectors. To study dynamic phenomena, economic structures must be explicitly considered. It is important to develop economic theories based on microeconomic mechanisms. Such theories must treat micro, intermediate, and macro variables as an interdependent whole. In this chapter, I build an economic growth model that includes an economic structure and heterogeneous households. The model determines the distribution and value of land. The model is based on three core theories of economics: Walrasian general equilibrium theory, Ricardian distribution theory, and neoclassical growth theory.

Walras's general equilibrium theory in pure exchange and pure production economies has played an important role in the development of modern general equilibrium theory. This general equilibrium theory was first proposed by Walras (1874). This theory was further formalized and developed by Arrow (Arrow and Debreu 1954; Arrow and Hahn 1971; Arrow 1974, and Debreu) and others (Gale 1955; Nikaido 1956, 1968; Debreu 1959; McKenzie 1959; Mas-Colell et al. 1995). General equilibrium theory is essential to understand economic mechanisms such as production, consumption, and exchange with heterogeneous industries and households. However, this theory has not been further developed to explain modern economic phenomena. For example, endogenous wealth has not been fully introduced into general equilibrium theory. Walras introduced savings and capital accumulation into general equilibrium theory. However, his treatment of capital accumulation is not adequate, especially in light of modern neoclassical growth models (Impicciatore

W. Zhang, *A Dynamic Economic Theory of Heterogenous Households*,
https://doi.org/10.1007/978-981-95-8918-0_2

et al. 2012). Over the years, many attempts have been made to further develop Walrasian capital accumulation within the Walrasian framework (Morishima 1964, 1977; Diewert 1977; Eatwell 1987; Dana et al. 1989; Montesano 2008). These approaches have not been successful because they are not based on a proper microeconomic foundation of wealth accumulation. Recently, Impicciatore et al. (2012) proposed a model in which consumers save capital goods and provide services to the productive sector in the next period. Capital goods that disappear in a period are assumed to be fully depreciated at the end of that period. This work does not adequately explain household saving behavior. This chapter uses Zhang's alternative approach to model household behavior with wealth accumulation (Zhang 2014f, 2014g, 2015d, 2017b). The model further develops traditional Walrasian general equilibrium theory by considering wealth accumulation and heterogeneous households.

The Walrasian general equilibrium theory determines economic equilibrium. But it fails to address important issues about interdependence between economic growth, structural change, and wealth and income distribution. Ricardo dealt with income distribution. He tried to explain how a shift in this distribution could affect accumulation. His On the Principles of Political Economy and Taxation of 1817 made a very valuable contribution to economics. Applying the law of diminishing returns in agriculture, Ricardo made an important development of the theory of rent. Ricardo's study shows how that wages, interest rates, and rent can be determined within a compact theory. Ricardo considered three different production factors: labor, capital, and land. He provided a theory to determine the functional income shares of labor share, the capital, and the land rent in the total income. Ricardo (1821: preface) stated: "The produce … is divided among three classes of the commodity, namely, the proprietor of land, the owners of the stock or capital necessary for its cultivation, and laborers by whose industry it is cultivated. But in different stages of the society, the proportions of the whole produce of the earth which will be allotted to each of these classes, under the names of rent, profits, and wages, will be essentially different; depending mainly on the actual fertility of the soil, on the accumulation of capital and population, and on the skill, ingenuity, and the instruments in agriculture." Since the publication of the Principles, many efforts have been made to generalize and extend the system. The beginning of modeling the Ricardian system perhaps dates back to 1833 with the model of Whewell (Barkai 1959, 1966). Economists extended and generalized Ricardo's system in different ways (Cochrane 1970; Caravale and Tosato 1980; Marglin 1984; Negish 1989; Morishima 1989). For instance, Samuelson (1959) studied Ricardo-like models to reveal validity and limitations of the Ricardian propositions in a wider setting than that assumed by Ricardo; Brems (1970) considered fixed capital in the Ricardian problem of machinery; Pasinetti (1960, 1974) dealt with the validity of what Ricardo meant by making the necessary assumptions for Ricardian conclusions; Casarosa (1985) reformed the Pasinetti model to give a new interpretation of Ricardo with respect to the role of the market wages. What Ricardo (1821: preface) observed long time ago is still proper to state the contemporary situation: "To determine the laws which regulate this distribution, is the principal problem in Political Economy: much as the science has been improved by the writings of Turgot, Stuart, Smith, Say, Sismondi, and others, they afford very little satisfactory information respecting the natural course of rent, profit, and wages." This chapter will make a further contribution to literature on the laws of wealth and income distribution with capital accumulation and land value in a general equilibrium framework.

Neither the Walrasian theory nor the Ricardian theory provides a profound microeconomic mechanism of wealth accumulation. The neoclassical growth theory explicitly deals with endogenous wealth accumulation with microeconomic foundation. The representative model is the Ramsey model. This chapter applies an alternative approach to households by Zhang to examine dynamic interdependence between growth, wealth, and income distribution, and economic structures. It synthesizes the neoclassical growth theory, the Walrasian general equilibrium theory, and the Ricardian theory of distribution into a single compact analytical framework. Although there are some studies on integrating the neoclassical growth theory with the general equilibrium analysis (Jensen and Larsen 2005), Shoven and Whalley (1992:1) observed: "Most contemporary applied general models are numerical analogs of traditional two-sector general equilibrium models popularized by James Meade, Harry Johnson, Arnold Harberger, and others in the 1950s and 1960s." Only a few formal models have been developed to explicitly deal with distribution issues in the neoclassical growth theory (Solow 1956; Kurz 1968; Burmeister and Dobell 1970; Wang and Yip 1992; Barro and Sala-i-Martin 1995; Zhang 2015e). It is a well-known difficult problem to study economic growth, wealth, and income distribution. As mentioned before, the Arrow-Debreu general economic theory studies economic equilibrium problems in economies of heterogeneous households and firms. It is desirable to integrate the economic mechanisms of the three core theories in economics into an integrated analytical framework. This chapter synthesizes the ideas in the three-sector model with economic structure and land by Zhang (1996a) and the growth model of heterogeneous groups by Zhang (2013a). In Zhang's 1996 paper, the population is homogeneous, while in Zhang's 2013 paper, neither land nor housing are considered. This chapter is based on Zhang (2017c). The rest of the chapter is structured as follows. Section 2.1 shows the growth model of income and wealth distribution with heterogeneous households. Section 2.2 studies the dynamics and the properties of the economic system. Section 2.3 shows how a rise in group 1's propensity to save affects the motion of the economic system. Section 2.4 studies how a rise in group 1's human capital impacts the dynamics of economic structure and income and wealth distribution between heterogeneous households. Section 2.5 examines the effects of a rise in group 3's propensity to consume agricultural goods on the economic system. Section 2.6 shows the effects of a rise in group 3's population on the system. Section 2.7 analyzes the effects of a rise in group 1's population on the economic system. Section 2.8 concludes the chapter. The appendix proves Lemma 2.1.

2.1 The Growth Model with Income and Wealth Distribution

This chapter deals with an economy with three—agricultural, capital goods, and consumer goods—sectors. The agricultural sector supplies goods, such as vegetables, rice, and corn, for consumption. I follow the Uzawa two-sector model in describing the capital goods and consumer goods sectors (Uzawa 1961). Services are treated as consumer goods. This chapter applies the neoclassical growth theory to describe the production sectors (Zhang 1990, 1996b; Azariadis 1993). Capital goods are employed as input factors in the three sectors. Capital is assumed to depreciate at a fixed rate δ_k, which is not related to the manner of use. The assets of the economy are owned by households. They use their incomes to consume and save. All the markets are assumed to be perfectly competitive. Factors are inelastically supplied. All factors are assumed to be fully utilized at every moment. Savings are not undertaken by firms.

The population is classified into multiple groups. Each group has a fixed population, $\overline{N}_j$, $(j = 1, \cdots, J)$. In the Walrasian general equilibrium theory, $\overline{N}_j = 1$. The prices are measured in terms of capital goods. Let the wage rate of worker of type j and rate of interest be denoted by $w_j(t)$ and $r(t)$, respectively. Capital goods are selected to serve as numeriare. Let $p_a(t)$ and $p_s(t)$ denote respectively the prices of agricultural commodity and consumer goods at time t. As all the markets are perfectly competitive and the land, capital, and labor force, are fully employed, the wage rate, $w_j(t)$, land rent $R(t)$, and $r(t)$, are identical in the economy. I denote the fixed land by L. The total capital stock $K(t)$ is allocated among the three sectors. Subscript index a, i, and s represent the agricultural sector, the capital good sector, and the consumer goods sector, respectively. Let $N_m(t)$ and $K_m(t)$ stand for the labor force and capital stocks employed by sector m. The total population $\overline{N}$ and total qualified labor supply N are

$$\overline{N} = \sum_{j=1}^{J} \overline{N}_j, N = \sum_{j=1}^{J} h_j \overline{N}_j, \tag{2.1}$$

in which h_j is the human capital of group j. The assumption of labor force being fully employed implies

$$N_a(t) + N_i(t) + N_s(t) = N. \tag{2.2}$$

I introduce

$$k_m(t) \equiv \frac{K_m(t)}{N_m(t)}, k(t) \equiv \frac{K(t)}{N(t)}, m = a, i, s.$$

Agricultural sector

There are three input factors, land, labor force, and capital, in the agricultural production. I use $L_a(t)$ to denote the land used by the agricultural sector. Let $F_m(t)$ stand for the production function of sector m, $m = a, i, s$. The agricultural sector's production function is specified as follows:

$$F_a(t) = A_a K_a^{\alpha_a}(t) N_a^{\beta_a}(t) L_a^{\varsigma}(t), \alpha_a, \beta_a, \varsigma > 0, \alpha_a + \beta_a + \varsigma = 1, \tag{2.3}$$

where A_a, α_a ,β_a, and ζ_a are parameters. The marginal conditions imply

$$r(t) + \delta_k = \frac{\alpha_a p_a(t) F_a(t)}{K_a(t)}, w(t) = \frac{\beta_a p_a(t) F_a(t)}{N_a(t)},$$
$$R(t) = \frac{\varsigma p_a(t) F_a(t)}{L_a(t)}. \tag{2.4}$$

Capital goods sector

The production function of the industrial sector is specified as follows:

$$F_i(t) = A_i K_i^{\alpha_i}(t) N_i^{\beta_i}(t), \alpha_i, \beta_i > 0, \alpha_i + \beta_i = 1, \tag{2.5}$$

where A_i, α_i, and β_i are positive parameters. The capital goods sector employs two input factors, capital and labor force. Here, the possible land use by the capital goods and consumer goods sectors is neglected. The marginal conditions for the capital goods sector are given by

$$r(t) + \delta_k = \frac{\alpha_i F_i(t)}{K_i(t)}, w(t) = \frac{\beta_i F_i(t)}{N_i(t)}. \tag{2.6}$$

Consumer goods sector

The production function of the consumer goods sector is as follows:

$$F_s(t) = A_s K_s^{\alpha_s}(t) N_s^{\beta_s}(t), \alpha_s + \beta_s = 1, \alpha_s, \beta_s > 0, \tag{2.7}$$

where A_s, α_s, and β_s are the technological parameter of the service sector. The marginal conditions are as follows:

$$r(t) + \delta_k = \frac{\alpha_s p_s(t) F_s(t)}{K_s(t)}, w(t) = \frac{\beta_s p_s(t) F_s(t)}{N_s(t)}. \tag{2.8}$$

Consumer behaviors and wealth dynamics

This book applies my approach to household behavior. The approach is explained in Zhang (2020b). The rest of this book applies the approach. The assumption of the public land ownership is applied. It means that the revenue of land is distributed among the population equally. The total land revenue is given by $R(t)L$. Let $\overline{K}_j(t)$ and $\overline{r}(t)$ stand for per capita wealth of group j and per capita land revenue. I have

$$\overline{K}_j(t) = \frac{\overline{K}_j(t)}{\overline{N}_j}, \overline{r}(t) = \frac{R(t)L}{\overline{N}},$$

where $\overline{K}_j(t)$ is the total wealth held by group j. Per capita current income from the interest payment $r(t)\overline{k}_j(t)$, the wage payment $hw(t)$, and land ownership $\overline{r}(t)$ is given by

$$y_j(t) = r(t)\overline{k}_j(t) + h_j w(t) + \overline{r}(t).$$

The per capita disposable income is the current disposable income plus the value of wealth. That is

$$\hat{y}_j(t) = y_j(t) + \overline{k}_j(t). \tag{2.9}$$

The household uses the disposable income for saving and consumption. The value, $\overline{k}_j(t)$, (i.e., $p(t)\overline{k}_j(t)$ with $p(t) = 1$) is a flow variable. It is assumed that selling wealth is conducted instantaneously, and there is no transaction cost. I consider $\overline{k}_j(t)$ as the income that the household gets by selling the wealth. Accordingly, the household has the total amount of income $\hat{y}_j(t)$ to distribute between consumption and saving.

A representative household from group j would distribute the total available budget among savings $s_j(t)$, consumption of agricultural goods $c_{aj}(t)$, , housing (measured by lot size $l_j(t)$), and consumption of consumer goods $c_{sj}(t)$. The budget constraint is as follows:

$$R(t)l_j(t) + p_a(t)c_{aj}(t) + p_s(t)c_{sj}(t) + s_j(t) = \hat{y}_j(t) \tag{2.10}$$

at each point in time, consumers have four variables to decide. It is assumed that the utility level $U_j(t)$ is a function of $l_j(t)$, $c_{aj}(t)$, $c_{sj}(t)$, and $s_j(t)$, as follows:

$$U_j(t) = l_j^{\eta_{0j}}(t)c_{aj}^{\mu_{0j}}(t)c_{sj}^{\xi_{0j}}(t)s_j^{\lambda_{0j}}(t),\ \eta_{0j}, \mu_{0j}, \xi_{0j}, \lambda_{0j} > 0,$$

where η_{0j} is the propensity to consume housing, ξ_{0j} is the propensity to consume agricultural goods, ξ_{0j} is the propensity to consume consumer goods, and λ_{0j} the propensity to save. It should be remarked that heterogeneous households are considered in some growth models of endogenous wealth accumulation. But the heterogeneity in these approaches is due to the differences in the initial endowments of wealth rather than in preferences (Chatterjee 1994; Caselli and Ventura 2000; Maliar and Maliar 2001; Turnovsky and Penalosa 2006; Penalosa and Turnovsky 2006). Households in this approach are essentially homogeneous as all the households are described with the same preference utility function. Our approach considers the heterogeneity due to differences in utility functions.

Maximizing the utility subject to (2.10) yields

$$R(t)l_j(t) = \eta_j \hat{y}_j(t), p_a(t)c_{aj}(t) = \mu_j \hat{y}_j(t), p_s(t)c_{sj}(t) = \xi_j \hat{y}_j(t),$$
$$s_j(t) = \lambda_j \hat{y}_j(t), \tag{2.11}$$

where

$$\eta_j \equiv \rho_j \eta_{0j}, \mu_j \equiv \rho_j \mu_{0j}, \xi_j \equiv \rho_j \xi_{0j}, \lambda_j \equiv \rho_j \lambda_{0j}, \rho_j \equiv \frac{1}{\eta_{0j} + \mu_{0j} + \xi_{0j} + \lambda_{0j}}.$$

From the definition of $s_j(t)$, I have the household's change of wealth as follows:

$$\dot{\bar{k}}_j(t) = s_j(t) - \bar{k}_j(t) = \lambda_j \hat{y}_j(t) - \bar{k}_j(t). \tag{2.12}$$

This equation implies that the change in wealth equals the saving minus dissaving.

Demand and supply of the three sectors

The equilibrium of demand and supply for agricultural goods is

$$\sum_{j=1}^{J} c_{aj}(t) \overline{N}_j = F_a(t). \tag{2.13}$$

The demand and supply equilibrium for the consumer goods sector is

$$\sum_{j=1}^{J} c_{sj}(t) \overline{N}_j = F_s(t). \tag{2.14}$$

The output of the capital goods sector equals the net savings and the depreciation of capital stock. I have

$$S(t) - K(t) + \delta_k K(t) = F_i(t), \tag{2.15}$$

where

$$S(t) \equiv \sum_{j=1}^{J} s_j(t) N_j, K(t) = \sum_{j=1}^{J} k_j(t) N_j.$$

Capital being fully utilized

Total capital stock $K(t)$ is allocated to the three sectors

$$K_a(t) + K_i(t) + K_s(t) = K(t). \tag{2.16}$$

Land being fully used

The land is fully used:

$$L_a(t) + \sum_{j=1}^{J} l_j(t)\overline{N}_j = L. \tag{2.17}$$

The construction of the model is complete. Irrespective of the obvious strict assumptions in our model, the model structurally is general as some well-known models in economics are its special cases. For instance, if housing, agricultural sector, and land are omitted and the population is homogeneous, our model is structurally similar to the models by Solow (1956) and Uzawa (1961). Our model is structurally similar to the Ricardian models formed by Pasinetti and Samuelson. The model is structurally similar to the growth models for the dual economy (Todaro 1969; Kaiyama 1973; Marino 1975; Amano 1980).

2.2 The Dynamics and Its Properties

As the dynamic system consists of any (finite) number of households, it is nonlinear and highly dimensional. In general, it is difficult to analyze properties of such nonlinear dynamic systems. Nevertheless, I can simulate the motion of the economy. The following lemma shows that the dimension of the dynamical system is equal to the number of types of households. It also provides a computational procedure for calculating all the variables at any point in time. First, I define a new variable $z(t)$ by

$$z(t) \equiv \frac{r(t) + \delta_k}{w_j(t)/h_j}.$$

Lemma 2.1 The motion of the economic system is determined by J differential equations with $z(t)$ and $\left\{\overline{k}_j(t)\right\}$, where $\left\{\overline{k}_j(t)\right\} \equiv \left(\overline{k}_2(t), \cdots, \overline{k}_J(t)\right)$, as the variables:

$$\begin{aligned} \dot{z}(t) &= \Lambda_1\left(z(t), \left\{\overline{k}_j(t)\right\}\right), \\ \dot{\overline{k}}_j(t) &= \Lambda_j\left(z(t), \left\{\overline{k}_j(t)\right\}\right), j = 2, \cdots, J, \end{aligned} \tag{2.18}$$

in which $\Lambda_j(t)$ are unique functions of $z(t)$ and $\left\{\overline{k}_j(t)\right\}$ defined in the appendix. The following procedure determines the other variables uniquely as functions of $z(t)$ and $\left\{\overline{k}_j\right\}$ as follows: $r(t)$ and $w_j(t)$ by (A2.3) $\rightarrow$ $\overline{k}_1(t)$ by (A2.17) $\rightarrow$ $N_i(t)$ by (A2.14) $\rightarrow$ $N_a(t)$, $N_s(t)$, and $\overline{r}(t)$ by (A2.13) $\rightarrow$ $R(t) = \overline{r}(t)\overline{N}/L \rightarrow w(t) = w_1(t)/h_1 \rightarrow$ $\hat{y}_j(t)$ by (A2.6) $\rightarrow$ $K_a(t)$, $K_s(t)$, and $K_i(t)$ by (A2.1) $\rightarrow$ $F_i(t)$, $F_s(t)$ and $F_a(t)$ by the definitions $\rightarrow p_s(t)$ by (A2.4) $\rightarrow p_a(t)$ by (2.4) $\rightarrow l_j(t)$, $c_{sj}(t)$, $c_{aj}(t)$, and $s_j(t)$ by (2.11) $\rightarrow K(t)$ by (2.16).

The lemma gives a computational procedure for plotting the motion of the economy with any number of types of households. It is well known that calibration of general equilibrium involves solving high-dimensional nonlinear equations. With regard to the Arrow-Debreu concept of general equilibrium the final stage of analysis is to find a price vector at which excess demand is zero (Judd 1988). There are numerical approaches for calculating equilibria (Scarf 1967; Scarf and Hansen 1973). As it is difficult to interpret the analytical results, to study properties of the system the model is simulated with the following parameters:

$$A_i = 1.3, A_s = 1, A_a = 0.8, L = 10, \alpha_i = 0.34, \alpha_s = 0.3,$$
$$\alpha_a = 0.17, \beta_a = 0.2, \delta_k = 0.05,$$
$$\begin{pmatrix} N_1 \\ N_2 \\ N_3 \end{pmatrix} = \begin{pmatrix} 12 \\ 40 \\ 20 \end{pmatrix}, \begin{pmatrix} h_1 \\ h_2 \\ h_3 \end{pmatrix} = \begin{pmatrix} 3 \\ 1.5 \\ 0.6 \end{pmatrix}, \begin{pmatrix} \lambda_{10} \\ \lambda_{20} \\ \lambda_{30} \end{pmatrix} = \begin{pmatrix} 0.78 \\ 0.75 \\ 0.7 \end{pmatrix}, \begin{pmatrix} \xi_{10} \\ \xi_{20} \\ \xi_{30} \end{pmatrix} = \begin{pmatrix} 0.12 \\ 0.16 \\ 0.18 \end{pmatrix},$$
$$\begin{pmatrix} \eta_{10} \\ \eta_{20} \\ \eta_{30} \end{pmatrix} = \begin{pmatrix} 0.2 \\ 0.16 \\ 0.14 \end{pmatrix}, \begin{pmatrix} \mu_{10} \\ \mu_{20} \\ \mu_{30} \end{pmatrix} = \begin{pmatrix} 0.06 \\ 0.08 \\ 0.09 \end{pmatrix}. \tag{2.19}$$

The population of group 2 is the largest, while the population of group 3 is the next. The human capital level of group 1 is highest, while the human capital level of group 3 is lowest. The total factor productivities of the capital goods, agricultural, and consumer goods sectors are, respectively, 1.3, 1, and 0.8. The values of the parameters, α_j, in the Cobb–Douglas productions for the capital goods and consumer goods sectors are approximately equal to 0.3 (Miles and Scott 2005; Abel et al. 2007). The depreciation rate of physical capital is specified at 0.05. Group 1'*s* propensity to save is 0.78, and group 3'*s* propensity to save is 0.7. The value of group 2'*s* propensity is between the two groups. The initial conditions are as follows:

$$z(0) = 0.045, \bar{k}_2(0) = 15, \bar{k}_3(0) = 8.5.$$

The motion of the variables is plotted in Fig. 2.1. In the figure, the national income is

$$Y(t) = F_i(t) + p_s(t)F_s(t) + p_a(t)F_a(t) + (L_0 - L_a(t))R(t).$$

The output level of the capital goods sector rises, and the output levels of the consumer goods and agricultural sectors fall overtime. The rate of interest rises. The wage rates of the three groups fall. The national capital stocks and output fall. The consumption levels of the three groups also vary over time. The economic structure

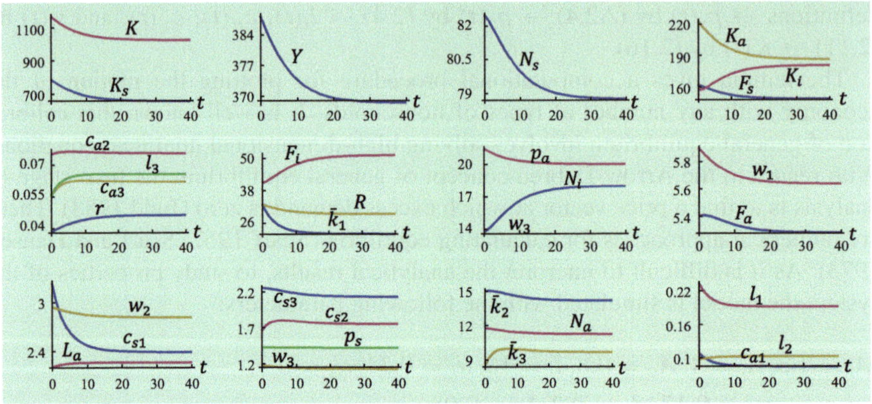

Fig. 2.1 The motion of the economic system

varies over time. After confirming the existence of a unique equilibrium and its stability, I will examine how the dynamic patterns are affected by different variables.

It is straightforward to confirm that the variables become stationary. The simulation shows that the system has a unique equilibrium. The equilibrium values are listed in (2.20):

$$\begin{gathered}Y = 596.2, K = 1025.6, F_i = 51.28, F_s = 148.9, F_a = 5.28, r = 0.046, \\ R = 29.42, p_a = 20.02, p_s = 1.42, w_1 = 5.64, w_2 = 2.82, w_3 = 1.13, \\ L_a = 2.26, N_a = 11.25, N_i = 18.0, N_s = 78.75, K_a = 186.5, \\ K_i = 180.9, K_s = 658.2, \bar{k}_1 = 22.07, \bar{k}_2 = 14.18, \bar{k}_3 = 9.67, \\ c_{s1} = 2.39, c_{s2} = 2.13, c_{s3} = 1.75, c_{a1} = 0.085, c_{a2} = 0.075, \\ c_{a3} = 0.062, l_1 = 0.192, l_2 = 0.103, l_3 = 0.066.\end{gathered} \tag{2.20}$$

It is straightforward to calculate the three eigenvalues as follows:

$$\{-0.335, -0.303, -0.159\}.$$

The real parts of the eigenvalues are negative. The unique equilibrium is locally stable. As the lemma gives the computational procedure to simulate the motion of the economic variables, it is straightforward to examine effects of change in any parameter on transitory processes as well as stationary states of all the variables. I introduce a variable $\overline{\Delta} x_j(t)$ which stands for the change rate of the variable, $x_j(t)$, in percentage due to changes in the parameter value.

2.2.1 Group 1 Augmenting the Propensity to Save

Preferences of different households are important for understanding economic structures. First, I examine the case where group 1 increases its propensity to save in the following way:

$$\lambda_{01} : 0.78 \Rightarrow 0.8.$$

The simulation results are given in Fig. 2.2. Group 1's per capita wealth is increased. The levels of agricultural and service consumption and lot size are lessened initially and subsequently increased. This occurs as the group saves more from the disposable income, the household consumes less. Nevertheless, as the household has more wealth and the wage rate is also increased, the disposable income is increased in the long term, which leads to the rises in the consumption levels. Hence, group 1 benefits from saving more from the disposable income in the long term. As far as the transitory effects are concerned, the effects on the other two groups are different. The two groups' per capita wealth and service consumption levels are slightly affected, initially being reduced and augmented in the long term. The lot sizes and consumption levels of agricultural goods are initially increased and subsequently lowered. Although the two groups' wage rates are increased, as the land rent and price of agricultural goods fall initially and rise subsequently, the net effects on the two variables for the two groups are negative. As more capital is accumulated as a consequence of the rise in the propensity to save, the rate of interest falls. As more capital goods are produced, labor force is shifted from the service and agricultural goods sectors to the capital good sector. The capital stock employed by the capital goods sector increases. The capital stocks employed by the other two sectors fall initially but rise subsequently (as a consequence of the rise in the two capital stocks). As group 1 (the rich group) reduces the demand for lot size and agricultural goods initially, the land rent and price of consumer goods sector fall; subsequently as the group has more disposable income and its demand for lot size and agricultural goods are increased, the land rent and price of consumer goods sector rise. The output level of the capital good sector increases, while the output levels of the other two sectors are slightly reduced. The impact on the national output is negative initially and positive in the long term.

2.3 Group 1 Improving Human Capital

The impact of human capital is currently a main topic in economic theory and empirical research. In modern economies, one of the key determinants of economic growth is human capital (Hanushek and Kimko 2000; Krueger and Lindahl 2001; Barro 2001; Castelló-Climent and Hidalgo-Cabrillana 2012). There are many studies on estimating the impact of education on earnings since Mincer's seminal work in

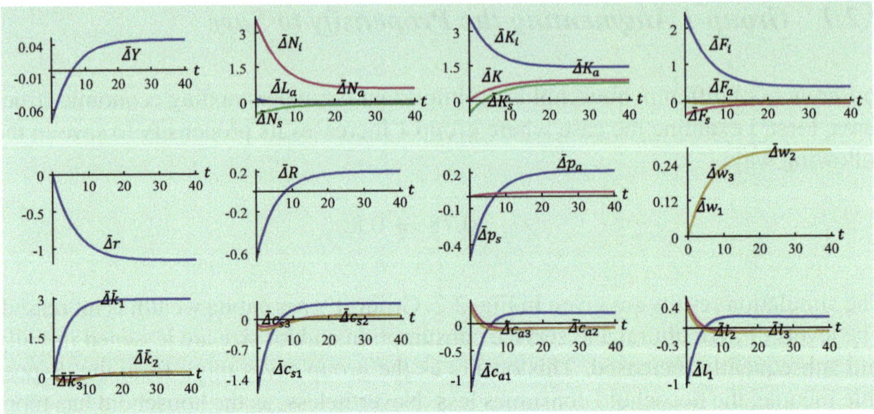

Fig. 2.2 A rise in group 1's propensity to save

1974 (Mincer 1974). Earlier studies (Tilak 1989) demonstrate that inequality within countries can be reduced in association with the spread of education. Could et al. (2001) constructed an economic model, concluding that increasing randomness is the primary factor for inequality growth among uneducated workers, but inequality growth within educated workers is mainly due to changes in the composition and return to ability (Tselios 2008; Fleisher et al. 2011). I now re-examine issues related to how differences in human capital affect wealth and income distribution among heterogeneous households during transitory processes and in long-term steady state. Let group 1 improve its human capital as follows:

$$h_1 : 3 \Rightarrow 3.1.$$

The simulation result is plotted in Fig. 2.3. The rise in group 1'*s* human capital leads to a rise in the group's wage rate, while the other two groups' wage rates are slightly affected. Hence, the wage gaps between group 1 and the other two groups are enlarged. It should be remarked that the wage gaps due to the change in the propensity to save just analyzed are not so strongly affected like in the case of change in the human capital. As group 1 increases its wage, its lot size, wealth level and the consumption levels of the two goods are all increased both in the short term and in the long term. The other two groups' lot sizes are reduced. The other two groups reduce their consumption levels of agricultural goods. As the households accumulate more wealth, one observes falls in the rate of interest. The land rent and the price of agricultural goods increase, while the price of consumer goods is almost not affected. The output levels of the three sectors and the national output are increased.

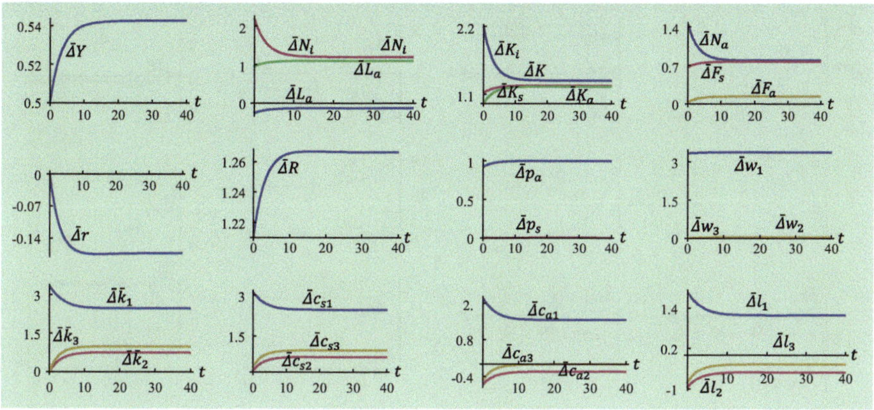

Fig. 2.3 A rise in group 1's human capital

2.4 Group 3 Increasing the Propensity to Consume Agricultural Goods

This section examines how group 3'*s* preference for agricultural goods may affect the economic structure and growth. I allow group 3 to increase their propensity to consume agricultural goods as follows:

$$\mu_{03} : 0.09 \Rightarrow 0.11.$$

The results are plotted in Fig. 2.4. The preference change leads to more consumption of agricultural goods by the group. The increased demand results in a rise in supply in the agricultural sector. The agricultural sector employs more labor, capital, and land. The land rent and the price of agricultural goods are thus increased. The increased price of agricultural goods makes the other groups consume less agricultural goods. As more land is employed by the agricultural sector and the land rent is increased, the other two groups use less lot sizes. Group 3 consumes less consumer good and has lower wealth, while each of the other two groups consumes more consumer good and has lower wealth. The price of consumer goods is slightly lowered. The national capital and capital stocks employed by the capital good and consumer good sectors are reduced. The reduced national capital stock is associated with rises in the rate of interest. The national output increases, even though the output levels of the consumer good and capital good sectors are reduced.

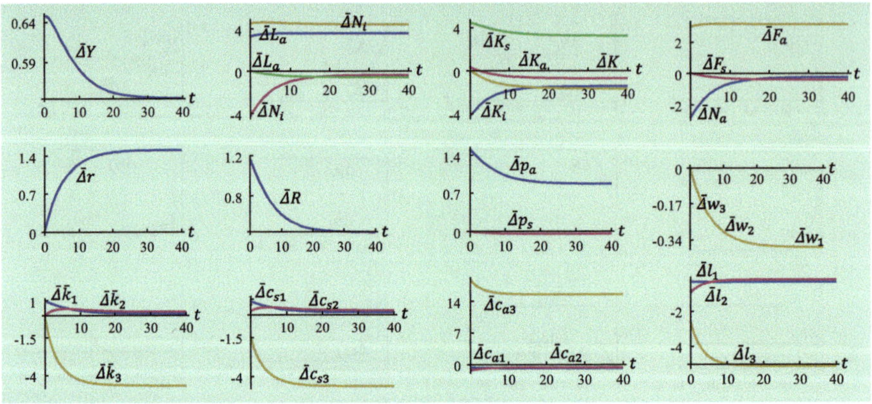

Fig. 2.4 A rise in group 3's propensity to consume agricultural goods

2.5 Group 3's Population Increases

The relationship between population changes and economics is a challenging area. Although this study assumes the population is fixed, it is important to examine effects of changes in the population sizes. As different countries have different levels of knowledge utilization efficiency and creativity, increases in the population sizes may have different effects upon the global economy. It has been observed that the effect of population growth varies with the level of economic development and can be positive for some developed economies. Theoretical models with human capital predict situation-dependent interdependence of population and economic development (Ehrlich and Lui 1997; Galor and Weil 1999; Boucekkine et al. 2002; Bretschger 2013). One reads different mixed conclusions from empirical studies related to the issue (Furuoka 2009; Yao et al. 2013). I now allow group 3'*s* population to increase as follows:

$$N_3 : 20 \Rightarrow 22.$$

The results are plotted in Fig. 2.5. As far as the aggregate real variables are concerned, in the long term the national output, the total capital stock, the capital inputs, the labor inputs, and the land input, the output levels of the three sectors are all increased. Group 3 has the lowest level of human capital. Hence, a rise in the population lowers the average level of human capital of the population. It is expected that the wage rates fall as a consequence of the fall in group 3'*s* population. The rise in the unskilled population lowers the wealth levels, consumption levels of consumer and agricultural goods, and lot sizes for all the groups. The land rent and the prices of the two goods are enhanced.

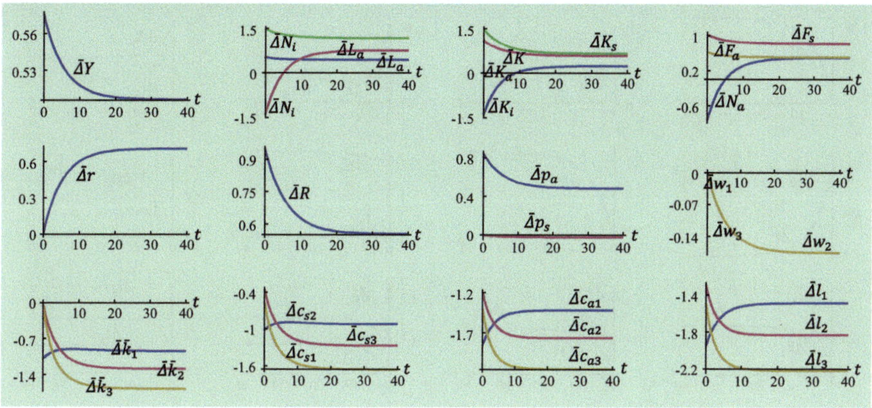

Fig. 2.5 A rise in group 3's population

2.6 Group 1's Population Increases

This section analyzes the effects of change in group 3'*s* population. It is interesting to compare effects of changes the populations with the highest and lowest levels of human capital. Group 1'*s* population increases as follows:

$$N_1 : 12 \Rightarrow 13.$$

The results are plotted in Fig. 2.6. As far as the aggregate real variables are concerned, in the long term the national output, the total capital stock, the capital inputs, the labor inputs, and the land input, the output levels of the three sectors are all increased. Hence, the aggregated variables are affected similarly by the changes in the two group's population. In contrast to the rise in the rise in group 3'*s* population, a rise in group 1'*s* population enhances the wage rates. The rise in the skilled population lowers the consumption levels of agricultural goods and lot sizes for all the groups as the rise in the unskilled population; but different from the case of the rise in unskilled population, the rise in the skilled population raises the wealth levels and consumption levels of consumer good for all the groups.

2.7 Concluding Remarks

This chapter proposed an economic growth model with economic structure and heterogeneous households. The framework is influenced by the three core theories in economics—Walrasian general equilibrium theory, Ricardian theory of distribution, and neoclassical growth theory. The economic system of heterogeneous households consists of one consumer goods sector and one capital goods sector. This chapter

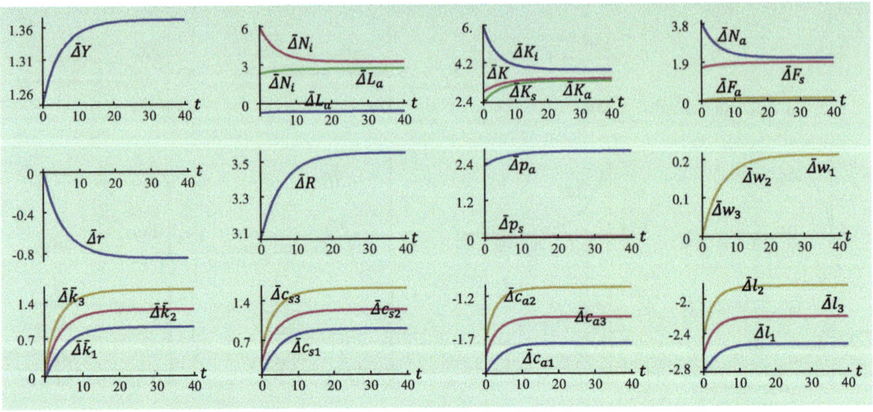

Fig. 2.6 A rise in group 1's population

studied economic growth and structural change with exogenous land resource, population, and human capital. The motion is described by a set of differential equations. For illustration, the chapter simulated the motion of the economic system with three groups. I identified the existence of a unique stable equilibrium point. By the comparative analysis, I illustrated the complexity of dynamic interdependence between economic growth, economic structural change, and wealth and income distribution. For instance, there are many studies on relations between wealth and income distribution and development. Kaldor (1956) holds that as income gap is larger, growth is faster because of more savings. The positive relation between income inequality and growth is tested by, for instance, Bourguignon (1981), Forbes (2000), and Frank (2009). There are other studies which find negative relations between income distribution and growth. Solow (1992) argues for a negative relationship between income inequality and growth. There are some formal models which show negative relations (e.g., Galor and Zeira 1993; Galor and Moav 2004; Benabou 2002). Some empirical studies find negative relations (e.g., Persson and Tabellini 1994). From our simulation, it can be seen that relations between inequality and economic growth are complicated in the sense that these relations are determined by many factors. For instance, from Fig. 2.2 it is observed that in initial transitory process the rich group's and the other two groups' wealth levels are enlarged, the national output experiences negative growth; while in the long term the rich group's and the other two groups' wealth levels continue to be enlarged, the national output experiences positive growth. Our comparative analysis also shows that in order to understand growth and development processes it is important to classify the population into different types according to their preferences and human capital. For instance, if the population of the group with the lowest (highest) level of human capital is increased, the wage rates and the wealth levels and consumption levels of consumer good of all the groups are reduced (enhanced). There are also extensive studies on income and wealth distribution between heterogeneous households (Atkinson et al. 2011;

Attanasio and Pistaferri 2014; Piketty and Zucman 2014; Saez and Zucman 2016; Coibion et al. 2017; Kaplan and Violante 2018; Clemens and Heinemann 2015; Zidar 2019; Garbinti et al. 2021; Lee 2023). Those studies provide different directions for generalizing the model in this chapter.

Appendix: Proving Lemma 2.1

By (2.4), (2.6), and (2.8), I obtain

$$z \equiv \frac{r + \delta_k}{w} = \frac{N_a}{\overline{\beta}_a K_a} = \frac{N_i}{\overline{\beta}_i K_i} = \frac{N_s}{\overline{\beta}_s K_s}, \tag{A2.1}$$

where $\overline{\beta}_j \equiv \beta_m / \alpha_m$. From (A2.1) and (2.15):

$$\overline{\beta}_a K_a + \overline{\beta}_i K_i + \overline{\beta}_s K_s = \frac{N}{z}. \tag{A2.2}$$

Insert (A2.1) in (2.4):

$$r = \alpha_r z^{\beta_i} - \delta_k, \; w_j = \alpha_j z^{-\alpha_i}, \tag{A2.3}$$

where

$$\alpha_r = \alpha_i A_i \overline{\beta}_i^{\beta_i}, \; \alpha_j = h_j \beta_i A_i \overline{\beta}_i^{-\alpha_i}.$$

Hence, the rate of interest and the wage rates are obtained as functions of z. From (2.7) and (2.8), I have

$$p_s = \frac{\overline{\beta}_s^{\alpha_s} z^{\alpha_s} w}{\beta_s A_s}. \tag{A2.4}$$

From (2.4), I have

$$L_a = \frac{w \varsigma N_a}{\beta_a R}. \tag{A2.5}$$

From (A2.3) and the definitions of $\hat{y}_j$, I have

$$\hat{y}_j = (1 + r)\overline{k}_j + h_j w + \overline{r}. \tag{A2.6}$$

Insert $p_s c_{sj} = \xi_j \hat{y}_j$ in (2.13):

$$\sum_{j=1}^{J} \xi_j \overline{N}_j \hat{y}_j = p_s F_s. \tag{A2.7}$$

Substituting (A2.6) in (A2.7) yields

$$\frac{wN_s}{\beta_s} - \overline{r}\tilde{g}_0 = \sum_{j=1}^{J} \tilde{g}_j \overline{k}_j + \tilde{g}w, \tag{A2.8}$$

where $p_s F_s = wN_s / \beta_s$ is applied and

$$\tilde{g}_j(z) \equiv (1+r)\xi_j \overline{N}_j, \ \tilde{g} \equiv \sum_{j=1}^{J} h_j \xi_j \overline{N}_j, \ \tilde{g}_0 \equiv \sum_{j=1}^{J} \xi_j \overline{N}_j.$$

Insert $p_a c_{aj} = \mu_j \hat{y}_j$ from (2.11) in (2.13):

$$\sum_{j=1}^{J} \mu_j \hat{y}_j \overline{N}_j = \frac{wN_a}{\beta_a}, \tag{A2.9}$$

where $p_a F_a = wN_a / \beta_a$ is applied. Insert (A2.6) in (A2.9):

$$\frac{wN_a}{\beta_a} - \tilde{h}_0 \overline{r} = \sum_{j=1}^{J} \tilde{h}_j \overline{k}_j + w\tilde{h}, \tag{A2.10}$$

where

$$\tilde{h}_j(z) \equiv (1+r)\mu_j \overline{N}_j, \ \tilde{h} \equiv \sum_{j=1}^{J} h_j \mu_j \overline{N}_j, \ \tilde{h}_0 \equiv \sum_{j=1}^{J} \mu_j \overline{N}_j.$$

Insert (A2.5) and $Rl_j = \eta_j \hat{y}_j$ from (2.11) in (2.17):

$$\frac{w\varsigma N_a}{\beta_a} + \sum_{j=1}^{J} \eta_j \hat{y}_j \overline{N}_j = RL. \tag{A2.11}$$

Insert (A2.6) in (A2.11):

$$-\frac{w\varsigma N_a}{\beta_a} + \left(\overline{N} - \overline{h}_0\right)\overline{r} = \sum_{j=1}^{J} \overline{h}_j \overline{k}_j + \overline{h}w, \tag{A2.12}$$

where

$$\overline{h}_j(z) \equiv (1 + r)\eta_j\overline{N}_j, \overline{h} \equiv \sum_{j=1}^{J} h_j\eta_j\overline{N}_j, \overline{h}_0 \equiv \sum_{j=1}^{J} \eta_j\overline{N}_j.$$

From (A2.8), (A2.10), and (A.12), it is straightforward to see that the left-hand sides of the three equations contain three variables, N_a, N_s, and $\overline{r}$. The three equations are linear in N_a, N_s, and $\overline{r}$. It is also noted that the right-hand sides of the three equations contain $\overline{k}_j$ which don't appear on the left-hand sides of the equations. These imply that I can get the solution of (A2.8), (A2.10), and (A2.12) with N_a, N_s, and $\overline{r}$ as the variables in the following form:

$$N_a\left(z, \left(\overline{k}_j\right)\right) = \sum_{j=1}^{J} \phi_{aj}(z)\overline{k}_j,$$

$$N_s\left(z, \left(\overline{k}_j\right)\right) = \sum_{j=1}^{J} \phi_{sj}(z)\overline{k}_j, \quad \text{(A2.13)}$$

$$\overline{r}\left(z, \left(\overline{k}_j\right)\right) = \sum_{j=1}^{J} \phi_{Rj}(z)\overline{k}_j.$$

I don't provide explicit expressions of $\phi_{..}(z)$ as they are tedious. From (2.2) and (A2.13), I solve

$$N_i\left(z, \left(\overline{k}_j\right)\right) = \sum_{j=1}^{J} \phi_{ij}(z)\overline{k}_j. \quad \text{(A2.14)}$$

From (A2.1), (2.16) and $K = \sum_{j=1}^{J} \overline{k}_j\overline{N}_j$, I get

$$\frac{N_a}{\overline{\beta}_a} + \frac{N_i}{\overline{\beta}_i} + \frac{N_s}{\overline{\beta}_s} = z\sum_{j=1}^{J} \overline{k}_j\overline{N}_j. \quad \text{(A2.15)}$$

Substituting N_a, N_s, and N_i in (A2.13 and (A2.14) yields

$$\sum_{j=1}^{J} \phi_j(z)\overline{k}_j = 0, \quad \text{(A2.16)}$$

where

$$\phi_j(z) \equiv \frac{\phi_{aj}(z)}{\overline{\beta}_a} + \frac{\phi_{ij}(z)}{\overline{\beta}_i} + \frac{\phi_{sj}(z)}{\overline{\beta}_s} - z\overline{N}_j.$$

Hence, solve (A2.16) with $\overline{k}_1$ as the variable:

$$\overline{k}_1 = \phi\left(z, \left\{\overline{k}_j\right\}\right) \equiv -\frac{1}{\phi_1(z)} \sum_{j=2}^{J} \phi_j(z)\overline{k}_j, \tag{A2.17}$$

where $\left\{\overline{k}_j\right\} \equiv \left(\overline{k}_2, \cdots, \overline{k}_J\right)$. It is straightforward to confirm that all the variables can be expressed as functions of z and $\left\{\overline{k}_j\right\}$ by the following procedure: r and w_j by (A2.3) $\rightarrow \overline{k}_1$ by (A2.17) $\rightarrow N_i$ by (A2.14) $\rightarrow N_a$, N_s, and $\overline{r}$ by (A2.13) $\rightarrow R = \overline{r}\overline{N}/L$ $\rightarrow w = w_1/h_1 \rightarrow \hat{y}_j$ by (A2.6) $\rightarrow K_a$,K_s, and K_i by (A2.1) $\rightarrow F_i$, F_s and F_a by the definitions $\rightarrow p_s$ by (A2) $\rightarrow p_a$ by (2.4) $\rightarrow l_j$, c_{sj}, c_{aj}, and s_j by (2.11) $\rightarrow K$ by (2.16). From this procedure, (A2.21), and (2.12), I have

$$\dot{\overline{k}}_1 = \overline{\Omega}_1\left(z, \left\{\overline{k}_j\right\}\right) \equiv \lambda_1 \hat{y}_1 - \phi, \tag{A2.18}$$

$$\dot{\overline{k}}_j = \Lambda_j\left(z, \left\{\overline{k}_j\right\}\right) \equiv \lambda_j \overline{y}_j - \overline{k}_j, j = 3, \cdots, J. \tag{A2.19}$$

Taking derivatives of equation (A2.17) with respect to t and combining with (A2.18) implies

$$\dot{\overline{k}}_1 = \frac{\partial \phi}{\partial z}\dot{z} + \sum_{j=2}^{J} \Lambda_j \frac{\partial \phi}{\partial \overline{k}_j}. \tag{A2.20}$$

Equaling the right-hand sides of equations (A2.18) and (A2.20), I get

$$\dot{z} = \left[\overline{\Omega}_1 - \sum_{j=2}^{J} \Lambda_j \frac{\partial \phi}{\partial \overline{k}_j}\right] \left(\frac{\partial \phi}{\partial z}\right)^{-1}. \tag{A2.21}$$

In summary, the lemma is confirmed.

Chapter 3
Growth and Distribution with Endogenous Leisure Time

> And while the law of competition may be sometimes hard for the individual, it is best for the race, because it ensures the survival of the fittest in every department.
>
> Andrew Carnegie (1835-1919)

This chapter examines the dynamic interdependence between economic growth and structural change, considering endogenous time allocation and durable consumer goods. It is well known that traditional neoclassical growth theory is unable to adequately model structural change with heterogeneous capital based on microeconomic foundations (Takayama 1963, 1965; Burmeister and Dobell 1970; Echevarria 1997; Jones and Manuelli 1997; Acemoglu 2009; Acemoglu and Guerrieri 2008). This chapter develops a two-sector, two-group growth model and examines the dynamics of wealth and income distribution in a world in which capital accumulation is the main driving force of economic growth. This approach is influenced by neoclassical growth theory, but also by post-Keynesian growth and distribution theory (Pasinetti 1962, 1974; Brems 1970; Salvadori 1991; Reati 1998; Ciarli et al. 2010; Cimoli and Procile 2010; Gabardo 2017). In most post-Keynesian growth models with heterogeneous classes, the economic system has a single productive sector. There are exceptions, for example Stiglitz (1967) who proposes a two-sector, two-class growth model. The Stiglitz model is a synthesis of post-Keynesian theory and Uzawa's two-sector model. However, there is little further work along with this line of research. In this chapter, I address similar economic problems to those addressed by the Stiglitz model with a different approach to household behavior. Moreover, in this model, labor supply is an endogenous variable, whereas in the Stiglitz model, labor supply is fixed.

The Solow model in the neoclassical growth theory was proposed for one sector economy; it is not proper to deal with economic structural change and price changes of various goods. The initial extensions of the Solow model were proposed by Uzawa (1961, 1963), Meade (1961) and Kurz (1963). The Uzawa model has been applied as a standard model for modeling two-sector economic growth. The two sectors use

W. Zhang, *A Dynamic Economic Theory of Heterogenous Households*,
https://doi.org/10.1007/978-981-95-8918-0_3

capital and labor to produce, respectively, capital and consumer goods. In the traditional two-sector economy, output of the capital sector is used entirely for investment and that of the consumption sector for consumption. Economists have made many efforts in generalizing and extending the Uzawa two-sector model by, for instance, introducing more general production functions, money, externalities, knowledge, human capital, and fictions in different markets (Takayama 1985; Galor 1992; Mino 1996; Drugeon and Venditti 2001; Harrison 2003; Cremers 2006; Herrendorf and Valentinyi 2006; Li and Lin 2008; Stockman 2009; Herrendorf et al. 2015; Mutreja et al. 2018; Buera *et.al.* 2020; Comin et al. 2021; Jones and Liu 2022). The two-sector economic structure is recognized as not proper for dealing with issues of heterogeneous capital goods and multiple services. Many empirical studies demonstrate that economic sectors are different in their dynamic interactions with the economic system. Acconcia and Simonelli (2008: 3010) found out that the early literature on empirical studies of business fluctuations implicitly assumes that "a one-sector model is sufficient in order to correctly interpret the business cycle." Nevertheless, the recent literature emphasizes the necessity of dividing production into different sectors (Baxter 1996; Whelan 2003; Erceg et al. 2005; Fisher 2006). This chapter introduces consumer durable goods into the traditional two-sector model. Consumer durable goods, such as cars, home appliances, consumer electronics, furniture, sports equipment, and toys, are important in terms of households' expenditure shares in modern economies. The Uzawa model is not proper for dealing with non-durable and durable goods differently. This chapter applies Zhang's approach to household behavior to extend the two-sector economic structure by distinguishing consumer non-durable goods and durable goods (Zhang 1993b, 2005b). The model also includes housing as consumer durable goods. Housing is essential for proper living. Housing is the largest component of nonhuman wealth for households. Housing is the largest expense for many households. For instance, as described in DiPasquale and Wheaton (1996) real estate investment is over 50% of total private investment and real estate assets represent just under 60% of the nation's wealth and almost 70% of U.S. real estate is residential. More than 60 percent of total net worth held by all households in Korea are housing assets (Cho 2010). There are many studies on interactions between housing markets and macroeconomy (Henderson et al. 2001; Leung 2004; Leamer 2007; Ghent and Owyang 2010). This chapter provides some insights into demand and supply of housing markets. The model in this chapter synthesizes the ideas in the two-sector model with endogenous labor by Zhang (2005a), the growth model with durable consumer good by Zhang (2008a), and the growth model with heterogeneous households by Zhang (2014a). This chapter is based on Zhang (2017b). It is organized as follows. Section 3.1 develops the two-sector two-group model with endogenous wealth accumulation and time distribution between work and leisure. Section 3.2 shows the dynamics and equilibrium of the economic system. Section 3.3 examines how an improvement in the capital goods sector's productivity affects the motion of the economic system. Section 3.4 analyses the impact of a rise in group 1's human capital on the economic system. Section 3.5 shows how an enhancement in group 2's propensity to save affects the wealth distribution and time distribution. Section 3.6 concludes the chapter. The appendix proves Lema 3.1.

3.1 The Two-Sector Two-Group Model with Leisure Time

The production side of the economic system is according to the Uzawa model. The two sectors produce respectively consumption and capital goods. This chapter extends the Uzawa model in that capital goods can be used not only as input in the two sectors but also as consumer durable goods by the household. Capital is assumed to depreciate at a constant exponential rate δ_k.

3.1.1 Production Sectors

The two sectors use labor and capital goods as input. The two inputs are smoothly substitutable for each other in each sector and are freely transferable from one sector to the other. The technology of each sector is neoclassical. Subscripts i and s are used to stand for the capital goods sector and the consumer goods sector respectively. The production functions are:

$$F_q(t) = A_q K_q^{\alpha_q}(t) N_q^{\beta_q}(t), \, q = i, s,$$

where F_q are the output of sector q, and $K_q(t)$ and $N_q(t)$ are respectively the capital and labor used by sector q.

The labor force is classified into two groups. Let $T_j(t)$ stand for the work time of a representative household of group j and $N(t)$ for the flow of labor services used at time t for production. It is assumed that labor is fully employed. I measure $N(t)$ as follows:

$$N(t) = h_1 T_1(t) \overline{N}_1 + h_2 T_2(t) \overline{N}_2, \tag{3.1}$$

where h_j are the levels of human capital of group j, $j = 1, 2$. Markets are perfectly competitive. The capital good that is selected serves as a medium of exchange and is taken as numeraire. Let $p(t)$ stand for the price of consumer goods. The rate of interest $r(t)$ and wage rate $w(t)$ of per unit qualified labor force are determined by markets. Hence for any individual firm $r(t)$ and $w(t)$ are given at each point of time. The production sector chooses the two variables $K_j(t)$ and $N_j(t)$ to maximize its profit. The marginal conditions are given by:

$$\begin{aligned} r + \delta_k &= f_i'(k_i) = p f_s'(k_s), \, w(t) = f_i(k_i) - k_i f_i'(k_i) \\ &= p(t)\left[f_s(k_s) - k_s f_s'(k_s)\right], \end{aligned} \tag{3.2}$$

where $f_q(t) \equiv F_q(t)/N_q(t)$. The wage rate of group j is equal to $w_j(t) = h_j w(t)$.

3.1.2 Full Employment of the Input Factors

Total capital stock $K(t)$ is distributed between the two sectors and the households. Full employment of labor and capital is expressed as

$$K_i(t) + K_s(t) + \tilde{K}_1(t) + \tilde{K}_2(t) = K(t), N_i(t) + N_s(t) = N(t), \qquad (3.3)$$

where $\tilde{K}_j(t)$ is the level of consumer durables used by group j, $j = 1, 2$. I rewrite (3.3) as:

$$\begin{gathered} n_i(t)k_i(t) + n_s(t)k_s(t) + \tilde{n}_1(t)\tilde{k}_1(t) + \tilde{n}_2(t)\tilde{k}_2(t) = k(t), \\ n_i(t) + n_s(t) = 1, \end{gathered} \qquad (3.4)$$

where

$$k(t) \equiv \frac{K(t)}{N(t)}, n_q(t) \equiv \frac{N_q(t)}{N(t)}, q = i, s, \tilde{k}_j(t) \equiv \frac{\tilde{K}_j(t)}{\overline{N}_j}, \tilde{n}_j(t) \equiv \frac{\overline{N}_j}{N(t)},$$

$$j = 1, 2.$$

I use $\bar{k}_j(t)$ to represent per capita wealth of group j at t. According to the definitions, it follows:

$$K(t) = \bar{k}_1(t)\overline{N}_1 + \bar{k}_2(t)\overline{N}_2. \qquad (3.5)$$

3.1.3 Current and Disposable Incomes

Consumers make decisions on choice of levels of consumer durables, services, commodities, and saving. Group j's per capita current income $y_j(t)$ from the interest payment $r(t)\bar{k}_j(t)$ and the wage payment $T_j(t)w_j(t)$ are:

$$y_j(t) = r(t)\bar{k}_j(t) + T_j(t)w_j(t).$$

The sum that consumers spend for consuming and saving is not necessarily equal to the current income. Consumers may sell wealth to buy, for instance, goods for having a party at home. A retired man may live on the accumulated wealth in the past. What consumer j can sell is equal to $\bar{k}_j(t)$, if there is no borrowing from others. The per capita disposable income of consumer j is equal to the sum of the current income and the wealth:

$$\hat{y}_j(t) = y_j(t) + \bar{k}_j(t) = (1 + r(t))\bar{k}_j(t) + T_j(t)w_j(t), j = 1, .2. \qquad (3.6)$$

The disposable income is spent on saving and consuming. The disposable income is distributed between saving $s_j(t)$, consumer durables $\tilde{k}_j(t)$, and consumer good $c_j(t)$. The budget constraint of consumer j is:

$$p(t)c_j(t) + (r(t) + \delta_k)\tilde{k}_j(t) + s_j(t) = \hat{y}_j(t) = (1 + r(t))\overline{k}_j(t) + T_j(t)w_j(t). \tag{3.7}$$

Let $T_{hj}(t)$ represent the leisure time at time t and T_0 the (fixed) available time for work and leisure. The time constraint is:

$$T_j(t) + T_{hj}(t) = T_0.$$

Substituting this relation into (3.7) yields:

$$T_{hj}(t)w_j(t) + p(t)c_j(t) + (r(t) + \delta_k)\tilde{k}_j(t) + s_j(t) = \overline{y}_j(t) \equiv (1 + r(t))\overline{k}_j(t) + T_0 w_j(t). \tag{3.8}$$

3.1.4 Utility Function and Optimal Decision

The utility level $U_j(t)$ is dependent on $c_j(t)$, $\tilde{k}_j(t)$, and $s_j(t)$. The utility level of group j is specified as follows:

$$U_j(t) = T_{hj}^{\sigma_{0j}}(t)c_j^{\xi_{0j}}(t)\tilde{k}_j^{\eta_{0j}}(t)s_j^{\lambda_{0j}}(t),\ \sigma_{0j},\ \xi_{0j},\ \eta_{0j},\ \lambda_{0j} > 0,\quad j = 1, \ldots J, \tag{3.9}$$

where σ_{0j}, ξ_{0j}, η_{0j} and λ_{0j} are respectively group j's propensities to use leisure time, to consume consumer good, to utilize consumer durables, and to own wealth. Maximizing U_j subject to the budget constraints (3.8), I obtain the following first-order conditions:

$$w_j(t)T_{hj}(t) = \sigma_j\overline{y}_j(t), p(t)c_j(t) = \xi_j\overline{y}_j(t), (r(t) + \delta_k)\tilde{k}_j(t) = \eta_j\overline{y}_j(t), s_j(t) = \lambda_j\overline{y}_j(t), \tag{3.10}$$

where

$$\sigma_j \equiv \rho_j\sigma_{0j}, \xi_j \equiv \rho_j\xi_{0j}, \mu_j \equiv \rho_j\mu_{0j}, \lambda_j \equiv \rho_j\lambda_{0j}, \rho_j \equiv \frac{1}{\sigma_{0j} + \xi_{0j} + \mu_{0j} + \lambda_{0j}}.$$

3.1.5 Wealth Accumulation

According to the definitions of $s_j(t)$, the wealth accumulation of the consumer of group j is:

$$\dot{\bar{k}}_j(t) = s_j(t) - \bar{k}_j(t). \tag{3.11}$$

Equation (3.11) implies that the change in wealth is equal to the saving minus dissaving.

3.1.6 Demand and Supply

What the consumer goods sector produces is consumed by the households:

$$\sum_{j=1}^{J} c_j(t)\overline{N}_j = F_s(t). \tag{3.12}$$

The output of the capital goods sector is equal to the depreciation of capital stock and the net saving:

$$\sum_{j=1}^{J} s_j(t)\overline{N}_j - K(t) + \delta_k K(t) = F_i(t). \tag{3.13}$$

I built the economic growth model of physical capital distribution wealth and income distribution in the economy in which the markets are perfectly competitive. The model synthesizes some main ideas in economic growth theory.

3.2 The Dynamics and Equilibrium of the Economic System

This section examines the dynamic properties of the two-sector two-group model. Although the system consists of many equations and interactions between variables are complicated, the following lemma shows that the motion of the economic system is solved with two differential equations.

Lemma 3.1 The motion of the two-sector two-group economic system is governed by the following two nonlinear differential equations with $k_i(t)$ and $k(t)$ as the variables.

$$\dot{k}_i(t) = \Lambda(k_i(t), k(t)),$$
$$\dot{k}(t) = \Omega(k_i(t), k(t)), \tag{3.14}$$

where Λ and Ω are functions of $k_i(t)$ and $k(t)$ defined in the appendix. Moreover, all the other variables can be determined as functions of $k_i(t)$ and $k(t)$ at any point in time by the following procedure: $\bar{k}_j(t), j = 1, 2$ by (A3.18) $\rightarrow k_s(t) = \alpha k_i(t) \rightarrow f_q(t)$ by (A3.1) $\rightarrow \bar{y}_j(t)$ by (A3.20) $\rightarrow p(t)$ by (A3.3) $\rightarrow n_i(t)$ and $n_s(t)$ by (A3.9) $\rightarrow r(t)$ and $w(t)$ by (3.2) $\rightarrow w_j(t) = h_j w(t), j = 1, 2 \rightarrow T_j(t)$ by (A3.12) $\rightarrow \tilde{k}_j(t), c_j(t)$ and $s_j(t)$ by (3.10) $\rightarrow N(t)$ by (A3.16) $\rightarrow \tilde{n}_j(t) = \overline{N}_j/N(t) \rightarrow N_q(t) = n_q(t)N_q(t)$, $q = i, s \rightarrow K(t) = k(t)N(t) \rightarrow K_q(t) = k_q(t)N_q(t) \rightarrow F_q(t) = f_q(t)N_q(t) \rightarrow U_j(t)$ by (3.9).

As the lemma provides the procedure to determine all the variables, it is straightforward to follow the motion of the system with computer. For simulation, the parameter values are as follows:

$$\begin{aligned} &\overline{N}_1 = 6, \overline{N}_2 = 18, A_i = 2, A_s = 1, \alpha_i = 0.38, \alpha_s = 0.34, h_1 = 2,\\ &h_2 = 0.5, \delta_k = 0.05, \lambda_{01} = 0.7, \sigma_{01} = 0.1, \eta_{01} = 0.1, \xi_{01} = 0.1,\\ &\lambda_{02} = 0.65, \sigma_{02} = 0.1, \eta_{02} = 0.07, \xi_{02} = 0.08. \end{aligned} \tag{3.15}$$

Group $2's$ population is 3 times as many as group $1's$. Group $1's$ level of human capital is 4 times as high as group $2's$. Group 1 has lower (relative) propensity to save (which equals 0.7) than group $2's$ (which equals $0.65/0.9 \approx 0.72$) and group 1 has lower propensity to enjoy leisure time than group 2. We choose the initial conditions, $k(0) = 18$ and $k_i(0) = 8$. The motion of the variables is plotted in Fig. 3.1 with Mathematica.

In Fig. 3.1, $F(t) \equiv F_i(t) + p(t)F_s(t)$ stands for the national product. The labor share of the service sector rises as time passes. Group 1 works shorter hours, while Group 2 works longer hours. The price of the consumer good changes slightly over

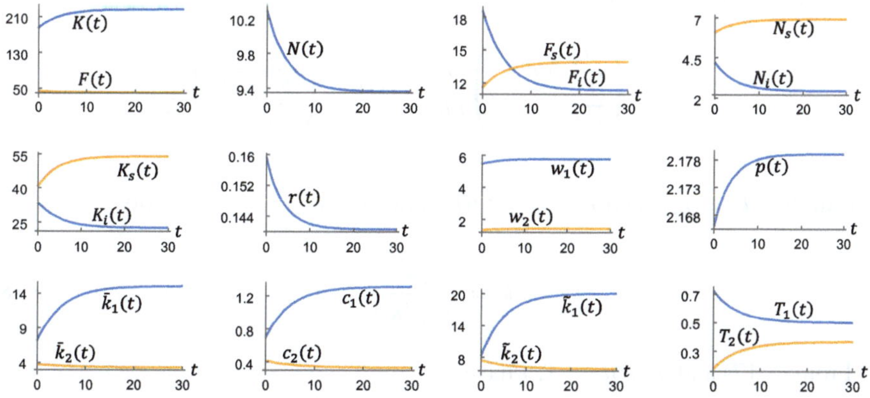

Fig. 3.1 The motion of the economic system

time. The wealth per capita, the consumption levels of durable goods and consumer goods and wage rate of group 1 are augmented, while the corresponding variables of group 2 are lessened. Hence, due to the initial conditions group 2 works longer hours, but their living conditions and wealth are not improved. The rate of interest lowers in associating in rising in the capital intensities. The output and two inputs of the consumer goods sector are increased, while the corresponding variables of the capital goods sector are lessened. The national output decreases. As the per capita wealth of the economy is enhanced and the per capita wealth group 2 is reduced, the wealth capita is enlarged.

From Fig. 3.1, all the variables become stationary in the long term. This implies that the system has an equilibrium point. It is shown now that the system has a unique equilibrium point. By (3.11), $s_j = \bar{k}_j$ at equilibrium. From $s_j = \bar{k}_j$ and $s_j = \lambda_j \bar{y}_j$, I solve $\bar{k}_j = \lambda_j \bar{y}_j$. From $\bar{k}_j = \lambda_j \bar{y}_j$ and the definition of $\bar{y}_j$, the following holds:

$$\bar{k}_j = \varphi_j(k_i) \equiv \frac{\bar{h}_j k_i}{\bar{\lambda}_j k_i^{\beta_i} - \alpha_i A_i}, \tag{3.16}$$

where $\bar{\lambda}_j \equiv 1/\lambda_j - 1 + \delta_k$ and $\bar{h}_j \equiv T_0 \beta_i A_i h_j$. From the definition of k and (3.5), it follows:

$$k = \left(\sum_{j=1}^{J} \bar{k}_j \bar{N}_j\right) \frac{1}{N}.$$

By this equation, (3.12) and (3.13) are rewritten as:

$$n_s = \frac{\phi_s(k_i)}{N}, \; n_i = \frac{\phi_i(k_i)}{N}, \tag{3.17}$$

where $c_j = \xi_j \bar{k}_j / \lambda_j p$ is applied, $s_j = \bar{k}_j$ and

$$\phi_s(k_i) \equiv \left(\sum_{j=1}^{J} \frac{\bar{N}_j \xi_j \bar{k}_j}{\lambda_j}\right) \frac{1}{p f_s}, \; \phi_i(k_i) \equiv \left(\sum_{j=1}^{J} \bar{N}_j \bar{k}_j\right) \frac{\delta_k}{f_i}.$$

Substituting $\bar{k}_j = \lambda_j \bar{y}_j$ and $r + \delta_k = f_i{\prime}(k_i)$ into $(r + \delta_k)\tilde{k}_j = \eta_j \bar{y}_j$, I solve:

$$\tilde{k}_j = \frac{\eta_j \bar{k}_j}{\lambda_j f_i{\prime}(k_i)}. \tag{3.18}$$

From (3.17) and $n_i + n_s = 1$, I have:

$$N = \phi(k_i) \equiv \phi_s(k_i) + \phi_i(k_i). \tag{3.19}$$

By $w_j T_{hj} = \sigma_j \bar{y}_j$, $\bar{k}_j = \lambda_j \bar{y}_j$ and $w_j = h_j \beta_i f_i$, it follows:

$$T_{hj} = \frac{\overline{\sigma}_j \bar{k}_j}{f_i}, \tag{3.20}$$

where $\overline{\sigma}_j \equiv \sigma_j / \lambda_j h_j \beta_i$. From (3.20) and the definition of N, I solve:

$$N = \sum_{j=1}^{J} \left(T_0 - \frac{\overline{\sigma}_j \bar{k}_j}{f_i} \right) h_j \overline{N}_j, \tag{3.21}$$

where $T_j(t) + T_{hj}(t) = T_0$ is applied. Equalizing the right-hand sides of (3.19) and (3.21) yields

$$\Omega(k_i) \equiv \phi(k_i) - \sum_{j=1}^{J} \left(T_0 - \frac{\overline{\sigma}_j \bar{k}_j}{f_i} \right) h_j \overline{N}_j = 0. \tag{3.22}$$

Summarizing the above analysis, I determine all the variables at the equilibrium point by the following computing procedure: k_i by (3.22) $\to \bar{k}_j$.. by (3.16) $\to k_s = \alpha k_i$ $\to f_j$ by (A3.1) $\to \bar{y}_j = \bar{k}_j / \lambda_j \to p$ by (A3.3) $\to N$ by (3.19) $\to n_j$ by (3.17) $\to$ $N_j = n_j N \to r$ and w by (3.2) $\to w_j = h_j w \to T_{hj}$ by (3.20) $\to \tilde{k}_j$, c_j and s_j by (3.10) $\to K = kN \to K_j = k_j N_j \to F_j = f_j N_j$.

Figure 3.2 demonstrates that Eq. (3.22) has a unique meaningful solution. The equation has actually two positive solutions, $k_i = 2.29$, $k_i = 9.30$, as demonstrated in Fig. 3.1. Nevertheless, at $k_i = 2.29$ the work times of the two groups do not belong to [0, 1].

Under (3.15), I have the equilibrium values in (3.23). As $p = 2.18$ and $F_s = 13.9$, the consumer goods sector makes more contribution to the national economy than the capital goods sector ($F_i = 11.37$). Most of the labor force is employed by the consumer goods sector. The representative household from group 1 consumes more consumer good, holds more wealth, utilizes more consumer durables than the household from group 2. The representative household of group 2 works less hours

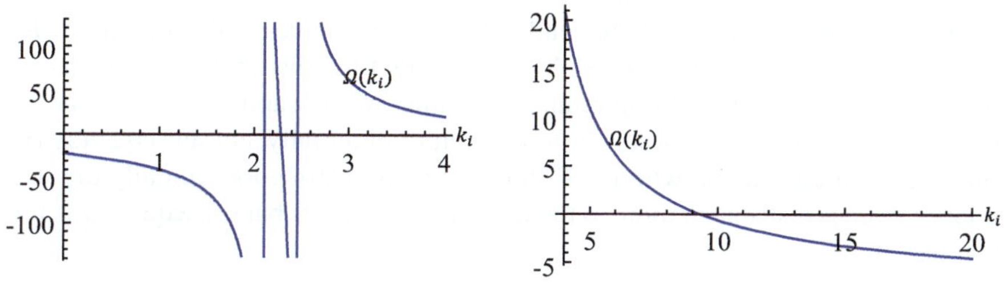

Fig. 3.2 A unique meaningful solution of Eq. (3.22)

than group 1.

$$\begin{aligned}
&F = 41.74, F_i = 11.37, F_s = 13.94, K = 227.40, K_i = 22.65,\\
&K_s = 54.14, N = 9.37, N_i = 2.44, N_s = 6.93, f_i = 4.67, f_s = 2.01,\\
&k_i = 9.30, k_s = 7.81, n_i = 0.26, n_s = 0.74, p = 2.18, r = 0.141,\\
&w_1 = 5.79, w_2 = 1.45, c_1 = 1.32, c_2 = 0.34, T_{h1} = 0.50, T_{h2} = 0.63,\\
&\bar{k}_1 = 20.10, \bar{k}_2 = 5.93, \tilde{k}_1 = 15.06, \tilde{k}_2 = 3.35.
\end{aligned} \tag{3.23}$$

The two eigenvalues are $\{-0.293, 3 \times 10^{-17}\}$.

3.3 An Improvement in the Capital Goods Sector's Productivity

This section studies what will happen to the economic system if the capital goods sector's total productivity is enhanced in the following way:

$$A_i : 2 \Rightarrow 2.1.$$

Following the lemma, I plot the shifts of the transitional paths as in Fig. 3.3. As the productivity is improved, the capital goods sector's output level is enhanced. Although the total capital increases, the rate of interest rises initially but subsequently comes back to its original value. In the long term the change in the total productivity has no impact on the rate of interest. As the capital supply is increased, the price of consumer goods is enhanced. Although the two groups' wage rates are changed at the same rate (because the change is due to the total productivity improvement in the Cobb–Douglas production function), group $1's$ wage income is increased far more than group $2's$, irrespective of that group $2s$ work longer hours than before. Group $1's$ wage rate, consumption levels of consumer good and durable goods, and per capita wealth are all increased, but the values of the corresponding variables are lowered initially but subsequently augmented. The total labor supply and two sector's labor inputs are all increased initially but end in the original values in the long term. This occurs because in the long term each household's time distribution is invariant in the long term. The national output and the output of the capital goods sector rise, but the output level of the consumer goods sector fall initially and subsequently rise. This occurs in association with the shift of the labor distribution. Initially the share of labor force is distributed more to the capital goods sector but subsequently is little affected.

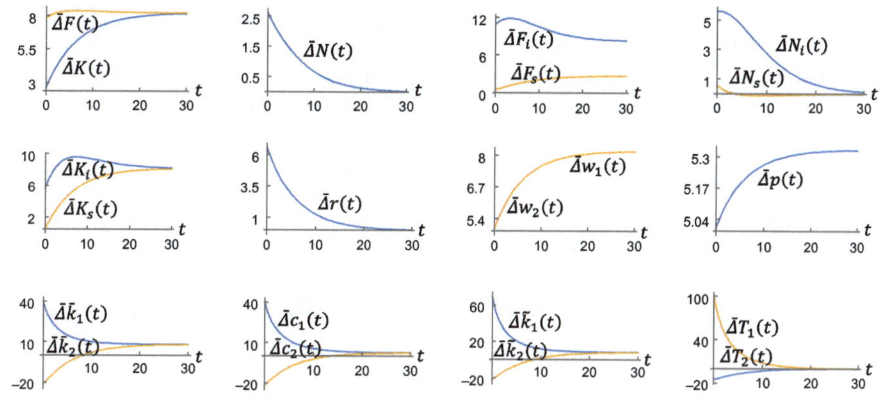

Fig. 3.3 An improvement in the capital goods sector's technology

3.4 An Enhancement in Group 1's Human Capital

Group $1's$ human capital is enhanced in the following way: $h_1 : 2 \Rightarrow 2.2$. The result is plotted in Fig. 3.4. The immediate result of a rise in group $1's$ human capital is the rise in the group's wage rate. This leads to a slight fall in the group $2's$ wage rate because the gap in human capital is enlarging. Group 1 works longer hours as the opportunity cost of leisure falls, while group 2 works shorter hours in association with falling in the group's opportunity cost of leisure. Nevertheless, the work hours are slightly affected by the parameter change. The price of consumer goods is slightly affected. The human capital improvement enhances the total labor supply and labor input of the two sectors. The share of the labor force of the consumer goods sector is increased. The enhanced human capital reduces the capital intensities of the two sectors, which is associated with the rise in the rate of interest. From the group's improved human capital group 1 benefits in terms of wealth, consumption levels of the two goods in the transitional process as well as the long term. But this does not happen to the other group. Group 1 benefits in the transitional process but not in the long term.

3.5 An Enhancement in Group 2's Propensity to Save

This section studies the effects of the following rise in group $2's$ propensity to save:

$$\lambda_{02} : 0.65 \Rightarrow 0.69.$$

The simulation is plotted in Fig. 3.5. As group 1 increases the propensity to save, the per capita wealth of the group falls initially but subsequently rises. This occurs as the increased propensity to save leads to the enhancement in the total capital in

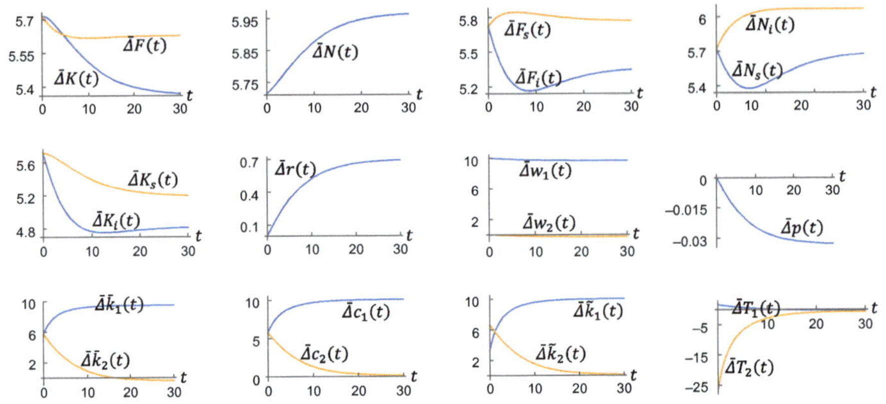

Fig. 3.4 An enhancement in group 1's human capital

association with falling in the rate of interest. As more capital is saved, the price of consumer goods is enhanced. The augmented capital and labor supply increase the output levels of the two sectors. It is concluded that even group 2 does not benefit initially, in the long term all the households in the economy benefit.

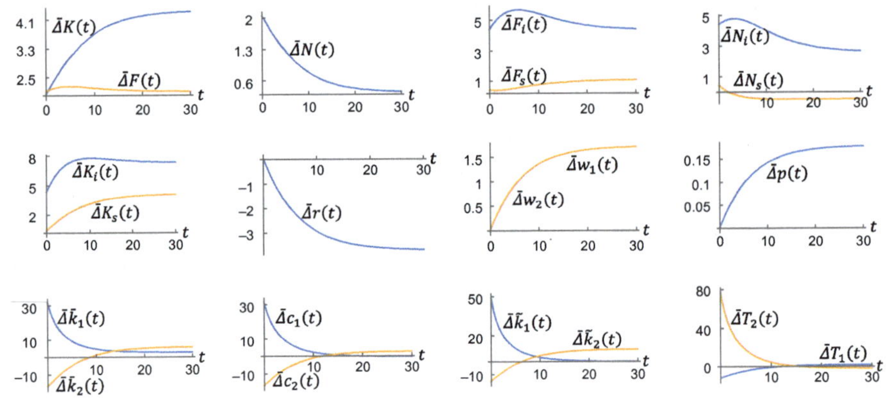

Fig. 3.5 Group 2's propensity to save being enhanced

3.6 Concluding Remarks

This chapter introduced heterogeneous households, endogenous time and durable consumer good into the traditional Uzawa two-sector growth model. This chapter does not only model the economic structure like the Uzawa's model but also determines endogenous income and wealth distribution between heterogeneous households. The model is influenced by the neoclassical growth theory and the post-Keynesian theory of growth and distribution. As the model is influenced by the core models in the neoclassical and post-Keynesian approaches and these core models have been extended and generalized in different ways, it is not difficult to generalize the model on the basis of these extensions and generalizations. For instance, it is straightforward to introduce externalities into the two-sector model on the basis of the approaches taken by Benhabib and Farmer (1994) and Boldrin et al. (2001a).

Appendix: Proving Lemma 3.1

The production functions are expressed as

$$f_j(k_j) = A_j k_j^{\alpha_j}, A_j > 0, 0 < \alpha_j < 1, j = i, s. \quad \text{(A3.1)}$$

From the equations (A3.1) and (3.2), I directly obtain:

$$k_s = \alpha k_i, \quad \text{(A3.2)}$$

where

$$\alpha \equiv \frac{\beta_i \alpha_s}{\beta_s \alpha_i}, \beta_j \equiv 1 - \alpha_j, j = i, s.$$

The capital intensity of the consumer goods sector is proportional to that of the capital goods sector. By $k_s = \alpha k_i$ and $\beta_i f_i = \beta_s p f_s$, I solve:

$$w = \beta_i f_i, p = \frac{\beta_i A_i}{\beta_s \alpha^{\alpha_s} A_s} k_i^{\alpha_i - \alpha_s}. \quad \text{(A3.3)}$$

The price of consumer goods is positively related to the technological level of the capital goods sector but negatively related to that of the consumer goods sector. The price is positively or negatively related to the capital intensity of the capital goods sector, depending on the sign of $\alpha_i - \alpha_s$. If $\alpha_i = \alpha_s$, then the price is constant, $p = A_i / A_s$. In the remainder of this section, $\alpha_i > \alpha_s$.is required If the equality holds, then labor distribution is invariant in time. The analysis of $\alpha_i \leq \alpha_s$ is similar. The condition $\alpha_i > \alpha_s$ (which implies $\alpha < 1$) guarantees $k_s(t) < k_i(t)$ for any t.

According to the definitions, (3.12) and (3.13) are rewritten as:

$$\sum_{j=1}^{2} \tilde{n}_j(t)c_j(t) = n_s(t)f_s(t),$$
$$\sum_{j=1}^{2} \tilde{n}_j(t)s_j(t) - \delta k(t) = n_i(t)f_i(t). \tag{A3.4}$$

Substitute $pc_j = \xi_j \overline{y}_j$ and $s_j = \lambda_j \overline{y}_j$ into (A3.4):

$$\begin{bmatrix} \xi_1 \tilde{n}_1 & \xi_2 \tilde{n}_2 \\ \lambda_1 \tilde{n}_1 & \lambda_2 \tilde{n}_2 \end{bmatrix} \begin{bmatrix} \overline{y}_1 \\ \overline{y}_2 \end{bmatrix} = \begin{bmatrix} pn_s f_s \\ n_i f_i + \delta k \end{bmatrix}, \tag{A3.5}$$

where I omit time in the expressions. I solve the above linear equations as

$$\overline{y}_1 = \frac{\beta_i \lambda_2 n_s f_i / \beta_s - (n_i f_i + \delta k)\xi_2}{\lambda \tilde{n}_1},$$
$$\overline{y}_2 = \frac{\xi_1 (n_i f_i + \delta k) - \beta_i \lambda_1 n_s f_i / \beta_s}{\lambda \tilde{n}_2}, \tag{A3.6}$$

where $pf_s = \beta_i f_i / \beta_s$ and $\lambda \equiv \xi_1 \lambda_2 - \xi_2 \lambda_1$ ($\neq 0$) are applied. It is tedious to examine these conditions because of lengthy and complicated expressions.

Substituting (A3.6) and $r + \delta_k = f_i\prime(k_i)$ into $(r + \delta_k)\tilde{k}_j = \eta_j \overline{y}_j$, I solve:

$$\tilde{k}_1 = \left(\overline{\xi}_2 n_s f_i - n_i f_i - \delta k\right) \frac{\xi_2 \tilde{\lambda}_1 k_i^{\beta_i}}{\tilde{n}_1},$$
$$\tilde{k}_2 = \left(n_i f_i + \delta k - \overline{\xi}_1 n_s f_i\right) \frac{\xi_1 \tilde{\lambda}_2 k_i^{\beta_i}}{\tilde{n}_2}, \tag{A3.7}$$

where

$$\tilde{\lambda}_j \equiv \frac{\eta_j}{\lambda \alpha_i A_i}, \ \overline{\xi}_j \equiv \frac{\lambda_j \beta_i}{\xi_j \beta_s}, j = 1, 2.$$

Substitute (A3.7) into (3.4)

$$\psi_i(k_i) n_i + \psi_s(k_i) n_s = k, \tag{A3.8}$$

where

$$\psi_i(k_i) \equiv \left(\frac{1 - A_i \xi_2 \tilde{\lambda}_1 + A_i \xi_1 \tilde{\lambda}_2}{1 + \delta \xi_2 \tilde{\lambda}_1 k_i^{\beta_i} - \delta \xi_1 \tilde{\lambda}_2 k_i^{\beta_i}} \right) k_i,$$
$$\psi_s(k_i) \equiv \left(\frac{\alpha + A_i \overline{\xi}_2 \xi_2 \tilde{\lambda}_1 - A_i \overline{\xi}_1 \xi_1 \tilde{\lambda}_2}{1 + \delta \xi_2 \tilde{\lambda}_1 k_i^{\beta_i} - \delta \xi_1 \tilde{\lambda}_2 k_i^{\beta_i}} \right) k_i.$$

From (A3.8) and $n_i + n_s = 1$, I get:

$$n_i = \overline{\psi}_i(k_i, k) \equiv \frac{\psi_s(k_i) - k}{\psi_s(k_i) - \psi_i(k_i)},$$
$$n_s = \overline{\psi}_s(k_i, k) \equiv \frac{k - \psi_i(k_i)}{\psi_s(k_i) - \psi_i(k_i)}. \tag{A3.9}$$

The labor distribution between the two sectors is uniquely determined by k and k_i. I consider $n_i(t)$ and $n_s(t)$ as functions of $k(t)$ and $k_i(t)$.

Substitute (A3.6) into $w_j T_{hj} = \sigma_j \overline{y}_j$:

$$w_1 T_{h1} = \frac{\beta_i \sigma_1 \lambda_2 n_s f_i - (n_i f_i + \delta k)\beta_s \sigma_1 \xi_2}{\beta_s \lambda \tilde{n}_1},$$
$$w_2 T_{h2} = \frac{(n_i f_i + \delta k)\beta_s \sigma_2 \xi_1 - \beta_i \sigma_2 \lambda_1 n_s f_i}{\beta_s \lambda \tilde{n}_2}, \tag{A3.10}$$

where $pf_s = \beta_i f_i / \beta_s$ is applied. Inserting $T_j + T_{hj} = T_0$, $w_j = h_j \beta_i A_i k_i^{\alpha_i}$ and

$$\tilde{n}_j = \frac{\overline{N}_j}{\sum_{j=1}^{2} h_j \overline{N}_j T_j},$$

in (A3.10), I obtain:

$$T_0 = \left(\Gamma_1 h_1 \overline{N}_1 + 1\right) T_1 + \Gamma_1 h_2 \overline{N}_2 T_2,$$
$$T_0 = h_1 \overline{N}_1 \Gamma_2 T_1 + \left(h_2 \overline{N}_2 \Gamma_2 + 1\right) T_2, \tag{A3.11}$$

where $T_j + T_{hj} = T_0$ is applied and

$$\Gamma_1(k_i, k) \equiv \frac{\beta_i \sigma_1 \lambda_2 n_s f_i - (n_i f_i + \delta k)\beta_s \sigma_1 \xi_2}{\beta_s \lambda h_1 \beta_i A_i \overline{N}_1 k_i^{\alpha_i}},$$
$$\Gamma_2(k_i, k) \equiv \frac{(n_i f_i + \delta k)\beta_s \sigma_2 \xi_1 - \beta_i \sigma_2 \lambda_1 n_s f_i}{h_2 \beta_i A_i \beta_s \lambda \overline{N}_2 k_i^{\alpha_i}}.$$

Solving (A3.11) with T_j as variables, I have:

$$T_1 = \Gamma_{T1}(k_i, k) \equiv \left(h_2 \overline{N}_2 \Gamma_2 - \Gamma_1 h_2 \overline{N}_2 + 1\right) \Gamma_0(k_i, k) T_0,$$
$$T_2 = \Gamma_{T2}(k_i, k) \equiv \left(\Gamma_1 h_1 \overline{N}_1 - h_1 \overline{N}_1 \Gamma_2 + 1\right) \Gamma_0(k_i, k) T_0, \tag{A3.12}$$

where

$$\Gamma_0(k_i, k) \equiv \frac{1}{\left(h_2\overline{N}_2\Gamma_2 - \Gamma_1 h_2\overline{N}_2 + 1\right)h_1\overline{N}_1\Gamma_2 + \left(h_2\overline{N}_2\Gamma_2 + 1\right)\left(\Gamma_1 h_1\overline{N}_1 - h_1\overline{N}_1\Gamma_2 + 1\right)}.$$

Insert $s_j = \lambda_j \overline{y}_j$ into the second equation in (3.13):

$$\sum_{j=1}^{2} \tilde{n}_j \lambda_j \overline{y}_j - \delta k = A_i k_i^{\alpha_i} n_i. \tag{A3.13}$$

Substituting (3.6) into (A3.13) yields:

$$\sum_{j=1}^{2} \tilde{n}_j \lambda_j (1+r)\overline{k}_j + \sum_{j=1}^{2} \tilde{n}_j \lambda_j w_j - \delta k = A_i k_i^{\alpha_i} n_i.$$

Insert $r = \alpha_i A_i k_i^{-\beta_i} - \delta_k$ and $w_j = h_j \beta_i A_i k_i^{\alpha_i}$ in the above equation:

$$\sum_{j=1}^{2} \tilde{n}_j \lambda_j \left(\alpha_i A_i k_i^{-\beta_i} + \delta\right)\overline{k}_j + \beta_i A_i k_i^{\alpha_i} \sum_{j=1}^{2} \tilde{n}_j \lambda_j h_j - \delta k = A_i k_i^{\alpha_i} n_i. \tag{A3.14}$$

Insert n_i in (A3.8) in (A3.10)

$$\sum_{j=1}^{2} \tilde{n}_j \lambda_j \left(\alpha_i A_i k_i^{-\beta_i} + \delta\right)\overline{k}_j + \left(\beta_i A_i \sum_{j=1}^{2} \tilde{n}_j \lambda_j h_j - \frac{A_i \psi_s(k_i)}{\psi_s(k_i) - \psi_i(k_i)}\right) k_i^{\alpha_i} = \left(\delta - \frac{A_i k_i^{\alpha_i}(k_i)}{\psi_s(k_i) - \psi_i(k_i)}\right) k. \tag{A3.15}$$

According to the definitions, I can rewrite (3.5) as:

$$k\hat{N}(k_i, k) = \sum_{j=1}^{2} \overline{N}_j \overline{k}_j, \tag{A3.16}$$

where
$\hat{N}(k_i, k) \equiv h_1\overline{N}_1\Gamma_{T1}(k_i, k) + h_2\overline{N}_2\Gamma_{T2}(k_i, k)$.
Substitute (A3.16) into (A3.15):

$$\Omega_1(k_i)\overline{k}_1 + \Omega_2(k_i)\overline{k}_2 = \Omega_0(k_i, k), \tag{A3.17}$$

where $\tilde{n}_j = \overline{N}_j / N$ is applied and

$$\Omega_j(k_i) \equiv \left(\frac{A_i k_i^{\alpha_i}}{\psi_s(k_i) - \psi_i(k_i)} + \lambda_j \alpha_i A_i k_i^{-\beta_i} + \lambda_j \delta - \delta \right) \overline{N}_j, j = 1, 2,$$

$$\Omega_0(k_i, k) \equiv \left(\frac{A_i \psi_s(k_i) \hat{N}(k_i, k)}{\psi_s(k_i) - \psi_i(k_i)} - \beta_i A_i \sum_{j=1}^{2} \lambda_j h_j \overline{N}_j \right) k_i^{\alpha_i}.$$

I solve (A3.16) and (A3.17) with $\overline{k}_1$ and $\overline{k}_2$ as variables:

$$\begin{aligned} \overline{k}_1 &= \overline{\Omega}_1(k_i, k) \equiv \frac{\overline{N}_2 \Omega_0(k_i, k) - k\Omega_2(k_i)\hat{N}(k_i, k)}{\overline{N}_2 \Omega_1(k_i) - \overline{N}_1 \Omega_2(k_i)}, \\ \overline{k}_2 &= \overline{\Omega}_2(k_i, k) \equiv \frac{k\hat{N}(k_i, k)\Omega_1(k_i) - \overline{N}_1 \Omega_0(k_i, k)}{\overline{N}_2 \Omega_1(k_i) - \overline{N}_1 \Omega_2(k_i)}. \end{aligned} \tag{A3.18}$$

Hence, $\overline{k}_1(t)$ and $\overline{k}_2(t)$ are expressed as functions of $k_i(t)$ and $k(t)$ at any point of time. Taking derivatives of (A3.18) with respect to t yields:

$$\begin{aligned} \dot{\overline{k}}_1 &= \overline{\Omega}_{1k_i}(k_i, k)\dot{k}_i + \overline{\Omega}_{1k}(k_i, k)\dot{k}, \\ \dot{\overline{k}}_2 &= \overline{\Omega}_{2k_i}(k_i, k)\dot{k}_i + \overline{\Omega}_{2k}(k_i, k)\dot{k}. \end{aligned} \tag{A3.19}$$

Insert (A3.9) and $\tilde{n}_j = \overline{N}_j / \hat{N}(k_i, k)$ into (A3.6):

$$\begin{aligned} \overline{y}_1 &= \left(\frac{A_i \beta_i \lambda_2 \overline{\psi}_s(k_i) k_i^{\alpha_i} - \left(A_i \overline{\psi}_i(k_i) k_i^{\alpha_i} + \delta k\right) \beta_s \xi_2}{\lambda \beta_s \overline{N}_1} \right) \hat{N}(k_i, k), \\ \overline{y}_2 &= \left(\frac{\left(A_i \overline{\psi}_i(k_i) k_i^{\alpha_i} + \delta k\right) \beta_s \xi_1 - A_i \beta_i \lambda_1 \overline{\psi}_s(k_i) k_i^{\alpha_i}}{\lambda \beta_s \overline{N}_2} \right) \hat{N}(k_i, k). \end{aligned} \tag{A3.20}$$

I express $\overline{y}_j(t)$ as functions of $k_i(t)$ and $k(t)$.
Insert $s_j = \lambda_j \overline{y}_j$ and (A3.20) into (3.11):

$$\begin{aligned} \dot{\overline{k}}_1 &= \tilde{s}_1(k_i, k) \equiv -\overline{\Omega}_1(k_i, k) + \\ &\left(\frac{A_i \beta_i \lambda_2 \overline{\psi}_s(k_i) k_i^{\alpha_i} - \left(A_i \overline{\psi}_i(k_i) k_i^{\alpha_i} + \delta k\right) \beta_s \xi_2}{\lambda \beta_s \overline{N}_1} \right) \lambda_1 \hat{N}(k_i, k), \\ \dot{\overline{k}}_2 &= \tilde{s}_2(k_i, k) \equiv -\overline{\Omega}_2(k_i, k) + \\ &\left(\frac{\left(A_i \overline{\psi}_i(k_i) k_i^{\alpha_i} + \delta k\right) \beta_s \xi_1 - A_i \beta_i \lambda_1 \overline{\psi}_s(k_i) k_i^{\alpha_i}}{\lambda \beta_s \overline{N}_2} \right) \lambda_2 \hat{N}(k_i, k). \end{aligned} \tag{A3.21}$$

Delete $\overline{k}_1(t)$ and $\overline{k}_2(t)$ from (A3.19) and (A3.21)

$$\overline{\Omega}_{1k_i}(k_i, k)\dot{k}_i + \overline{\Omega}_{1k}(k_i, k)\dot{k} = \tilde{s}_1(k_i, k),$$
$$\overline{\Omega}_{2k_i}(k_i, k)\dot{k}_i + \overline{\Omega}_{2k}(k_i, k)\dot{k} = \tilde{s}_2(k_i, k). \tag{A3.22}$$

Solving (A3.13) with $\dot{k}_i(t)$ and $\dot{k}(t)$ as variables, I get:

$$\dot{k}_i = \Lambda(k_i, k) \equiv \frac{\tilde{s}_1(k_i, k)\overline{\Omega}_{2k}(k_i, k) - \tilde{s}_2(k_i, k)\overline{\Omega}_{1k}(k_i, k)}{\overline{\Omega}_{1k_i}(k_i, k)\overline{\Omega}_{2k}(k_i, k) - \overline{\Omega}_{1k}(k_i, k)\overline{\Omega}_{2k_i}(k_i, k)},$$
$$\dot{k} = \Omega(k_i, k) \equiv \frac{\tilde{s}_2(k_i, k)\overline{\Omega}_{1k_i}(k_i, k) - \tilde{s}_1(k_i, k)\overline{\Omega}_{2k_i}(k_i, k)}{\overline{\Omega}_{1k_i}(k_i, k)\overline{\Omega}_{2k}(k_i, k) - \overline{\Omega}_{1k}(k_i, k)\overline{\Omega}_{2k_i}(k_i, k)}. \tag{A3.23}$$

The two differential equations contain two variables $k_i(t)$ and $k(t)$. Summarizing the above analysis, I confirmed the lemma.

Chapter 4
Income and Wealth Distribution with Endogenous Wealth and Human Capital

> Knowledge is power. Information is liberating. Education is the premise of progress, in every society, in every family.
>
> Kofi Annan (1938-2018)

Dynamic interdependence between economic growth and human capital is a main topic in economic theory and empirical research. It is not enough to be only concerned with physical capital accumulation as in the neoclassical growth theory in order to explain why countries grow differently. As observed by Easterlin (1981), in 1850 there were few people outside North-Western Europe and North America who had any formal education. The spread of formal school seems to have preceded the beginning of modern economic growth. Estimating the impact of education on earnings has caused great attention in empirical studies in economics since Mincer (1974) published the seminal work in 1974. He finds that for white males not working on farms, an extra year of education raises the earnings by about 7%. Earlier studies (Tilak 1989) show that spread education can substantially reduce inequality within countries. Could et al. (2001) build a model to provide insights into the evolution of wage inequality within and between industries and education groups in the past few decades. The model shows that increasing randomness is the primary source of inequality growth within uneducated workers, but inequality growth within educated workers is determined more by changes in the composition and return to ability (which is closely related to education). Tselios (2008) studies the relationship between income and educational inequalities in the regions of the European Union, using the European Community Household Panel data survey for 94 regions over the period 1995–2000. The research finding suggests a positive relationship between income and educational inequalities. Fleisher et al. (2011) examine the role of education on worker productivity and firms' total factor productivity on the basis of firm-level data from China. The study shows that an additional year of schooling raises marginal product by 30.1 percent, and the CEO's education increases TFP for foreign-invested firms. The return is also closely related to the ownership. For

W. Zhang, *A Dynamic Economic Theory of Heterogenous Households*,
https://doi.org/10.1007/978-981-95-8918-0_4

instance, the effect of schooling on productivity is highest in foreign-invested firms. A significant conclusion is that market mechanisms contribute to a more efficient use of human capital within firms. Zhu (2011) studies the individual heterogeneity in returning to education in China from 1995 to 2002. The study highlights heterogeneity within and between gender groups. Zhu shows that heterogeneity in school enrollment rates declined between 1995 and 2002, despite a large increase in school enrollment rates for both boys and girls in China's cities. One reason for the decline in heterogeneity is the improved functioning and increased integration of China's urban labor markets.

The literature on endogenous knowledge and economic growth has increasingly expanded since Romer (1986) re-examined issues of endogenous technological change and economic growth in his 1986 paper (Lucas 1988; Grossman and Helpman 1991; Aghion and Howitt 1998). The first formal dynamic growth model with education was actually proposed by Uzawa (1965). Over years the Uzawa-Lucas model has been extended and generalized in various directions (Jones et al. 1993; Stokey and Rebelo 1995; de la Croix and Licandro 1999; Mino 1996; Lagerlof 2003; Alonso-Carrera and Freire-Sere 2004; Galor 2005; De Hek 2005; Chakraborty and Gupta 2009; Sano and Tomoda 2010; Naz and Chaudhry 2017 2018; Sasakura 2022). Their other issues related to innovation, diffusion of technology, and behavior of economic agents under various institutions have been discussed in the literature (Bovenberg and Smulders 1995; Bovenberg et al. 2008; Baldnzi et al. 2019). In the Uzawa-Lucas model and many of their extensions and generalizations, it implicitly assumes that all skills and human capital is formed due to formal schooling. Nevertheless, much of human capital may be accumulated in family and many other social and economic activities. For instance, the human capital of a graduate student from a rich family in the US may be quite the human capital of a graduate student from a middle class in India. Ignoring non-school factors may make people misunderstand the role of formal education in economic development. Another issue is described by Chen and Chevalier (2008), "Making and exploiting an investment in human capital requires individuals to sacrifice not only consumption, but also leisure. When estimating the returns to education, existing studies typically weigh the monetary costs of schooling (tuition and forgone wages) against increased wages, neglecting the associated labor/leisure tradeoff." This chapter introduces other sources of learning into the Uzawa-Lucas two-sector growth model.

Households have different propensities to save and receive education, and different abilities to absorb knowledge and increase human capital through education, practical learning, and consumption learning. Extensions and generalizations of the Uzawa-Lucas model have been limited to representative single households. In fact, there are endogenous human capital models that take heterogeneous households into account. For instance, Galor and Zeira (1993) propose a model to study the relationship between growth and inequality with human capital as the driving force of economic growth. A main conclusion of their study is that in the presence of credit constraints on human capital investments high initial inequality may reduce long-run growth, while redistribution may increase the growth rate. Maoz and Moav (1999) build a similar model and show that impact of income redistribution is situation dependent.

In another model by Galor and Moav (2004), it is demonstrated that at the early stage of modern economic development high inequality encourages growth as the rich have a higher propensity to save, whereas at later stages high inequality may discourage growth as human capital becomes increasingly important and high inequality may be an impediment to human capital accumulation. Fender and Wang (2003) build an overlapping-generations model with endogenous education choice with credit or without credit constraints. In their model, credit constraints are associated with lower education and a lower rate of interest. Laitner (2000) examines dynamics of earnings within education groups and overall productivity with a model with endogenous human capital and a distribution of natural abilities. In a model of education where the distribution of abilities is the source of heterogeneity, Cardak (2004) shows that private education results in higher incomes and less income inequality than in the public education model. Erosa et al. (2010) build a model of endogenous human capital accumulation with education to explain the variation in per capita income across countries. Heterogeneous households make investments in schooling quantity and quality. Further literature can be found in the studies cited. A main deviation of my approach from the previous models is that I derive demand of education in an alternative approach to the typical Ramsey approach. The model is built on the three main growth models—Solow's one-sector growth model, Arrow's learning by doing model, and the Uzawa-Lucas's growth model with education—in the growth literature. The main mechanisms of economic growth in these three models are integrated into a single framework with heterogeneous households. It is also based on the growth model with heterogeneous groups by Zhang (2009b). In Zhang's model, human capital is fixed. The synthesis of the three growth models within a single framework is still analytically tractable because I propose an alternative approach to consumers' behavior. The chapter is based on Zhang (2013b) and is organized as follows. Section 4.1 constructs the dynamic model with endogenous wealth and human capital. Section 4.2 shows the dynamics of the economic system and its properties. Section 4.3 studies how a rise in the RC's propensity to obtain education affects the motion of the economic system. Section 4.4 studies the impact of a rise in the RC's propensity to save on the income and wealth distribution between the groups of the population. Section 4.5 analyses the effects of a rise in the RC's population on the system. Section 4.6 follows the changes in the path of the system as the total factor productivity rises. Section 4.7 concludes the chapter. The appendix proves Lemma 4.1

4.1 The Dynamic Model with Endogenous Wealth and Human Capital

The economy has one production sector and one education sector. Most aspects of the production sector are similar to the standard one-sector growth model. It is assumed that there is only one (durable) good in the economy under consideration. Households own assets of the economy and distribute their incomes to consume and save. Firms use inputs such as labor with varied levels of human capital, different kinds of capital, knowledge and natural resources to produce material goods or services. Exchanges take place in perfectly competitive markets. Factor markets work well; factors are inelastically supplied, and the available factors are fully utilized at every moment. Savings are undertaken only by households. All earnings of firms are distributed in the form of payments to factors of production, labor, managerial skill and capital ownership. Each group has a fixed population, $\overline{N}_j$, $(j = 1, \cdots, J)$. Let prices be measured in terms of the commodity and the price of the commodity be unity. Let wage and interest rates be denoted by $w_j(t)$ and $r(t)$, respectively. The variable $H_j(t)$ stands for group j's level of human capital.

The total capital stock $K(t)$ is allocated between the two sectors. Let $N_i(t)$ and $K_i(t)$ stand for the labor force and capital stocks employed by the production sector, and $N_e(t)$ and $K_e(t)$ for the labor force and capital stocks employed by the education sector. I use $T_j(t)$ and $T_{je}(t)$ to stand for, respectively, the work time and study time of a typical worker in group j. As full employment of labor and capital is assumed, it follows:

$$K_i(t) + K_e(t) = K(t), N_i(t) + N_e(t) = N(t), \tag{4.1}$$

where $N(t)$ is the total qualified labor supply defined by:

$$N(t) = \sum_{j=1}^{J} T_j(t) H_j^{m_j}(t) \overline{N}_j. \tag{4.2}$$

I rewrite (4.1) as follows:

$$n_i(t)k_i(t) + n_e(t)k_e(t) = k(t), n_i(t) + n_e(t) = 1, \tag{4.3}$$

in which

$$k_j(t) \equiv \frac{K_j(t)}{N_j(t)}, n_j(t) \equiv \frac{N_j(t)}{N(t)}, k(t) \equiv \frac{K(t)}{N(t)}, j = i, e.$$

4.1.1 Production Sector

It is assumed that production is to combine the labor force $N_i(t)$ and physical capital $K_i(t)$. The function $F_i(t)$ is specified as:

$$F_i(t) = A_i K_i^{\alpha_i}(t) N_i^{\beta_i}(t), A_i, \alpha_i, \beta_i > 0, \alpha_i + \beta_i = 1.$$

Markets are competitive; thus, labor and capital earn their marginal products, and firms earn zero profits. The rate of interest and wage rate are determined by markets. For any individual firm $r(t)$ and $w_j(t)$ are given at each point of time. The production sector chooses the two variables $K_i(t)$ and $N_i(t)$ to maximize its profit. The marginal conditions are given by:

$$r(t) + \delta_k = \alpha_i A_i k_i^{-\beta_i}(t), \; w_j(t) = \beta_i A_i H_j^{m_j}(t) k_i^{\alpha_i}(t), \tag{4.4}$$

where δ_k is depreciation rate of physical capital.

4.1.2 Education Sector

It is assumed that the education sector is also characterized by perfect competition. Here, I neglect any government's financial support for education. Students pay the education fee $p(t)$ per unit of time. The education sector pays teachers and capital with the market rates. The total education service is measured by the total education time received by the population. I specify the production function of the education sector as follows:

$$F_e(t) = A_e K_e^{\alpha_e}(t) N_e^{\beta_e}(t), \; \alpha_e, \beta_e > 0, \; \alpha_e + \beta_e = 1, \tag{4.5}$$

where A_e, α_e and β_e are positive parameters. The marginal conditions for the education sector are:

$$r + \delta_k = \frac{\alpha_e p F_e}{K_e} = \alpha_e A_e p k_e^{-\beta_e}, \; w_j = \beta_e A_e p H_j^{m_j} k_e^{\alpha_e}. \tag{4.6}$$

The demand for labor force from the education sector increases in the price and level of human capital and decreases in the wage rate.

4.1.3 The Consumer Behaviors and Wealth Dynamics

Consumers make decisions on choice of consumption levels of education, services and commodities as well as on how much to save. Family plays an important role in decisions about investment in education. There are different models about decisions on education in a family. For instance, in Becker (1981), parents and children share a single unified utility function. In Cox (1987), the family is a nexus for transactions–the old lend to their children who repay them with old age care. There is also a range of formations that are in between these two formulations where parents put some weight on the income, consumption or human capital of their children (Behrman et al. 1982, Fernandez and Rogerson 1998; Banerjee 2004). This chapter follows Zhang

(2007b) in modeling the choice of education time. The preference over current and future consumption is reflected in the consumer's preference structure over education, consumption, and saving. Let $\bar{k}_j(t)$ stand for the per capita wealth of group j. I have $\bar{k}_j(t) = \bar{K}_j(t)/\bar{N}_j$. Per capita current income from the interest payment $r(t)\bar{k}_j(t)$ and the wage payment $T_j(t)w_j(t)$ is given by:

$$y_j(t) = r(t)\bar{k}_j(t) + T_j(t)w_j(t).$$

I call $y_j(t)$ the current income in the sense that it comes from consumers' payment for human capital and efforts and consumers' current earnings from ownership of wealth. The per capita disposable income is given by:

$$\hat{y}_j(t) = y_j(t) + \bar{k}_j(t) = (1 + r(t))\bar{k}_j(t) + T_j(t)w_j(t). \tag{4.7}$$

The disposable income is used for saving, consumption, and education. The consumer has the total amount of income equaling $\hat{y}_j(t)$ to distribute among saving, consumption, and education. At each point of time, a consumer would distribute the total available budget among saving $s_j(t)$, consumption of goods $c_j(t)$, and education $p_j(t)T_{je}(t)$. The budget constraint is given by:

$$c_j(t) + s_j(t) + p_j(t)T_{je}(t) = \hat{y}_j(t) = (1 + r(t))\bar{k}_j(t) + T_j(t)w_j(t). \tag{4.8}$$

The consumer is faced with the following time constraint:

$$T_j(t) + T_{je}(t) = T_0,$$

where T_0 is the total available time for work and study. Substituting this function into (4.8) yields:

$$c_j(t) + s_j(t) + \big(p_j(t) + w_j(t)\big)T_{je}(t) = \bar{y}_j(t) \equiv (1 + r(t))\bar{k}_j(t) + T_0 w_j(t). \tag{4.9}$$

I will now introduce the utility function. Here, I consider that education has two kinds of returns. As education raises labor productivity, its effect is reflected in higher wages. As Lazear (1977: 570) describes: "education is simply a normal consumption good and that, like all other normal goods, an increase in wealth will produce an increase in the amount of schooling purchased. Increased incomes are associated with higher schooling attainment as the simple result of an income effect." Education also brings about direct pleasure, more knowledge, higher social status and so on (Heckman 1976; Lazear 1977; Malchow-Møller et al. 2011). The relative importance of these returns may vary across different types of education with different individuals. This chapter introduces education time as a normal good into the utility function. In the model, at each point of time, consumers have three variables, the level of consumption, the level of saving, and the education time to decide. It is assumed that consumers' utility function is a function of level of goods $c_j(t)$ and level of saving $s_j(t)$ and education level $T_{je}(t)$ as follows:

$$U(t) = c^{\xi_{j0}}(t) s^{\lambda_{j0}}(t) T_e^{\eta_{j0}}(t),\ \xi_{j0}, \lambda_{j0}, \eta_{j0} > 0, \tag{4.10}$$

where ξ_{j0} is called the propensity to consume, λ_{j0} the propensity to own wealth, and η_{j0} the propensity to obtain education.

For the representative consumer, wage rate $w_j(t)$ and rate of interest $r(t)$ are given in markets and wealth $\bar{k}_j(t)$ is predetermined before decision. Maximizing $U_j(t)$ subject to (4.9) yields:

$$c_j = \xi_j \bar{y}_j,\ s_j = \lambda_j \bar{y}_j,\ \left(p + w_j\right) T_{je} = \eta_j \bar{y}_j, \tag{4.11}$$

where

$$\xi_{j0} \equiv \rho_j \xi_{j0},\ \lambda_{j0} \equiv \rho_j \lambda_{j0},\ \eta_{j0} \equiv \rho_j \eta_{j0},\ \rho_j \equiv \frac{1}{\xi_{j0} + \lambda_{j0} + \eta_{j0}}.$$

The demand for education is given by $T_{je} = \eta_j \bar{y}_j / \left(p_j + w_j\right)$. The demand for education decreases in the price of education and the wage rate and increases in $\bar{y}_j$. An increase in the propensity to get educated increases the education time when the other conditions are fixed. In this dynamic system, as any factor is related to all the other factors over time, it is difficult to see how one factor affects any other variable over time in the dynamic system.

According to the definitions of $s_j(t)$, the wealth accumulation of the representative household in group j is given by:

$$\dot{\bar{k}}_j(t) = s_j(t) - \bar{k}_j(t). \tag{4.12}$$

This equation simply states that the change in wealth is equal to the savings minus dissaving.

4.1.4 Dynamics of Human Capital

As empirically tested by Aakvik et al. (2010), different forms of learning have different effects of human capital accumulation. It is assumed that there are three sources of improving human capital, through education, "learning by producing", and "learning by leisure". Arrow (1962) first introduced learning by doing into growth theory; Uzawa (1965) took account of trade-offs between investment in education and capital accumulation, and Zhang (2007b) introduced the impact of consumption on human capital accumulation (via the so-called creative leisure) into growth theory. In fact, Arrow (1962: 172) recognizes the necessity to extend his idea to include other sources of human capital accumulation: "It has been assumed here that learning takes place only as a by-product of ordinary production. In fact, society has created institutions, education and research, whose purpose is to enable learning to take place more rapidly. A fuller model would take account of these as additional variables." In the literature on education and economic growth, there are some growth models with public or private education (Dee 2004; Guvenen et al. 2014; Becker et al. 2016; Bhattacharya and Chakraborty 2017; Cigno et al. 2017; Futagami and Konishi 2019; Bishnu et al. 2021; Bishnu et al. 2023). Eckstein and Zilcha (1994) propose an overlapping model with compulsory schooling. According to Kaganovich and Zilcha (1999), the government allocates tax revenues towards public investment in education and social security benefits. Epple and Romano (1998) and Caucutt (2002) examine school choice with peer effects. In Chen (2005), mixed education systems are presented.

I propose that human capital dynamics is given by:

$$\dot{H}_j = \frac{\upsilon_{je} F_e^{a_{je}} \left(H_j^{m_j} T_{je} \overline{N}_j \right)^{b_{je}}}{H_j^{\pi_{je}} \overline{N}_j} + \frac{\upsilon_{ji} F_i^{a_{ji}}}{H_j^{\pi_{ji}} \overline{N}_j} + \frac{\upsilon_{jh} C_j^{a_{jh}}}{H_j^{\pi_h} \overline{N}_j} - \delta_{jh} H_j, \tag{4.13}$$

where $\delta_{jh}(> 0)$ is the depreciation rate of human capital, υ_{je}, υ_{ji}, υ_{jh}, a_{je}, b_{je}, a_{ji}, and a_{jh} are non-negative parameters. The signs of the parameters π_{je}, π_{ji}, and π_{jh} are not specified as they may be either negative or positive.

The above equation is a synthesis and generalization of Arrow's, Uzawa's, and Zhang's ideas about human capital accumulation. The term $\upsilon_{je} F_e^{a_{je}} \left(H_j^{m_j} T_{je} \overline{N}_j \right)^{b_{je}} / H_j^{\pi_{je}} \overline{N}_j$ describes the contribution to human capital improvement through education. Human capital tends to increase with an increase in the level of education service, F_e, and in the (qualified) total study time, $H_j^{m_j} T_{je} \overline{N}_j$. The population $\overline{N}_j$ in the denominator measures the contribution in terms of per capita. The term $H^{\pi_{je}}$ indicates that as the level of human capital of the population increases, it may be more difficult (in the case of π_{je} being large) or easier (in the case of π_{je} being small) to accumulate more human capital via formal education. The term $\overline{N}_j$ in the denominator term measures the contribution in terms of per capita. I take account of learning by producing effects in human capital accumulation by the term $\upsilon_{ji} F_i^{a_{ji}} / H_j^{\pi_{ji}}$. This term implies that contribution of the production sector to human capital improvement is positively related to its production scale F_{ji} and is dependent on the level of human capital. The term $H^{\pi_{ji}}$ takes account of returns to scale effects in human capital accumulation. The case of $\pi_{ji} > (<) 0$ implies that as human capital is increased it is more difficult (easier) to further improve the level of human capital. I take account of learning by consuming by the term $\upsilon_{jh} C_j^{a_{jh}} / H_j^{\pi_{jh}} \overline{N}_j$. This term can be interpreted similarly as the term for learning by producing. Zhang (2007b) introduced this term into the human capital accumulation equation. In contemporary (in particular, developed) economies, human capital is evidently closely related to leisure activities such as different club activities, travelling different parts of the world, playing computer games, watching TV, and doing sports. Playing games in leisure time and using mobile phones to communicate with friends enables people to accumulate skills for operating computers. Travelling makes people aware of differences in, for instance, geography and cultures. People born in poverty and rich obviously have different human capital because of different living conditions. Neither Arrow's learning by doing nor Uzawa's formal education take account of this source of human capital accumulation.

It should be noted that in the literature on education and economic growth, it is assumed that human capital evolves according to the following equation (see Barro and Sala-i-Martin 1995):

$$\dot{H}(t) = H^{\eta}(t)G(T_e(t)),$$

where the function G is increasing as the effort rises with $G(0) = 0$. In the case of $\eta < 1$, there is diminishing return to the human capital accumulation. This formation is due to Lucas (1988). As $\dot{H}/H < H^{\eta-1}G(1)$, the growth rate of human capital must eventually tend to zero no matter how much effort is devoted to accumulating human capital. Uzawa's model may be considered a special case of the Lucas model with $\gamma = 0$, $U(c) = c$, and the assumption that the right-hand side of the above equation is linear in the effort. It seems reasonable to consider diminishing returns in human capital accumulation: people accumulate it rapidly early in life, then less rapidly, then not at all–as though each additional percentage increment were harder to gain than the preceding one. Solow adapts the Uzawa formation to the following form:

$$\dot{H}(t) = H(t)\kappa T_e(t).$$

This is a special case of the above equation. The new formation implies that if no effort is devoted to human capital accumulation, then $\dot{H}(0) = 0$ (human capital does not vary as time passes; this results from depreciation of human capital being ignored); if all effort is devoted to human capital accumulation, then $g_H(t) = \kappa$ (human capital grows at its maximum rate; this results from the assumption of potentially unlimited growth of human capital). Between the two extremes, there is no diminishing return to the stock $H(t)$. To achieve a given percentage increase in $H(t)$ requires the same effort. As remarked by Solow (2000), the above formulation is very far from a plausible relationship. If the above equation is considered as a production for new human capital (i.e., $\dot{H}(t)$), and if the inputs are already accumulated human capital and study time, then this production function is homogenous of degree two. It has strong increasing returns to scale and constant returns to $H(t)$ itself. It can be seen that our approach is more general to the traditional formation with regard to education. Moreover, I treat teaching also as a significant factor in human capital accumulation. Efforts in teaching are neglected in the Uzawa-Lucas model.

For the education sector, the demand and supply balance at any point of time:

$$\sum_{j=1}^{J} T_{je}\overline{N}_j = F_{je}(t). \tag{4.14}$$

The total capital stocks employed by the world are equal to the wealth owned by the world:

$$K(t) = K_i(t) + K_e(t) = \sum_{j=1}^{J} \overline{k}_j(t)\overline{N}_j. \tag{4.15}$$

The world production is equal to the world consumption and world net savings. That is:

$$C(t) + S(t) - K(t) + \delta_k K(t) = F_i(t), \tag{4.16}$$

where

$$C(t) \equiv \sum_{j=1}^{J} c_j(t)\overline{N}_j,\ S(t) \equiv \sum_{j=1}^{J} s_j(t)\overline{N}_j.$$

It is straightforward to show that this equation can be derived from the other equations in the system. The construction of the dynamic model is complete.

4.2 The Dynamics and Its Properties

Because the system has heterogeneous type of households, the dynamics is highly dimensional. The following lemma shows that the motion of the economy is expressed by $2J$ dimensional differential equations.

Lemma 4.1 The dynamics of the economy is governed by the following $2J$ dimensional differential equations system with $k_{1i}(t)$, $\left\{\overline{k}_j(t)\right\}$, and $\left(H_j(t)\right)$, where $\left\{\overline{k}_j\right\} \equiv \left(\overline{k}_2, \cdots, \overline{k}_J\right)$ and $\left(H_j\right) \equiv (H_1, \cdots, H_J)$, as the variables

$$\dot{k}_{1i} = \overline{\Lambda}_1\left(k_{1i}, \left(H_j\right), \left\{\overline{k}_j\right\}\right),$$

$$\dot{\overline{k}}_j = \overline{\Lambda}_j\left(k_{1i}, \left(H_j\right), \left\{\overline{k}_j\right\}\right), j = 2, \cdots, J,$$

$$\dot{H}_j = \Lambda_j\left(k_{1i}, \left(H_j\right), \left\{\overline{k}_j\right\}\right), j = 1, \cdots, J,$$

in which $\overline{\Lambda}_j$ and Λ_j are unique functions of $k_{1i}(t)$, $\left\{\overline{k}_j(t)\right\}$, and $\left(H_j(t)\right)$ at any point of time, defined in Appendix. For any given positive values of $k_{1i}(t)$, $\left\{\overline{k}_j(t)\right\}$, and $\left(H_j(t)\right)$ at any point of time, the other variables are uniquely determined by the following procedure: k_{ji} by (A4.1) $\rightarrow$ k_{je} by (A4.3) $\rightarrow$ r and w_j by (A4.2) $\rightarrow$ p by (A4.4) $\rightarrow$ $\bar{k}_1$ by (A4.12) $\rightarrow$ K_j by (A4.12) $\rightarrow$ k_j by (A4.9) $\rightarrow$ T_j by (A4.10) $\rightarrow$ T_{je} by (A4.8) $\rightarrow$ $N_j = T_j\overline{N}_j$ $\rightarrow$ n_{ji} and n_{je} by (A4.5) $\rightarrow$ $N_{ji} = n_{ji}N_j$ and $N_{je} = n_{je}N_j$ $\rightarrow$ $K_{ji} = k_{ji}N_{ji}$ and $K_{je} = k_{je}N_{je}$ $\rightarrow$ F_{ji} by (4.2) $\rightarrow$ F_{je} by (4.12) $\rightarrow$ $\bar{y}_j$ by (4.7) $\rightarrow$ c_j and s_j by (4.9).

I have the dynamic equations for the economy with any number of types of households. To illustrate motion of the system, the parameters are as follows:

$$\begin{pmatrix} N_1 \\ N_2 \\ N_3 \end{pmatrix} = \begin{pmatrix} 10 \\ 30 \\ 60 \end{pmatrix}, \begin{pmatrix} m_1 \\ m_2 \\ m_3 \end{pmatrix} = \begin{pmatrix} 0.5 \\ 0.4 \\ 0.3 \end{pmatrix}, \begin{pmatrix} \xi_{10} \\ \xi_{20} \\ \xi_{30} \end{pmatrix} = \begin{pmatrix} 0.12 \\ 0.18 \\ 0.2 \end{pmatrix}, \begin{pmatrix} \lambda_{10} \\ \lambda_{20} \\ \lambda_{30} \end{pmatrix} = \begin{pmatrix} 0.8 \\ 0.75 \\ 0.7 \end{pmatrix},$$
$$\begin{pmatrix} \eta_{10} \\ \eta_{20} \\ \eta_{30} \end{pmatrix} = \begin{pmatrix} 0.015 \\ 0.010 \\ 0.008 \end{pmatrix}, \begin{pmatrix} v_{1e} \\ v_{2e} \\ v_{3e} \end{pmatrix} = \begin{pmatrix} 0.8 \\ 0.7 \\ 0.5 \end{pmatrix}, \begin{pmatrix} v_{1i} \\ v_{2i} \\ v_{3i} \end{pmatrix} = \begin{pmatrix} 2.5 \\ 2 \\ 1.7 \end{pmatrix}, \begin{pmatrix} v_{1h} \\ v_{2h} \\ v_{3h} \end{pmatrix} = \begin{pmatrix} 0.8 \\ 0.6 \\ 0.5 \end{pmatrix},$$
$$\begin{pmatrix} a_{1e} \\ a_{2e} \\ a_{3e} \end{pmatrix} = \begin{pmatrix} 0.3 \\ 0.4 \\ 0.45 \end{pmatrix}, \begin{pmatrix} b_{1e} \\ b_{2e} \\ b_{3e} \end{pmatrix} = \begin{pmatrix} 0.5 \\ 0.55 \\ 0.6 \end{pmatrix}, \begin{pmatrix} a_{1i} \\ a_{2i} \\ a_{3i} \end{pmatrix} = \begin{pmatrix} 0.4 \\ 0.45 \\ 0.5 \end{pmatrix},$$
$$\begin{pmatrix} a_{1h} \\ a_{2h} \\ a_{3h} \end{pmatrix} = \begin{pmatrix} 0.1 \\ 0.15 \\ 0.2 \end{pmatrix}, \begin{pmatrix} b_{1h} \\ b_{2h} \\ b_{3h} \end{pmatrix} = \begin{pmatrix} 0.3 \\ 0.35 \\ 0.4 \end{pmatrix}, \begin{pmatrix} \pi_{1e} \\ \pi_{2e} \\ \pi_{3e} \end{pmatrix} = \begin{pmatrix} -0.2 \\ -0.15 \\ -0.1 \end{pmatrix},$$
$$\begin{pmatrix} \pi_{1i} \\ \pi_{2i} \\ \pi_{3i} \end{pmatrix} = \begin{pmatrix} 0.7 \\ 0.75 \\ 0.8 \end{pmatrix}, \begin{pmatrix} \pi_{1h} \\ \pi_{2h} \\ \pi_{3h} \end{pmatrix} = \begin{pmatrix} 0.1 \\ 0.15 \\ 0.2 \end{pmatrix},$$
$$A_i = 0.9, A_e = 0.8, \alpha_i = 0.32, \alpha_e = 0.37, T_0 = 1, \delta_k = 0.05,$$
$$\delta_{1h} = 0.04, \delta_{2h} = 0.05, \delta_{3h} = 0.06. \tag{4.17}$$

Group 1, 2, and $3's$ populations are respectively 10, 30, and 60. Group 3 has the largest population. The industrial sector and education sector's total productivity are respectively 0.9 and 0.8. Group 1, 2 and $3's$ utilization efficiency parameters, m_j, are respectively 0.5, 0.4, and 0.3. Group 1 utilizes human capital most effectively; group 2 next and group 3 lest effectively. The three groups are called, rich, middle, and poor class (RC, MC, PC), respectively. I specify the values of the parameters, α_j, in the Cobb–Douglas productions approximately equal to 0.3. The RC's learning by doing parameter, v_{1i}, is the highest. The returns to scale parameters in learning by doing, π_{ji}, are all positive, which implies that knowledge exhibits decreasing returns to scale in learning by doing. The depreciation rates of physical capital and knowledge are specified to be about 0.05. The RC's propensity to save is 0.8 and the PC's propensity to save is 0.7. The value of the MC's propensity is between the other groups. The RC's propensity to obtain education is highest among the three classes; the PC has the lowest propensity to obtain education. Under (4.17) the system has a unique equilibrium. The equilibrium values are listed in (4.18). The national industrial output is 292.25 and the interest rate is about 3.9 percent. The human capital levels of the RC, MC, and PC are respectively 22.62, 6.63, and 3.64. The wage rates of the three groups are respectively 22.62, 6.63, and 3.64. The RC has the highest human capital as well as a higher wage rate. The RC also spends much more time on education than the other two groups. According to Dur and Glazer (2008), rich people tend to attend college at a higher rate than poor people as the rich people get more benefits from the consumption content of education. The PC spends longest time on working. The RC's consumption level and wealth are also highest.

$$\begin{aligned}
&r = 0.039, p = 1.026, k = 5.67, N = 189.09, K = 1071.22,\\
&F_i = 292.25, F_e = 4.09, N_i = 186.61, N_e = 2.48, K_i = 1053.74,\\
&K_e = 17.48, k_i = 5.65, k_e = 7.07, f_i = 1.56, f_e = 1.65, H_1 = 22.62,\\
&H_2 = 6.63, H_3 = 3.64, w_1 = 5.07, w_2 = 2.27, w_3 = 1.57,\\
&\bar{k}_1 = 38.96, \bar{k}_2 = 10.57, \bar{k}_3 = 6.07, T_{1e} = 0.12, T_{2e} = 0.04,\\
&T_{3e} = 0.03, c_1 = 5.84, c_2 = 2.54, c_3 = 1.74.
\end{aligned} \tag{4.18}$$

It is straightforward to calculate the six eigenvalues as follows:

$$-0.20, -0.18, -0.13, -0.09, -0.06, -0.03.$$

As all the eigenvalues are negative, the equilibrium is locally stable. In Fig. 4.1, the motion of the system is plotted with the following initial conditions:

$$k_{1i}(0) = 11, \underset{2}{k}(0) = 4.5, \underset{3}{k}(0) = 2, H_1(0) = 3.5, H_2(0) = 1.9,$$

$$H_3(0) = 0.5.$$

The system approaches its equilibrium point in the long term.

4.3 A Rise in the RC's Propensity to Obtain Education

It is important to ask questions such as how a change in one group's propensity to save or to obtain education affects the economy and each group's wealth and consumption. This section examines the case that all the parameters, except the RC's propensity to obtain education, η_{10}, are the same as in (4.17). The propensity rises in the following way:

$$\eta_{10} : 0.015 \Rightarrow 0.018.$$

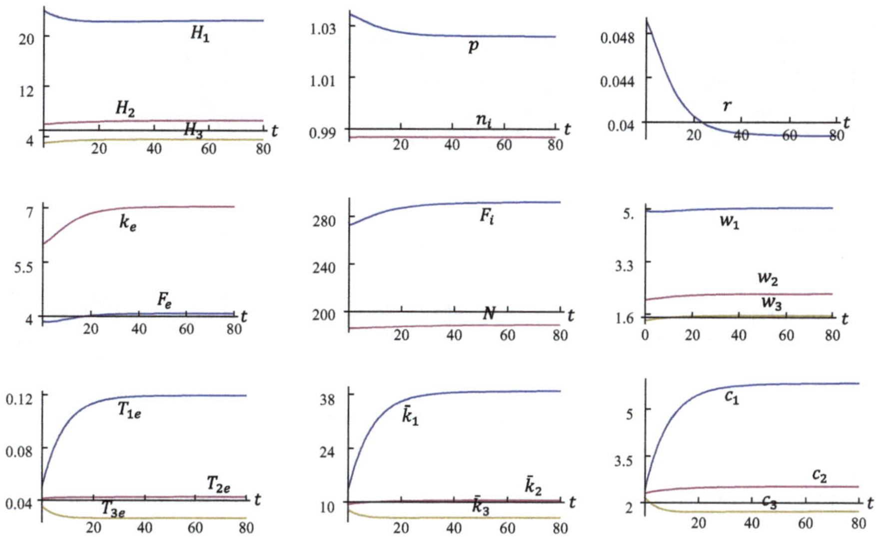

Fig. 4.1 The motion of some variables

The simulation results are plotted in Fig. 4.2. From Fig. 4.2, it is seen that as the RC increases the propensity to obtain education, the RC's level of human capital is increased. To examine the process of the change in the human capital, it is important to follow how all the variables in the system react to the parameter shift. Initially as the rich class increases the preference for formal education, the rich people would spend more time on schooling (with the other conditions remaining the same). Hence, the human capital of the rich class will be increased. The rise in human capital increases the total labor force, but the fall in the work time reduces the labor force. As shown in Fig. 4.2, the total labor force is reduced. Hence, the total output of the industrial sector falls. As the demand for education is increased, the education fee increases and output of the education sector is increased. The labor share of the education sector increases. Although the RC increases the education time, the education time by the other two classes is slightly affected. The other two classes' human capital levels are increased, but the PC's human capital is much less affected. The wage rate of the RC increases, but the wage rates of the other two classes are reduced. As the education hours of the MC and PC are slightly affected, it can be concluded that the returns from schooling in terms of wage rate are reduced for the two classes. As the RC puts more resources into schooling, the wealth and consumption are reduced. It should be noted that in a model with education and inequality by Nakajima and Nakamura (2009), it is found that the educational expenditure of rich households could prevent poor households from escaping poverty. Their model tries to explain the possible effects of high prices of education on growth and inequality in countries, like Japan, Korea and the U.S. The basic insight from the model is that as the rich households demand higher education, the price should be pushed up. Consequently, the poor are excluded from higher education. This also leads to enlarged inequality between the

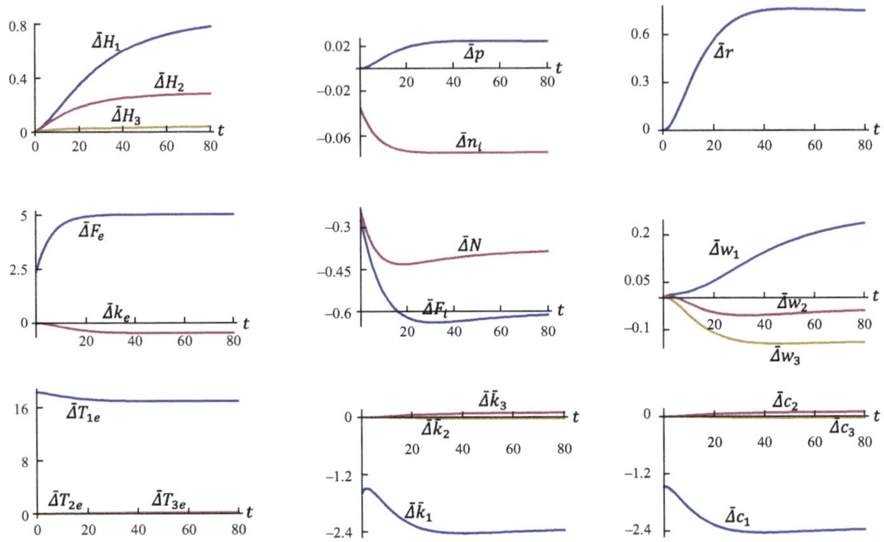

Fig. 4.2 A rise in the rich class's propensity to receive education

rich and poor in the long term. Our model predicts similar effects within a country with heterogeneous households.

4.4 A Rise in the RC's Propensity to Obtain Education

The propensity rises in the following way:

$$\lambda_{10} : 0.8 \Rightarrow 0.81.$$

The simulation results are plotted in Fig. 4.3. A rise in the RC's propensity to save tends to enlarge the gaps with the other two classes in terms of wealth and consumption levels but tends to reduce gaps of human capital among the classes. In reality, as extremely rich people have "too much" money to spend, the propensity to save tends to increase in the long term. It should be remarked that that the propensity to save in our model is different than defined in the neoclassical growth theory. In our model, the propensity to save is equal to the share of the disposable income saved for the future; while in the Solow model the propensity to save is equal to the share of the current income saved for the future. Hence, in the Solow model how much people accumulate wealth has much weaker impact on saving behavior than in our model when the wealth per capita is extremely high. It can be seen that our model predicts enlarged income gaps between the rich and the poor over time, even though the human capital level differences may not vary much between the two groups.

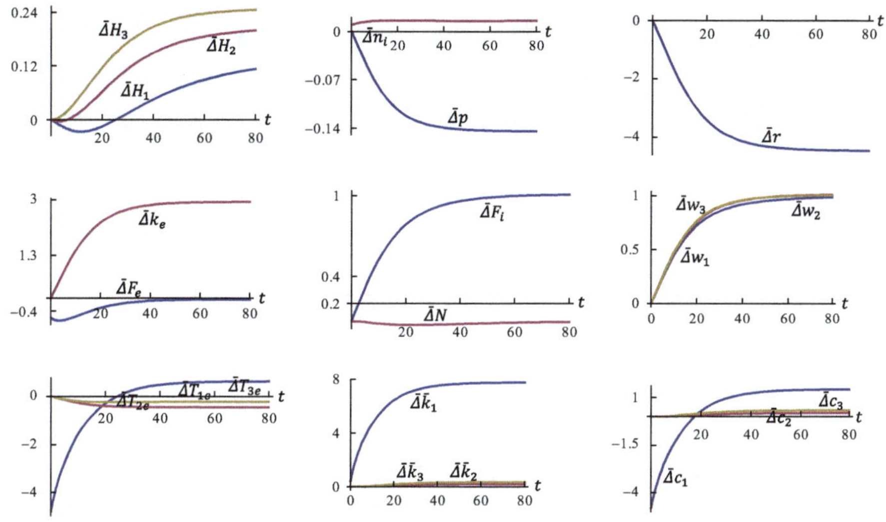

Fig. 4.3 A rise in the rich class's propensity to save

4.5 A Rise in the RC's Population

It has been observed that the effect of population growth varies with the level of economic development and can be positive for some developed economies. Theoretical models with human capital predict situation-dependent interactions between population and economic growth. I now increase the RC's population in the following way:

$$\overline{N}_1 : 10 \Rightarrow 15.$$

The simulation results are plotted in Fig. 4.4. As the RC increases the population, the RC's human capital and wage rate falls over time. The schooling time, consumption level, and wealth per capita of the RC rise initially and fall in the long term. The price of education falls, which benefits the MC and PC. As the output of the industrial sector is increased as a consequence of the population increase, the MC and PC learn more effectively through learning by producing. The human capital levels of both the MC and the PC increase. In the long term the consumption and wealth levels per capita of the MC and the PC are increased. The MC and PC benefit in the long term. It is concluded that an increase in the RC's population reduces the gaps in income, wealth and consumption between the rich and the poor in the long term.

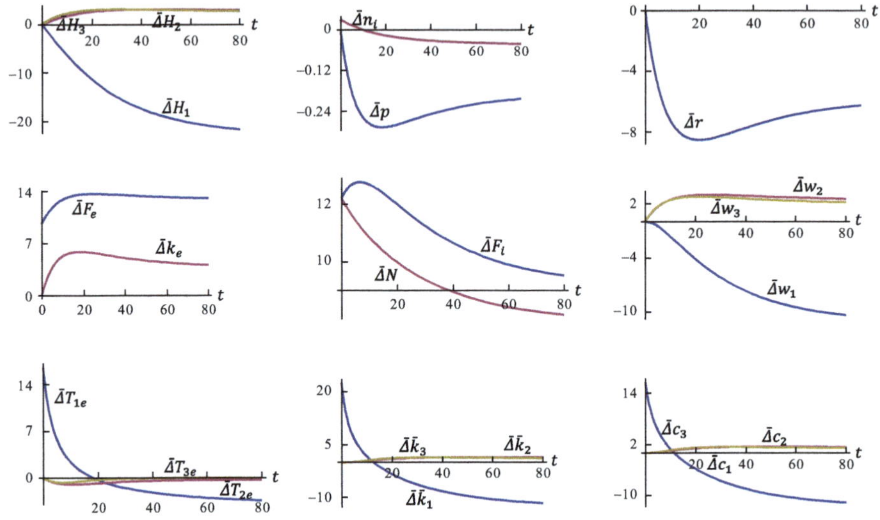

Fig. 4.4 A rise in the rich class's population

4.6 A Rise in the Total Factor Productivity

Another important question is what will happen to different people and the national economy if the total productivity of the education sector is increased. The total productivity rises in the following way:

$$A_e : 0.8 \Rightarrow 0.9.$$

The simulation results are plotted in Fig. 4.5. The rise in the productivity increases human capital of all the groups and reduces the price of education. As all the classes' human capital levels are increased and the differences of these increases are not large, the distribution of the total labor force is slightly affected. The two sectors increase the output levels in the long term. The education time, wage rates, wealth and consumption levels of all the groups are increased in the long term. It is concluded that an improvement in the efficiency of the educational system will benefit different people in the long term.

4.7 Concluding Remarks

This chapter proposed a growth model of heterogeneous households with wealth accumulation and human capital accumulation. The economic system consists of one production sector and one education sector. I took account of three ways of improving human capital: learning by producing, learning by education, and learning

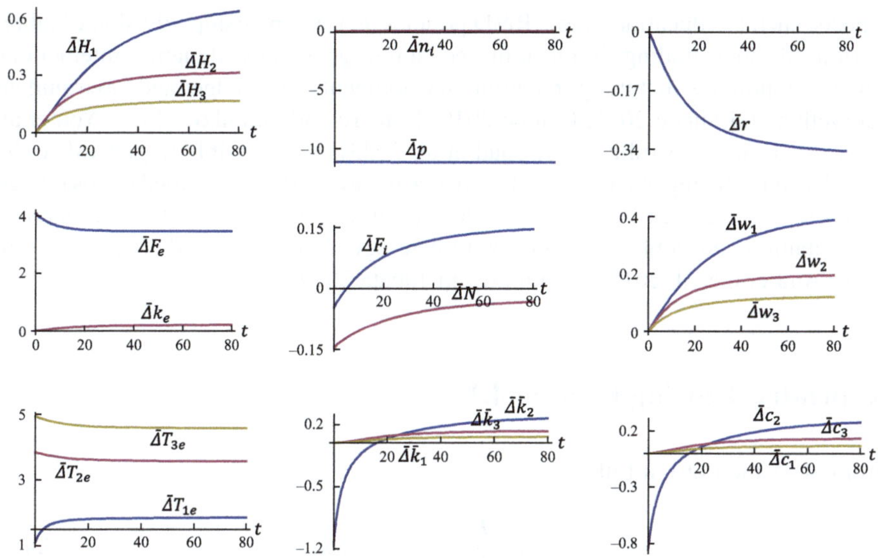

Fig. 4.5 A rise in the education sector's total productivity

by consuming. The model describes a dynamic interdependence among wealth accumulation, human capital accumulation, and division of labor under perfect competition. It is possible to extend the model in some directions. For instance, as mentioned by Bertocchi and Spagat (2004), the specific structure of the educational system is largely unexplored. Education may be privately or publicly provided. An education system may also be founded on a hierarchical differentiation between vocational and general education. As demonstrated by Bertocchi and Spagat, the educational structure varies over time. I may introduce some kind of government intervention in education into the model. I don't consider public provision or subsidies of education. In the literature of education and economic growth, many models with heterogeneous households are proposed to address issues related to taxation, education policy, distribution of income and wealth, and economic growth. For instance, Benabou (2002) studied the effects of progressive income taxes and education finance in a dynamic heterogeneous-agent model. As shown in Glomm and Kaganovich (2008), public provision may have significant impact on growth and inequality across households. They examine the relationship between growth and inequality with public education in the context of an overlapping generation economy with heterogeneous agents. The government collects a tax on labor income to finance education. The model predicts that the government spending on education reduces income inequality. Another study by Dur and Glazer (2008) shows that rich people tend to attend college at a higher rate than poor people as the rich people get more benefits from the consumption content of education. They conclude that colleges should make sure to attract the most able students and not only the riches, and also charge higher intuition fees from the rich students. There are also many other models emphasizing different aspects, such as education, trade, R&D policies, entrepreneurship, division of labor, learning through trading, brain drain, economic geography, dynamic interactions among economic structure, population, development, knowledge, and environment (Cervellati and Sunde 2015; Osiobe 2019; Romero and Gramkow 2021; You et al. 2022; Madsen and Strulik 2023; Saad et al. 2023). It is possible to generalize the model by introducing other factors. For instance, Levy (2005) examined issues related to how society chooses the tax rate and the allocation of the revenues between income redistribution and public education with heterogeneous households (Grembi et al. 2016; Andreoli et al. 2018; Morimoto and Tabata 2019).

Appendix: Proving Lemma 4.1

From (4.4) and (4.6), it follows:

$$\frac{K_e}{N_e} = \alpha \frac{K_i}{N_i}, \text{ i.e.}, k_e = \alpha k_i, \tag{A4.1}$$

where $\alpha \equiv \alpha_e \beta_i / \alpha_i \beta_e$ ($\neq 1$ assumed). From (A4.1), (4.4) and (4.6), I obtain:

$$p = \frac{\alpha^{\beta_e} \alpha_i A_i}{\alpha_e A_e} k_i^{\beta}, \tag{A4.2}$$

where $\beta \equiv \beta_e - \beta_i$. From (A4.1) and (4.1), I solve the labor distribution as functions of k_i and k:

$$n_i = \frac{\alpha k_i - k}{(\alpha - 1) k_i}, \quad n_e = \frac{k - k_i}{(\alpha - 1) k_i}. \tag{A4.3}$$

From $(p + w_j) T_{je} = \eta_j \overline{y}_j$ in (4.11) and the definition of $\overline{y}_j$, it follows:

$$T_{je} = \phi_{jp} \overline{k}_j + \phi_{j0}, \tag{A4.4}$$

where

$$\phi_{jp}(k_i, H_j) \equiv \frac{(1 + r)\eta_j}{p + w_j}, \quad \phi_{j0}(k_i, H_j) \equiv \frac{\eta_j T_0 w_j}{p + w_j}.$$

From (A4.4) and (4.14):

$$\phi \sum_{j=1}^{J} \left(\phi_{jp} \overline{k}_j + \phi_{j0} \right) \overline{N}_j = N(k - k_i), \tag{A4.5}$$

where $F_e = A_e k_e^{\alpha_e} n_e N$, (A4.3), $k_e = \alpha k_i$, are applied, and

$$\phi(k_i) \equiv \frac{(\alpha - 1)k_i^{\beta_e}}{\alpha^{\alpha_e} A_e}.$$

From $T_j + T_{je} = T_0$ and (A4.4), I have:

$$T_j = T_0 - \phi_{jp}\overline{k}_j - \phi_{j0}. \tag{A4.6}$$

From (A4.6), I have:

$$N = \sum_{j=1}^{J}\left(T_0 - \phi_{jp}\overline{k}_j - \phi_{j0}\right)H_j^{m_j}\overline{N}_j. \tag{A4.7}$$

From (4.2) and $K = kN$, it follows:

$$K = k\left(\sum_{j=1}^{J}\left(T_0 - \phi_{jp}\overline{k}_j - \phi_{j0}\right)H_j^{m_j}\overline{N}_j\right). \tag{A4.8}$$

From (A4.8) and (4.15):

$$kN = k\left(\sum_{j=1}^{J}\left(T_0 - \phi_{jp}\overline{k}_j - \phi_{j0}\right)H_j^{m_j}\overline{N}_j\right) = \sum_{j=1}^{J}\overline{k}_j\overline{N}_j. \tag{A4.9}$$

Insert (A4.9) and (A4.7) in (A4.5):

$$\overline{k}_1 = \Lambda_k\left(k_i, (H_j), \left\{\overline{k}_j\right\}\right) \equiv \frac{\Lambda_0 - \phi\phi_{10} - (T_0 - \phi_{10})k_i H_1^{m_1}}{\phi\phi_{1p} - 1 - \phi_{1p}k_l H_1^{m_1}}, \tag{A4.10}$$

where

$$\Lambda_0\left(k_i, (H_j), \left\{\overline{k}_j\right\}\right) \equiv$$

$$\frac{1}{\overline{N}_1}\sum_{j=2}^{J}\left[\overline{k}_j - \left(T_0 - \phi_{jp}\overline{k}_j - \phi_{j0}\right)k_i H_j^{m_j} - \phi\left(\phi_{jp}\overline{k}_j + \phi_{j0}\right)\right]\overline{N}_j,$$

where $\left(H_j\right) \equiv (H_1, \cdots, H_J)$ and $\left\{\overline{k}_j\right\} \equiv \left(\overline{k}_2, \cdots, \overline{k}_J\right)$. It is straightforward to confirm that all the variables can be expressed as functions of k_i, $\left(H_j\right)$ and $\left\{\overline{k}_j\right\}$ by the following procedure: k_e by (A4.1) $\rightarrow$ r and w_j by (4.4) $\rightarrow$ p by (A4.2) $\rightarrow$ $\overline{k}_1$ by (A4.10) $\rightarrow$ k by (A4.9) $\rightarrow$ K by (A4.8) $\rightarrow$ T_j by (A4.6) $\rightarrow$ T_{je} by (A4.4) $\rightarrow$ N

by (A4.7) $\to n_i$ and n_e by (A4.3) $\to N_i = n_i N$ and $N_e = n_e N \to K_i = k_i N_i$ and $K_e = k_e N_e \to F_i$ by (4.4) $\to F_e$ by (4.5) $\to \overline{y}_j$ by (4.9) $\to c_j$ and s_j by (4.11). From this procedure and (4.11), it follows:

$$\dot{H}_j = \Lambda_j\left(k_{1i}, (H_j), \left\{\overline{k}_j\right\}\right) \equiv \frac{\upsilon_{je} F_e^{a_{je}} \left(H_j^{m_j} T_{je} \overline{N}_j\right)^{b_{je}}}{H_j^{\pi_{je}} \overline{N}_j} + \frac{\upsilon_{ji} F_i^{a_{ji}}}{H_j^{\pi_{ji}} \overline{N}_j} + \frac{\upsilon_{jh} C_j^{a_{jh}}}{H_j^{\pi_h} \overline{N}_j} - \delta_{jh} H_j. \tag{A4.11}$$

Here, I don't provide explicit expressions of the functions as they are tedious. Substituting $\overline{y}_j = (1 + r)\overline{k}_j + T_O w_j$ into $s_j = \lambda_j \overline{y}_j$ yields:

$$s_j = (1 + r)\lambda_j \overline{k}_j + \lambda_j T_O w_j. \tag{A4.12}$$

Substituting (A4.12) into (4.12) yields:

$$\dot{\overline{k}}_1 = \lambda_1 T_O w_1 - R(k_i, H_1)\overline{k}_1, \tag{A4.13}$$

$$\dot{\overline{k}}_j = \overline{\Lambda}_j\left(k_i, (H_j), \left\{\overline{k}_j\right\}\right) \equiv \lambda_j T_O w_j - \left(1 - \lambda_j - \lambda_j r\right)\overline{k}_j, \quad j = 2, \cdots, J, \tag{A4.14}$$

in which $R(k_i, H_1) \equiv 1 - \lambda_1 - \lambda_1 r$.Taking derivatives of equation (A4.10) with respect to t yields:

$$\dot{\overline{k}}_1 = \frac{\partial \Lambda_k}{\partial k_i} \dot{k}_i + \sum_{j=1}^{J} \Lambda_j \frac{\partial \Lambda_k}{\partial H_j} + \sum_{j=2}^{J} \overline{\Lambda}_j \frac{\partial \Lambda_k}{\partial \overline{k}_j}, \tag{A4.15}$$

where (A4.11) and (A4.14) are applied. Equal the right-hand sizes of equations (A4.13) and (A4.15):

$$\dot{k}_i = \overline{\Lambda}_1\left(k_i, (H_j), \left\{\overline{k}_j\right\}\right) \equiv \left[\lambda_1 T_O w_1 - R\Lambda_k - \sum_{j=1}^{J} \Lambda_j \frac{\partial \Lambda_k}{\partial H_j} - \sum_{j=2}^{J} \overline{\Lambda}_j \frac{\partial \Lambda_k}{\partial \overline{k}_j}\right] \left(\frac{\partial \Lambda_k}{\partial k_i}\right)^{-1}. \tag{A4.16}$$

In summary, the lemma is confirmed.

Chapter 5
Growth, Trade, and Knowledge with National Research

> Against stupidity we are defenseless. Neither protests nor force can touch it; arguments fall on deaf ears. Evil always carries the seeds of its own undoing – it creates unease. But stupidity feels self-satisfied, immune, and convinced of its own rightness. And that makes it far more dangerous.
>
> Dietrich Bonhoeffer (1906-1945)

Income and wealth inequality and its dynamics among different groups, regions, and countries are important topics in economics. This chapter considers the impact of trade on income distribution among countries in a globalizing world economy. Many studies have shown that much of the income disparity among countries is explained by productivity differences, and that technology plays an important role in determining productivity (Jaffe, 1989; Krugman and Venables, 1995; Manasse and Turrini, 2001; Agénor, 2004; Aghion et al., 2009; Gersbach et al., 2013; Zhang, 2015c; Zhang, 2016b; Mutreja et al., 2018). To understand contemporary world economy, it is necessary to deal with global economies as an integrated whole (Ömer et al., 2018; Yazdi, 2019; Gedikli et al., 2022; Saad et al., 2023; Cárdenas-García et al., 2024). The pattern of worldwide technical change is determined largely by international technology diffusion. Moreover, a few rich countries account for most of the world's creation of new technology. It is important to have analytical frameworks for analyzing global economic interactions with microeconomic foundations. As developed, industrializing and developing economies are well connected with trades, it is important to examine how changes in preference or technology in one country can affect the country as well as other countries in a well-connected world economy. For instance, an underdeveloped economy with large population, like India or China, may affect different economies as its technology is improved or population is increased. This chapter is also concerned with how trade patterns may be affected as technologies are further improved or propensities to save are reduced in developed economies like the US or Japan. It is well known that only a few formal economic theories properly address inequalities in income and wealth among nations with microeconomic foundation. This chapter deals with the effects of free trade and

W. Zhang, *A Dynamic Economic Theory of Heterogenous Households*,
https://doi.org/10.1007/978-981-95-8918-0_5

national governments' research policies on global growth and inequalities among nations.

As far as modelling production and trade patterns are concerned, this chapter follows the neoclassical growth trade model, particularly the Oniki-Uzawa model (Oniki and Uzawa, 1965). As reviewed by Findlay (1984), the pure theory of international trade developed before the 1960s failed to properly analyze the connection between economic growth and international trade. The classic Ricardian theory of comparative advantage and the Heckscher-Ohlin theory did not consider labor and capital stocks (or land) as endogenously changeable variables. In the last three or four decades, trade theory has made some systematic treatment of capital accumulation or technological changes in the context of international economics. A dynamic model with endogenous capital accumulation and capital movements was initially developed by Oniki and Uzawa and others (e.g., Oniki and Uzawa, 1965; Johnson, 1971), in terms of the two-country, two-good, two-factor model of trade. The model has been extended and generalized to analyze the interdependence between trade patterns and economic growth (e.g., Jones and Kenen, 1984; Ethier and Svensson, 1986; Bhagwati, 1991; Wong, 1995; Sorger, 2002; Vellutini; 2003). Zhang (2008b) provides an extensive review on the literature by then. Irrespective of analytical difficulties involved in analyzing two-country, dynamic-optimization models with capital accumulation, many efforts have been made to examine the impact of saving, technology, and various policies upon trade patterns within this framework (Frenkel and Razin, 1987; Jensen, 1994; Valdés, 1999; Nishimura and Shimomura, 2002). As far as capital accumulation and trade pattern determination are concerned, our study follows the Oniki-Uzawa framework (Ikeda and Ono, 1992), even though this chapter deviates from the traditional approach in modeling behavior of households.

In the model economic dynamics are fueled by public investment in research, learning by doing and physical investment. The model is to integrate the basic economic growth mechanisms in the neoclassical growth theory with capital accumulation and growth theory with endogenous knowledge. I consider knowledge as an international public good in the sense that all countries access knowledge and the utilization of knowledge by one country does not affect that by others. Trade economists have recently developed different trade models with endogenous knowledge (Chari and Hopenhayn, 1991; Martin and Ottaviano, 2001; Brecher *et al.*, 2002; Ben-David and Loewy, 2003; Nocco, 2005; Hinloopen, 2014; Akcigit and Kerr, 2018; Jones, 2019). These studies attempted to formalize trade patterns with endogenous technological change and monopolistic competition. They often link trade theory with increasing-returns growth theory. These approaches deal with dynamic interdependence between trade patterns, R&D efforts, and various economic policies. Although these studies explore the relationship between trade policy and long-run growth either with knowledge or with capital, in most of them it is not with both capital and knowledge in a unified framework.A common limitation in most trade models with endogenous capital and/or knowledge is that they deal with the world economy with only two national economies (Grossman and Helpman, 1991; Wong, 1995; Jensen and Wong, 1998; Obstfeld and Rogoff, 1998). The world consists of different countries and different countries have different preferences, technologies and resources. Conclusions made from analyzing a two-country model might provide limited or even misleading insights into the complexity of multi-country economy. It is necessary to deal with a world economy with any number of national economies. It is well known that dynamic-optimization models with capital accumulation are associated with analytical difficulties. To avoid these difficulties, this chapter applies an alternative approach to consumer behavior. The model is a further development of the studies by Zhang. Zhang (1992) proposed a multi-country model with capital accumulation and knowledge creation. The study does not consider research and does not simulate the behavior of the model. Zhang (1993b) develops an endogenous growth model with wealth accumulation and knowledge dynamics. This chapter does not simulate the model and is limited to a national economy. Zhang (2014c) considers different sources of knowledge dynamics for a national economy without interregional or international trade and simulates the model so that one can observe the dynamic behavior of the economic system. This study synthesizes the basic ideas for a multi-country global economy with wealth accumulation and knowledge dynamics. This chapter models the behavior of households in an alternative way for a multi-country economy with free trade and assumes that knowledge creation is through learning by doing and research. This chapter is based on Zhang (2018a) and is organized as follows. Section 5.1 defines the multi-country model with capital accumulation and knowledge creation. Section 5.2 shows that the dynamics of the world economy with J countries can be described by $(J + 1)$-dimensional differential equations. Section 5.3 shows how the economic system is affected when the DE's knowledge utilization efficiency rises. Section 5.4 shows the effects of a rise in the DE's tax rate on the motion of the economic system. Section 5.5 analyses what happens in the system where the UE's tax rate is increased. Section 5.6 analyses the impact of a rise in the DE's propensity to save. Section 5.7 concludes the chapter. The analytical results in sect. 5.2 are confirmed in Appendix A1. Appendix A2 examines the case when all the countries have the same preference.

5.1 The Multi-Country Trade Model with Capital and Knowledge

I consider a global economy with any number of countries. Each country has one production sector and one university. Subscript indexes i and r are used to denote the production sector and the university, respectively. The university is financially supported by the government through taxing the production sector. The governments fix the tax rates and obtain tax incomes from the private sectors. The research sector employs labor and capital in such a way that the research output is maximized with the government's tax income. Knowledge growth is through learning by doing by the production sector and research activities by the university. It is assumed that the countries produce a homogenous commodity. Most aspects of production sectors in the model are similar to the neo-classical one-sector growth model. There is only one (durable) good in the global economy under consideration. Households own assets of the economy and distribute their incomes to consume and save. Production sectors or firms use knowledge, capital, and labor. Exchanges take place in perfectly competitive markets. Production sectors sell their product to households or to other sectors and households sell their labor and assets to production sectors. Factor markets work well; factors are inelastically supplied and the available factors are fully utilized at every moment. Saving is undertaken only by households, which implies that all earnings of firms are distributed in the form of payments to factors of production. The possibility of hoarding output in the form of non-productive inventories held by households is neglected. All savings volunteered by households are absorbed by firms. The system consists of multiple countries, indexed by $j = 1, \ldots, J$. Each country has a fixed labor force, N_j, ($j = 1, \ldots, J$). Let prices be measured in terms of the commodity and the price of the commodity be unity. The wage and interest rates are denoted by $w_j(t)$ and $r_j(t)$, respectively, in the j th country. In the free trade system, the interest rate is identical throughout the world economy, i.e., $r(t) = r_j(t)$. For convenience, I call the people working in the production sector as workers and the people working in the university as scientists. The population is classified into workers and scientists. Let $N_{qj}(t)$ and $K_{qj}(t)$ stand for the labor force and capital stocks employed by sector q, $q = i, r$, in country j.

5.2 Behavior of Producers

There are three factors, physical capital, labor, and knowledge at each point of time t. Let $F_j(t)$ stand for the output level of the production sector by country j. The production functions are given by:

$$F_j(t) = A_j Z^{m_j}(t) K_{ij}^{\alpha_j}(t) N_{ij}^{\beta_j}(t),\ A_j > 0,\ \alpha_j + \beta_j = 1,\ \alpha_j, \beta_j > 0,$$

$$j = 1, \cdots, J,$$

In which $Z(t)(>0)$ is the knowledge stock at time t. Here, m_j is called country $j's$ knowledge utilization efficiency parameter. If I interpret $Z^{m_j/\beta}(t)N_j(t)$ as country $j's$ human capital or qualified labor force (e.g., Iacopetta, 2011), the production function is a neoclassical one and homogeneous of degree one with the inputs. Many studies show that basic research positively affects applied research (Nelson and Winter, 1982; Jaffe, 1989; Nelson, 2002; Adams, 1990; Acs et al., 1992; Mansfield, 1998). It is also possible to interpret the above formation as follows. A company's applied knowledge is a nonlinear function of general knowledge. I consider that the total productivity factor is proportionally related to $Z^{m_j}(t)$.

Markets are competitive; thus labor and capital earn their marginal products, and firms earn zero profits. The rate of interest, $r(t)$, and wage rates, $w_j(t)$, are determined by markets. Hence, for any individual firm $r(t)$ and $w_j(t)$ are given at each point of time. The production sector chooses the two variables $K_{ij}(t)$ and $N_{ij}(t)$ to maximize its profit. The marginal conditions are given by:

$$r(t) + \delta_{kj} = \bar{\tau}_j A_j \alpha_j Z^{m_j}(t) k_j^{-\beta_j}(t),\ w_j(t) = \bar{\tau}_j A_j \beta_j Z^{m_j}(t) k_j^{\alpha_j}(t) \tag{5.1}$$

where δ_{kj} are the depreciation rate of physical capital in country j and

$$k_j(t) \equiv \frac{K_{ij}(t)}{N_{ij}(t)},\ \bar{\tau}_j \equiv 1 - \tau_j$$

in which τ_j is country $j's$ tax rate on its production sector.

5.3 Behavior of Consumers

Each household gets income from wealth ownership and wages. Consumers make decisions on consumption levels of goods as well as on how much to save. Let $\bar{k}_j(t)$ stand for the per capita wealth in country j. Each consumer of country j obtains income:

$$y_j(t) = r(t)\bar{k}_j(t) + w_j(t), j = 1, \cdots, J \tag{5.2}$$

from the interest payment $r(t)\bar{k}_j(t)$ and the wage payment $w_j(t)$. I call $y_j(t)$ the current income in the sense that it comes from consumers' wages and consumers' current earnings from ownership of wealth. The disposable income that consumers are using for consuming, saving, or transferring are not necessarily equal to the current income because consumers can sell wealth to pay, for instance, the current consumption if the current income is not sufficient for buying food and touring the country. The maximum value of wealth is when a consumer can sell to purchase goods equal to $\bar{k}_j(t)$. The disposable income is as follows:

$$\hat{y}_j(t) = y_j(t) + \bar{k}_j(t) \tag{5.3}$$

The disposable income is used for saving and consumption. It should be noted that the value, $\bar{k}_j(t)$, (i.e., $p(t)\bar{k}_j(t)$ with $p(t) = 1$), in the above equation is a flow variable.

At each point of time, a consumer distributes the total available budget between savings, $s_j(t)$, and consumption of goods, $c_j(t)$. The budget constraint is:

$$c_j(t) + s_j(t) = \hat{y}_j(t) = r\bar{k}_j(t) + w_j(t) + \bar{k}_j(t) \tag{5.4}$$

At each point of time, consumers have two variables to decide. Eq. (5.4) means that consumption and savings exhaust the consumer's disposable income.

The utility levels that the consumers obtain are dependent on the consumption level of commodity, $c_j(t)$, and the savings, $s_j(t)$. The utility level of the consumer in country j, $U_j(t)$, is specified as follows:

$$U_j(t) = c_j^{\xi_{0j}}(t) s_j^{\lambda_{0j}}(t),\ \xi_{0j},\ \lambda_{0j} > 0 \tag{5.5}$$

where ξ_{0j} and λ_j are respectively household j's propensities to consume and to hold wealth. Here, the preference structure is assumed invariant. It is quite reasonable to assume that one's attitude towards the future is dependent on factors such as capital gains, the stock of durables owned by oneself, income distribution, and demographic factors.

Maximizing U_j subject to the budget constraints (5.4) yields:

$$c_j(t) = \xi_j \hat{y}_j(t),\ s_j(t) = \lambda_j \hat{y}_j(t) \tag{5.6}$$

in which

$$\xi_j \equiv \frac{\xi_{0j}}{\xi_{0j} + \lambda_{0j}},\ \lambda_j \equiv \frac{\lambda_{0j}}{\xi_{0j} + \lambda_{0j}}.$$

According to the definitions of $s_j(t)$, the wealth accumulation of the representative household in country j is given by:

$$\dot{\bar{k}}_j(t) = s_j(t) - \bar{k}_j(t) \tag{5.7}$$

This equation states that the change in wealth is the saving minus dissaving.

5.4 Knowledge Creation

Bresnahan and Trajtenberg (1995) argued that technologies have a treelike structure, with a few prime movers located at the top and all other technologies radiating out from them. They characterize general purpose technologies by pervasiveness (which means that such a technology can be used in many downstream sectors), technological dynamism (which means that it can support continuous innovational efforts and learning), and innovational complementarities (which exist because productivity of R&D in downstream sectors increases as a consequence of innovation in the general purpose technology, and vice versa). Like capital, a refined classification of knowledge and technologies tend to lead new conceptions and modeling strategies. This study uses knowledge in a highly aggregated sense. It is assumed as a conventional production function of knowledge in which labor, capital, and knowledge are combined to create new knowledge in a deterministic way. This is an approximate description of the idea that devoting more resources to research yields more rapidly new knowledge. There does not appear to have certain evidence for supporting any form of how increases in the stock of knowledge affect the creation of new knowledge. Research is carried out only by the universities. It is more realistic to assume that the research sector consists of two sub-sectors: a private research sector and a government research sector as in, for instance, Park (1998). In Park's model, the government may create knowledge useful for defense, space, and environment and the private sector for industrial, agricultural, and consumption goods (Kline and Rosenberg, 1987; Porter, 1990, 1998; Jaffe et al., 1993; Anselin et al., 1997, 2000; Fujita and Thisse, 2002; Henderson, 2003). Some overlapping knowledge, like mathematical and scientific knowledge, may be tailored for research as particular activities. The equation for knowledge growth is taken on the following form:

$$\dot{Z}(t) = \sum_{j=1}^{J}\left\{\frac{\tau_{ij}F_j(t)}{Z^{\varepsilon_{ij}}(t)} + \tau_{rj}Z^{\varepsilon_{rj}}(t)K_{rj}^{\alpha_{rj}}(t)N_{rj}^{\beta_{rj}}(t)\right\} - \delta_z Z(t) \tag{5.8}$$

in which $\delta_z(\geq 0)$ is the depreciation rate of knowledge, and ε_{qj}, τ_{qj}, α_{rj} and β_{rj} are parameters. It is required that $\tau_{qj,}$ α_{rj}, and β_{rj} are non-negative. To interpret eq. (5.8), consider a special case that knowledge accumulation is through learning by doing. The parameters τ_{ij} and δ_z are non-negative. The term $\tau_{ij}F(t)/Z^{\varepsilon_{ij}}(t)$ is interpreted as the contribution to knowledge accumulation through learning by doing by country $j's$ production sector. To see how learning by doing occurs, assume that knowledge is a function of country $j's$ total industrial output during some period:

$$Z(t) = a_1\left\{\int_0^t F_j(\theta)d\theta\right\}^{a_2} + a_3$$

in which a_1, a_2 and a_3 are positive parameters. The above equation implies that the knowledge accumulation through learning by doing exhibits decreasing (increasing) returns to scale in the case of $a_2 < (>)1$. The parameters, a_1 and a_3, are interpreted as the measurements of the efficiency of learning by doing by the production sector. Taking the derivatives of the equation yields::

$$\dot{Z}(t) = \frac{\tau_{ij}F_j(t)}{Z^{\varepsilon_{ij}}(t)}$$

in which

$$\tau_{ij} \equiv a_1 a_2,\ \varepsilon_{ij} \equiv 1 - a_2.$$

The term, $\tau_{rj}Z^{\varepsilon_{rj}}(t)K_{rj}^{\alpha_{rj}}(t)N_{rj}^{\beta_{rj}}(t)$, is the contribution to knowledge growth by country $j's$ university. It means that knowledge production of the university is positively related to the capital stocks, $K_{rj}(t)$, employed by the university and the number of scientists $N_{rj}(t)$. To interpret the parameter, ε_{rj}, on the one hand, as the knowledge stock is increased, the university may more effectively utilize traditional knowledge to discover new theorems, on the other hand, a large stock of knowledge may make discovery of new knowledge difficult. This implies that ε_{rj} may be either positive or negative. It is reasonable to assume that the more equipment, books, and buildings, and scientists the university employs, the more productive it becomes. That is, α_{rj} and β_{rj}, are positive. I do not require that the creation function for knowledge has constant returns to scale in capital and labor. It is possible that doubling the number of computers and scientists increases three times of the knowledge creation than before–the university's knowledge creation exhibits increasing returns to scale in scientist and capital. It is also possible for the university to have decreasing returns to scale. There are thus three possibilities—increasing, constant, decreasing returns to scale in scientists and capital—in the university's knowledge creation.

5.5 University Maximizing its Output With the Research Fund

The universities are financially supported by the governments. In our model, the governments collect taxes to support the universities. As tax income is used only for supporting the utilities, it follows:

$$\left(r(t) + \delta_{kj}\right)K_{rj}(t) + w_j(t)N_{rj}(t) = \tau_j F_j(t), j = 1, \ldots, J \tag{5.9}$$

The university pays the interest, $(r(t) + \delta_{kj})K_{rj}(t)$, the scientists' wage, $w_j(t)N_{rj}(t)$, with the research fund, $\tau_j F_j(t)$. $K_{rj}(t)$ and $N_{rj}(t)$ are determined by assuming that country $j's$ university utilizes its financial resource, $\tau_j F_j(t)$, in such a way that its output–contribution to knowledge growth–is maximized. The behavior of the university is thus formulated by:

$$\mathrm{Max}\,\tau_{rj} Z^{\varepsilon_{rj}}(t) K_{rj}^{\alpha_{rj}}(t) N_{rj}^{\beta_{rj}}(t)$$

s.t.: $(r(t) + \delta_{kj})K_{rj}(t) + w_j(t)N_{rj}(t) = \tau_j F_j(t)$.

Country $j's$ university allocates the financial resources as follows:

$$K_{rj}(t) = \frac{\bar{\alpha}_j \tau_j F_j(t)}{r(t) + \delta_{kj}}, N_{rj}(t) = \frac{\bar{\beta}_j \tau_j F_j(t)}{w_j(t)} \tag{5.10}$$

where

$$\bar{\alpha}_j \equiv \frac{\alpha_{rj}}{\alpha_{rj} + \beta_{jr}}, \bar{\beta}_j \equiv \frac{\beta_{rj}}{\alpha_{rj} + \beta_{rj}}.$$

If the other conditions remain the same, an increase in the tax rate or output enables the university to utilize more equipment and to employ more people. An increase in factor price will reduce the employment level of the factor.

5.6 Full Employment and the Demand and Supply Balance

I use $K_j(t)$ and $\bar{K}_j(t)$ to stand for the capital stocks employed and the wealth owned by country j. The assumption that the labor force and capital are always fully employed in each country is represented by:

$$N_{ij}(t) + N_{rj}(t) = N_j, \quad K_{ij}(t) + K_{rj}(t) = K_j(t) \tag{5.11}$$

Let $K(t)$ stand for the capital stocks of the world economy. The total capital stocks employed by the world is equal to the wealth owned by the world:

$$K(t) = \sum_{j=1}^{J} K_j(t) = \sum_{j=1}^{J} \bar{k}_j(t) N_j \tag{5.12}$$

The world production is equal to the world consumption and world net savings. That is

$$C(t) + S(t) - K(t) + \sum_{j=1}^{J} \delta_{kj} K_j(t) = F(t)$$

where

$$C(t) = \sum_{j=1}^{J} c_j(t) N_j, \quad S(t) = \sum_{j=1}^{J} s_j(t) N_j, \quad F(t) = \sum_{j=1}^{J} F_j(t)$$

I have thus built the model with trade, economic growth, capital accumulation, knowledge creation and utilization in the world economy in which the domestic markets of each country are perfectly competitive, international product and capital markets are freely mobile, and labor is internationally immobile.

5.7 The Economic Dynamics of the Global Economy

Appendix A2 examines the dynamic properties when all the households in the global economy have identical preference. I can obtain analytical properties of the dynamic analysis as the world economy is controlled only by two-dimensional differential equations. I now examine the behavior of the system when the households have different preferences among countries. It is shown now that the dynamics of the world economy can be expressed by $(J + 1)$ differential equations.

5.7.1 Lemma 5.1

The dynamics of the world economy is governed by the following $(J + 1)$ differential equations with $Z(t)$, $k_1(t)$ and $\bar{k}_j(t)$, $j = 2, \cdots, J$, as the variables

$$\dot{Z}(t) = \Lambda\left(k_1(t), \left\{\bar{k}_j(t)\right\}, Z(t)\right),$$

$$\dot{k}_1(t) = \Lambda_1\left(k_1(t), \left\{\bar{k}_j(t)\right\}, Z(t)\right),$$

$$\dot{\bar{k}}_j(t) = \Lambda_j\left(k_1(t), \bar{k}_j(t), Z(t)\right), j = 2, \ldots, J,$$

In which $\left\{\bar{k}_j(t)\right\} \equiv \left(\bar{k}_2(t), , \bar{k}_J(t)\right)$, and $\Lambda(t)$ and $\Lambda_j(t)$ are unique functions of $Z(t)$, $k_1(t)$ and $\bar{k}_j(t)$ at any point of time, defined in Appendix A1. For any given positive values of $Z(t)$, $k_1(t)$ and $\bar{k}_j(t)$ at any point of time, the other variables are uniquely determined by the following procedure: $\bar{k}_1(t)$ by (A5.7) $\rightarrow k_j(t)$, by (A5.1) $\rightarrow r(t)$ $\rightarrow w_j(t)$ by (A5.2) $\rightarrow N_{qj}(t)$ by (A5.4) $\rightarrow K_j(t)$ by (A5.5) $\rightarrow K_{qj}(t)$ by (A5.4) $\rightarrow$ $\hat{y}_j(t)$ by (A5.8) $\rightarrow c_j(t)$ and $s_j(t)$ by (5.6) $\rightarrow F_j(t)$ by the definition $\rightarrow U_j(t)$ by (5.5).

I have the dynamic equations for the world economy with any number of countries. The system is nonlinear and is of high dimension. It is difficult to generally analyze the behavior of the system. The parameters are specified as follows:

$$\begin{pmatrix} N_1 \\ N_2 \\ N_3 \end{pmatrix} = \begin{pmatrix} 3 \\ 4 \\ 8 \end{pmatrix}, \begin{pmatrix} A_1 \\ A_2 \\ A_3 \end{pmatrix} = \begin{pmatrix} 1 \\ 0.8 \\ 0.7 \end{pmatrix}, \begin{pmatrix} m_1 \\ m_2 \\ m_3 \end{pmatrix} = \begin{pmatrix} 0.4 \\ 0.2 \\ 0.1 \end{pmatrix}, \begin{pmatrix} \tau_1 \\ \tau_2 \\ \tau_3 \end{pmatrix} = \begin{pmatrix} 0.05 \\ 0.04 \\ 0.02 \end{pmatrix},$$

$$\begin{pmatrix} \alpha_1 \\ \alpha_2 \\ \alpha_3 \end{pmatrix} = \begin{pmatrix} 0.3 \\ 0.32 \\ 0.31 \end{pmatrix}, \begin{pmatrix} \alpha_{1r} \\ \alpha_{2r} \\ \alpha_{3r} \end{pmatrix} = \begin{pmatrix} 0.4 \\ 0.4 \\ 0.4 \end{pmatrix}, \begin{pmatrix} \beta_{1r} \\ \beta_{2r} \\ \beta_{3r} \end{pmatrix} = \begin{pmatrix} 0.4 \\ 0.3 \\ 0.2 \end{pmatrix},$$

$$\begin{pmatrix} \tau_{i1} \\ \tau_{i2} \\ \tau_{i3} \end{pmatrix} = \begin{pmatrix} 0.02 \\ 0.01 \\ 0.01 \end{pmatrix}, \begin{pmatrix} \tau_{r1} \\ \tau_{r2} \\ \tau_{r3} \end{pmatrix} = \begin{pmatrix} 0.08 \\ 0.06 \\ 0.03 \end{pmatrix}, \begin{pmatrix} \varepsilon_{i1} \\ \varepsilon_{i2} \\ \varepsilon_{i3} \end{pmatrix} = \begin{pmatrix} 0.1 \\ 0.2 \\ 0.3 \end{pmatrix},$$

$$\begin{pmatrix} \varepsilon_{r1} \\ \varepsilon_{r2} \\ \varepsilon_{r3} \end{pmatrix} = \begin{pmatrix} 0.4 \\ 0.3 \\ 0.2 \end{pmatrix}, \begin{pmatrix} \xi_{01} \\ \xi_{02} \\ \xi_{0.3} \end{pmatrix} = \begin{pmatrix} 0.2 \\ 0.2 \\ 0.3 \end{pmatrix}, \begin{pmatrix} \lambda_{01} \\ \lambda_{02} \\ \lambda_{03} \end{pmatrix} = \begin{pmatrix} 0.75 \\ 0.7 \\ 0.65 \end{pmatrix},$$

$$\delta_k = 0.05, \delta_Z = 0.04 \tag{5.13}$$

Country 1, 2 and $3^{'}s$ populations are respectively 3, 4 and 8. Country 3 has the largest population. Country 1, 2 and $3^{'}s$ total productivities, A_j, are respectively 1,0.8 and 0.7. Country 1, 2 and $3^{'}s$ knowledge utilization efficiency parameters, m_j, are respectively 0.4, 0.2 and 0.1. Country 1 utilizes knowledge mostly effectively; country 2 next and country 3 utilizes knowledge lest effectively. The three countries are called, developed, industrializing, and underdeveloped economies, respectively (DE, IE, UE). The DE has the highest tax rate for supporting research and the UE has the lowest tax rate. It is required that $\delta_k = \delta_{kj}, j = 1, 2, 3$. The values of the parameters, α_j, in the Cobb-Douglas productions are approximately equal to 0.3. The DE's learning by doing and university creativity parameters, τ_{i1} and τ_{r1}, are the highest among the countries. The returns to scale parameters in learning by doing, ε_{ij}, are all positive, which implies that knowledge exhibits decreasing returns to scale in learning by doing. The depreciation rates of physical capital and knowledge are specified respectively at 0.05 and 0.04. The DE's propensity to save is 0.75 and the UE's propensity to save is 0.65. The value of the IE's propensity is between the two other countries. In Fig. 5.1, the motion of the system is plotted with the following initial conditions:

$$k_1(0) = 19.5, \bar{k}_2(0) = 6.5, \bar{k}_3(0) = 2.2, Z(0) = 20.$$

In Fig. 5.1, the trade balances of the three countries are given by

$$E_j(t) = \left(\bar{K}_j(t) - K_j(t)\right)r(t), j = 1, 2, 3.$$

When $E_j(t)$ is positive (negative),thatcountry j is in trade surplus (deficit). When $E_j(t)$ is zero, country $j^{'}s$ trade is in balance. The worker in the DE has the highest wage rate,

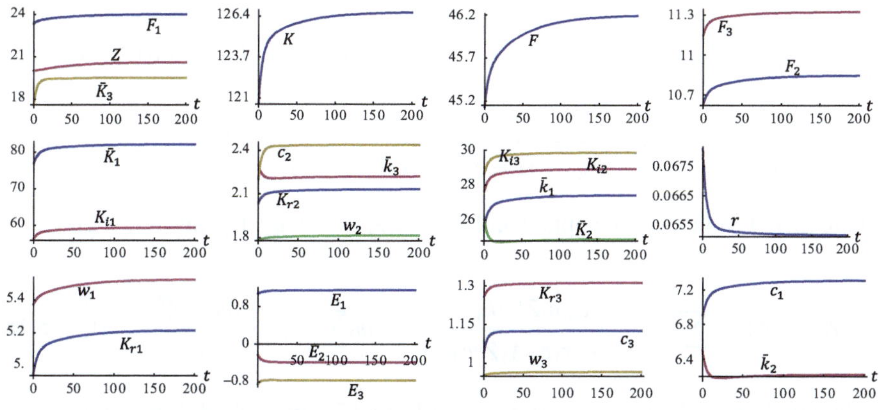

Fig. 5.1 The motion of the system

and wealth and consumption levels, while the worker in the UE has the lowest wage rate, and wealth and consumption levels. The DE is in trade surplus, while the other two economies are in trade deficits. Due to their initial values, most of the variables in the system are increased over time till they approach their equilibrium values. Figure 5.1 shows that the system is approaching its equilibrium point. Nevertheless, it is difficult to confirm whether this equilibrium point is unique. I further simplify equilibrium conditions to discuss the uniqueness. First, from eqs. (A5.1) and (A5.2), the equilibrium point is given by:

$$k_j = \varphi_j(k_1, Z) = \tau_{kj} Z^{\bar{m}_j} k_1^{\beta_1/\beta_j},$$

$$w_j = \bar{\varphi}_j(k_1, Z) = \tau_{wj} Z^{m_{0j}} k_1^{\alpha_{wj}}, j = 1, \cdots, J \tag{5.14}$$

where

$$\tau_{kj} \equiv \left(\frac{\bar{\tau}_j A_j \alpha_j}{\bar{\tau}_1 A_1 \alpha_1}\right)^{\frac{1}{\beta_j}}, \bar{m}_j \equiv \frac{m_j - m_1}{\beta_j}, \tau_{wj} \equiv \bar{\tau}_j A_j \beta_j \tau_{kj}^{\alpha_j},$$

$$m_{0j} \equiv m_j + \alpha_j \bar{m}_j, \alpha_{wj} \equiv \frac{\beta_1 \alpha_j}{\beta_j}.$$

By eqs. (5.7), $s_j = \bar{k}_j$. By the definition of R and eqs. (5.1), it follows:

$$R(k_1, Z) = \lambda_1 \left(\lambda_{u1} - \bar{\tau}_1 A_1 \alpha_1 Z^{m_1} k_1^{-\beta_1}\right) \tag{5.15}$$

in which $\lambda_{u1} \equiv 1/\lambda_1 - 1 + \delta_k$. From the equations for k_j in (5.14) and eqs. (A5.5):

$$K = \psi = \sum_{j=1}^{J} \frac{\tau_{kj} N_{ij} k_1^{\beta_1/\beta_j} Z^{\bar{m}_j}}{a_{ij}} \tag{5.16}$$

From $s_j = \bar{k}_j$ and eqs. (5.6), $\hat{y}_j = \bar{k}_j/\lambda_j$. Substituting $\hat{y}_j = \bar{k}_j/\lambda_j$ into (A5.8) yields:

$$\bar{k}_j = \frac{\tau_{wj} Z^{m_{0j}} k_1^{\alpha_{wj}}}{\lambda_{uj} - \bar{\tau}_1 \alpha_1 A_1 Z^{m_1} k_1^{-\beta_1}}, j = 2, \ldots, J \tag{5.17}$$

where (5.14) and (5.1) are applied and $\lambda_{uj} \equiv 1/\lambda_j - 1 + \delta_k$. By eqs. (A5.12):

$$\Omega_k(k_1, Z) \equiv \sum_{j=1}^{J} \frac{\tau_{wj} n_j Z^{m_{0j}} k_1^{\alpha_{wj}}}{\lambda_{uj} - \bar{\tau}_1 \alpha_1 A_1 Z^{m_1} k_1^{-\beta_1}} - n_0 \sum_{j=1}^{J} \frac{\tau_{kj} N_{ij} k_1^{\frac{\beta_1}{\beta_j}} Z^{\bar{m}_j}}{a_{ij}} = 0 \tag{5.18}$$

in which $n_1 = 1$, $\Lambda = \Lambda_j = 0$, and (5.14)–(5.17) are applied. Substituting $\varphi_j = \tau_{kj} Z^{\bar{m}_j} k_1^{\beta_1/\beta_j}$ into eq. (A5.13) and setting the resulted equation at the equilibrium point, it follows:

$$\Omega_Z(k_1, Z) \equiv \sum_{j=1}^{J} \left(\bar{\tau}_{ij} \tau_{kj}^{\alpha_{ij}} Z^{x_{ij}} k_1^{\frac{\beta_1 \alpha_j}{\beta_j}} + \bar{\tau}_{rj} \tau_{kj}^{\alpha_{rj}} Z^{x_{rj}} k_1^{\frac{\beta_1 \alpha_{rj}}{\beta_j}} \right) - \delta_z = 0 \tag{5.19}$$

in which

$$x_{ij} \equiv m_j - \varepsilon_{ij} + \alpha_{ij} \bar{m}_j - 1, x_{rj} \equiv \varepsilon_{rj} + \alpha_{rj} \bar{m}_j - 1.$$

The two equations:

$$\Omega_k(k_1, Z) = 0, \Omega_Z(k_1, Z) = 0,$$

Contain two variables, k_1 and Z. The two equations determine equilibrium values of k_1 and Z. By eqs. (5.17), I determine $\bar{k}_j$ for $j = 2, \ldots, J$. Following the procedure in the lemma, I determine all the other variables at equilibrium point. It is seen that the main problem is to solve $\Omega_k(k_1, Z) = 0$ and $\Omega_Z(k_1, Z) = 0$, for $k_1 > 0$ and $Z > 0$. Fig. 5.2 plots the two equations, $\Omega_k(k_1, Z) = 0$ and $\Omega_Z(k_1, Z) = 0$, for $k_1 > 0$ and $Z > 0$, under (5.13). The solid lines represent $\Omega_k(k_1, Z) = 0$ and the dashed line stands for $\Omega_Z(k_1, Z) = 0$.

Figure 5.2 shows that the two equations have multiple solutions. Nevertheless, it can be shown that only the following solution:

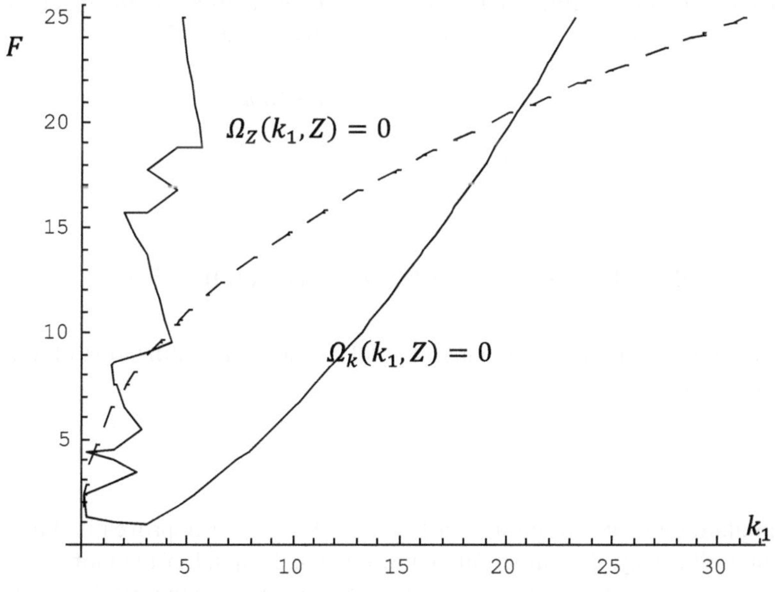

Fig. 5.2 Confirming the uniqueness of equilibrium

$$k_1 = 20.567, Z = 20.610.$$

is meaningful. All the other variables are economically meaningful. For instance, the system has another solution, $k_1 = 2.195$ and $Z = 7.726$. This point is economically meaningless because at this point:

$$\bar{k}_1 = -34.230, \bar{k}_2 = 22.546, \bar{k}_3 = 3.557.$$

As $\hat{y}_1 = \lambda_1 \bar{k}_1 < 0$, the disposable income is negative, which means negative consumption in country 1.

The dynamic system has a unique equilibrium. The other variables at $k_1 = 20.567$ and $Z = 20.610$, are listed in Table 5.1. The global output is 46.2 and the rate of interest is about 6.5 percent. The shares of the global outputs by the DE, IE, and UE are respectively 8.31,2.78, and 1.43. The differences in labor productivity are mainly due to the differences in knowledge utilization efficiency. The table also gives the labor and capital distributions between the sectors in each country and the capital distribution among the three countries. More than half of the global capital stocks is employed by the DE. The DE uses more capital stocks in research than the IE, even though its number of scientists is less than the number in the IE. The wage rates in the DE, ID, and UD are respectively 5.53, 1.82, and 0.97. The trade balances at the equilibrium point are as follows:

$$E_1 = 1.146, E_2 = -0.385, E_3 = -0.761.$$

The DE is in trade surplus and the other two economies are in trade deficit.

It is straightforward to calculate the four eigenvalues as follows

$$\{-0.27, -0.21, -0.18, -0.02\}.$$

The equilibrium point is stable.

5.8 The DE'S Knowledge Utilization Efficiency Rises

This section examines the case where the DE's knowledge utilization efficiency is increased as follows:

$$m_1 : 0.4 \Rightarrow 0.42.$$

The simulation results are plotted in Fig. 5.3. As the DE improves its knowledge utilization efficiency, the output, the knowledge and capital of the global economy are increased. The DE's output level rises, the other two countries' output levels fall initially and then rise. As the rate of interest rises initially and knowledge rises

Table 5.1 The equilibrium values of the global economy

Z		K		F		C	
20.610		126.665		46.199		39.831	
Country 1		Country 2		Country 3		National shares	
F_1	24.03	F_2	10.85	F_3	11.3	F_1/F	0.52
F_1/N_{i1}	8.310	F_2/N_{i2}	2.78	F_3/N_{i3}	1.43	F_2/F	0.24
K_1	64.68	K_2	30.79	K_3	31.2	F_3/F	0.25
K_{i1}	59.47	K_{i2}	28.94	K_{i3}	29.9	K_1/K	0.51
K_{r1}	5.22	K_{r2}	2.13	K_{r3}	1.31	K_2/K	0.24
N_{i1}	2.89	N_{i2}	3.90	N_{i3}	7.92	K_3/K	0.25
N_{r1}	0.11	N_{r2}	0.15	N_{r3}	0.08	$\bar{K}_1/\bar{K}$	0.65
$\bar{K}_1$	82.27	$\bar{K}_2$	24.89	$\bar{K}_3$	19.51	$\bar{K}_2/\bar{K}$	0.196
C_1	21.94	C_2	8.89	C_3	9.0	$\bar{K}_3/\bar{K}$	0.154
w_1	5.53	w_2	1.82	w_3	0.97	C_1/C	0.551
$\bar{k}_1$	27.42	$\bar{k}_2$	6.22	$\bar{k}_3$	2.44	C_2/C	0.223
$\hat{y}_1$	34.73	$\hat{y}_2$	8.44	$\hat{y}_3$	3.57	C_3/C	0.226
c_1	7.313	c_2	2.222	c_3	1.13		

but not much initially, the costs of production are high for the IE and UE and their productivities are not much improved, the two economies' output levels fall initially. As time passes, the world accumulates more knowledge and the rate of interest falls, the IE's and UE's output levels are increased. It is seen that in the long term the DE's trade balance is improved and the other two economies' trade balances slightly deteriorate. In the long term the wage rates and the levels of per capita consumption and wealth in the three economies are all improved. Hence, it is concluded that as UE improves its knowledge utilization efficiency, all the consumers in the globe benefit in the long term. I also conduct comparative dynamic analysis with regard to the UE's knowledge utilization efficiency. It can be shown that the effects on the global economy are similar.

5.9 The DE'S Tax Rate Is Enhanced

This section studies what happens in the global economy if the DE increases its tax rate as follows:

$$\tau_1 : 0.05 \Rightarrow 0.06.$$

The simulation results are plotted in Fig. 5.4. As the DE increases its tax rate to support its research activities, the knowledge, global wealth and output level are increased.

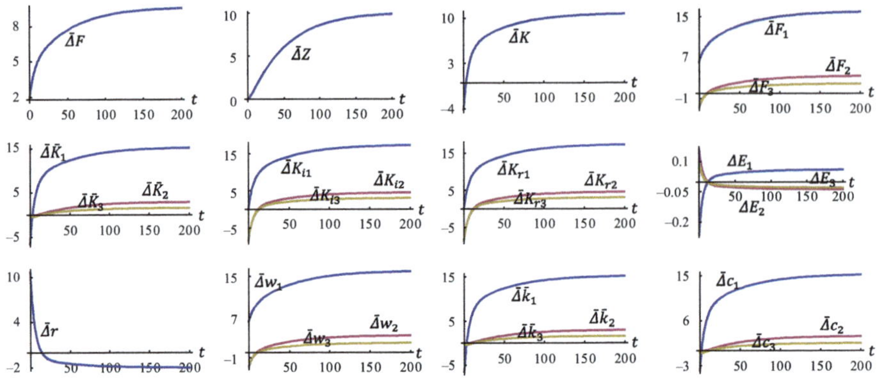

Fig. 5.3 The DE's knowledge utilization efficiency being enhanced

The rate of interest is reduced initially and then increased in the long term. The DE's output level falls initially but rises in the long term. The other two countries' output levels are increased. As the DE's production sector has to pay more tax initially, its output level is reduced initially. As the world accumulates more knowledge and the DE applies knowledge most effectively, its output growth rate is higher than the other two countries in the long term. The DE's wage rate, consumption level, and wealth level fall initially but rise in the long term. The other two countries' wage rates, consumption levels, and wealth levels are increased. The IE's trade balance is improved and the other two countries' trade balances deteriorate.

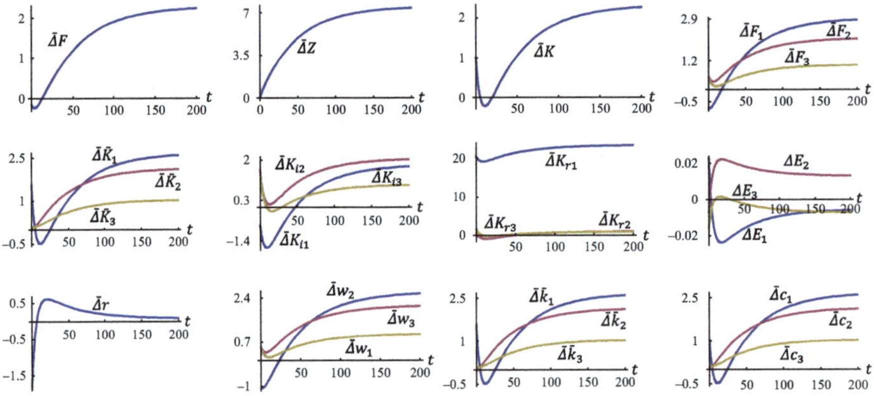

Fig. 5.4 The DE's tax rate being enhanced

5.10 The UE'S Tax Rate Is Increased

This section studies what happens to the global economy if the UE increases its tax rate as follows:

$$\tau_3 : 0.02 \Rightarrow 0.05.$$

The result is plotted in Fig. 5.5. As the UE strengthens its research policy, the knowledge stock is increased as more research is carried out by the UE. The global output and wealth are reduced initially as the UE puts more resources to research. Nevertheless, the global output and wealth are increased in the long term as a consequence of improved productivity in all the economies. The rate of interest is increased. This implies that capital costs are increased for all the economies. The UE increases its efforts in research as it increases capital and labor inputs. Nevertheless, the UE does not so effectively apply the knowledge as the other two economies. The net economic consequences on the UE are that its national output, national wealth and capital input of the production sector are all reduced. On micro level, the UE's wage rate and per capita levels of consumption and wealth are reduced. These conclusions on the UE imply that it will benefit the UE if its research resources are targeted at the fields which increase its abilities to apply the international public capital rather than to make contribution to the public capital with low abilities to using it. Moreover, the efforts in increasing the public capital will enlarge the gaps in income and wealth between the UE and the other two economies. The UE's trade balance is slightly affected, the DE's trade balance is improved, and the IE's trade balance is deteriorated. The DE and IE benefit from the increased efforts in research by the UE in terms of wage rate, wealth, national wealth, and national output. It should be remarked that according to Gersbach et al. (2013), "higher investment in basic research for a particular generation has three effects on the economy. First, basic research draws skilled labor from the production sector, thereby making skilled labor more costly and reducing consumption. Second, as basic research fosters innovation, it has a positive effect on the productivity and consumption level of the economy. And third, by increasing innovation success basic research also helps to prevent foreign entry, thereby raising innovation rents and income." (Arnold, 1997; Cozzi and Galli, 2009, 2011). Our conclusions from analyzing effects of encouraging research for the DE and the UE also provide insights into the complexity of research and knowledge as global public capital.

5.11 The DE'S Propensity to Save Is Enhanced

This section studies the effects of a rise in the DE's propensity to save as follows:

$$\lambda_{01} : 0.75 \Rightarrow 0.77.$$

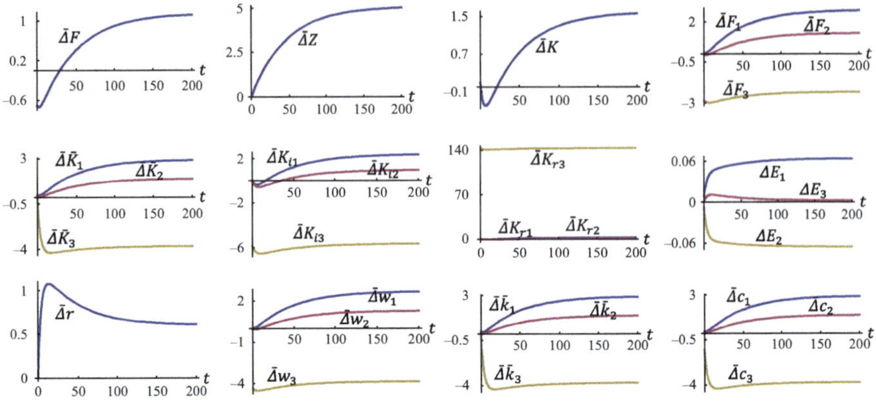

Fig. 5.5 The UE's tax rate being enhanced

The results are plotted in Fig. 5.6. As the DE increases its propensity to save, the knowledge, global wealth, global output, and output of all three economies are increased. The rate of interest falls, and the wage rates of the three economies are increased. As the DE saves more out of its disposable income, its per capita consumption is reduced initially. The consumption level as a consequence of increased productivity. The wealth levels of the three economies are all increased. The consumption levels of the other two economies are increased. The DE trade balance is slightly improved, and the IE's and UE's trade balances are slightly deteriorated.

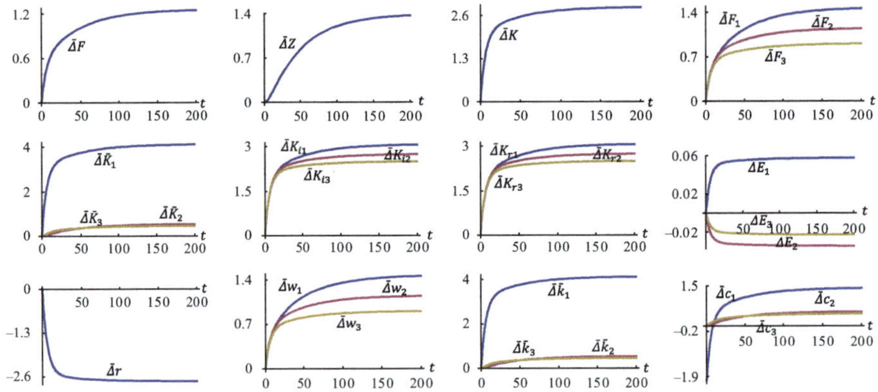

Fig. 5.6 The DE's propensity to save being enhanced

5.12 Concluding Remarks

This chapter proposed a multi-country growth model with capital accumulation and knowledge dynamics. Capital accumulation is through saving, while knowledge is through learning by doing and research. Knowledge is international public good, and research is financially supported and conducted nationally. Production is neoclassical and is the same as in the one-sector growth Solow model. International trade is free and trade patterns are determined like in the Oniki-Uzawa model. The dynamics of J-country world economy is controlled by a $(J + 1)$-dimensional differential equations system. The chapter carried out comparative dynamic analysis with regards to the knowledge utilization efficiency, the rates of tax for encouraging research, and the propensity to save. The comparative analysis provides some insight into the complexity of international trade with endogenous wealth and knowledge. For instance, it is demonstrated that as the UE encourages research by increasing its tax rate, the knowledge stock is increased; the global output and wealth are reduced initially and are increased in the long term; the rate of interest is increased; the UE increases its efforts in research; the net economic consequences on the UE are that its national output, national wealth and capital input of the production sector are all reduced; the UE's wage rate and per capita levels of consumption and wealth are reduced; the trade balances are slightly affected; the other economies benefit from the increased efforts in research by the UE in terms of wage rate, wealth, national wealth, and national output. These conclusions imply that it will benefit the UE if its resources are targeted at the fields which increase its abilities to apply the international public capital rather than to make contribution to the public capital with low abilities to using it. Moreover, the efforts in increasing the public capital will enlarge the gaps in income and wealth between the UE and the other economies. Our model may be extended and generalized in different directions. It is straightforward to develop the model in discrete time. It is possible to analyze the behavior of the model with other forms of production or utility functions. In the contemporary literature, private research and endogenous population have been emphasized. It is also extending our model by learning from modeling some aspects of trade in the literature of gravity models (Yotov et al., 2016).There are growth models with multiple sectors and increasing returns to scale (e.g., Young, 1928; Mulligan and Sala-I-Martin, 1993; Baierl et al., 1998; Boldrin et al., 2001b; Kim et al., 2005; Combes et al., 2008; Glaeser and Gottlieb, 2009; Delgado et al., 2010; Minniti and Parello, 2011; Desmet *and* Rossi-Hansberg, 2012; Davis and Hashimoto, 2015; McCann and Ortega-Argilés, 2015; Desmet et al., 2018; Peretto, 2018; Beenstock, 2021; Bond-Smith, 2021, 2024). The rest of this book will explore some issues related to economic structure and return to scale. Those studies provide further directions for generalizing the model in this chapter.

Appendix A1: Proving Lemma 5.1

First, from eqs. (5.1) I obtain:

$$k_j = \varphi_j(k_1, Z) \equiv \left(\frac{\bar{\tau}_j A_j \alpha_j Z^{m_j}}{\bar{\tau}_1 A_1 \alpha_1 Z^{m_1} k_1^{-\beta_1} + \delta_j} \right)^{\frac{1}{\beta_j}}, j = 1, \ldots, J \quad \text{(A5.1)}$$

where $\delta_j \equiv \delta_{k1} - \delta_{kj}$. It should be noted that $\varphi_1 = k_1$. From (5.1) and (A5.1), I determine the wage rates as functions of $k_1(t)$ and $Z(t)$ as follows:

$$w_j = \bar{\varphi}_j(k_1, Z) \equiv \bar{\tau}_j A_j \beta_j Z^{m_j} \varphi_j^{\alpha_j}(k_1, Z), j = 1, \cdots, J \quad \text{(A5.2)}$$

From (5.1) and (5.10), it follows:

$$\frac{K_{rj}}{K_{ij}} = \frac{\bar{\alpha}_j \tau_j}{\bar{\tau}_j \alpha_j}, \frac{N_{rj}}{N_{ij}} = \frac{\bar{\beta}_j \tau_j}{\bar{\tau}_j \beta_j} \quad \text{(A5.3)}$$

From (5.11) and (A5.3), I solve the capital and labor distribution between the production sector and the university in country j as follows:

$$K_{qj} = a_{qj} K_j, N_{qj} = b_{qj} N_j, q = i, r, j = 1, \ldots, J \quad \text{(A5.4)}$$

where

$$a_{rj} \equiv \frac{\bar{\alpha}_j \tau_j}{\bar{\alpha}_j \tau_j + \bar{\tau}_j \alpha_j}, a_{ij} \equiv \frac{\bar{\tau}_j \alpha_j}{\bar{\alpha}_j \tau_j + \bar{\tau}_j \alpha_j}, b_{rj} \equiv \frac{\bar{\beta}_j \tau_j}{\bar{\beta}_j \tau_j + \bar{\tau}_j \beta_j}, b_{ij} \equiv \frac{\bar{\tau}_j \beta_j}{\bar{\beta}_j \tau_j + \bar{\tau}_j \beta_j}.$$

The labor distribution is constant as it is determined by the tax rate and capital distribution is proportional to the total capital stocks employed by the country.

By $k_j = K_{ij}/N_{ij}$ and (A5.4), it follows:

$$K_j = \frac{N_{ij} k_j}{a_{ij}}, j = 1, \ldots, J \quad \text{(A5.5)}$$

As k_j are functions of $k_1(t)$ and $Z(t)$, $K_j(t)$ are also functions of $k_1(t)$ and $Z(t)$. From (A5.4), I also solve $K_{rj}(t)$ as functions of $k_1(t)$ and $Z(t)$. The capital distribution among the countries and between sectors in each country are uniquely determined as functions of $k_1(t)$ and $Z(t)$. By $K = \sum_{j=1}^{J} K_j$, K is uniquely determined as a function of k_1 and Z. I denote this function as follows:

$$K = \psi(k_1, Z).$$

Substituting $F_j = Z^{m_j} K_{ij}^{\alpha_j} N_{ij}^{\beta_j}$ into (5.8) yields:

$$\dot{Z} = \Lambda(k_1, Z) \equiv$$

$$\sum_{j=1}^{J}\left(\tau_{ij}A_jN_{ij}^{\beta_j}Z^{m_j-\varepsilon_{ij}}K_{ij}^{\alpha_j} + \tau_{rj}N_{rj}^{\beta_{rj}}Z^{\varepsilon_{rj}}K_{rj}^{\alpha_{rj}}\right) - \delta_z Z \tag{A5.6}$$

It is seen that the motion of Z can be described as a unique function of k_1 and Z. From (5.12):

$$\bar{k}_1 = n_0\psi(k_1, Z) - \sum_{j=2}^{J} n_j\bar{k}_j \tag{A5.7}$$

in which

$$n_0 \equiv \frac{1}{N_1}, n_j \equiv \frac{N_j}{N_1}, j = 2, \ldots, J.$$

Country 1's per capita wealth, $\bar{k}_1(t)$, can be expressed as a unique function of the knowledge, country 1's capital intensity of production function and the other countries' per capita wealth, $\{\bar{k}(t)\}$, at any point of time.

From (5.2) and (5.3), I have:

$$\hat{y}_j = (1 + r)\bar{k}_j + w_j \tag{A5.8}$$

Substituting $s_j = \lambda_j\hat{y}_j$ and (A5.8) into (5.7) yields:

$$\dot{\bar{k}}_1 = \Lambda_1(k_1, \bar{k}_1, Z) \equiv \lambda_1 w_1 - R(k_1, Z)\bar{k}_1 \tag{A5.9}$$

$$\dot{\bar{k}}_j = \Lambda_j(k_1, \bar{k}_j, Z) \equiv \lambda_j w_j - (1 - \lambda_j - \lambda_j r)\bar{k}_j, j = 2, \ldots, J \tag{A5.10}$$

in which $R(k_1, Z) \equiv 1 - \lambda_1 - \lambda_1 r$. Eqs. (A5.10) are the differential equations for $\bar{k}_j(t)$ in Lemma 2, $j = 2, \ldots, J$. Taking derivatives of (A5.7) with respect to t yields:

$$\dot{\bar{k}}_1 = n_0\psi_{k_1}\dot{k}_1 + n_0\psi_Z\dot{Z} - \sum_{j=2}^{J} n_j\dot{\bar{k}}_j \tag{A5.11}$$

where ψ_{k_1} and ψ_Z are the partial derivatives of $\psi(k_1, Z)$ with respect to k_1 and Z. Equaling the right-hand sizes of (A5.9) and (A5.11), I get:

$$n_0\psi_{k_1}\dot{k}_1 + n_0\psi_Z\dot{Z} - \sum\nolimits_{j=2}^{J} n_j\dot{\bar{k}}_j = \lambda_1 w_1 - R\bar{k}_1.$$

Substitute (A5.7) into the above equation:

$$\dot{k}_1 = \Lambda_1\left(k_1, \{\bar{k}_j\}, Z\right) \equiv$$

$$\left[\sum_{j=2}^{J} n_j \Lambda_j + \lambda_1 w_1 - n_0 R\psi + R\sum_{j=2}^{J} n_j \bar{k}_j - n_0 \psi_Z \Lambda\right] \frac{1}{n_0 \psi_{k_1}} \tag{A5.12}$$

where (A5.10) and (A5.6) are applied. This is the differential equation for $k_1(t)$ in Lemma 2. Substitute eqs. (A5.4), (A5.5), (A5.1), and (A5.12) into (A5.6):

$$\dot{Z} = \Lambda(k_1, Z) = \sum_{j=1}^{J}\left(\bar{\tau}_{ij} Z^{m_j - \varepsilon_{ij}} \varphi_j^{\alpha_j} + \bar{\tau}_{rj} Z^{\varepsilon_{rj}} \varphi_j^{\alpha_{rj}}\right) - \delta_z Z \tag{A5.13}$$

where

$$\bar{\tau}_{ij} \equiv \tau_{ij} A_j N_{ij}, \; \bar{\tau}_{rj} \equiv \tau_{rj} a_{rj}^{\alpha_{rj}} a_{ij}^{-\alpha_{rj}} N_{rj}^{\beta_{rj}} N_{ij}^{\alpha_{rj}}.$$

This is the differential equation for $Z(t)$ in the lemma. The lemma is confirmed.

Appendix A2: Examining the Dynamic Properties With Identical Preference

I now analyze the case where all the households in the world have an identical preference and the depreciation rates are the same in the global economies:

$$\xi = \xi_j, \lambda = \lambda_j, \delta_k = \delta_{kj}, \alpha = \alpha_j, j = 1, \ldots, J.$$

First, it is shown that all the variables in the dynamic system can be expressed as functions of $k_1(t)$ and $Z(t)$ at any point. From (5.1):

$$k_j(t) = M_j Z^{\bar{m}_j}(t) k_1(t), j = 1, \ldots, J \tag{A5.14}$$

in which

$$M_j \equiv \left(\frac{A_j \bar{\tau}_j}{A_1 \bar{\tau}_1}\right)^{1/\beta}, \bar{m}_j \equiv \frac{m_j - m_1}{\beta}.$$

Country $j's$ capital intensity can be expressed as a unique function of the knowledge and country $1's$ capital intensity. The ratio between any two countries' capital intensities is related to the two countries' tax rates and the knowledge utilization efficiency. I determine the rate of interest and the wage rates as functions of $k_1(t)$ and $Z(t)$ as follows:

$$r(t) = \bar{\tau}_1(t)A_1\alpha Z^{m_1}(t)k_1^{-\beta}(t) - \delta_k,\ w_j(t) = \bar{\tau}_j A_j \beta \bar{\alpha}_j^{\alpha} Z^{\alpha\bar{m}_j + m_j}(t)k_1^{\alpha}(t), j = 1, \cdots, J \tag{A5.15}$$

From (5.1) and (5.10), it follows:

$$\frac{K_{rj}(t)}{K_{ij}(t)} = \frac{\bar{\alpha}_j\tau_j(t)}{\bar{\tau}_j\alpha_j(t)},\ \frac{N_{rj}(t)}{N_{ij}(t)} = \frac{\bar{\beta}_j\tau_j}{\bar{\tau}_j\beta_j} \tag{A5.16}$$

From (5.11) and (A5.16), I solve the capital and labor distribution between the production sector and the university in country j as follows:

$$K_{qj}(t) = \bar{a}_{qj}K_j(t), N_{qj} = \bar{b}_{qj}N_j, q = i, r, j = 1, \ldots, J \tag{A5.17}$$

where

$$\bar{a}_{rj} \equiv \frac{\bar{\alpha}_j\tau_j}{\bar{\alpha}_j\tau_j + \bar{\tau}_j\alpha},\ \bar{a}_{ij} \equiv \frac{\bar{\tau}_j\alpha_j}{\bar{\alpha}_j\tau_j + \bar{\tau}_j\alpha},\ \bar{b}_{rj} \equiv \frac{\bar{\beta}_j\tau_j}{\bar{\beta}_j\tau_j + \bar{\tau}_j\beta},\ \bar{b}_{ij} \equiv \frac{\bar{\tau}_j\beta}{\bar{\beta}_j\tau_j + \bar{\tau}_j\beta}.$$

The labor distribution is constant as it is determined by the tax rate and capital distribution is proportional to the total capital stocks employed by the country. By $k_j(t) = K_{ij}(t)/N_{ij}$ and (A5.17) and (A5.14), I have:

$$K_j(t) = \bar{M}_j Z^{m_j}(t)k_1(t), j = 1, \ldots, J \tag{A5.18}$$

where $\bar{M}_j = N_{ij}M_j/\bar{a}_{ij}$.A5.18 Adding all the equations in () yields:

$$K(t) = k_1(t)\Lambda_0(Z(t)) \tag{A5.19}$$

where $K(t) = \sum_{j=1}^{J} K_j(t)$ is applied and:

$$\Lambda \equiv -\delta_z Z(t) + \sum_{j=1}^{J}\{\tau_{rj1}(t) + \tau_{rj2}(t)\}$$

From $F_j(t) = A_j Z^{m_j}(t)K_{ij}^{\alpha}(t)N_{ij}^{\beta}$ and (A5.17) and (A5.18), it follows:

$$F_j(t) = \bar{a}_{ij}^{\alpha}A_j N_{ij}^{\beta}\bar{M}_j^{\alpha}Z^{m_j+\alpha\bar{m}_j}(t)k_1^{\alpha}(t) \tag{A5.20}$$

Substituting (A5.17), (A5.18) and (A5.20) into (5.8) yields:

$$\dot{Z}(t) = \Lambda(k_1(t), Z(t)) \tag{A5.21}$$

where

$$\Lambda \equiv -\delta_z Z(t) + \sum_{j=1}^{J} \{\tau_{rj1}(t) + \tau_{rj2}(t)\}$$

where

$$\tau_{rj1}(t) \equiv \tau_{ij}\bar{a}_{ij}^{\alpha} A_j N_{ij}^{\beta} \bar{M}_j^{\alpha}(t) Z^{m_j+\alpha\bar{m}_j-\varepsilon_{ij}}(t) k_1^{\alpha}(t),$$

$$\tau_{rj2}(t) \equiv \tau_{rj}\bar{a}_{rj}^{\alpha_{rj}} \bar{M}_j^{\alpha_{rj}} N_{rj}^{\beta_{rj}} Z^{\alpha_{rj}\bar{m}_j+\varepsilon_{rj}}(t) k_1^{\alpha_{rj}}(t).$$

The motion of $Z(t)$ can be described as a unique function of $k_1(t)$ and $Z(t)$. From eqs. (5.2) and (5.3):

$$\hat{y}_j(t) = (1 + r(t))\bar{k}_j(t) + w_j(t).$$

Substituting $s_j(t) = \lambda \hat{y}_j(t)$ and the above equation into (5.7) yields:

$$\dot{\bar{k}}_j(t) = \lambda w_j(t) - (1 - \lambda - \lambda r(t))\bar{k}_j(t) \tag{A5.22}$$

Multiplying the equation for $\bar{k}_j(t)$ by N_j and then adding the J resulted equations yield:

$$\dot{K}(t) = \lambda \beta k_1^{\alpha}(t)$$

$$\sum_{j=1}^{J} \bar{\tau}_j A_j \bar{\alpha}_j^{\alpha} Z^{\alpha\bar{m}_j+m_j}(t) - \left(\bar{\lambda} - \bar{\tau}_1 A_1 \alpha \lambda Z^{m_1}(t) k_1^{-\beta}(t)\right) K(t) \tag{A5.23}$$

where (A5.15) and $K(t) = \sum_{j=1}^{J} \bar{k}_j(t) N_j$ and $\bar{\lambda} \equiv 1 - \lambda + \lambda\delta_k$ are applied.
Taking derivatives of (A5.19) with respect to t yields:

$$\dot{K}(t) = \frac{K(t)\dot{k}_1(t)}{k_1(t)} + \left(k_1(t)\sum_{j=1}^{J} \bar{m}_1 \bar{M}_j Z^{\bar{m}_j-1}(t)\right)\dot{Z}(t) \tag{A5.24}$$

Substituting (A5.23), (A5.19), and (A5.23) into (A5.24) yields:

$$\dot{k}_1(t) = \tilde{\Lambda}(t) - \left(k_1(t)\sum_{j=1}^{J} \bar{m}_1 \bar{M}_j Z_{\square}^{\bar{m}_j-1}(t)\right)\frac{\Lambda(t)}{\Lambda_0(t)} \tag{A5.25}$$

where

$$\tilde{\Lambda}(t) \equiv \frac{\lambda\beta k_1^{\alpha}(t)}{\Lambda_0(t)}$$

$$\sum_{j=1}^{J} \bar{\tau}_j A_j \bar{\alpha}_j^{\alpha} Z^{\alpha\bar{m}_j+m_j}(t) - \left(\bar{\lambda} - \bar{\tau}_1 A_1 \alpha\lambda Z^{m_1} k_1^{-\beta}(t)\right) k_1(t)$$

Summarizing the above results, I obtain the following lemma.

Lemma A1

Assume that all the households in the world have the same preference. The motion of the two variables, $k_1(t)$ and $Z(t)$, are given by two differential equations, (A5.21) and (A5.25). For any given $k_1(t)$ and $Z(t)$, $r(t)$ and $w_j(t), j = 1, \cdots, J$, are determined by (A5.15). The variables, $\bar{k}_j(t)$, are solved by eqs. (A5.22) as follows:

$$\bar{k}_j(t) = e^{-\int(1-\lambda-\lambda r)d\tau}\left(h_j + \lambda \int w_j(\tau) e^{\int(1-\lambda-\lambda r)d\tau} d\tau\right),$$

$$j = 1, \cdots, J \tag{A5.26}$$

where h_j are constant to be determined by initial conditions. For any given positive values of $Z(t)$, $k_1(t)$ and $\bar{k}_j(t)$ at any point of time, the other variables are uniquely determined by the following procedure: $k_j(t)$, $j = 2, \cdots, J$ by (A5.14) $\to N_{qj}$, $q = i, r, j = 1, \cdots, J$ by (A5.17) $\to K_j(t)$ by (A5.18) $\to K_{qj}(t)$ by (A5.17) $\to$ $\hat{y}_j(t) = (1 + r(t))\bar{k}_j(t) + w_j(t)$ by (A5.21) $\to c_j(t)$ and $s_j(t)$ by (5.6) $\to F_j(t) = Z^{m_j}(t) K_{ij}^{\alpha}(t) N_{ij}^{\beta}(t)$.

The dynamic properties of the world economy are determined by the two differential equations. Equilibrium is determined by:

$$\sum_{j=1}^{J}\left\{\tau_{ij}\bar{a}_{ij}^{\alpha} A_j N_{ij}^{\beta} \bar{M}_j^{\alpha} Z^{m_j+\alpha\bar{m}_j-\varepsilon_{ij}} k_1^{\alpha} + \tau_{rj}\bar{a}_{rj}^{\alpha_{ri}} \bar{M}_j^{\alpha_{ri}} N_{rj}^{\beta_{ri}} Z^{\alpha_{rj}\bar{m}_j+\varepsilon_{ij}} k_1^{\alpha_{rj}}\right\}$$

$$= \delta_z Z,$$

$$\lambda\beta k_1^{\alpha} \sum_{j=1}^{J} \bar{\tau}_j A_j \bar{\alpha}_j^{\alpha} Z_{\square}^{\alpha\bar{m}_j+m_j} - \left(\bar{\lambda} - \bar{\tau}_1 A_1 \alpha\lambda Z_{\square}^{m_1} k_1^{-\beta}\right) k_1 \Lambda_0 = 0 \tag{A5.27}$$

By the second equation in (A5.27), I solve:

$$k_1 = \Omega_0^{1/\beta}\left(\frac{\lambda}{\bar{\lambda}}\right)^{1/\beta} \tag{A5.28}$$

where

$$\Omega_0(Z) \equiv \frac{\beta}{\Lambda_0} \sum_{j=1}^{J} \bar{\tau}_j A_j \bar{\alpha}_j^{\alpha} Z^{\alpha \bar{m}_j + m_j} + \bar{\tau}_1 A_1 \alpha Z^{m_1}$$

Substitute (A5.28) into the first equation in (A5.27)

$$\Omega(Z) \equiv \sum_{j=1}^{J} \left\{ \bar{\tau}_{ij} Z^{m_j + \alpha \bar{m}_j - \varepsilon_{ij} - 1} \Omega_0^{\frac{\alpha}{\beta}} + \bar{\tau}_{rj} Z^{\alpha_{rj} \bar{m}_j + \varepsilon_{rj} - 1} \Omega_0^{\frac{\alpha_{rj}}{\beta}} \right\} - \delta_z = 0 \qquad \text{(A5.29)}$$

where

$$\bar{\tau}_{ij} \equiv \tau_{ij} \bar{a}_{ij}^{\alpha} A_j N_{ij}^{\beta} \bar{M}_j^{\alpha} \left(\frac{\lambda}{\bar{\lambda}} \right)^{\alpha/\beta} > 0, \; \bar{\tau}_{rj} \equiv \tau_{rj} \bar{a}_{rj}^{\alpha_{rj}} \bar{M}_j^{\alpha_{rj}} N_{rj}^{\beta_{rj}} \left(\frac{\lambda}{\bar{\lambda}} \right)^{\alpha_{rj}/\beta} > 0.$$

From Lemma A1 and the above discussions, I have the following corollary.

Corollary A1

The number of equilibrium points is the same as the number of solutions of $\Omega(Z) = 0$, for $Z > 0$. For any solution $Z > 0$, all the other variables are uniquely determined by the following procedure: k_1 by (A5.28) $\rightarrow$ r and $w_j, j = 1, \cdots, J$, by (A5.15) $\rightarrow$ $\bar{k}_j = \lambda w_j / (1 - \lambda - \lambda r) \rightarrow k_j, j = 2, \cdots, J$ by (A5.14) $\rightarrow N_{qj}, q = i, r, j = 1, \cdots, J$ by (A5.17) $\rightarrow K_j$ by (A5.18) $\rightarrow K_{qj}$ by (A5.17) $\rightarrow \hat{y}_j = (1 + r)\bar{k}_j + w_j$ by (A5.21) $\rightarrow c_j$ and s_j by (5.6) $\rightarrow F_j = A_j Z^{m_j} K_{ij}^{\alpha} N_{ij}^{\beta}$.

The number of equilibrium points is the same as the number of solutions of $\Omega(Z) = 0$, for $Z > 0$. As the expression is tedious, it is difficult to explicitly judge under what conditions the equation has a unique or multiple equilibrium points. To see that eq. (A5.29) may have either a unique or multiple equilibrium points, I am concerned with a case that all the countries have identical population, identical production function, equal tax rate, and identical learning by doing and university's knowledge creation functions. In this case, the world economy is the same as a single economy. It is straightforward to show that in this case eq. (A5.29) becomes:

$$\Omega(Z) = \bar{\tau}_{0i} Z^{x_i} + \bar{\tau}_{0r} Z^{x_r} - \delta_z = 0,$$

in which index j is omitted as all the countries are identical and:

$$x_i \equiv \frac{m}{\beta} - \varepsilon_i - 1, \; x_r \equiv \frac{\alpha_r m}{\beta} + \varepsilon_r - 1,$$

$$\bar{\tau}_{0i} \equiv J \bar{\tau}_i A (\beta \bar{a}^{\alpha} \bar{\tau} + \alpha \bar{\tau})^{\alpha/\beta} > 0, \; \bar{\tau}_{0r} \equiv J \bar{\tau}_r (\beta \bar{a}^{\alpha} \bar{\tau} + \alpha \bar{\tau})^{\alpha_r/\beta} > 0.$$

It can be shown that the model in this case is a special case of the national growth model proposed by Zhang (2005a: Chap. 9). The dynamic properties of the model are thoroughly examined. The properties are summarized in the following corollary.

Corollary A2

If $x_i < 0$ and $x_r < 0$ (or $x_i > 0$ and $x_r < 0$), the system has a unique stable (unstable) equilibrium point; and if $x_i < 0$ and $x_r < 0$ ($x_i > 0$ and $x_r < 0$), the system may have none, one, or two equilibrium points. When the system has two equilibrium points, the one with the higher value of Z is unstable and the other one is stable.

I interpret x_i and x_r respectively as measurements of returns to scale of the production sector and university in the dynamic system. When $x_j < (>)0$, sector j displays decreasing (increasing) returns to scale in the dynamic economy. Hence, if the both sectors display decreasing (increasing) returns, the dynamic system has a unique equilibrium; if one sector displays decreasing (increasing) returns and the other sector exhibits increasing (decreasing), the system may have none, one, or two equilibrium points.

Chapter 6
Group-Based Human Capital Externalities and Inequality

> I do not believe in race as such. Race is a fraud. All modern people are the conglomeration of so many ethnic mixtures that no pure race remains.
>
> Albert Einstein

Classification is the first step in creating knowledge. Classification of, for instance, people, classes, nations, races, ages, and gender, for instance, are essential for comprehending and explaining variations and dynamics of human societies. Ethnicity, for instance, is important for understanding economic growth and development of different people within countries or across countries. There are great differences in living conditions and income among different ethnic groups in the USA. Although Japan and China shared similar cultural values over centuries, the per capita income and wealth are greatly different between the two countries in modern times. There are many studies on the role of ethnic differences on, for instance, human capital, cooperativeness and trust (Fershtma and Weiss, 1993; Cutler and Glaeser, 1997; Grugan, 2004; Sethi and Somanathan, 2004; Bleakley and Chin, 2008). In a study on ethnic human-capital externalities, Borjas (1995, 1998) argues that the individual economic performance depends not only on parental skills and education, but also on the average skills of the ethnic group in the ethnic capital. The study by Borjas (1995: 365) demonstrates that "Ethnicity has an external effect, even among persons who grow up in the same neighborhood, when children are exposed frequently to persons who share the same ethnic background." In another study of impact of ethnic externalities, Yaman (2011) investigates how regional ethnic capital—which is defined as the average years of schooling of ethnic groups—affects the educational attainment of young second-generation immigrants in Germany. The research identifies the existence of externalities of ethnic capital for different groups and shows that a higher average education of ethnic groups makes attendance of higher-quality secondary schools more likely. Yaman also confirms that the marginal effect of externality is increasing in the ethnic concentration. In his influential book *The End of History and the Last Man*, Fukuyama (1992) studies the role of culture on economic

W. Zhang, *A Dynamic Economic Theory of Heterogenous Households*,
https://doi.org/10.1007/978-981-95-8918-0_6

performance. He argues that the level of trust or cooperative behavior based on shared norms has significant effects on a nation's prosperity. Fukuyama characterizes China, Italy, Korea, and France as low-trust societies and German and Japan as high-trust societies. According to Fukuyama (1996), the high-trust societies are capable of building innovative organizations and holding down the cost of doing business, while in the low-trust societies, negotiations are costly, and rules and regulations are often not well obeyed. The common point in the studies just referred is that they identify the importance of externalities associated with social relations and interactions within the group on economic performance (Becker, 1974; Basu, 1989; Akerlof, 1997; Mailath and Postlewaite, 2006; Lee, 2007; Currarini et al. 2009). Irrespective of this empirical research, there are only a few theoretical growth models which formally deal with interactions of group-based human capital externalities, income and wealth distribution among groups and economic growth in a comprehensive framework. The chapter is to introduce group-based human capital externalities into an integrated Walrasian-general-equilibrium and neoclassical growth theory. The economy consists of any number of groups. The production side is neoclassical. The way that human-capital externalities are introduced is influenced by how production externalities are introduced in the literature of economic growth and spatial agglomeration (Eicher and Turnovsky, 2000; Gómez, 2008; Zhang, 2013e). I integrate the neoclassical growth theory with Walrasian general equilibrium theory for studying dynamic interactions among growth, wealth and income distribution, and economic structures. Zhang (2013d) integrated Walrasian general equilibrium theory and neoclassical growth theory. This chapter introduces group-based human capital externalities into the integrated theoretical framework. It is based on Zhang (2014b). It is closely related to formal studies on ethnicity. One can also apply the model to comprehend growth with multiple social classes. The chapter is organized as follows. Section 6.1 proposes the basic model with group-based human capital externalities and inequality. Section 6.2 shows the dynamics and its properties. Section 6.3 shows how the system reacts to a rise in group 1's human capital externalities. Section 6.4 shows the effects of a rise in group 1's population on the economic system. Section 6.5 studies the impact of a rise in group 1's decreasing returns to scale in human capital accumulation. Section 6.6 shows how the system reacts to a rise in the consumer goods sector's total factor productivity. Section 6.7 studies how a rise in group 1's propensity to save affects the system. Section 6.8 concludes the chapter. The appendix confirms Lemma 6.1.

6.1 The Basic Model With Group-Based Human Capital Externalities and Inequality

I consider an economic system consisting of capital goods and consumer goods sectors. The capital goods and consumer goods sectors are the same as in the Uzawa two sector model (Uzawa, 1961). Services are classified as consumer goods. Most aspects of the production sector are neoclassical. Capital goods are used as inputs in the two sectors. Capital depreciates at a constant exponential rate δ_k, which is independent of the manner of use. It is required: $0 < \delta_k < 1$.Households own assets of the economy and distribute their incomes to consume and save. Exchanges take place in perfectly competitive markets. Factor markets work well; factors are inelastically supplied, and the available factors are fully utilized at every moment. Savings are undertaken only by households. All earnings of firms are distributed in the form of payments to factors of production, labor, managerial skill and capital ownership. Each group has a fixed population, $\bar{N}_j$, $(j = 1, \ldots, J)$. In the Walrasian general equilibrium theory, $\bar{N}_j = 1$. Let prices be measured in terms of capital goods and the price of the commodity be unit. The wage rate of group j and rate of interest be denoted by $w_j(t)$ and $r(t)$, respectively. Let $p(t)$ denote the price of consumer goods. The total capital stock $K(t)$ is allocated between the two sectors. Let subscript index, i and s stand for capital goods and consumer goods sectors, respectively. I use $N_m(t)$ and $K_m(t)$ to stand for the labor force and capital stocks employed by sector m. The total population $\bar{N}$ and total qualified labor supply $N(t)$ are:

$$\bar{N} = \sum_{j=1}^{J} \bar{N}_j, N(t) = \sum_{j=1}^{J} h_j(t)\bar{N}_j \tag{6.1}$$

In which $h_j(t)$ is the human capital of group j. I will specify group-based human capital externalities on $h_j(t)$ later on. The assumption of the labor force being fully employed implies:

$$N_i(t) + N_s(t) = N(t) \tag{6.2}$$

6.1.1 Capital Goods Sector

There are two input factors, labor force and capital, in production. Let $F_m(t)$ stand for the production function of sector m, $m = i, s$. The production function of the industrial sector is specified as follows:

$$F_i(t) = A_i K_i^{\alpha_i}(t) N_i^{\beta_i}(t), \alpha_i, \beta_i > 0, \alpha_i + \beta_i = 1 \tag{6.3}$$

where A_i, α_i, and β_i are the positive parameters. The marginal conditions for the capital goods sector are given by:

$$r(t) + \delta_k = \frac{\alpha_i F_i(t)}{K_i(t)}, w(t) = \frac{\beta_i F_i(t)}{N_i(t)} \tag{6.4}$$

where $w(t)$ is the wage rate of per qualified labor input. The wage rate of group j is:

$$w_j(t) = h_j(t)w(t)$$

6.1.2 Consumer Goods Sector

The production function of the consumer goods sector is:

$$F_s(t) = A_s K_s^{\alpha_s}(t) N_s^{\beta_s}(t), \alpha_s + \beta_s = 1, \alpha_s, \beta_s > 0 \tag{6.5}$$

where A_s, α_s, and β_s are the technological parameter of the service sector. The marginal conditions are:

$$r(t) + \delta_k = \frac{\alpha_s p(t) F_s(t)}{K_s(t)}, w(t) = \frac{\beta_s p(t) F_s(t)}{N_s(t)} \tag{6.6}$$

6.1.3 Consumer Behaviors and Wealth Dynamics

Let $\bar{k}_j(t)$ stand for the per capita wealth of group j. I have $\bar{k}_j(t) = \bar{K}_j(t)/\bar{N}_j$, where $\bar{K}_j(t)$ is the total wealth held by group j. Per capita current income from the interest payment $r(t)\bar{k}_j(t)$, and the wage payment $h_j(t)w(t)$, is:

$$y_j(t) = r(t)\bar{k}_j(t) + h_j(t)w(t)$$

The per capita disposable income is the sum of the current disposable income and the value of wealth. That is

$$\hat{y}_j(t) = y_j(t) + \bar{k}_j(t) \tag{6.7}$$

The disposable income is used for saving and consumption. It should be noted that the value, $\bar{k}_j(t)$, (i.e., $p(t)\bar{k}_j(t)$ with $p(t) = 1$), in the above equation is: a flow variable. Under the assumption that selling wealth can be conducted instantaneously without any transaction cost, $\bar{k}_j(t)$ is the amount of income that the consumer obtains at time t by selling all of his wealth. Hence, at time t the consumer has the total amount of income equaling $\hat{y}_j(t)$ to distribute between saving and consumption.

The representative household from group j would distribute the available budget between $s_j(t)$ and $c_j(t)$. The budget constraint is:

$$p(t)c_j(t) + s_j(t) = \hat{y}_j(t) \tag{6.8}$$

At each point of time, consumers have two variables to decide. It is assumed that the utility level $U_j(t)$ is dependent on $c_j(t)$ and $s_j(t)$ as follows:

$$U_j(t) = c_j^{\xi_{0j}}(t)s_j^{\lambda_{0j}}(t),\ \xi_{0j},\ \lambda_{0j} > 0$$

where ξ_{0j} is the propensity to consume consumer goods and λ_{0j} the propensity to save. Some growth models with endogenous wealth accumulation consider heterogeneous households. Nevertheless, the heterogeneity in these studies is by the differences in the initial endowments of wealth among different types of households rather than in preferences (Chatterjee, 1994; Caselli and Ventura, 2000; Maliar and Maliar, 2001; Penalosa and Turnovsky, 2006; Turnovsky and Penalosa, 2006). Different households are essentially homogeneous in the sense that all the households have the same preference utility function in the traditional Ramsey approach. I consider different groups have different utility functions.

Maximizing the utility subject to (6.8) yields:

$$p(t)c_j(t) = \xi_j\hat{y}_j(t),\ s_j(t) = \lambda_j\hat{y}_j(t) \tag{6.9}$$

where

$$\xi_j \equiv \rho_j\xi_{0j},\ \lambda_j \equiv \rho_j\lambda_{0j},\ \rho_j \equiv \frac{1}{\xi_{0j} + \lambda_{0j}}$$

According to the definition of $s_j(t)$, the change in the household's wealth is given by:

$$\frac{d\bar{k}_j(t)}{dt} = s_j(t) - \bar{k}_j(t) = \lambda_j\hat{y}_j(t) - \bar{k}_j(t) \tag{6.10}$$

This equation simply states that the change in wealth is equal to saving minus dissaving.

6.1.4 Demand and Supply of the Two Sectors

The demand and supply equilibrium for the consumer goods sector is:

$$\sum_{j=1}^{J} c_j(t)\bar{N}_j = F_s(t) \tag{6.11}$$

As output of the capital goods sector is equal to the depreciation of capital stock and the net savings, it follows:

$$S(t) - K(t) + \delta_k K(t) = F_i(t) \tag{6.12}$$

where

$$S(t) \equiv \sum_{j=1}^{J} s_j(t)\bar{N}_j,\ K(t) = \sum_{j=1}^{J} \bar{k}_j(t)\bar{N}_j$$

6.1.5 Capital Being Fully Utilized

Total capital stock $K(t)$ is allocated to the two sectors:

$$K_i(t) + K_s(t) = K(t) \tag{6.13}$$

6.1.6 Human Capital With Group-Based Human Capital Externalities

This chapter specifies the change in human capital $h_j(t)$ as follows:

$$\frac{dh_j(t)}{dt} = \frac{\upsilon_j c_j^{a_j}(t)\bar{K}_j^{\upsilon_j}(t)}{h_j^{\pi_j}(t)}\left(\frac{\bar{K}_j(t)}{K(t)}\right)^{\theta_j} - \delta_j h_j(t) \tag{6.14}$$

The depreciation rates of human capital satisfy $0 < \delta_j < 1$. It is also required that groups may have different depreciation rates of human capital. The human capital accumulation in this study is affected by different approaches to human capital accumulation in the literature of endogenous human capital. Zhang (2007b) introduces the impact of consumption on human capital accumulation (via the so-called creative leisure) into growth theory. The specification of $\left(\bar{K}_j/K\right)^{\theta_j}\bar{K}_j^{\upsilon_j}$ is influenced by production externalities by, for instance, Eicher and Turnovsky (2000). The term $\bar{K}_j^{\upsilon_j}$ implies that the group experiences positive (negative) human capital externalities if $\upsilon_j > (<)0$. For instance, if the group becomes richer, the people within the group may make more efforts on their children's education and adults might encourage and learn more effectively from each other within the group. It is commonly observed that in an economy with multiple groups one group may strengthen its cultural tradition by spending more on its own cultural infrastructure. The term $\left(\bar{K}_j/K\right)^{\theta_j}$ measures possible effects on the relative share of wealth (or relative economic conditions) of the group in the whole economy. It may also be considered as an index of social status of the group. If $\theta_j > (<)0$, the relative social status has a positive (negative) impact on the human capital accumulation. Here, the possible direct effects of other groups upon the group's human capital accumulation are neglected. The members of the entire population interact and affect each other in markets.

The model is complete. Irrespective of the obvious strict assumptions in our model, from a structural point of view the model is quite general in the sense that some well-known models in economics can be considered as its special cases.

6.2 The Dynamics and its Properties

As the dynamic system consists of any (finite) number of (types of) households, it should be nonlinear and highly dimensional with both human capital and wealth accumulation. It is difficult to get explicitly analytical properties of the nonlinear dynamic system. The following lemma shows that the dimension of the dynamical system is twice as many as the number of groups. The following lemma provides a computational procedure for calculating all the variables at any point of time. First, I introduce a new variable $z(t)$:

$$z(t) \equiv \frac{r(t) + \delta_k}{w_j(t)/h_j}.$$

6.2.1 *Lemma 6.1*

The motion of the economic system is determined by $2J$ differential equations with $z(t)$ and $\{\bar{k}_j(t)\}$, where $\{\bar{k}_j(t)\} \equiv (\bar{k}_2(t), \cdots, \bar{k}_J(t))$ and $(h_j(t)) \equiv (h_1(t), \cdots, h_J(t))$ as the variables:

$$\frac{dz(t)}{dt} = \Lambda_1\big(z(t), \{\bar{k}_j(t)\}, (h_j(t))\big)\frac{d\bar{k}_j(t)}{dt} = \Lambda_j\big(z(t), \{\bar{k}_j(t)\}, (h_j(t))\big), j = 2, \ldots, J$$

$$\frac{dh_j(t)}{dt} = \Omega_j\big(z(t), \{\bar{k}_j(t)\}, (h_j(t))\big) \tag{6.16}$$

In which $\Lambda_j(t)$ are unique functions of $z(t)$, $\{\bar{k}_j(t)\}$ and $(h_j(t))$ defined in the appendix. At any point of time the other variables are unique functions of $z(t)$, $\{\bar{k}_j(t)\}$ and $(h_j(t))$ by the following procedure: $r(t)$ and $w_j(t)$ by (A6.3) $\rightarrow \bar{k}_1(t)$ by (A6.11) $\rightarrow N_i(t)$ by (A6.9) $\rightarrow N_s(t)$ by (A6.7)$\rightarrow w(t) = w_1(t)/h_1(t) \rightarrow \hat{y}_j(t)$ by (A6.5) $\rightarrow K_s(t)$ and $K_i(t)$

by (A6.1) $\rightarrow N(t)$ by (6.1) $\rightarrow F_i(t)$ and $F_s(t)$ by the definitions $\rightarrow p(t)$ by (A6.4) $\rightarrow$ $c_j(t)$ and $s_j(t)$ by (6.11) $\rightarrow K(t) = K_i(t) + K_s(t)$.

The lemma presents a computational procedure for following the motion of the economic system with any number of types of households. As it is difficult to interpret the analytical results, to study the properties of the system I simulate the model with the following parameter values:

$$A_i = 1.3, A_s = 1, \alpha_i = 0.34, \alpha_s = 0.3, \delta_k = 0.05$$

$$\begin{pmatrix} \bar{N}_1 \\ \bar{N}_2 \\ \bar{N}_3 \end{pmatrix} = \begin{pmatrix} 10 \\ 30 \\ 60 \end{pmatrix}, \begin{pmatrix} \lambda_{10} \\ \lambda_{20} \\ \lambda_{30} \end{pmatrix} = \begin{pmatrix} 0.8 \\ 0.75 \\ 0.7 \end{pmatrix}, \begin{pmatrix} \xi_{10} \\ \xi_{20} \\ \xi_{30} \end{pmatrix} = \begin{pmatrix} 0.12 \\ 0.18 \\ 0.2 \end{pmatrix}$$

$$\begin{pmatrix} \delta_1 \\ \delta_2 \\ \delta_3 \end{pmatrix} = \begin{pmatrix} 0.04 \\ 0.05 \\ 0.06 \end{pmatrix}, \begin{pmatrix} v_1 \\ v_2 \\ v_3 \end{pmatrix} = \begin{pmatrix} 0.8 \\ 0.6 \\ 0.5 \end{pmatrix}, \begin{pmatrix} a_1 \\ a_2 \\ a_3 \end{pmatrix} = \begin{pmatrix} 0.1 \\ 0.15 \\ 0.2 \end{pmatrix}, \begin{pmatrix} \pi_1 \\ \pi_2 \\ \pi_3 \end{pmatrix} = \begin{pmatrix} 0.1 \\ 0.2 \\ 0.3 \end{pmatrix}$$

$$\begin{pmatrix} \theta_1 \\ \theta_2 \\ \theta_3 \end{pmatrix} = \begin{pmatrix} 0.2 \\ 0.1 \\ 0.01 \end{pmatrix}, \begin{pmatrix} \upsilon_1 \\ \upsilon_2 \\ \upsilon_3 \end{pmatrix} = \begin{pmatrix} 0.2 \\ 0.1 \\ 0.01 \end{pmatrix} \tag{6.17}$$

The population of group 3 is the largest, while the population of group 2 is the next. The capital goods and consumer goods sector's total productivities are respectively 1.3 and 1. The depreciation rate of physical capital is specified at 0.05. Group $1's$ propensity to save is 0.8 and group $3's$ propensity to save is 0.7. The depreciation rates of human capital of groups 1, 2, and 3 are respectively 0.04, 0.05, and 0.06. The decreasing returns to scale effects in human capital of groups 1, 2, and 3 are respectively 0.01, 0.02, and 0.03. Group 1 (3) has the lowest (highest) depreciation rate and lowest (highest) decreasing return to scale in human capital. Group 1 learns least effectively from consuming, while group 3 learns most effectively from consuming. Group 1's human capital externality is the strongest, while group 3's is the weakest. The relative social status has the strongest impact on group 1's human capital accumulation, while the relative social status has negligible impact on group 3's human capital accumulation. The initial conditions are: as follows:

$$z(0) = 0.03, \bar{k}_2(0) = 225, \bar{k}_3(0) = 64, h_1(0) = 150, h_2(0) = 22,$$

$$h_3(0) = 8,$$

The motion of the variables is plotted in Fig. 6.1. In Fig. 6.1, the national income is:

$$Y(t) = F_i(t) + p(t)F_s(t)$$

The output levels of the two sectors fall slightly overtime. As the price of the consumer goods sector also falls, the national output falls as all its three components are lowered over time. The human capital level of group 1 is changed slightly, the human capital level of group 2 is augmented, and the human capital level of group 3 is lowered. The total labor supply is slightly increased. The total capital stock is reduced in association with rises in the rate of interest. The capital and labor inputs of the capital goods sector are augmented and the capital and labor inputs of the

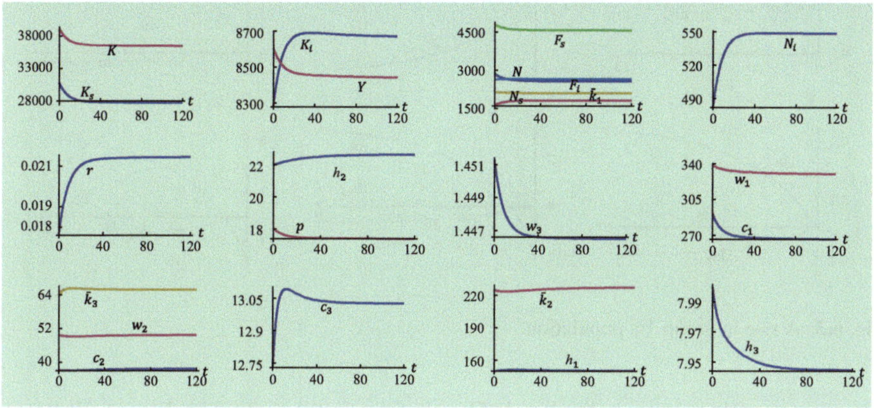

Fig. 6.1 The motion of the economic system

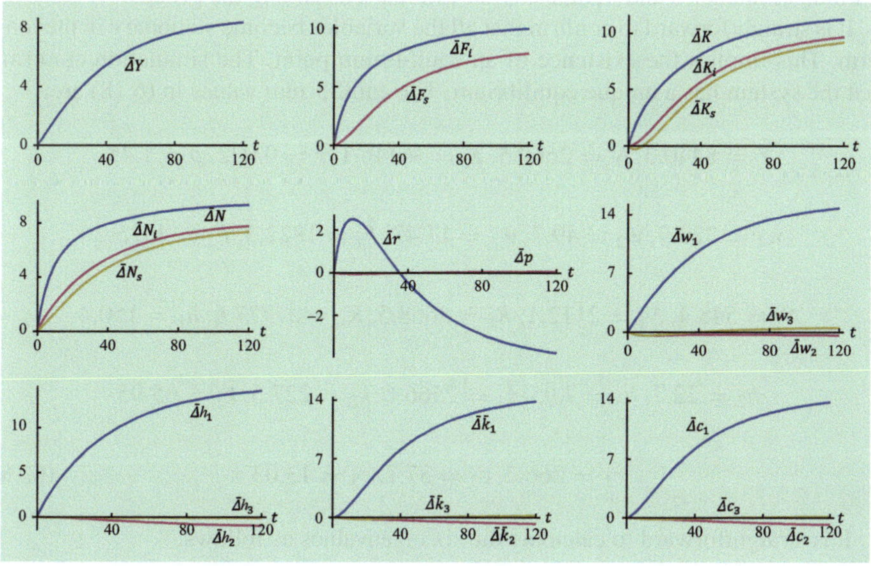

Fig. 6.2 Group 1 strengthens its human capital externalities

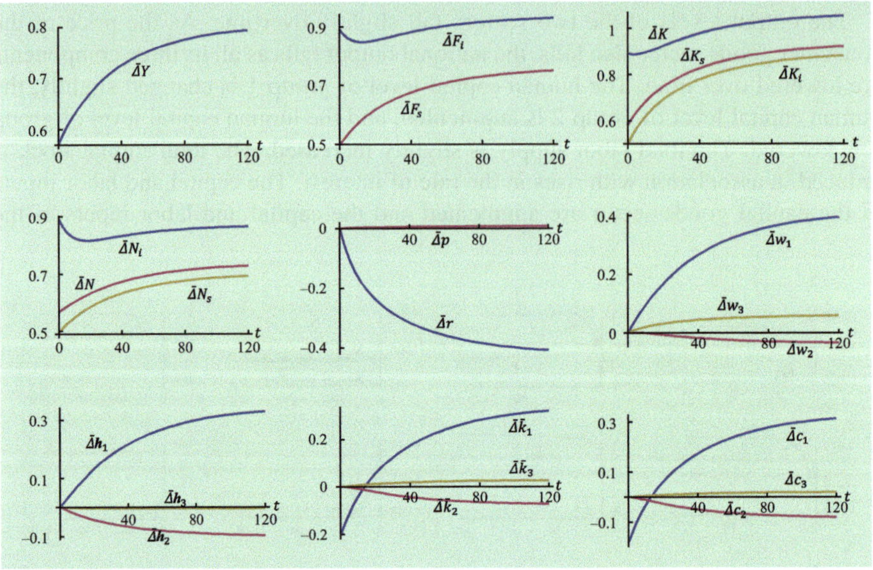

Fig. 6.3 A rise in group 1's population

consumer goods sector are lessened. The changes in the rest variables are illustrated in Fig. 6.1. What is important here is that there are gaps in wages and wealth among the groups. These differences come from the differences in the propensities to save, learning efficiencies and human capital externalities among the groups.

It is straightforward to confirm that all the variables become stationary in the long term. This implies the existence of an equilibrium point. The simulation confirms that the system has a unique equilibrium. The equilibrium values in (6.18) are:

$$Y = 8440.3, N = 2660.5, K = 36446.1, r = 0.022, p = 1.45$$

$$w_1 = 329.9, w_2 = 49.7, w_3 = 17.43, F_i = 1822.3, F_s = 4575.2$$

$$N_i = 548.4, N_s = 2112.1, K_i = 8668.5, K_s = 27777.6, h_1 = 150.4$$

$$h_2 = 22.7, h_3 = 7.95, \bar{k}_1 = 2566.6, \bar{k}_2 = 227.5, \bar{k}_3 = 65.95$$

$$c_1 = 266.2, c_2 = 37.7, c_3 = 13.03 \tag{6.18}$$

It is straightforward to calculate the six eigenvalues as follows:

$$\{-0.22, -0.19, -0.13, -0.06, -0.04, -0.03\}$$

The eigenvalues are real and negative. The unique equilibrium is locally stable. This guarantees the validity of exercising comparative dynamic analysis.

6.3 Group 1 Strengthening Human Capital Externalities

The impact of human capital is currently a main topic in economic theory and empirical research (Bandyopadhyay and Tang, 2011; Castelló-Climent and Hidalgo-Cabrillana, 2012). Could et al. (2001) build an economic model, concluding that the primary source of inequality growth within uneducated workers is due to increasing randomness, but inequality growth within educated workers is mainly due to changes in the composition and return to ability (Tselios, 2008; Fleisher et al. 2011). If educated and uneducated are treated as two different groups, I may give some insights into economic inequalities among different groups classified according by different criteria. This section studies the case that group 1 strengthens its human capital externalities as follows:

$$\upsilon_1 : 0.2 \Rightarrow 0.21$$

The simulation result is plotted as in Fig. 6.2. As human capital externalities of group 1 are strengthened; the group's human capital is increased. The rise in group 1's human capital leads to increases in the group's wage rate. Group $1'$ $s$per capita levels of wealth and consumption are increased. Group $2'$ $s$human capital, wage rate, and per capita levels of wealth and consumption are slightly reduced, while group $3'$ $s$human capital, wage rate, and per capita levels of wealth and consumption are slightly increased. The change has positive effects on the macroeconomic variables. The GDP, the two sectors' output levels, the total labor and capital, and labor and capital inputs are all increased. The price of consumer goods slightly changes, while the rate of interest rises initially and falls in the long term. The strengthened human capital extensities benefit greatly the group itself and national economy, while in regard to the other two groups one group suffers and the other groups' benefits. The inequalities in income and wealth between group 1 and the other groups are enlarged.

6.4 Group 1's Population Being Increased

The relationship between population changes and economic development is empirically ambiguous and theoretically difficult. Theoretical models with human capital predict situation-dependent interactions between population and economic growth (Galor and Weil, 1999; Bretschger, 2013). There are also mixed conclusions in empirical studies on the issue (Furuoka, 2009; Yao et al., 2013). Although I now allow group $1'$ s population to be increased as follows:

$$N_1 : 10 \Rightarrow 10.1$$

The results are plotted in Fig. 6.3. As far as the aggregate real variables are concerned, during the transitory process as well as in the long term the national output, the total capital stock, the total labor supply, the capital inputs, the labor inputs, and the output levels of the two sectors are all increased. As group $1's$ population increases, its capita wealth and consumption levels fall initially, but they are increased in the long term. The rise in the population enlarges the wealth stocks and tends to increase the relative social status. The net result of strengthened human capital externalities and increased relative social status augments the group's human capital. Consequently, the group's wage rate is increased. It should be emphasized that the effects on the other two groups are opposite. Group $2's$ human capital, wage rate, and per capita levels of wealth and consumption are all reduced, while group $3's$ human capital is slightly reduced and group $3's$ wage rate, and per capita levels of wealth, consumption are increased. This group-based conclusion is due to complicated interactions of macro-related and group-based forces.

6.5 Group 1's Decreasing Returns to Scale in Human Capital Accumulation Being Strengthened

This section allows group $1's$ decreasing returns to scale to be changed as follows:

$$\pi_1 : 0.1 \Rightarrow 0.12$$

The changes are given in Fig. 6.4. Group $1's$human capital is lowered, and the other two groups' human capital levels are slightly affected. Group $1's$wage rate is lowered, the other two groups' human capital levels increased. The increases in the wage rates result from the falls in the capital intensity of the capital goods sector. The total labor supply is reduced due to the reduction in human capital. The labor force is shifted from the consumer goods sector to the capital goods sector. The total capital is increased. More capital is employed by the capital goods sector and less by the consumer goods sector. The rate of interest falls in association with rising capital stocks. The price is slightly affected. The output of the capital goods sector is reduced, while the output of the consumer goods sector rises. The GDP rises slightly but soon falls. The wealth of each group is increased. Group $1's$ consumption levels are reduced, while group $2's$ and group $3's$ consumption levels are increased.

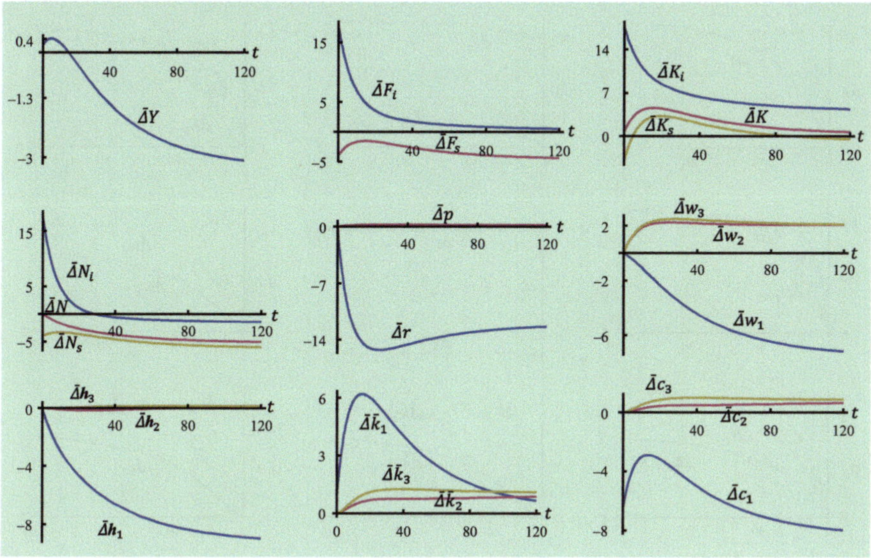

Fig. 6.4 Group 1's decreasing returns to scale being strengthened

6.6 The Consumer Goods Sector's Total Factor Productivity Being Augmented

I specify the change in the consumer goods sector's total factor productivity as follows:

$$A_s : 1 \Rightarrow 1.1$$

The effects are given in Fig. 6.5. The total capital stock, total labor supply, capital inputs, labor inputs, output levels of the two sectors, and GDP are all increased. The rate of interest slightly increases initially but is not affected in the long term. The price of consumer goods decreases. The human capital, wage rate and wealth and consumption levels of each group are increased.

6.7 Group 1 Increasing its Propensity to Save

Preferences of different households are important for understanding economic structures as demonstrated in the Walrasian general equilibrium theory. Nevertheless, economics does not yet an effective analytical framework for analyzing effects of changes in one type of household on national economic growth as well as wealth and income distribution among different households. As our analytical framework

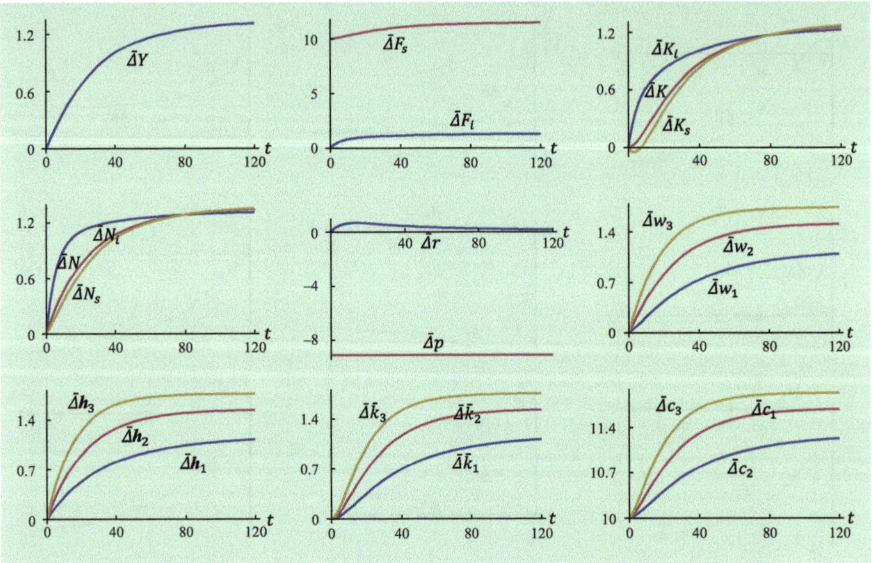

Fig. 6.5 The consumer goods sector's total factor productivity being augmented

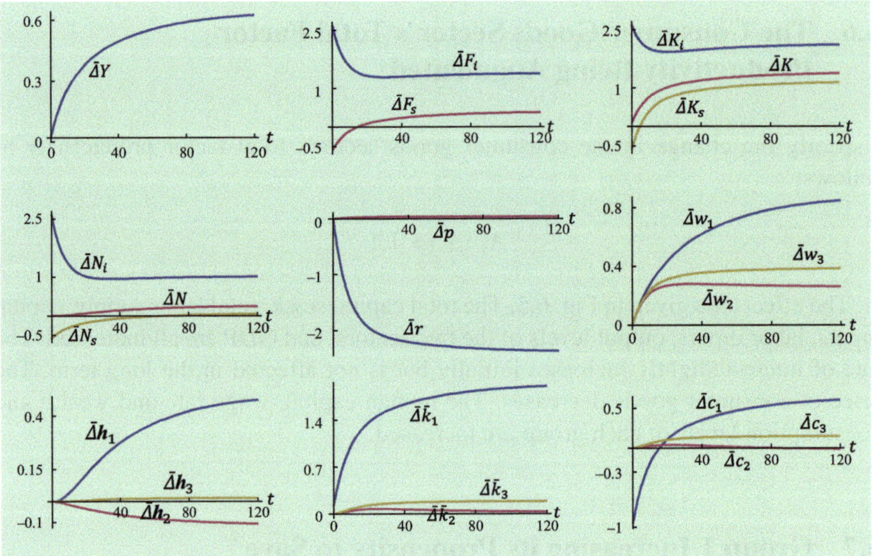

Fig. 6.6 Group 1 increasing its propensity to save

integrates the economic mechanism of the Walrasian general equilibrium theory and neoclassical growth theory, I can analyze the effects of a change in the preference of any people on the dynamic path of economic growth. I now allow group 1 to increase its propensity to save in the following way:

$$\lambda_{01} : 0.8 \Rightarrow 0.81$$

The simulation results are given in Fig. 6.6. As group $1's$ increases its patience for the future consumption, its wealth is increased. The consumption level of consumer goods is lessened initially and subsequently increased. As the typical household from the group initially saves more, it consumes less. Nevertheless, as the household has more wealth and the wage rate is also increased, the disposable income is increased in the long term, which leads to the rises in the consumption level. Hence, group 1 benefit from saving more from the disposable income in the long term. Group $3's$ human capital, wage rate and consumption and wealth levels are increased. Group $2'$swage rate is increased, while its human capital is reduced. Group $2's$ wealth and consumption levels are slightly affected. The total capital stock, total labor supply, capital inputs, labor inputs, output levels of the two sectors, and GDP are all increased in the long term. The rate of interest is reduced. The price of consumer goods changes slightly.

6.8 Concluding Remarks

This chapter proposed an economic growth model of heterogeneous households with economic structure and group-based human capital accumulation in an integrated Walrasian-general-equilibrium and neoclassical growth framework. The model emphasizes the role of group-based human capital externalities on economic structural change and wealth and income distribution. The model is influenced by learning by doing ideas by Arrow (1962) and the two theories in economics - Walrasian general equilibrium theory and neoclassical growth theory. The economic system consists of one capital goods sector, one consumer goods sector, and any number (of types) of households. The motion is described by a set of differential equations. The motion of the economic system is simulated with three groups. The chapter carried out the comparative dynamic analysis. Comparative analyses provide some insights into the complexity of economic growth with group-based human capital externalities. For instance, economists have been concerned with the relations between wealth and income distribution and growth have since long time ago. Kaldor (1956) argues that as income inequality is enlarged, growth should be encouraged as savings are promoted. This positive relation between income inequality and growth is also observed in studies, for instance, by Bourguignon (1981), Forbes (2000), and Frank (2009). There are other studies which find negative relations between income inequality and economic growth. Some mathematical models which predicate negative relations are: referred to, for instance, Galor and Zeira (1993), Galor and Moav (2004), and Benabou (2002). Some empirical studies by, for instance, Persson and Tabellini (1994), also confirm negative relations. From our simulation, the relations between inequality and economic growth are complicated in the sense that these relations are: determined by many factors. The relations are: expectably ambiguous or development-dependent in the sense that one may observe positive or negative relations according to the parameter values combinations and state of economic development.

Appendix: Proving Lemma 6.1

By (6.4) and (6.6), I obtain:

$$z \equiv \frac{r + \delta_k}{w} = \frac{N_i}{\bar{\beta}_i K_i} = \frac{N_s}{\bar{\beta}_s K_s} \tag{A6.1}$$

where $\bar{\beta}_j \equiv \beta_m / \alpha_m$. From (A6.1) and (6.13), it follows:

$$\bar{\beta}_i K_i + \bar{\beta}_s K_s = \frac{N}{z} \tag{A6.2}$$

Insert (A6.1) in (6.4):

$$r = \alpha_r z^{\beta_i} - \delta_k, \; w_j = \alpha_w h_j z^{-\alpha_i} \tag{A6.3}$$

where

$$\alpha_r = \alpha_i A_i \bar{\beta}_i^{\beta_i}, \alpha_w = \beta_i A_i \bar{\beta}_i^{-\alpha_i}$$

Hence, I determine the rate of interest and the wage rates as functions of z and h_j. From (6.5) and (6.6), it follows:

$$p = \frac{\bar{\beta}_s^{\alpha_s} z^{\alpha_s} w}{\beta_s A_s} \tag{A6.4}$$

where $w = w_1/h_1$. From (A6.3) and the definitions of $\hat{y}_j$, I have:

$$\hat{y}_j = (1 + r)\bar{k}_j + h_j w \tag{A6.5}$$

Insert $pc_j = \xi_j \hat{y}_j$ in (6.11):

$$\sum_{j=1}^{J} \xi_j \bar{N}_j \hat{y}_j = pF_s \tag{A6.6}$$

Substituting (A6.5) in (A6.6) yields:

$$N_s = \sum_{j=1}^{J} \tilde{g}_j \bar{k}_j + \tilde{g} \tag{A6.7}$$

where $pF_s = wN_s/\beta_s$ is applied and

$$\tilde{g}_j(z) \equiv \left(\frac{1+r}{w}\right)\beta_s \xi_j \bar{N}_j,\ \tilde{g}\big((h_j)\big) \equiv \beta_s \sum_{j=1}^{J} h_j \xi_j \bar{N}_j$$

From (A6.1), (6.1) and $K = \sum_{j=1}^{J} \bar{k}_j \bar{N}_j$ I get:

$$\frac{N_i}{\bar{\beta}_i} + \frac{N_s}{\bar{\beta}_s} = z \sum_{j=1}^{J} \bar{k}_j \bar{N}_j \tag{A6.8}$$

From (A6.7) and (A6.8), I solve:

$$N_i = \bar{\beta}_i z \sum_{j=1}^{J} \bar{k}_j \bar{N}_j - \frac{\bar{\beta}_i}{\bar{\beta}_s} \sum_{j=1}^{J} \tilde{g}_j \bar{k}_j - \frac{\bar{\beta}_i \tilde{g}}{\bar{\beta}_s} \tag{A6.9}$$

From (A6.7) and (A6.9), I have:

$$N_i + N_s = \sum_{j=1}^{J} \phi_j \bar{k}_j + \bar{\beta} \tilde{g} \tag{A6.10}$$

where

$$\phi_j = \bar{\beta} \tilde{g}_j + z \bar{\beta}_i \bar{N}_j,\ \bar{\beta} \equiv 1 - \frac{\bar{\beta}_i}{\bar{\beta}_s}$$

From (6.1) and (A6.10), it follows:

$$\bar{k}_1 = \phi\big(z, \{\bar{k}_j\}, (h_j)\big) \equiv \left(N - \sum_{j=2}^{J} \phi_j \bar{k}_j - \bar{\beta} \tilde{g}\right) \frac{1}{\phi_1} \tag{A6.11}$$

where $\{\bar{k}_j\} \equiv (\bar{k}_2, \ldots, \bar{k}_J)$. It is straightforward to confirm that all the variables can be expressed as functions of z, $\{\bar{k}_j\}$ and (h_j) by the following procedure: r and w_j by (A6.3) $\to \bar{k}_1$ by (A6.11) $\to N_i$ by (A6.9) $\to N_s$ by (A6.7)$\to w = w_1/h_1 \to \hat{y}_j$ by (A6.5) $\to K_s$, and K_i by (A6.1) $\to N$ by (6.1) $\to F_i$ and F_s by the definitions $\to$ p by (A6.4) $\to c_j$ and s_j by (6.11) $\to K = K_i + K_s$. From this procedure, (A6.21), (6.12) and (6.14), I have:

$$\frac{d\bar{k}_1}{dt} = \bar{\Omega}_1\left(z, \{\bar{k}_j\}, (h_j)\right) \equiv \lambda_1 \hat{y}_1 - \phi \tag{A6.18}$$

$$\frac{d\bar{k}_j}{dt} = \Lambda_j\left(z, \{\bar{k}_j\}, (h_j)\right) \equiv \lambda_j \bar{y}_j - \bar{k}_j, j = 3, \ldots, J$$

$$\frac{dh_j}{dt} = \Omega_j\left(z, \{\bar{k}_j\}, (h_j)\right) \equiv \frac{\upsilon_j c_j^{a_j} \bar{K}_j^{\bar{\theta}_j}}{h_j^{\pi_j}} \left(\frac{\bar{K}_j}{K}\right)^{\theta_j} - \delta_j h_j \tag{A6.19}$$

Taking derivatives of eq. (A6.17) with respect to t and combining with (A6.18) implies:

$$\frac{d\bar{k}_1}{dt} = \frac{\partial \phi}{\partial z}\dot{z} + \sum_{j=2}^{J} \Lambda_j \frac{\partial \phi}{\partial \bar{k}_j} + \sum_{j=1}^{J} \Omega_j \frac{\partial \phi}{\partial h_j} \tag{A6.20}$$

Equaling the right-hand sizes of eqs. (A6.18) and (A6.20), I get:

$$\frac{dz}{dt} = \Lambda_1\left(z, \{\bar{k}_j\}, (h_j)\right) \equiv \left[\bar{\Omega}_1 - \sum_{j=2}^{J} \Lambda_j \frac{\partial \phi}{\partial \bar{k}_j} - \sum_{j=1}^{J} \Omega_j \frac{\partial \phi}{\partial h_j}\right] \left(\frac{\partial \phi}{\partial z}\right)^{-1} \tag{A6.21}$$

In summary, the lemma is proved.

Chapter 7
How Do the Richest 1% Own 50% of Wealth?

> Cultural patterns of oppression are not only interrelated but are bound together and influenced by the intersectional systems of society. Examples of this include race, gender, class, ability, and ethnicity.
>
> Kimberle Williams Crenshaw (1950-)

It has been reported that the richest 1% of the world's population owns almost half of the world's wealth. Moreover, it does seem that inequality will be enlarged in the near future in tandem with rapid economic globalization. There is a need-to-know determinants of inequality and dynamics of inequality. This need is emphasized by Forbes (2000) as follows: "careful reassessment of the relationship between these two variables (growth rate and income inequality) needs further theoretical and empirical work evaluating the channels through which inequality, growth, and any other variables are related." Surprisingly, theoretical economics still has little to say about determinants and dynamics of economic growth and inequality. In a systematic review on the literature of economic growth and inequality of income and wealth, Zhang (2006a) argued that although the importance of issues related to growth and inequality was well recognized a long time ago by economists such as Marx and Kaldor, the mainstream of modern theoretical economics has failed in providing a proper analytical framework to analyze relations between growth and inequality. Without a proper analytical framework, economics can hardly analyze the complicated dynamic issues with nonlinear interactions among many variables over time. The chapter addresses the issues related to growth and inequality with Zhang's concept of disposable income and utility function. I am especially interested in the phenomenon of contemporary free-market economies where the richest 1% of the population own more than half of the wealth. By comparative dynamic analysis it is demonstrated that inequalities will not be shrunk but will be enlarged in free-market economies with rapid technological changes and connected markets. In order to analyze these issues, this chapter introduces endogenous human capital and human capital externalities into the general equilibrium theory with heterogeneous households and endogenous wealth.

W. Zhang, *A Dynamic Economic Theory of Heterogenous Households*,
https://doi.org/10.1007/978-981-95-8918-0_7

This chapter is based on Zhang's integrated Walrasian general equilibrium and neoclassical growth theory (Zhang, 2006a). Both physical wealth and human capital are the determinants of economic growth and inequality. Wealth differs between households partly because people have different propensities to save, and human capital differs between people partly because they have different abilities and preferences in accumulating human capital. It integrates neoclassical growth theory with the Walrasian general equilibrium theory for studying dynamic interactions among growth, wealth and income distribution, and economic structures. In economic theory there are only a few theoretical models which study inequality and growth with both endogenous wealth and human capital accumulation. This chapter extends the models on economic growth with heterogeneous households by Zhang (2012b). This chapter is based on Zhang (2015a). It is organized as follows. Section 7.1 develops the neoclassical growth model with heterogeneous households. Section 7.2 examines the dynamics of the economic system and its properties. Section 7.3 illustrates what happens to the economic system when the rich apply human capital more effectively. Section 7.4 shows the effects of a rise in the rich's propensity to save. Section 7.5 shows the impact of an increase in the rich's propensity to consume. Section 7.6 studies the change in the path of economic development when the rich's propensity to enjoy leisure rises. Section 7.7 shows how the inequality of income and wealth is affected when the total factor productivity of the capital goods sector rises. Section 7.8 analyses the effects of a rise in the rich's learning through consumption. Section 7.9 concludes the chapter. The appendix proves Lemma 7.1.

7.1 The Neoclassical Growth Model With Heterogeneous Households

The economy consists of one capital goods sector and one consumer goods sector. Households have assets of the economy and distribute their incomes to consumption and to save. Firms use labor and physical capital inputs to supply goods and services. Exchanges take place in perfectly competitive markets. Factor markets work well, and the available factors are fully utilized at every moment. Savings are undertaken only by households. All earnings of firms are distributed in the form of payments to factors of production, labor, managerial skill, and capital ownership. The population is classified into J groups. Each group has a fixed population, $\bar{N}_j$, $(j = 1, \ldots, J)$. Let prices be measured in terms of the commodity and the price of the commodity be unit. Let $p(t)$ denote the price of consumer goods at time t. The wage and interest rates are denoted by $w_j(t)$ and $r(t)$, respectively. Let $H_j(t)$ stand for group j's level of human capital. The variable $H_j(t)$ may consist of not only human capital such as skills and knowledge but also intangible assets such as social status, reputation, and social relations.

Let subscript index i and s stand for capital goods and consumer goods, respectively. I use $N_m(t)$ and $K_m(t)$ to stand for the labor force and capital stocks employed by sector m. Let $T_j(t)$ stand for the work time of a typical worker in group j. The variable $N(t)$ represents the total qualified labor force. A worker's labor force is $T_j(t)H_j^{m_j}(t)$, where m_j is a parameter measuring utilization efficiency of human capital by group j. The labor input is the work time by the effective human capital. A group's labor input is the group's population by each member in the labor force, that is, $T_j(t)H_j^{m_j}(t)\bar{N}_j$. As the total qualified labor force is the sum of all the groups' labor forces, $N(t)$ is as follows:

$$N(t) = \sum_{j=1}^{J} T_j(t)H_j^{m_j}(t)\bar{N}_j, \quad j = 1, \ldots, J \tag{7.1}$$

7.2 Full Employment of Labor and Capital

The total labor force is employed by the two sectors. The condition of full employment of labor force implies

$$N_i(t) + N_s(t) = N(t) \tag{7.2}$$

The total capital stock $K(t)$ is allocated between the two sectors. As full employment of capital is assumed, it follows:

$$K_i(t) + K_s(t) = K(t) \tag{7.3}$$

Let $\bar{k}_j(t)$ denote per capita wealth of group j at t. Group j's wealth is $\bar{k}_j(t)\bar{N}_j$. As wealth is held by the households, I have

$$K(t) = \sum_{j=1}^{J} \bar{k}_j(t)\bar{N}_j \tag{7.4}$$

7.3 Capital Goods Sector

Let $F_m(t)$ stand for the production function of sector m, $m = i, s$. The production function of the capital goods sector is specified as follows:

$$F_i(t) = A_i K_i^{\alpha_i}(t)N_i^{\beta_i}(t), \alpha_i, \beta_i > 0, \alpha_i + \beta_i = 1 \tag{7.5}$$

where A_i, α_i, and β_i are positive parameters. The capital goods sector employs two input factors, capital and labor force. It is assumed that all the markets are perfectly competitive. The marginal conditions for the capital goods sector are

$$r(t) + \delta_k = \frac{\alpha_i F_i(t)}{K_i(t)}, \; w(t) = \frac{\beta_i F_i(t)}{N_i(t)} \tag{7.6}$$

7.4 Consumer Goods Sector

The production function of the consumer goods sector is specified as follows:

$$F_s(t) = A_s K_s^{\alpha_s}(t) N_s^{\beta_s}(t), \alpha_s + \beta_s = 1, \alpha_s, \beta_s > 0 \tag{7.7}$$

where A_s, α_s, and β_s are technological parameters. The marginal conditions are

$$r(t) + \delta_k = \frac{\alpha_s p(t) F_s(t)}{K_s(t)}, \; w(t) = \frac{\beta_s p(t) F_s(t)}{N_s(t)} \tag{7.8}$$

7.5 Consumer Behaviors and Wealth Dynamics

Consumers make decisions on choice of leisure time, consumption levels of services and commodities as well as on how much to save. The wage rate of group j is

$$w_j(t) = w(t) H_j^{m_j}(t), j = 1, \cdots, J \tag{7.9}$$

Per capita current income from the interest payment $r(t)\bar{k}_j(t)$ and the wage payment $T_j(t) w_j(t)$ is

$$y_j(t) = r(t)\bar{k}_j(t) + T_j(t) w_j(t)$$

The variable $y_j(t)$ is the current income in the sense that it comes from consumers' payment for human capital and efforts and consumers' current earnings from ownership of wealth. The total value of wealth that consumers can use is $\bar{k}_j(t)$. Here, it is assumed that selling and buying wealth can be conducted instantaneously without any transaction cost. The per capita disposable income is given by:

$$\hat{y}_j(t) = y_j(t) + \bar{k}_j(t) = (1 + r(t))\bar{k}_j(t) + W_j(t) \tag{7.10}$$

where $W_j(t) \equiv T_j(t)w_j(t)$ is the wage income. The disposable income is used for saving, consumption, and education. It should be noted that the value, $\bar{k}_j(t)$, (i.e., $p(t)\bar{k}_j(t)$ with $p(t) = 1$), in (7.10) is a flow variable. Under the assumption that selling wealth can be conducted instantaneously without any transaction cost, $\bar{k}_j(t)$ can be considered as the amount of income that the consumer obtains at time t by selling all of his wealth. Hence, at time t the consumer has the total amount of income equaling $\hat{y}_j(t)$ to distribute between saving and consumption. It should be noted that in the traditional neoclassical growth theory and most empirical studies disposable income is defined as the income that a household earns each period of time after taxes and transfers. It is supposed to be the money available to the household for spending on goods and services. Indeed, when wealth plays a minor role in analyzing behavior of households the traditional concept is not misleading. Nevertheless, when wealth is large and plays an important role in affecting household behavior, the omission in the money available for spending may be misleading. Obviously, a rich man with the net value of wealth US$70 billions will save a lot even if he had no current income (no pension and wealth earning a net zero rate of return) as common sense tells us. According to the neoclassical growth theory (such as the most well-known Solow model in growth theory), the rich man makes neither consumption nor saving as his disposable income is zero. In our model, the man's disposable income is $0 + 70 = 70$. If his consumption annually is 0.1 billion, his saving is 70–0.1 = 69.9 billion US dollars. His actual saving rate is saving/(disposable income) = 69.9/70, rather than 0 as in a national statistical record. In our approach rich people have a high propensity to save poor people partly as the extremely rich have too much to spend. As our approach accumulated wealth will play another important role in protecting social status as wealth helps the rich to accumulate more physical capital (due to interest returns of wealth) as well as human capital (due to easy access to best education, for instance), to build more useful social networks, and to maintain reputation of being rich.

The typical consumer distributes the total available budget between saving $s_j(t)$ and consumption of consumer goods $c_j(t)$. The budget constraint is

$$p(t)c_j(t) + s_j(t) = \hat{y}_j(t) = (1 + r(t))\bar{k}_j(t) + w_j(t)T_j(t) \tag{7.11}$$

The time constraint for everyone is

$$T_j(t) + \bar{T}_j(t) = T_0 \tag{7.12}$$

where $\bar{T}_j(t)$ is the leisure time of the representative household and T_0 is the total available time. Substituting (7.12) into (7.11) yields

$$w_j(t)\bar{T}_j(t) + p(t)c_j(t) + s_j(t) = \bar{y}_j(t)$$

$$\equiv (1 + r(t))\bar{k}_j(t) + T_0 w_j(t) \tag{7.13}$$

The variable $\bar{y}_j(t)$ is the disposable income when the household spends all the available time on work. The consumer's utility function is dependent on $\bar{T}_j(t)$, $c_j(t)$, and $s_j(t)$ as follows:

$$U(t) = \bar{T}_j^{\sigma_{j0}}(t) c^{\xi_{j0}}(t) s^{\lambda_{j0}}(t), \ \sigma_{j0}, \xi_{j0}, \lambda_{j0} > 0 \tag{7.14}$$

where σ_{j0} is the propensity to use leisure time, ξ_{j0} is the propensity to consume, and λ_{j0} is the propensity to own wealth. Maximizing $U_j(t)$ subject to (7.13) yields

$$\bar{T}_j(t) = \frac{\sigma_j \bar{y}_j(t)}{w_j(t)}, \ c_j(t) = \frac{\xi_j \bar{y}_j(t)}{p_s(t)}, \ s_j(t) = \lambda_j \bar{y}_j(t) \tag{7.15}$$

where

$$\sigma_{j0} \equiv \rho_j \sigma_{j0}, \ \xi_{j0} \equiv \rho_j \xi_{j0}, \ \lambda_{j0} \equiv \rho_j \lambda_{j0}, \ \rho_j \equiv \frac{1}{\sigma_{j0} + \xi_{j0} + \lambda_{j0}}$$

7.6 Change in Household Wealth

According to the definitions of $s_j(t)$, the wealth accumulation of the representative household in group j is given by:

$$\dot{\bar{k}}_j(t) = s_j(t) - \bar{k}_j(t) \tag{7.16}$$

This equation simply states that the change in wealth is equal to saving minus dissaving.

7.7 Dynamics of Human Capital

In economic theory there are three sources of improving human capital, "through education," "learning by producing," and "learning by leisure." Arrow (1962) first introduced learning by doing into growth theory. The basic idea is that people accumulate more skills and have more ideas when they are engaged in economic production. Uzawa (1965) took account of trade-offs between investment in education and capital accumulation in his well-known two-sector model. The basic idea is that education uses social resources but enables people to have more skills and knowledge. Zhang (2007b) introduced the impact of consumption on human capital accumulation (via the so-called creative leisure) into growth theory. Arrow's idea of learning by doing is that useful knowledge can be obtained mainly through working experiences. His idea has narrow implications as there are many other sources of accumulating skills and knowledge. Activities which are classified neither as formal education as in the Uzawa model nor as production as in the Arrow model, such as playing computer games, having social parties, being brought up by rich and educated parents, living in a decent society, touring different parts of the world, and being extremely rich, may have strong effects on human capital. Influenced by the three approaches just mentioned and being concerned with providing a case of the richest 1% owning 50% wealth, I propose that the human capital accumulation is described as follows:

$$\dot{H}_j(t) = \frac{\tilde{\upsilon}_j c_j^{a_j}(t) \bar{k}_j^{\upsilon_j}(t) T_j^{\theta_j}(t)}{H_j^{\pi_j}(t)} - \delta_{hj} H_j(t) \tag{7.17}$$

where δ_{hj} is the depreciation rates of human capital, $0 < \delta_{hj} < 1$. In (7.17), $\tilde{\upsilon}_j$, a_j, υ_j, and θ_j are non-negative parameters, and π_j is a parameter. In our approach different groups may have different depreciation rates of human capital. The human capital accumulation in this study is influenced by different approaches to human capital accumulation in the literature of endogenous human capital. The item $c_j^{a_j}$ in $\tilde{\upsilon}_j c_j^{a_j} \bar{k}_j^{\upsilon_j} T_j^{\theta_j} / H_j^{\pi_j}$ implies a positive relation between human capital accumulation and consumption is influenced by Uzawa's learning through education and Zhang's learning through consumption. As education is classified as the consumption of services, a higher level of consumption may imply a higher investment in education. On the other hand, higher consumption also implies that the household may accumulate more through other consumption activities. The item $\bar{k}_j^{\upsilon_j}$ which implies a positive relation between wealth and human capital accumulation can be interpreted as meant that more wealth means, for instance, a higher social status. More wealth may also help one to maintain a professional reputation. The specification of $T_j^{\theta_j}$ is influenced by Arrow's learning by doing. More work accumulates more human capital. The term $H_j^{\pi_j}$ implies that more human capital makes it easier (more difficult) to accumulate knowledge in the case of $\pi_j < 0$ ($\pi_j > 0$).

7.8 Demand for and Supply of Consumer Goods

The output of the consumer goods sector is consumed only by the households. The demand for consumer goods from a group is $c_j(t)\bar{N}_j$. The condition that the total demand is equal to the total supply implies

$$\sum_{j=1}^{J} c_j(t)\bar{N}_j = F_s(t) \tag{7.18}$$

7.9 Demand for and Supply of Capital Goods

As output of the capital goods sector is used only as capital goods, the output equals the depreciation of capital stock and the net savings. That is:

$$\sum_{j=1}^{J} s_j(t)\bar{N}_j - K(t) + \delta_k K(t) = F_i(t) \tag{7.19}$$

The model construction is complete. The model is structurally general in the sense that some well-known models in theoretical economics can be considered as its special cases. For instance, if wealth and human capital are fixed and the number of types of households is equal to the population, then the model is a Walrasian general equilibrium model. If the population is homogeneous, our model is structurally similar to the neoclassical growth model. It is structurally similar to the multi-class models by Pasinetti and Samuelson (Samuelson, 1959; Pasinetti, 1960, 1974; Stiglitz, 1967).

7.10 The Dynamics and its Properties

As the system consists of any number of types of households, its dynamics is highly dimensional. The following lemma shows that the economic dynamics is represented by $2J$dimensional differential equations. First, I introduce a variable:

$$z(t) \equiv \frac{r(t) + \delta_k}{w(t)}$$

Lemma 7.1

The dynamics of the economy is governed by the following $2J$dimensional differential equations system with $z(t)$, $\{\bar{k}_j(t)\}$,and $(H_j(t))$, where $\{\bar{k}_j(t)\} \equiv (\bar{k}_2(t), \cdots, \bar{k}_J(t))$ and $(H_j(t)) \equiv (H_1(t), \cdots, H_J(t))$, as the variables:

$$\dot{z}(t) = \Lambda_1\left(z(t), (H_j(t)), \{\bar{k}_j(t)\}\right)$$

$$\dot{\bar{k}}_j(t) = \Lambda_j\left(z(t), (H_j(t)), \{\bar{k}_j(t)\}\right), j = 2, \ldots, J$$

$$\dot{H}_j(t) = \Omega_j\left(z(t), (H_j(t)), \{\bar{k}_j(t)\}\right), j = 1, \ldots, J$$

in which Λ_j and Ω_j are unique functions of $z(t)$, $\{\bar{k}_j(t)\}$,and $(H_j(t))$ at any point in time, defined in the appendix. For given $z(t)$, $\{\bar{k}_j(t)\}$,and $(H_j(t))$, the other variables are uniquely determined at any point in time by the following procedure: $r(t)$ and

$w(t)$ by (A7.3) $\to$ $w_j(t)$ by (A7.4) $\to$ $p(t)$ by (A7.5) $\to$ $\bar{k}_1(t)$ by (A7.18) $\to$ $N_i(t)$ by (A7.12) $\to$ $N(t)$ by (A7.11) $\to$ $N_s(t)$ by (A7.8) $\to$ $\bar{y}_j(t)$ by (A7.6) $\to$ $K_i(t)$ and $K_s(t)$ by (A7.1) $\to$ $F_i(t)$ and $F_s(t)$ by the definitions $\to$ $\bar{T}_j(t)$, $c_j(t)$, and $s_j(t)$ by (7.15) $\to$ $K(t)$ by (7.4).

The lemma gives a computational program to follow the motion of the dynamic economic system by simulating the dynamic equations with any number of types of households. As the system is nonlinear and is of high dimension, it is difficult to generally analyze behavior of the system. For illustration, the parameter values are specified as follows:

$$\begin{pmatrix} N_1 \\ N_2 \\ N_3 \end{pmatrix} = \begin{pmatrix} 1 \\ 69 \\ 20 \end{pmatrix}, \begin{pmatrix} m_1 \\ m_2 \\ m_3 \end{pmatrix} = \begin{pmatrix} 0.7 \\ 0.15 \\ 0.1 \end{pmatrix}, \begin{pmatrix} \xi_{10} \\ \xi_{20} \\ \xi_{30} \end{pmatrix} = \begin{pmatrix} 0.1 \\ 0.18 \\ 0.2 \end{pmatrix}$$

$$\begin{pmatrix} \lambda_{10} \\ \lambda_{20} \\ \lambda_{30} \end{pmatrix} = \begin{pmatrix} 0.94 \\ 0.65 \\ 0.6 \end{pmatrix}, \begin{pmatrix} \sigma_{10} \\ \sigma_{20} \\ \sigma_{30} \end{pmatrix} = \begin{pmatrix} 0.25 \\ 0.2 \\ 0.2 \end{pmatrix}, \begin{pmatrix} \bar{v}_1 \\ \bar{v}_2 \\ \bar{v}_3 \end{pmatrix} = \begin{pmatrix} 0.8 \\ 0.4 \\ 0.1 \end{pmatrix}$$

$$\begin{pmatrix} a_1 \\ a_2 \\ a_3 \end{pmatrix} = \begin{pmatrix} 0.3 \\ 0.2 \\ 0.1 \end{pmatrix}, \begin{pmatrix} v_1 \\ v_2 \\ v_3 \end{pmatrix} = \begin{pmatrix} 0.2 \\ 0.1 \\ 0.1 \end{pmatrix}, \begin{pmatrix} \theta_1 \\ \theta_2 \\ \theta_3 \end{pmatrix} = \begin{pmatrix} 0.3 \\ 0.35 \\ 0.4 \end{pmatrix}, \begin{pmatrix} \pi_1 \\ \pi_2 \\ \pi_3 \end{pmatrix} = \begin{pmatrix} 0.1 \\ 0.2 \\ 0.4 \end{pmatrix}$$

$$A_i = 1, A_s = 0.9, \alpha_i = 0.32, \alpha_s = 0.34, T_0 = 24, \delta_{h1} = 0.04$$

$$\delta_{h2} = 0.06, \delta_{h3} = 0.08, \delta_k = 0.05 \tag{7.20}$$

Group 1, 2,and 3's populations are respectively 1, 69, and 20. Group 2 has the largest population. The capital goods sector and consumer goods sector's total productivities are respectively 1 and 0.9. Group 1, 2,and 3's utilization efficiency parameters, m_j, are respectively 0.7, 0.15, and 0.1.Group 1 utilizes human capital most effectively; group 2 next and group 3 lest effectively. The three groups are called, respectively, the rich, the middle, and the poor. The rich's learning by doing parameter, $\bar{v}_1$, is the highest. The returns to scale parameters, π_j, are all positive, which implies that human capital accumulation exhibits decreasing returns to scale in human capital. The depreciation rates of human capital are specified in such a way that the rich has the lowest rate. The rich's propensity to save is 0.94, and the rich's propensity to save is 0.6. It is assumed that the rich is most effective in learning through consuming and working. The value of the middle's propensity is between the rich and the poor. In Figure 1, I plot the motion of the system with the following initial conditions:

$$z(0) = 0.135, \bar{k}_2(0) = 73, \bar{k}_3(0) = 45, H_1(0) = 460, H_2(0) = 17, H_3(0) = 3 \tag{7.21}$$

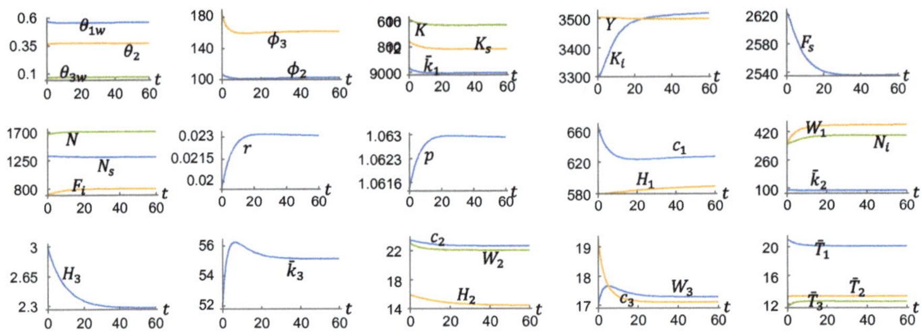

Fig. 7.1 The motion of the economic system

In Fig. 7.1, the national output Y,the share of each group's wealth in the national wealth θ_{jw}, and the ratio between group 1's and another group's wealth ϕ_j are respectively defined as:

$$Y(t) = F_i(t) + p(t)F_s(t), \theta_{jw}(t) \equiv \frac{\bar{K}_j(t)}{K(t)}, \phi_j(t) \equiv \frac{\bar{k}_1(t)}{\bar{k}_j(t)}, j = 1, 2, 3$$

With different initial conditions, the economy experiences different paths of development. Under (7.21), the national output and wealth experience negative growth over time. The rich's human capital is increased and the middle's and the poor's human capital fall over time. A rich household works more hours and a household from the other two groups works less. The rich own more than half of the national wealth with 1 percent of the population and the poor own less 10 percent of the national wealth with the 20% of the national population. The representative household from the rich owns 160 times more wealth than the household from the poor.

I start with different initial states not far away from the equilibrium point and find that the system approaches to an equilibrium point. Under (7.21) the system has a unique equilibrium. The equilibrium values are listed in (7.22). The rich has the highest human capital and highest wage income. The rich household spends the least hours working and the poor household spends the longest time working. The rich household's consumption level and wealth are also much higher than those of the households from the two other groups.

$$\theta_{1w} = 0.559, \theta_{2w} = 0.373, \theta_{3w} = 0.069, \phi_2 = 103.4, \phi_3 = 162.7$$

$$Y = 3503.5, K = 16092.3, N = 1708.4, F_i = 804.6, F_s = 2539.2$$

$$K_i = 3526, K_s = 12566.3, N_i = 401.4, N_s = 1306.9, r = 0.023$$

$$p = 1.06, w_1 = 118.9, w_2 = 2.04, w_3 = 1.48, W_1 = 462.4$$

$$W_2 = 22.1, W_3 = 17.13, H_1 = 591.9, H_2 = 14.47, H_3 = 2.28$$

$$\bar{k}_1 = 8988.23, \bar{k}_2 = 86.96, \bar{k}_3 = 55.19, c_1 = 629.7, c_2 = 22.66$$

$$c_3 = 17.31, \bar{T}_1 = 20.11, \bar{T}_2 = 13.15, \bar{T}_3 = 12.43 \tag{7.22}$$

It is straightforward to calculate the six eigenvalues as follows:

$$-0.38, -0.32, -0.18, -0.11, -0.07, -0.03$$

As all the eigenvalues are negative, the equilibrium point is locally stable.

7.11 The Rich Applying Human Capital more Effectively

Different people in society have different opportunities to apply their human capital. It is expected that the rich have more opportunities to utilize and tend to be more capable of applying human capital. There are many possible determinants of inequality of income and wealth in modern societies. It is expected that the rich will get richer in the near future. For instance, if society is developed in such a direction that enables the rich (and successful ones) to apply their human capital more effectively, one may expect changes in inequality between the rich and the poor. The rich's human capital utilization efficiency rises as follows:

$$m_1 : 0.7 \Rightarrow 0.71.$$

The simulation results are plotted in Fig. 7.2. As the rich increases their efficiency in applying human capital, the inequality between the rich and the poor is greatly enlarged. The rich get a higher share of the national wealth and the ratios of per household wealth between the poor and rich and between the middle and rich are increased. The improved efficiency by the rich benefits the growth of the national wealth, GDP, and total labor supply. The output levels and two input factors of the two sectors are augmented. The rate of interest falls in tandem with rising national wealth. The price of consumer goods decreases. The rich's human capital as well as the poor and the middle are all enhanced, with the rich's human capital being increased much higher than the poor and middles. It should be noted that an improvement in the rich's human capital utilization efficiency increases not only the rich's household wealth, consumption level of services, and wage income, but also the middles and the poor's. In summary, an improvement in the rich's human capital utilization efficiency enlarges the gaps between the rich and the poor and the rich and middle, and benefits everyone in society (except everyone working longer hours). By the way it should be remarked that the impact of human capital is currently a

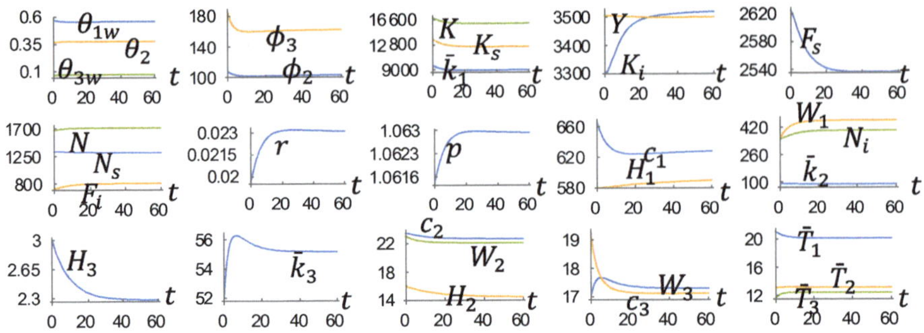

Fig. 7.2 The rich applying human capital more effectively

main topic in economic theory and empirical research. There are different empirical conclusions about inequalities and human capital. This model shows that a rise in the rich's efficiency in applying human capital benefits everyone and worsens equality.

7.12 The Rich's Propensity to Save Being Augmented

If the rich have become too rich to spend their wealth and become less interested in showing off with wealth, their propensity to save tends to be enhanced. The rich's propensity to save increases as follows:

$$\lambda_{10} : 0.94 \Rightarrow 0.95$$

The simulation results are plotted in Fig. 7.3. The effects caused by the rise in the rich's propensity to save are quite similar to the effects of an improvement in the rich's human capital utilization efficiently. As the rich increases their propensity to save, the inequality between the rich and the poor increases. The rich get a higher share of the national wealth and the ratios of household wealth between the poor and rich and between the middle and rich are increased. The national wealth, GDP, and total labor supply are augmented. The output levels and two input factors of the two sectors are increased. The rate of interest and the price of consumer goods are lowered. The rich's human capital as well as the poor and the middle are all enhanced. It should be noted that although the rich's consumption of consumer goods is reduced in the short term, it is enhanced in the long term. This occurs as in the short term the increased propensity to save makes the rich consume less of the disposable income. But their consumption is increased in the long term as more wealth enables the rich to accumulate more human capital and the rich work longer hours due to the change in the preference. In the long term any household's per household wealth, consumption level of services, and wage income are augmented. In summary, a rise in the rich's propensity to save benefits the national economic variables, enlarges the

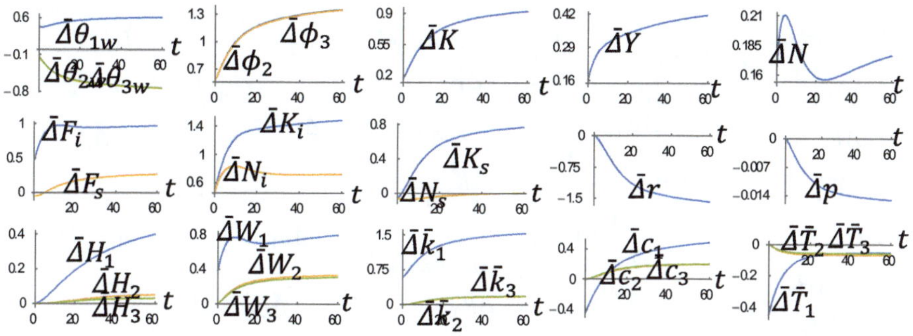

Fig. 7.3 The rich's propensity to save being augmented

gaps between the rich and the poor and the rich and the middle and benefits everyone in society (except everyone working longer hours).

7.13 The Rich's Propensity to Consume Being Increased

The rich's propensity to consume changes in the following way:

$$\xi_{10} : 0.07 \Rightarrow 0.08$$

The simulation results are plotted in Fig. 7.4. Per household of all the households is reduced by the rich's preference change. In the short term the inequalities are "improved" as the share of the rich in the national wealth falls and the ratios of the per household's wealth levels are shrunk. In the long term the inequalities are "deteriorated" as the share of the rich in the national wealth rises and the ratios of the per household's wealth levels are enhanced. This occurs partly because in our approach working experiences, owning wealth and consuming experiences all can affect human capital accumulation. As the rich consume more, they may grasp more business opportunities, learn more about business, and build more productive/useful human relations. The rich's human capital is thus enhanced. As they earn more income, their share of national wealth will be increased more rapidly than that of the other two groups. The rich work more hours, and the middle and the poor work less hours. The rich get more wage income, and the other two groups get less wage income. The national wealth is reduced, and the national GDP and labor supply are augmented. The rate of interest and price of consumer goods rise. The output of the consumer goods sector is enhanced, and the output of the capital goods sector is reduced.

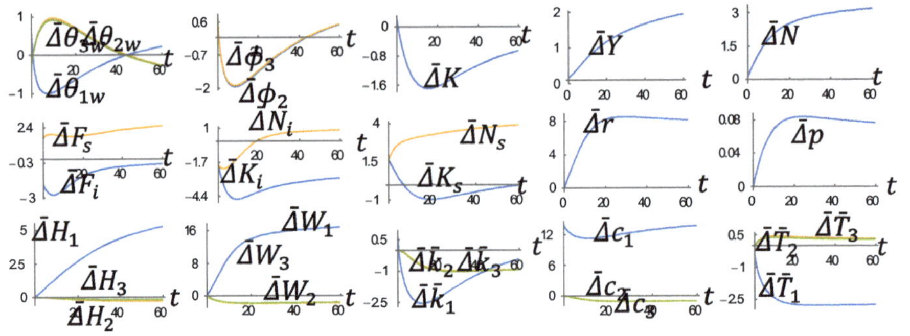

Fig. 7.4 The rich's propensity to consume being increased

7.14 The Rich's Propensity to Enjoy Leisure Being Increased

Another change in the rich's preference is that they prefer more consuming leisure. To examine the impact of their preference change, I now increase the rich's propensity to enjoy leisure as follows:

$$\sigma_{10} : 0.25 \Rightarrow 0.26$$

The simulation results are plotted in Fig. 7.5. The inequalities are improved as the share of the rich in the national wealth falls and the ratios of the per household's wealth levels are shrunk. As the rich spend more time on leisure, their human capital falls. The national wealth, GDP, and labor supply all fall. The rate of interest and price of consumer goods rise. The output levels of the two sectors and each sector's two inputs are enhanced. The household from any group has lower human capital, works less hours, consumes less goods, and owns less wealth. In summary as the rich tend to enjoy more leisure, the inequalities are reduced but everyone worsens off (except having more leisure hours).

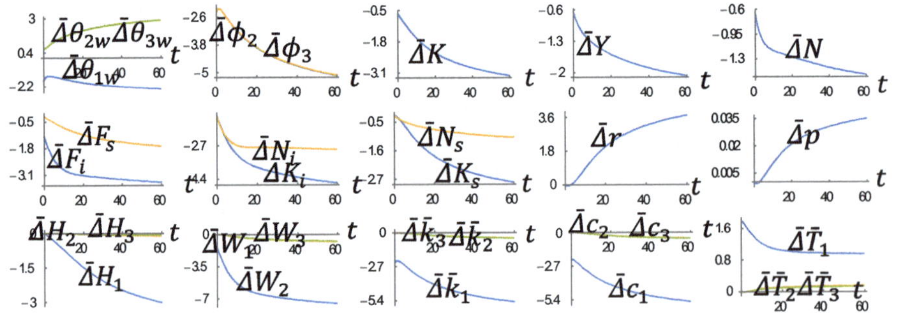

Fig. 7.5 The rich's propensity to enjoy leisure being increased

7.15 A Rise in the Total Factor Productivity of the Capital Goods Sector

Another important question is what will happen to different people and the national economy if the total productivity of the capital goods sector is increased. The total productivity rises as follows:

$$A_i : 1 \Rightarrow 1.05$$

The simulation results are plotted in Figure 7.6. The rise in productivity increases human capital and wage incomes of all the groups. The rate of interest rises initially and falls in the long term. The price of consumer goods rises. The distribution of the total labor force is slightly affected. The two sectors increase the output levels in the long term. The wealth and consumption levels of all the groups are increased in the long term. The national wealth, GDP, and total labor supply are all increased. The inequality between the rich and the poor is enlarged. The rich get higher share of the national wealth and the ratios of household wealth between the poor and the rich and between the middle and the rich are increased. It should be further noted that economists have been concerned with relations between wealth and income distribution and growth have long time ago. Kaldor (1956) argues that as income inequality is enlarged, growth should be encouraged as savings are promoted. There are other studies which find negative relations between income inequality and economic growth. From the simulation, it is seen that the relations between inequality and economic growth are complicated in the sense that these relations are determined by many factors. The relation is expectably ambiguous or development-dependent in the sense that one may observe positive or negative relations according to the parameter value combinations and state of economic development. It was demonstrated that if the rich increase their human capital utilization efficiency or the total factor productivity of the capital goods sector is increased, the economy experiences positive growth and inequalities are enlarged. It is also straightforward to show that if either the poor or the middle increases their human capital utilization efficiency, the economy will experience positive growth and inequalities between are shrunk.

7.16 The Rich's Learning through Consuming Being Strengthened

The impact of the rich's learning through consuming upon human capital accumulation changes as follows:

$$a_1 : 0.3 \Rightarrow 0.31$$

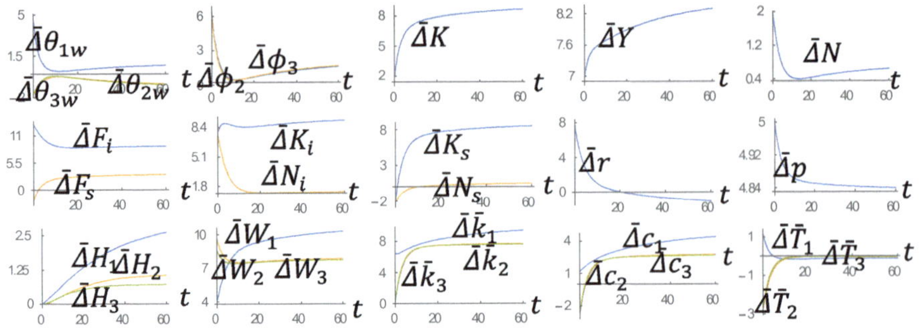

Fig. 7.6 A rise in the total productivity of the capital goods sector

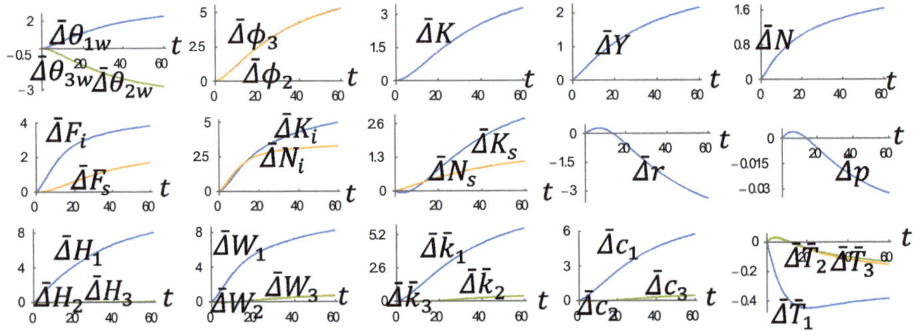

Fig. 7.7 The rich's learning through consuming being strengthened

The simulation results are plotted in Fig. 7.7. As the rich's consumption affects human capital accumulation more strongly, the wealth gap between the rich and the poor is enlarged. The rich get higher share of the national wealth and the ratios of per household wealth between the poor and the rich and between the middle and the rich are enhanced. The rich's human capital is augmented, which also increases the growth of the national wealth, GDP, and total labor supply. The output levels and two input factors of the two sectors are augmented. The rate of interest and the price of consumer goods decrease. The parameter change enlarges the gaps between the rich and the poor and the rich and the middle and benefits everyone in society.

7.17 Concluding Remarks

This chapter built a dynamic economic model of heterogeneous households to explain some economic mechanisms of how the richest one percent of the population own 50% of national wealth. The main determinants of growth and inequality are endogenous wealth and human capital accumulation under perfectly competitive conditions.

The production technologies and economic structure follow the Uzawa two-sector model. In this study a household's disposable income is the traditional disposable income (which is the income that a household earns each period of time after taxes and transfers in the Solow model and many empirical studies) plus the value of the household's wealth. By applying Zhang's concept of disposable income and utility approach, I describe consumers' wealth accumulation and consumption behavior. It was shown how wealth accumulation, human capital accumulation, division of labor, and time distribution interact with each other under perfect competition. I simulated the model with three groups of the population, the rich 1%, the middle 69%, and the poor 20%. It is shown the existence of an equilibrium point at which the rich 1% do own more than half of the national wealth and the poor 20% less than 10% of the national wealth. The system moves to the equilibrium from an initial state and confirms that the equilibrium point is stable. It is also demonstrated how changes in the total factor productivity of the capital goods sector, the rich's human capital utilization efficiency, the rich's efficiency of learning through consuming, and the rich's propensities to save, to consume, and to enjoy leisure affect growth and inequality. Although our comparative dynamic analysis does not find a situation of "the rich getting richer and the poor get poorer," the inequalities can be enlarged in tandem with economic growth, for instance, when the total factor productivity of the capital goods sector is increased. The study has many obvious limitations. For instance, it is assumed that there is no social mobility in the economic system. Although for a "mature" social and economic system, it is rare for the poor to become rich. In a case like China, about three decades ago there was almost no rich in the entire country. Today there are so many rich people who had never dreamt of becoming rich even two decades ago. The model does not explain this kind of phenomena. This chapter does not consider the role of the government in redistributing wealth and income. It is important to see how the government can affect distribution with various policies. It is more insightful to allow multiple parameters to be changed simultaneously. Another important issue is how to introduce endogenous change in preferences of different people.

Appendix: Proving Lemma 7.1

By (7.6) and (7.8), I obtain

$$z \equiv \frac{r + \delta_k}{w} = \frac{N_q}{\bar{\beta}_q K_q}, \; q = i, s \tag{A7.1}$$

where $\bar{\beta}_q \equiv \beta_q / \alpha_q$. From (A7.1) and (7.3), it follows:

$$\frac{N_i}{\bar{\beta}_i} + \frac{N_s}{\bar{\beta}_s} = z \sum_{j=1}^{J} \bar{k}_j \bar{N}_j \tag{A7.2}$$

where (7.4) is applied. Insert (A7.1) in (7.6):

$$r(z) = \alpha_r z^{\beta_i} - \delta_k,\ w(z) = \alpha z^{-\alpha_i} \tag{A7.3}$$

where

$$\alpha_r = \alpha_i A_i \bar{\beta}_i^{\beta_i},\ \alpha = \beta_i A_i \bar{\beta}_i^{-\alpha_i}$$

I have

$$w_j\big(z, H_j\big) = H_j^{m_j} w \tag{A7.4}$$

Hence, the rate of interest and the wage rates are determined as functions of z and (H_j). From (7.7) and (7.8), it follows:

$$p(z) = \frac{\bar{\beta}_s^{\alpha_s} z^{\alpha_s} w}{\beta_s A_s} \tag{A7.5}$$

From (A7.4) and the definitions of $\bar{y}_j$, I have

$$\bar{y}_j = (1 + r)\bar{k}_j + T_0 w_j \tag{A7.6}$$

Insert $pc_j = \xi_j \bar{y}_j$ in (7.18):

$$\sum_{j=1}^{J} \xi_j \bar{N}_j \bar{y}_j = pF_s \tag{A7.7}$$

Substituting (A7.6) in (A7.7) yields

$$N_s = \sum_{j=1}^{J} \tilde{g}_j \bar{k}_j + \tilde{g} \tag{A7.8}$$

where $pF_s = wN_s/\beta_s$ is applied and

$$\tilde{g}_j(z) \equiv \bar{r}\beta_s \xi_j \bar{N}_j,\ \bar{r}(z) \equiv \frac{1 + r}{w},\ \tilde{g}\big(z, (H_j)\big) \equiv \beta_s T_0 \sum_{j=1}^{J} H_j^{m_j} \xi_j \bar{N}_j$$

Insert $w_j \bar{T}_j = \sigma_j \bar{y}_j$ in (7.12):

$$T_j = T_0 - \frac{\sigma_j \bar{y}_j}{w_j} \tag{A7.9}$$

Insert (A7.6) in (A7.9):

$$T_j = \left(1 - \sigma_j\right)T_0 - \frac{(1+r)\sigma_j\bar{k}_j}{w_j} \tag{A7.10}$$

Insert (A7.10) in (7.1):

$$N = n_0 - \sum_{j=1}^{J} n_j\bar{k}_j \tag{A7.11}$$

where

$$n_0\left(z, (H_j)\right) \equiv T_0 \sum_{j=1}^{J}(1-\sigma_j)\bar{N}_j H_j^{m_j},\ n_j\left(z, (H_j)\right) \equiv \bar{r}\sigma_j\bar{N}_j$$

Substituting (A7.8) into (A7.11) yields

$$N_i\left(z, (H_j), (\bar{k}_j)\right) = n_0 - \tilde{g} - \sum_{j=1}^{J}(n_j + \tilde{g}_j)\bar{k}_j \tag{A7.12}$$

Insert (A7.12) and (A7.8) in (A7.2):

$$\bar{k}_1 = \phi\left(z, \{\bar{k}_j\}, (H_j)\right) \equiv \left(\frac{n_0 - \tilde{g}}{\bar{\beta}_i} + \frac{\tilde{g}}{\bar{\beta}_s} - \sum_{j=2}^{J}\varphi_j\bar{k}_j\right)\frac{1}{\varphi_1} \tag{A7.13}$$

in which

$$\varphi_j\left(z, \left(H_j\right)\right) \equiv z\bar{N}_j + \frac{n_j + \tilde{g}_j}{\bar{\beta}_i} - \frac{\tilde{g}_j}{\bar{\beta}_s},\ \left\{\bar{k}_j\right\} \equiv \left(\bar{k}_2, \ldots, \bar{k}_J\right)$$

It is straightforward to confirm that all the variables can be expressed as functions of z, $\left\{\bar{k}_j\right\}$, and (H_j) by the following procedure: r and w by (A7.3) $\rightarrow$ w_j by (A7.4) $\rightarrow$ p by (A7.5) $\rightarrow$ $\bar{k}_1$ by (A7.18) $\rightarrow$ N_i by (A7.12) $\rightarrow$ N by (A7.11) $\rightarrow$ N_s by (A7.8) $\rightarrow$ $\bar{y}_j$ by (A7.6) $\rightarrow$ K_i and K_s by (A7.1) $\rightarrow$ F_i and F_s, by the definitions $\rightarrow$ $\bar{T}_j$, c_j, and s_j by (7.15) $\rightarrow$$K$ by (7.4). From this procedure, (A7.13), (7.16), and (7.17), I have

$$\dot{\bar{k}}_1 = \bar{\Omega}_1\left(z, \left\{\bar{k}_j\right\}, \left(H_j\right)\right) \equiv \lambda_1\bar{y}_1 - \phi \ \text{(A7.14)}$$

$$\dot{\bar{k}}_j = \Lambda_j\left(z, \left\{\bar{k}_j\right\}, \left(H_j\right)\right) \equiv \lambda_j\bar{y}_j - \bar{k}_j, j = 2, \ldots, J$$

$$\dot{H}_j = \Omega_j\left(z, \left\{\bar{k}_j\right\}, \left(H_j\right)\right), j = 1, \ldots, J \tag{A7.15}$$

Taking derivatives of eq. (A7.13) with respect to t and combining with (A7.15), I get

$$\dot{\bar{k}}_1 = \frac{\partial \phi}{\partial z}\dot{z} + \sum_{j=2}^{J} \Lambda_j \frac{\partial \phi}{\partial \bar{k}_j} + \sum_{j=1}^{J} \Omega_j \frac{\partial \phi}{\partial H_j} \tag{A7.16}$$

Equaling the right-hand sides of eqs. (A7.14) and (A7.16), I get

$$\dot{z} = \Lambda_1\left(z, \{\bar{k}_j\}, (H_j)\right) \equiv \left[\bar{\Omega}_1 - \sum_{j=2}^{J} \Lambda_j \frac{\partial \phi}{\partial \bar{k}_j} - \sum_{j=1}^{J} \Omega_j \frac{\partial \phi}{\partial H_j}\right] \left(\frac{\partial \phi}{\partial z}\right)^{-1} \tag{A7.17}$$

In summary, I proved Lemma 7.1.

Chapter 8
Discrimination, Growth, and Inequality

> A people without the knowledge of their past history, origin and culture is like a tree without roots.
>
> Marcus Garvey (1887–1940)

Discrimination is conducted against different people in different forms over human history in different parts of the world. Discrimination may be conducted in different forms. For instance, discrimination in the form of slavery had a long history in the United States. After the end of slavery, discrimination under the embracement of the US legal system was continued for a long time in the form of state-sponsored racial segregation in schools, transportation, and public accommodations (Higgs 1977; Feagin 2000; Zhang 2003a, 2014e, 2017a, 2021a, 2024b). In modern times racial and gender discrimination is still conducted in different parts of the world (Coussey 2002). It is significant to introduce institutions in economic development theory (Nelson 2002). Arrow (1998) states the significance of economic study on discrimination as follows: "Racial discrimination pervades every aspect of a society in which it is found. It is found above all in attitudes of both groups, but also in social relations, in intermarriage, in residential location, and, frequently, in legal barriers. It is also found in levels of economic accomplishment, that is, income, wages, prices paid, and credit extended. This economic dimension hardly appears in general treatments of economics, outside of the specialized literature devoted to it." Although there are some studies about discrimination in economics (Becker 1957; Welch 1967, 1975; Bergmann 1971; Phelps 1972; Loury 1977; Borjas 1992; Whatley and Wright 1994; Carneiro *et al.* 2005; Shi 2006; Charles and Guryan 2008; Gabriel and Schmitz 2014; Zhang 2017e), it is argued that there are only a few formal economic models which explicitly deal with economic growth and distribution in income and wealth with discrimination. This chapter focuses on the role of discrimination in interdependence between growth and dynamics of inequality in income and wealth.

W. Zhang, *A Dynamic Economic Theory of Heterogenous Households*,
https://doi.org/10.1007/978-981-95-8918-0_8

To deal with economic effects of discrimination, it is necessary to make the analysis in a general framework with heterogeneous households. Nevertheless, traditional dynamic economic theories are poor at studying economic issues related to wealth and income distribution with endogenous saving between heterogeneous households. This study analyzes economic growth with discrimination by integrating the Walrasian general equilibrium theory and the neoclassical growth theory. The Walrasian general equilibrium is the underpinning of contemporary general equilibrium theory. It was initially formulated by Walras and further mathematically refined by Arrow, Debreu, and others. The general equilibrium theory provides an analytical framework for examining economic mechanisms of production, consumption, and exchanges with heterogeneous industries and households with the economic system as an integrated whole. Nevertheless, economists have not been very successful in generalizing and extending growth theory of heterogeneous households with endogenous wealth.

Walras attempted to include saving and capital accumulation in his general equilibrium theory. Nevertheless, he was not successful in introducing capital accumulation. Different attempts have been made to further develop Walras' capital accumulation theory within Walras' framework of heterogeneous households. But these attempts failed to solve the problem of giving microeconomic foundation for wealth accumulation. It should be noted that some models have been proposed in the literature of economic growth, trying to synthesize neoclassical growth theory and the general equilibrium analysis. As reviewed by Shoven and Whalley (1992): "Most contemporary applied general models are numerical analogs of traditional two-sector general equilibrium models popularized by James Meade, Harry Johnson, Arnold Harberger, and others in the 1950s and the 1960s. Earlier analytical work with these models has examined the distortionary effects of taxes, tariffs, and other policies, along with functional incidence questions." In fact, there are only a few formal dynamic models which explicitly deal with distribution issues among heterogeneous households in the neoclassical growth theory. Zhang (2012c, 2014c, 2018b) integrated the Walrasian general equilibrium and neoclassical growth theories. This chapter examines the effects of discrimination on economic growth and inequality in income and wealth. This chapter is based on Zhang (2017c) and is organized as follows. Section 8.1 introduces the basic model with wealth and income distribution with discrimination. Section 8.2 examines the dynamic properties of the model and simulates the model with three groups. Section 8.3 shows how the system changes its development path when there is a rise in the discrimination rate on wage income. Section 8.4 follows the changes in a rise in the discrimination rate on wealth. Section 8.5 studies how a rise in the discrimination rate on consumption affects the system. Section 8.6 examines the effects of a rise in discrimination associated with positive reactions of the discriminated against on economic growth and the distribution. Section 8.7 concludes the chapter. The appendix proves Lemma 8.1.

8.1 The Growth Model With Discrimination

Following the traditional two-sector growth model in the neoclassical growth theory, I consider that the economy has two sectors. Like in the Uzawa two-sector growth model, this study considers consumption and capital goods as different commodities. The two goods are produced in two distinct sectors. There is only one malleable capital good, and capital good can be used as an input in both sectors. Capital depreciates at a constant exponential rate δ_k. Households own assets of the economy and distribute their incomes to consume and save. Savings are undertaken only by households. Factors are inelastically supplied, and the available factors are fully utilized at every moment. All earnings of firms are distributed in the form of payments to factors of production, labor, and capital ownership. Consider that there are J types of households. Households are identical within each group and people from different groups are different in human capital, preference, and social power. A group's social power is reflected in whether it is discriminated by some other groups, discriminates some other groups, or has "neutral" relations with all the other groups. Each group has a fixed population, $\bar{N}_j$, $(j = 1, \ldots, J)$. It should be noted that in the Walrasian general equilibrium theory, $\bar{N}_j = 1$. Let prices be measured in terms of capital goods and the price of the commodity be unity. The wage rate of worker of group j and rate of interest are represented by $w_j(t)$ and $r(t)$, respectively. Let $K(t)$ stand for the total capital stock. The total capital stock is fully employed by the two sectors. Let index i and s stand for capital goods and consumer goods sectors, respectively. Let $N_j(t)$ and $K_j(t)$ stand for the labor force and capital stocks employed by sector q. Let $T_j(t)$ and $\bar{T}_j(t)$ represent the work time and leisure time of a typical worker in group j. The total qualified labor supply $N(t)$ of the economy is the sum of labor inputs of all the groups:

$$N(t) = \sum_{j=1}^{J} h_j T_j(t) \bar{N}_j. \tag{8.1}$$

I Introduce

$$k_q(t) \equiv \frac{K_q(t)}{N_q(t)}, \; n_q(t) \equiv \frac{N_q(t)}{N(t)}, \; k(t) \equiv \frac{K(t)}{N(t)}, \; q = i, s.$$

The assumption of labor force being fully employed implies

$$N_i(t) + N_s(t) = N(t). \tag{8.2}$$

Capital Goods Sector

It is assumed that production is to combine the labor force $N_i(t)$ and physical capital $K_i(t)$. I use the Cobb-Douglas production function which is widely applied in different issues related to economic growth. The function $F_i(t)$ is specified as:

$$F_i(t) = A_i K_i^{\alpha_i}(t) N_i^{\beta_i}(t), A_i, \alpha_i, \beta_i > 0, \alpha_i + \beta_i = 1, \tag{8.3}$$

where A_i, α_i, and β_i are parameters. The rate of interest and wage rate are determined by markets. Here, it is assumed that individual firms do not discriminate against workers from any group. Firms decide the factor input levels with $r(t)$ and $w_j(t)$ given at each point in time. The production sector chooses $K_i(t)$ and $N_i(t)$ to maximize its profit. The marginal conditions are

$$r(t) + \delta_k = \alpha_i A_i K_i^{-\beta_i}(t) N_i^{\beta_i}(t), w_j(t) = h_j w(t), \tag{8.4}$$

where

$$w(t) \equiv \beta_i A_i K_i^{\alpha_i}(t) N_i^{-\alpha_i}(t).$$

Consumer Goods Sector
The production function of the consumer goods sector is

$$F_s(t) = A_s K_s^{\alpha_s}(t) N_s^{\beta_s}(t), A_s, \alpha_s, \beta_s > 0, \alpha_s + \beta_s = 1. \tag{8.5}$$

The marginal conditions are

$$r(t) + \delta_k = \alpha_s p(t) A_s K_s^{-\beta_s}(t) N_s^{\beta_s}(t), w_j(t) = \beta_s h_j p(t) A_s K_s^{\alpha_s}(t) N_s^{-\alpha_s}(t), \tag{8.6}$$

where $p(t)$ is the price of consumer goods.

Consumer Behaviors and Wealth Dynamics
The preference over current and future consumption is reflected in the consumer's preference structure over leisure time, consumption, and saving. Let $\bar{k}_j(t)$ stand for the per capita wealth of group j. I have $\bar{k}_j(t) = \bar{K}_j(t)/\bar{N}_j$, where $\bar{K}_j(t)$ is the total wealth held by group j. Let $\phi_j(t)$ stand for the lump sum transfer that group $j's$ representative household receives from discrimination. If the group is discriminated, $\phi_j(t) \leq 0$. If the group discriminates other groups, $\phi_j(t) > 0$. It is assumed that discrimination is conducted against wage income, wealth, and consumer goods markets. For simplicity, this chapter neglects the possibility of any discrimination against interest income from wealth. It also neglects the possibility that a group discriminates against some other groups and at the same time is discriminated against by some other groups. Per capita current disposable income from the interest payment $r(t)\bar{k}_j(t)$ and the wage payment $T_j(t)w_j(t)$ is given by:

$$y_j(t) = r(t)\bar{k}_j(t) + \left(1 - \varphi_{wj}\right) T_j(t) w_j(t) + \varphi_j(t),$$

where φ_{wj} is the discrimination rate against group j in wage income. If there is no discrimination against group j in wage income, then $\varphi_{wj} = 0$; otherwise $\varphi_{wj} > 0$. It is assumed that the discrimination rates are constant during the study period. Similarly, introduce φ_{kj} as the discrimination rate on wealth against group j. If there is no discrimination on wealth against group j, then $\varphi_{kj} = 0$; otherwise $\varphi_{kj} > 0$. The per capita disposable income is the sum of the current disposable income and the value of net wealth:

$$\hat{y}_j(t) = y_j(t) + (1 - \varphi_{kj})\bar{k}_j(t). \tag{8.7}$$

The disposable income is used for saving and consumption. It should be noted that the value, $\bar{k}_j(t)$, (i.e., $\bar{p}(t)\bar{k}_j(t)$ with $\bar{p}(t) = 1$), in the above equation is a flow variable. Under the assumption that selling wealth can be conducted instantaneously without any transaction cost, I consider $\bar{k}_j(t)$ as the amount of the income that the consumer obtains at time t by selling all of his wealth. Hence, at time t the consumer has the available income equaling $\hat{y}_j(t)$ to distribute among saving and consumption.

The representative household of group j would distribute the total available budget between savings $s_j(t)$ and consumption of goods $c_j(t)$. Let the discrimination rate on group $j's$ consumption be φ_{cj}. The budget constraint is given by:

$$(1 + \varphi_{cj})p(t)c_j(t) + s_j(t) = \hat{y}_j(t). \tag{8.8}$$

Denote $\bar{T}_j(t)$ as the leisure time at time t and the (fixed) available time for work and leisure by T_0. The time constraint is

$$T_j(t) + \bar{T}_j(t) = T_0. \tag{8.9}$$

Substituting (8.9) into (8.8) yields

$$(1 - \varphi_{wj})w_j(t)\bar{T}_j(t) + (1 + \varphi_{cj})p(t)c_j(t) + s_j(t) - \bar{y}_j(t), \tag{8.10}$$

where

$$\bar{y}_j(t) \equiv (r(t) + 1 - \varphi_{kj})\bar{k}_j(t) + (1 - \varphi_{wj})T_0 w_j(t) + \varphi_j(t).$$

Consumers have three variables to decide. It is assumed that utility level $U_j(t)$ that the consumer from group j obtains is dependent on the leisure time $T_j(t)$, the consumption level of consumption goods $c_j(t)$, and the saving $s_j(t)$, as follows:

$$U_j(t) = \bar{T}_j^{\sigma_{0j}}(t)c_j^{\xi_{0j}}(t)s_j^{\lambda_{0j}}(t), \sigma_{0j}, \xi_{0j}, \lambda_{0j} > 0,$$

where σ_{0j} is the propensity to use leisure time, ξ_{0j} is the propensity to consume consumption goods, and λ_{0j} is propensity to own wealth. It should be noted that there are a few growth models of heterogeneous households with endogenous wealth accumulation. However, the heterogeneity in most of these studies is due to differences in initial endowments of wealth among different households rather than in preferences. The households are essentially homogeneous because all the households have the same preference utility function in these models.

Maximizing the utility subject to (8.10) yields

$$w_j(t)\bar{T}_j(t) = \sigma_j \bar{y}_j(t),\ p(t)c_j(t) = \xi_j \bar{y}_j(t),\ s_j(t) = \lambda_j \bar{y}_j(t), \tag{8.11}$$

where

$$\sigma_j \equiv \frac{\rho_j \sigma_{0j}}{1 - \varphi_{wj}},\ \xi_j \equiv \frac{\rho_j \xi_{0j}}{1 + \varphi_{cj}},\ \lambda_j \equiv \rho_j \lambda_{0j},\ \rho_j \equiv \frac{1}{\sigma_{0j} + \xi_{0j} + \lambda_{0j}}.$$

There are models which explicitly address relationships between the labor-leisure choice and portfolio and consumption decisions (Bodie 1992; Dessing 2002; Bodie *et al.* 2004; Farhi and Panageas 2007; Heijdra and Romp 2009; Martín 2010; Kim *et al.* 2014). The model in this chapter also determines the relationship between wealth and work time.

According to the definition of $s_j(t)$, the change in the household's wealth is given by:

$$\dot{\bar{k}}_j(t) = s_j(t) - \bar{k}_j(t) = \lambda_j \bar{y}_j(t) - \bar{k}_j(t). \tag{8.12}$$

This equation simply states that the change in wealth is equal to the saving minus dissaving.

Demand and Supply

The demand for and supply of consumer goods is equal:

$$\sum_{j=1}^{J} c_j(t)\bar{N}_j = F_s(t). \tag{8.13}$$

As the output of the capital goods sector equals the depreciation of capital stock and the net saving, it follows:

$$S(t) - K(t) + \delta_k K(t) = F_i(t), \tag{8.14}$$

where

$$S(t) \equiv \sum_{j=1}^{J} s_j(t)\bar{N}_j,\ K(t) = \sum_{j=1}^{J} \bar{k}_j(t)\bar{N}_j.$$

Capital Being Fully Utilized
As $K(t)$ is fully employed by the two sectors, it follows:

$$K_i(t) + K_s(t) = K(t). \tag{8.15}$$

Balance in Transfers Between the Groups due to Discrimination
The total income from discrimination is the sum of the total income $\Gamma_w(t)$ from discrimination in wage incomes, the total income $\Gamma_c(t)$ from discrimination in consumer goods market, and the total income $\Gamma_k(t)$ from discrimination in wealth, where

$$\Gamma_w(t) = \sum_{j=1}^{J} \varphi_{wj} T_j(t) w_j(t) \bar{N}_j, \ \Gamma_c(t) = \sum_{j=1}^{J} \varphi_{cj} p(t) c_j(t) \bar{N}_j,$$

$$\Gamma_k(t) = \sum_{j=1}^{J} \varphi_{kj} \bar{k}_j(t) \bar{N}_j.$$

The total income from discrimination is distributed between the discriminating groups:

$$\Gamma_w(t) + \Gamma_c(t) + \Gamma_k(t) = \sum_{j=1}^{J} \varphi_j(t) \bar{N}_j.$$

For simplicity, it is assumed that the per capita lump sum transfers $\varphi_j(t)$ are equal between the discriminating groups. Introduce $\delta_j = 1$ if j is a discriminating group, and $\delta_j = 0$ otherwise. I have

$$\varphi_j(t) = \delta_j \varphi(t).$$

This assumption simplifies the analysis as if the lump sum transfers vary between groups, indeed further distribution mechanisms for deciding distribution issues. From the definition, it follows

$$\varphi(t) = \frac{\Gamma_w(t) + \Gamma_c(t) + \Gamma_k(t)}{N_0}, \tag{8.16}$$

where

$$N_0 \equiv \sum_{j=1}^{J} \delta_j \bar{N}_j.$$

The model is complete. As far as economic structure and growth theory with endogenous capital are concerned, this is a very general model in the sense that it is closely related to some well-known models in the literature of economics. The model is built on the basis of economic mechanisms of the Walrasian general economic theory, the Solow growth model, and the Uzawa two-sector model. For instance, if the economic system has only two sectors, then the Walrasian general equilibrium theory (which treats capital exogenous) can be considered as a special case of our model with heterogeneous households with endogenous leisure time and wealth. It is straightforward to see that the Solow one-sector and the Uzawa two-sector model are special cases of our model. As our model also includes labor supply, it is closely related to some other growth models in the literature of, for instance, labor economics.

8.2 The Dynamics and Its Properties

The dynamic system consists of any number of groups, and each group has any number of households. As the population of each group is homogenous and the propensities to save vary between groups, it is reasonable to expect that the dimension of the dynamic is equal to the number of groups. The following lemma confirms that the dimension of the dynamical system is equal to the number of groups. The lemma also provides a computational procedure for calculating all the variables at any point in time. Introduce a new variable $z(t)$:

$$z(t) \equiv \frac{r(t) + \delta_k}{w(t)}.$$

Lemma 8.1
The motion of the economic system is determined by J differential equations with $z(t)$ and $\{\bar{k}_j(t)\}$, where $\{\bar{k}_j(t)\} \equiv (\bar{k}_2(t), \cdots, \bar{k}_J(t))$, as the variables:

$$\dot{z}(t) = \Lambda_1(z(t), \{\bar{k}_j(t)\}), \dot{\bar{k}}_j(t) = \Lambda_j(z(t), \{\bar{k}_j(t)\}), j = 2, \ldots, J, \tag{8.17}$$

in which $\Lambda_j(t)$ are unique functions of $z(t)$ and $\{\bar{k}_j(t)\}$ defined in the appendix. At any point in time the other variables are unique functions of $z(t)$ and $\{\bar{k}_j(t)\}$ determined by the following procedure: $\bar{k}_1(t)$ by (A8.21) $\rightarrow$ $r(t)$ and $w_j(t)$ by (A8.3) $\rightarrow$ $\varphi(t)$ by (A8.20) $\rightarrow$ $\bar{y}_j(t)$ by (A8.4) $\rightarrow$ $N(t)$ by (A8.13) $\rightarrow$ $K_i(t)$ and $K_s(t)$ by (A8.15) $\rightarrow$ $N_i(t)$ and $N_s(t)$ by (A8.1) $\rightarrow$ $F_i(t)$ by (8.3) $\rightarrow$ $F_s(t)$ by (8.5) $\rightarrow$ $p(t)$ by (A8.8) $\rightarrow$ $\bar{T}(t)_j$, $c_j(t)$, and $s_j(t)$ by (8.11) $\rightarrow$ $T_j(t) = T_0(t) - \bar{T}_j(t)$ $\rightarrow$ $K(t) = K_i(t) + K_s(t)$.

This lemma is important as it provides a computational procedure for simulating the motion of the economic system with any number of groups. Calibration of general equilibrium is mathematically not easy as it often involves solving high-dimensional nonlinear equations. For instance, when studying behavior of the Walrasian general equilibrium the final stage of analysis is to find a price vector at which excess demand is zero. Different methods for calculating equilibria are developed in mathematical economics. As our model is mathematically similar to the general equilibrium model at any point in time, it is possible for us to apply these traditional methods to find how the prices and other variables are related to the variables in the differential equations. I classify the population into 3 groups. The values of parameters are as follows:

$$A_i = 1.3, A_s = 1, \alpha_i = 0.29, \alpha_s = 0.32, T_0 = 1, \delta_k = 0.05, \delta_1 = 1.$$

$$\delta_2 = \delta_3 = 0, \varphi_{q1} = \varphi_{q2} = 0, \varphi_{q3} = 0.05, q = w, c, k.$$

$$\begin{pmatrix} N_1 \\ N_2 \\ N_3 \end{pmatrix} = \begin{pmatrix} 50 \\ 300 \\ 200 \end{pmatrix}, \begin{pmatrix} h_1 \\ h_2 \\ h_3 \end{pmatrix} = \begin{pmatrix} 2 \\ 1 \\ 0.6 \end{pmatrix}, \begin{pmatrix} \xi_{10} \\ \xi_{20} \\ \xi_{30} \end{pmatrix} = \begin{pmatrix} 0.12 \\ 0.16 \\ 0.18 \end{pmatrix}, \begin{pmatrix} \lambda_{10} \\ \lambda_{20} \\ \lambda_{30} \end{pmatrix} = \begin{pmatrix} 0.78 \\ 0.75 \\ 0.7 \end{pmatrix},$$
$$\begin{pmatrix} \sigma_{10} \\ \sigma_{20} \\ \sigma_{30} \end{pmatrix} = \begin{pmatrix} 0.25 \\ 0.18 \\ 0.15 \end{pmatrix}. \tag{8.18}$$

The population of group 2 is the largest, while the population of group 3 is the next. The human capital level of group 1 is the highest, while the human capital level of group 3 is the lowest. The capital goods sector and consumer goods sector's total productivity are respectively 1.3 and 1. Group 1 (called discriminator) discriminates group 3 (called discriminated group), while group 2 (called neutral group) discriminates no group and is not discriminated against. The depreciation rate of physical capital is specified at 0.05. The discriminator's propensity to save is 0.78, and discriminated group's propensity to save is 0.7. The value of the neutral group's propensity is between the other two groups. The discriminator's discrimination rates against the discriminated group are mild. The discrimination rates on consumption, wage income, and wealth are all fixed at 5%. The initial conditions are as follows:

$$z(0) = 0.048, k_{26}(0) = 6, \bar{k}_3(0) = 1.5.$$

The motion of the variables is plotted in Fig. 8.1. The output level of the capital goods sector rises over time, and the output level of the consumer goods sector falls. The price of consumer goods changes slightly. The national output falls as the fall in the value of the capital goods sector's output is larger than the rise in the value of the consumer goods sector's output. The wage rates of the three groups vary slightly over time. The discriminator's wage rate is higher than the neutral group's, and the neutral group's wage rate is higher than the discriminated group's. The discriminator gets increasingly more money from discriminating. The discriminator works less hours, and the discriminated group works more hours over time. The neutral group works more hours over time. The net impact on the total labor supply is that the labor supply falls over time. The labor force employed by the consumer goods sector is reduced, and the labor force employed by the capital goods sector is augmented slightly. The total capital and the capital input of the consumer goods sector are reduced slightly, and the capital input of the capital goods sector is increased. The rate of interest falls. The discriminator's and discriminated group's wealth levels are increased, and the neutral group's wealth is diminished. The discriminator's and the discriminated group's consumption levels are increased. The neutral group's consumption level is diminished. It should be noted that there are empirical studies which find negative relationships between wealth and labor supply (Holtz-Eakin *et al.* 1993; Cheng and French 2000; Coronado and Perozek 2003). In our model, the relationship is positive for some groups and negative for other groups. Another well-discussed issue is the relation between wealth and income distribution and growth. Kaldor (1956) held that as income inequality is enlarged, growth should be encouraged as savings are promoted. Some studies support this positive relation between income inequality and growth while some other studies argue for negative relations between income inequality and economic growth. From our simulation, the relations between inequality and economic growth are complicated in the sense that these relations are determined by many factors. For instance, as the economy experiences negative growth rate, the discriminator works less hours, and the other two groups work more hours. As the wage rates are almost not affected, the wage incomes between the groups are either enlarged or reduced.

It is straightforward to confirm that the variables become stationary in the long term. The simulation shows that the system has a unique equilibrium. The equilibrium values of the variables are listed in (8.19):

$$Y = 536.97, \varphi = 0.59, F_i = 105.77, F_s = 354.77, w_1 = 3.46,$$

$$w_2 = 1.73, w_3 = 1.04, r = 0.031, p = 1.22, N = 212.64, N_i = 43.36,$$

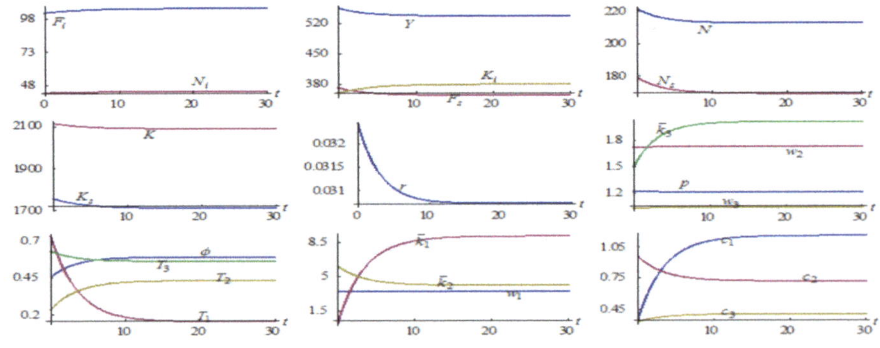

Fig. 8.1 The motion of the economic system

$$N_s = 169.28, K = 2089.17, K_i = 380, K_s = 1709.2, \bar{k}_1 = 9.14,$$

$$\bar{k}_2 = 4.1, \bar{k}_3 = 2.01, T_1 = 0.154, T_2 = 0.432, T_3 = 0.563,$$

$$c_1 = 1.16, c_2 = 0.72, c_3 = 0.41. \tag{8.19}$$

It is straightforward to calculate the three eigenvalues as follows:

$$\{-0.34, -0.30, -0.23\}.$$

The system has a unique equilibrium with real negative eigenvalues.

8.3 The Discrimination Rate on Wage Income Being Increased

This section studies the case where the discriminator increases the discrimination rate on wage income in the following way:

$$\varphi_{w3} : 0.05 \Rightarrow 0.1.$$

The simulation results are given in Fig. 8.2. As more wage income is transferred from the discriminated group to the discriminator, the lump sum transfer is increased. The wage rates, the price, and the rate of interest are slightly affected. The discriminator's work time is reduced, while the other two groups' work hours are slightly affected. The total labor supply, national wealth, and national output are reduced. The levels of the capital goods sector's two input factors are increased, and the levels of the consumer goods sector's two input factors are reduced. The discriminated group's consumption and wealth levels are reduced, the discriminator's consumption and wealth levels are increased, and the neutral group's consumption and wealth levels are slightly affected. Although the effects on the discriminating and discriminated groups are expectable, the strengthened discrimination has almost no impact the neutral group.

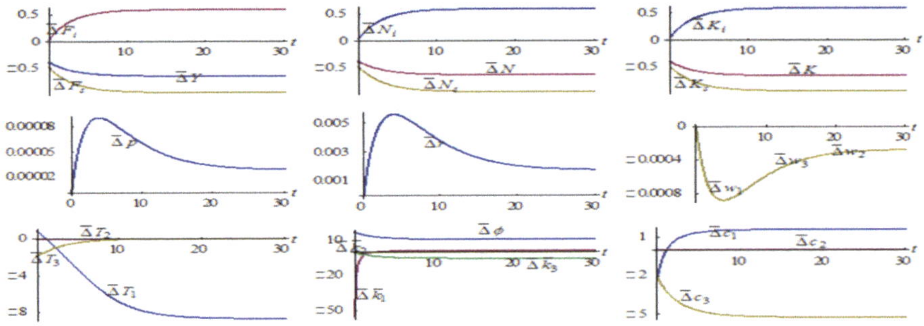

Fig. 8.2 A rise in the discrimination rate on wage income

8.4 The Discrimination Rate on Wealth Being Increased

The discriminator increases the discrimination rate on wealth in the following way.

$$\varphi_{k3} : 0.05 \Rightarrow 0.1.$$

The simulation results are given in Fig. 8.3. Like in the previous case, the lump sum transfer is increased. The wage rates are increased, while the price of consumer goods and the rate of interest are reduced. The discriminator's work time is reduced, the discriminated group's work time is increased, and the neutral group's work time is slightly affected. The total labor supply, national wealth, and national output are reduced. The levels of the capital goods sector's two input factors and the levels of the consumer goods sector's two input factors are reduced. The output level of the capital goods sector increases, while the output level of the consumer goods is reduced. The discriminated group's consumption and wealth levels are reduced, the discriminator's consumption and wealth levels are increased, and the neutral group's consumption and wealth levels are slightly affected. Like in the previous case, the strengthened discrimination has almost no impact on the neutral group.

8.5 The Discrimination Rate on Consumption Being Increased

This section analyzes what will happen to the economic system when the discriminator increases the discrimination rate on consumption in the following way.

$$\varphi_{c3} : 0.05 \Rightarrow 0.1.$$

The simulation results are given in Fig. 8.4 The effects are similar to the effects of the strengthened discrimination in wealth or wage income. It should be noted that

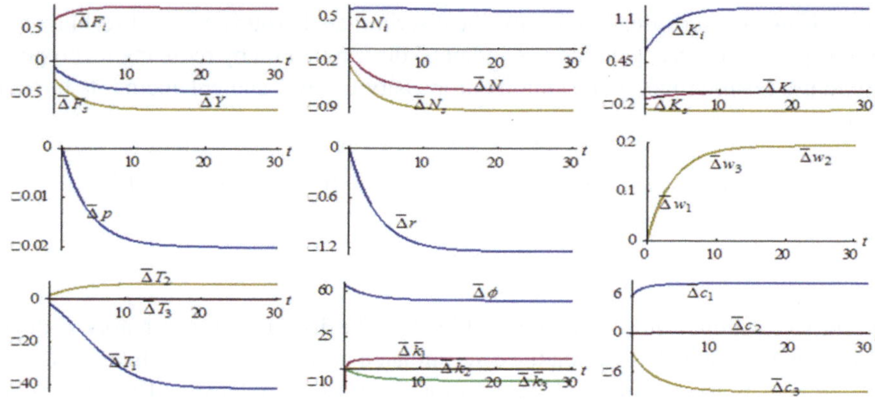

Fig. 8.3 A rise in the discrimination rate on wealth

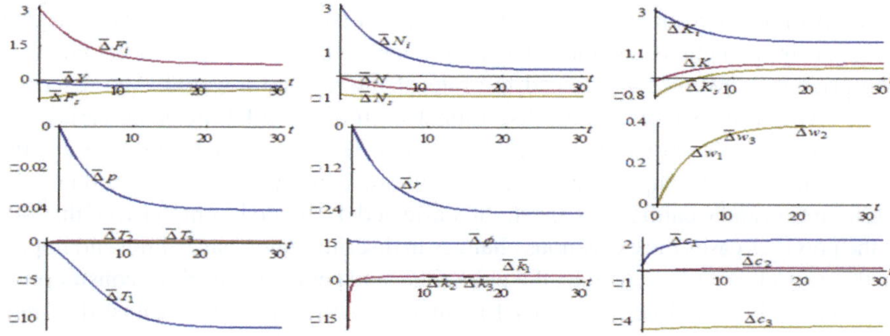

Fig. 8.4 A rise in the discrimination rate on consumption

the strengthened discrimination on consumption has also almost no impact on the neutral group.

8.6 Strengthened Discrimination Associated With Positive Reaction of the Discriminated

This chapter analyzed the effects of changes in a single parameter on the economic system. Nevertheless, multiple parameters may vary at the same time. For instance, when discriminating groups change attitudes toward discriminated groups, the discriminated groups may change their behavior and preferences. For instance, it is possible that when a group is more strongly discriminated against, it may make more investment in education and save more. Indeed, the opposite reaction is also possible. I examine what happens to the economic system when the discriminator strengthens its discrimination against the discriminated group and the discriminated group "positively" reacts to the strengthened discrimination by reducing its propensity to use leisure time, increasing its propensity to save, and enhancing its human capital as follows:

$$\varphi_{k3} = \varphi_{w3} = \varphi_{c3} : 0.05 \Rightarrow 0.1, h_3 : 0.6 \Rightarrow 0.7, \sigma_{03} : 0.15 \Rightarrow 0.13,$$

$$\lambda_3 : 0.7 \Rightarrow 0.73.$$

The simulation results are plotted in Fig. 8.5. The discriminator increases its three discrimination rates. In reaction the discriminated group increases its human capital and propensity to save and reduces its propensity to enjoy leisure. The simulation results are given in Fig. 8.5. The aggregated real variables are all increased. The national output, the national wealth, the total labor supply, the output levels, and the input factors of the two sectors are all increased. The lump sum transfer from the discriminated group to the discriminator is increased. The discriminated group's wage rate is augmented, and the other two groups' wage rates are almost not affected. The price of consumer goods and the rate of interest are lowered. The discriminator's work time is reduced, the discriminated group's work time is increased, and the neutral group's work time is slightly affected. The discriminated group's and the discriminator's consumption and wealth levels are increased, and the neutral group's consumption and wealth levels are slightly affected. It should be emphasized that like in the previous cases the exogenous changes in discrimination have almost no impact on the neutral group's wage rate, the work time, and per capita levels of consumption and wealth. It should be noted that I assume "positive" reaction against discrimination. It is possible to find the opposite trends. If the discriminated people react negatively, there may be more negative economic consequences of discrimination.

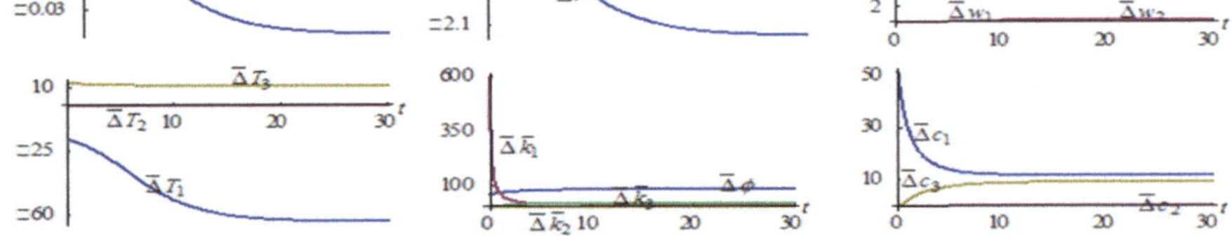

Fig. 8.5 Strengthened discrimination and positive reaction from the discriminated

8.7 Concluding Remarks

This chapter proposed a growth model of heterogeneous households with economic structure and discrimination. This chapter is mainly concerned with the role of discrimination in economic growth, income, and wealth distribution in an economy with endogenous wealth accumulation. The economic system consists of one capital goods sector, one consumer goods sector, and any number of groups. Different from the traditional two-sector growth model where the population is homogeneous, the population is classified into different groups. I built the model in which wealth accumulation, income, wealth distribution, time distribution, and division of labor interact with each other under a fixed pattern of discrimination. For illustration, the model is simulated with three groups, called the discriminator, the neutral group, and the discriminated group. The chapter discussed implications of discrimination for the relations between work time and wealth and the relations between wealth and income distribution and economic growth. For instance, it is shown that when the discriminator strengthens its discrimination against the discriminated group and the discriminated group "positively" reacts to the strengthened discrimination by reducing its propensity to use leisure time, increasing its propensity to save, and enhancing its human capital, I get the following effects: the national output, the national wealth, the total labor supply, the output levels, and the input factors of the two sectors are all increased; the lump sum transfer from the discriminated group to the discriminator is increased; the discriminated group's wage rate is augmented and the other two groups' wage rates are almost not affected; the price of consumer goods and the rate of interest are lowered; the discriminator's work time is reduced, the discriminated group's work time is increased, and the neutral group's work time is slightly affected; the discriminated group's and the discriminator's consumption and wealth levels are increased, and the neutral group's consumption and wealth levels are slightly affected. Another interesting conclusion from the comparative dynamic analysis is that the exogenous changes in the discriminator's discrimination against the discriminated group have almost no impact on the neutral group's wage rate, the work time, and per capita levels of consumption and wealth. This conclusion implies that as far as its economic self-interest is concerned, under certain conditions the neutral group has almost no incentive to join the discriminated group to be against the discriminator's discrimination. It should be noted that people even from the same group may react quiet differently toward the same discrimination according to their psychological, economic, and social conditions. Another important issue is to make discrimination endogenous variables. Further studies on endogenous discrimination should provide more insights into complexity of interrelations of different races and groups over time.

Appendix: Proving Lemma 8.1

From (8.4) and (8.6), it follows:

$$z \equiv \frac{r + \delta_k}{\frac{w_j}{h_j}} = \frac{N_i}{\bar{\beta}_i K_i} = \frac{N_s}{\bar{\beta}_s K_s}, \tag{A8.1}$$

in which $\bar{\beta}_j \equiv \beta_j/\alpha_j$. Insert (A8.1) in (8.2):

$$\bar{\beta}_i K_i + \bar{\beta}_s K_s = \frac{N}{z}. \tag{A8.2}$$

Insert (A8.1) in (8.4):

$$r = \alpha_r z^{\beta_i} - \delta_k, \ w_j = \alpha_j z^{-\alpha_i}, \tag{A8.3}$$

where

$$\alpha_r = \alpha_i A_i \bar{\beta}_i^{\beta_i}, \ \alpha_j = h_j \beta_i A_i \bar{\beta}_i^{-\alpha_i}.$$

The rate of interest and the wage rates are presented as functions of z. From (A8.3) and the definitions of $\bar{y}_j$, I get

$$\bar{y}_j = g_j \bar{k}_j + \bar{g}_j + \delta_j \varphi, \tag{A8.4}$$

where

$$g_j(z) \equiv \alpha_r z^{\beta_i} - \delta_k + 1 - \varphi_{kj}, \ \bar{g}_j(z) \equiv \left(1 - \varphi_{wj}\right) T_0 \alpha_j z^{-\alpha_i}.$$

Insert $pc_j = \xi_j \bar{y}_j$ in (8.13):

$$\sum_{j=1}^{J} \xi_j \bar{N}_j \bar{y}_j = pF_s. \tag{A8.5}$$

Substituting (A8.4) in (A8.5) yields

$$\sum_{j=1}^{J} \tilde{g}_j \bar{k}_j = pF_s - g - \xi_0 \varphi, \tag{A8.6}$$

where

$$\tilde{g}_j(z) \equiv \xi_j \bar{N}_j g_j,\ g(z) \equiv \sum_{j=1}^{J} \xi_j \bar{N}_j \bar{g}_j,\ \xi_0 \equiv \sum_{j=1}^{J} \delta_j \xi_j \bar{N}_j.$$

From (8.4) and (8.6):

$$r + \delta_k = \alpha_i A_i K_i^{-\beta_i} N_i^{\beta_i} = \alpha_s p A_s K_s^{-\beta_s} N_s^{\beta_s}. \tag{A8.7}$$

Inserting (A8.1) in (A8.7) yields

$$p = \frac{\alpha_i A_i \bar{\beta}_i^{\beta_i} z^{\beta_i - \beta_s}}{\alpha_s A_s \bar{\beta}_s^{\beta_s}}. \tag{A8.8}$$

From (8.6), it follows:

$$pF_s = \frac{w_1 N_s}{h_1 \beta_s}. \tag{A8.9}$$

From (A8.9) and (A8.1), it follows:

$$pF_s = \frac{\bar{\beta}_s w_1 z K_s}{h_1 \beta_s}. \tag{A8.10}$$

Insert (A8.10) in (A8.6):

$$\sum_{j=1}^{J} \tilde{g}_j \bar{k}_j = g_0 K_s - g - \xi_0 \varphi, \tag{A8.11}$$

where

$$g_0(z) \equiv \frac{\bar{\beta}_s w_1 z}{h_1 \beta_s}.$$

Using (8.1) and (8.9), I get

$$N = T_0 \sum_{j=1}^{J} h_j \bar{N}_j - \sum_{j=1}^{J} \frac{h_j \sigma_j \bar{y}_j \bar{N}_j}{w_j}, \tag{A8.12}$$

in which $w_j \bar{T}_j = \sigma_j \bar{y}_j$ is applied. Insert (A8.4) in (A8.12):

$$N = \tilde{\phi}_0 - \sum_{j=1}^{J} \tilde{\phi}_j \bar{k}_j - \hat{\phi}\varphi, \tag{A8.13}$$

where

$$\tilde{\phi}_0(z) \equiv \sum_{j=1}^{J} \left(T_0 - \frac{\sigma_j \bar{g}_j}{w_j} \right) h_j \bar{N}_j, \ \tilde{\phi}_j(z) \equiv \frac{h_j \sigma_j \bar{N}_j g_j}{w_j}, \ \hat{\phi} \equiv \sum_{j=1}^{J} \frac{\delta_j h_j \sigma_j \bar{N}_j}{w_j}.$$

From (8.15), it follows:

$$K_i + K_s = K = \sum\nolimits_{j=1}^{J} \bar{k}_j \bar{N}_j. \tag{A8.14}$$

From (A8.2) and (A8.14), I solve

$$K_i = \beta \bar{\beta}_s \sum_{j=1}^{J} \bar{k}_j \bar{N}_j - \frac{\beta N}{z}, \ K_s = \frac{\beta N}{z} - \beta \bar{\beta}_i \sum_{j=1}^{J} \bar{k}_j \bar{N}_j, \tag{A8.15}$$

where $\beta \equiv 1/(\bar{\beta}_s - \bar{\beta}_i)$. From (A8.3), I determine r and w_j as functions of z. Insert K_s from (A8.15) in (A8.11):

$$\sum_{j=1}^{J} \left(\tilde{g}_j + \frac{g_0 \beta \tilde{\phi}_j}{z} + \beta \bar{\beta}_i g_0 \bar{N}_j \right) \bar{k}_j = \frac{g_0 \beta \tilde{\phi}_0}{z} - g - \hat{\phi}_0 \varphi, \tag{A8.16}$$

where

$$\hat{\phi}_0 \equiv \xi_0 + \hat{\phi} \frac{g_0 \beta}{z}.$$

From (A8.16), it follows:

$$\varphi_1 \bar{k}_1 = \varphi_0 - \hat{\phi}_0 \varphi - \sum_{j=2}^{J} \varphi_j \bar{k}_j, \tag{A8.17}$$

where

$$\varphi_0(z, \varphi, \{\bar{k}_j\}) \equiv \frac{g_0 \beta \tilde{\phi}_0}{z} - g, \ \varphi_j(z) \equiv \tilde{g}_j + \frac{g_0 \beta \tilde{\phi}_j}{z} + \beta \bar{\beta}_i g_0 \bar{N}_j.$$

in which $\{\bar{k}_j\} \equiv (\bar{k}_2, \ldots \bar{k}_J)$. From (8.16):

$$\varphi N_0 = \sum_{j=1}^{J} (\varphi_{wj} T_j w_j + \varphi_{cj} p c_j + \varphi_{kj} \bar{k}_j) \bar{N}_j. \tag{A8.18}$$

Insert (8.11) in (A8.18):

$$\varphi N_0 = \sum_{j=1}^{J} (\bar{\sigma}_j \bar{y}_j + \varphi_{kj} \bar{k}_j) \bar{N}_j, \tag{A8.19}$$

where $\bar{\sigma}_j \equiv \varphi_{wj} \sigma_j + \varphi_{cj} \xi_j$. Substituting (A8.4) into (A8.19) yields

$$\varphi = n_0 \sum_{j=1}^{J} (\bar{\sigma}_j g_j + \varphi_{kj}) \bar{N}_j \bar{k}_j + n_0 \sum_{j=1}^{J} \bar{\sigma}_j \bar{g}_j \bar{N}_j, \tag{A8.20}$$

where

$$n_0 = \left(N_0 - \sum_{j=1}^{J} \delta_j \bar{\sigma}_j \bar{N}_j \right)^{-1}.$$

Insert (A8.20) in (A8.17):

$$\bar{k}_1 = \Phi(z, \{\bar{k}_j\}) \equiv \frac{\varphi_0 - \hat{\phi}_0 n_0 \sum_{j=1}^{J} \bar{\sigma}_j \bar{g}_j \bar{N}_j - \sum_{j=2}^{J} [\varphi_j + (\bar{\sigma}_j g_j + \varphi_{kj}) \hat{\phi}_0 n_0 \bar{N}_j] \bar{k}_j}{\varphi_1 + \hat{\phi}_0 n_0 (\bar{\sigma}_1 g_j + \varphi_{k1}) \bar{N}_1}. \tag{A8.21}$$

It is straightforward to confirm that all the variables can be expressed as functions of z and $\{\bar{k}_j\}$ by the following procedure: $\bar{k}_1$ by (A8.21) $\rightarrow r$ and w_j by (A8.3) $\rightarrow \varphi$ by (A8.20) $\rightarrow \bar{y}_j$ by (A8.4) $\rightarrow N$ by (A8.13) $\rightarrow K_i$ and K_s by (A8.15) $\rightarrow N_i$ and N_s by (A8.1) $\rightarrow F_i$ by (8.3) $\rightarrow F_s$ by (8.5) $\rightarrow p$ by (A8.8) $\rightarrow \bar{T}_j$, c_j, and s_j by (8.11) $\rightarrow T_j = T_0 - \bar{T}_j \rightarrow K = K_i + K_s$ by (8.15). From this procedure, (A8.21), and (8.12), I have

$$\dot{\bar{k}}_1 = \lambda_1 \bar{y}_1 - \Phi, \tag{A8.22}$$

$$\dot{\bar{k}}_j = \Lambda_j(z, \varphi, \{\bar{k}_j\}) \equiv \lambda_j \bar{y}_j - \bar{k}_j, j = 2, \ldots, J. \tag{A8.23}$$

Taking derivatives of (A8.21) with respect to t and combining with (A8.23) implies

$$\dot{\bar{k}}_1 = \frac{\partial \Phi}{\partial z}\dot{z} + \sum_{j=2}^{J} \Lambda_j \frac{\partial \Phi}{\partial \bar{k}_j}. \tag{A8.24}$$

Equating the right-hand sides of Eqs. (A8.24) and (A8.22), I get

$$\dot{z} = \left(\lambda_1 \bar{y}_1 - \Phi - \sum_{j=2}^{J} \Lambda_j \frac{\partial \Phi}{\partial \bar{k}_j}\right)\left(\frac{\partial \Phi}{\partial z}\right)^{-1}. \tag{A8.25}$$

From (A8.23) and (A8.25), I determine the motion of z and $\{\bar{k}_j\}$.

Chapter 9
Growth and Gender With Time Distribution

> Obviously there is no such thing as race, and in many ways, sex is a continuum, not a binary. So it doesn't make sense to label people in that way.
>
> Gloria Steinem (1934-)

This chapter models the gender division of labor in a framework of growth with heterogeneous households. There are many empirical studies on issues related to labor market and economic development with gender. For instance, Eckstein and Lifshitz (2011) find that the rise in education levels accounts for about 33% of the increase in female employment, and the rise in wages and narrowing of the gender wage gap account for another 20%, while about the 40% remains unexplained by observed household characteristics. They also show that this unexplained part can be accounted for by considering cohort-specific changes in preferences or the costs of childbearing and household maintenance. They do not empirically find that the decline in fertility and the increase in divorce rates are significant in explaining the increase in female employment. Antecol (2000) for the analysis of the differences among different groups of people and Fogli and Veldkamp (2011) among regions. The common trend occurs due to different factors. On the demand side, firms have become more willing to hire women due to factors such as the rise of service sectors, anti-discrimination policy measures, the increase of higher education among women, and the development of new technologies (which allow firms to substitute male for female workers). On the supply side, women tend to work more in labor markets as a consequence of lower fertility rates, the availability of new household technologies, and the emergence of flexible-time work. They observe great differences in women's participation rates in the labor market between the US and the EU. About 50% of the difference between the employment rates in the US and the EU can be attributed to differences in the educational attainments and the employment rates of women aged 25–54. Another study by Petrongolo (2005) examines gender segregation in employment contracts in 15 E.U. countries. It is found that women are overrepresented in part-time jobs in all the countries. There are gender differences in southern and

W. Zhang, *A Dynamic Economic Theory of Heterogenous Households*,
https://doi.org/10.1007/978-981-95-8918-0_9

northern Europe. In northern Europe, such allocation is affected by women's preferences and their need to combine their work with childcare, while in southern Europe part-time jobs are often involuntary and provide lower job satisfaction than full-time ones. Based on the EU-SILC data, Biagetti and Sergio (2009) examine the determinants of inequality in workers' formal life-long learning in Europe. Their analysis emphasizes gender differences. They show that for both men and women formal life-long learning incidence is significantly higher among better-educated young part-time and temporary workers, and lower among those who changed current jobs in the last year, working in small firms and having low-skilled occupations. They also observe gender differences among countries. For instance, Finland is the only country in their sample where less educated workers of both men and women are more likely to undertake formal life-long learning. This tends to reduce inequality in human capital among different groups. Further literature on theoretical and empirical studies related to gender, labor markets, and economic conditions can be found in many other studies as well (Zhang 1993a, 1995, 1997; Gomme *et al.* 2001; de la Croix and Doepke 2003; Gutierrez 2003; Choo and Siow 2006; Munshi and Myaus 2006; Bongaarts and Sobortka 2012: Cordoba *et al* 2016; Day 2016; Siegel 2017: Kleven *et al.* 2019; Strulik 2024). This chapter, which is based on Zhang (2012b) and Zhang (2025a: Chap.3), makes some theoretical insights into the complexity of growth and gender. This chapter is organized as follows. Section 9.1 defines the one-sector growth model with gender, leisure time, and heterogeneous groups. Section 9.2 analyzes the dynamic behavior of the three-group model. Section 9.3 shows how a rise in human capital of the women in group 1 affects the motion of the economic system. Section 9.4 follows what happens in the economic system when there is a rise group 1's female propensity to stay at home. Section 9.5 studies the impact of a rise in group 1's propensity to save on the time distribution and economic growth. Section 9.6 concludes the chapter. The appendix confirms Lemma 9.1.

9.1 The Growth Model with Endogenous Time Distribution

Most aspects of the production sector are similar to the standard one-sector growth model. There is only one (durable) good in the economy under consideration. Households have assets of the economy and distribute their incomes to consume and save. Production sectors or firms use labor and capital input to produce goods. Exchanges take place in perfectly competitive markets. Factor markets work well, and factors are fully utilized at every moment. Savings are undertaken only by households. I selected commodity to serve as numeraire, with all the other prices being measured relative to its price. I use family as a production unit in economic analysis. In addition to enjoyment, households also supply labor services, recreation, spiritual experiences, as well as conventional goods of the do-it-yourself variety. Household activities are conducted within houses as well as outside doors. There are J groups of households, indexed by $j, j = 1, \cdots, J$, in the economy. Each type of household has a fixed number, denoted by N_j. It should be noted that as the model exhibits constant returns to scale, the dynamics (in terms of per capita) will not be affected if the population of all the groups changes at a constant growth rate over time. It is further assumed that each family consists of four members—father, mother, son, and daughter. The total population of group j is equal to $4N_j$. I neglect complicated issues related to endogenous fertility rates. It can be seen that based on the literature on growth models with endogenous fertility (for instance, Barro and Becker 1989; Raut 1992; Doepke 2004; Conde-Ruiz *et al.* 2010; Daruich and Kozlowski 2020). This chapter does not address issues related to different households purchasing different goods as the model has only a single commodity (Hori 2011). It is assumed that only the adults may work. The children get educated before they get married and join the labor market. It is assumed that the husband and wife pass away at the same time. When the parents pass away, the son and the daughter respectively find their marriage partner within the same type of household and get married. The wealth left by the parents is shared equally between the two children. The children are educated so that they have the same human capital as their parents. When a new family is formed, the young couple joins the labor market and has two children. As all the families are identical, the family structure is invariant over time under these assumptions. Let subscripts $q = 1$ and $q = 2$ stand for man and woman respectively. Let $T_{1j}(t)$ and $T_{2j}(t)$ stand for the work time of husband and wife of a representative household of group j and $N(t)$ for the flow of labor services used at time t for production. I have $N(t)$ as follows:

$$N(t) = \sum_{j=1}^{J} \left[h_{1j}T_{1j}(t) + h_{2j}T_{2j}(t)\right]N_j, \tag{9.1}$$

where h_{qj} is the level of human capital of gender q of group j, where $q = 1$ and $q = 2$ stand respectively for husband and wife. I assume h_{qj} to be fixed. It is assumed that gender differences in productivity and social activities are measured by differences in human capital and preference. To simplify the analysis, this chapter uses highly aggregated indexes to measure gender differences. As pointed out by Truong (1997), there are different meanings and methodologies in dealing with gender differences in human development.

I use the conventional production function to describe a relationship between input and output. The production process is described by some sufficiently smooth function, $F(t) = F(K(t), N(t))$. I assume that $F(K(t), N(t))$ is neoclassical. A production function $F(K, N)$ is called neoclassical if it satisfies the following conditions: (i) $F(K, N)$ is non-negative if K and N are non-negative; (ii) $F(0, 0) = 0$; (iii) marginal products, F_K and F_N are non-negative; (iv) there exist second partial derivatives of F with respect to K and N; (v) the function is homogeneous of degree one: $F(\lambda K, \lambda N) = \lambda F(K, N)$ for all non-negative λ; (vi) the function is concave.

I may write output per capita as a function of capital intensity, $y(t) = f(k(t))$, where $k(t) \equiv K(t)/N(t)$. The function f has the following properties:

i. $f(0) = 0$;
ii. f is increasing, strictly concave on R^{+}, and C^2 on R^{++}; $f'(k) > 0$; and $f''(k) < 0$; and.
iii. $lim_{k \to 0} f'(k) = \infty$ and $lim_{k \to +\infty} f'(k) = 0$.

Markets are competitive; labor and capital earn their marginal products, and firms earn zero profits. I assume that the output good serves as a medium of exchange and is taken as numeraire. The rate of interest and wage rate are determined by markets. Hence, for any individual firm r and w_j are given at each point of time. The production sector chooses the two variables K and N to maximize its profit. Let $\delta_k (0 \le \delta_k < 1)$ denote the depreciation rate of physical capital. The marginal conditions are given by

$$r(t) + \delta_k = f'(k(t)), \; w_{qj}(t) = h_{qj} w(t),$$

$$w(t) \equiv f(k(t)) - k(t) f'(k(t)). \tag{9.2}$$

The ratio of wage rates between any two types of workers is equal to the ratio in their levels of human capital.

Let $k_j(t)$ denote per household wealth of group j at t. According to the definitions, the following equation holds:

$$K(t) = \sum_{j=1}^{J} k_j(t) N_j. \tag{9.3}$$

I follow the traditional approach of dividing the time available into leisure and work and assume that leisure is good in the family utility function. Hence, in the model, consumers make decisions on choice of leisure time, consumption levels of services, and commodities as well as on how much to save. There is no single purpose for people to make savings. Wealth may be accumulated for different reasons such as the capitalist spirit, old age consumption, providing education for children, power, and social status. Those different reasons determine preference structures. Group j 's per household current income $y_j(t)$ from the interest payment $r(t)k_j(t)$ and the wage payments, $w_{1j}(t)T_{1j}(t)$ and $w_{2j}(t)T_{2j}(t)$, is defined by:

$$y_j(t) = r(t)k_j(t) + w_{1j}(t)T_{1j}(t) + w_{2j}(t)T_{2j}(t).$$

The sum of money that consumers are using for consuming, saving, or transferring is not necessarily equal to the current income because consumers can sell wealth to pay, for instance, current consumption if the temporary income is not sufficient for purchasing goods and services. The total value of wealth that consumer j can sell to purchase goods and to save is equal to $p(t)k_j(t)$, where $p(t) = 1$ is the price of the single commodity. I assume that selling and buying wealth can be conducted instantaneously without any transaction cost. This is astrict assumption as it may take time to draw savings from a bank or to sell one's property. The per capita disposable income of consumer j is defined as the sum of the current income and the wealth available for purchasing consumption goods and saving:

$$\hat{y}_j(t) = (1 + r(t))k_j(t) + w_{1j}(t)T_{1j}(t) + w_{2j}(t)T_{2j}(t),$$

$$j = 1, \cdots, J. \tag{9.4}$$

The disposable income is used for saving and consumption. In this study, I omit possible gender-based taxation. There is an increasing number of publications on dynamics of time distribution between various activities (Aguiar and Hurst 2007; Olovsson 2009; Rogerson and Wallenius 2016; Bick and Fuchs-Schundeln 2018; Duernecker and Herrendorf 2018; Boerma and Karabarbounis 2020; Lei and Yang 2022). Focusing on the optimal linear-income taxation of two-earner households with exogenously given differences in labor supply elasticities between men and women, Boskin and Sheshinski (1983) suggest that women should be taxed at lower rates than men because women have higher labor supply elasticities. Alesina *et al.* (2011) recently proposed a model of gender-based taxation in which gender differences in labor supply elasticities are endogenous. They conclude that married women should be taxed lower than married men. Guner *et al.* (2012) empirically examine the qualitative implications and merits of gender-based tax rates. Relative to the current system of taxation in the US, setting a proportional tax rate on married females equal to 4% (8%) increases output and married female labor force participation by about 3.9% (3.4%) and 6.9% (4.0%), respectively.

At each point in time, a consumer would distribute the total available budget among savings $s_j(t)$ and consumption of goods $c_j(t)$. The budget constraint is given by:

$$c_j(t) + s_j(t) = \hat{y}_j(t). \tag{9.5}$$

Denote $\bar{T}_{qj}(t)$ as the leisure time of gender q of group j at time t and the (fixed) available time for work and leisure by T_0. The time constraint is expressed by:

$$T_{qj}(t) + \bar{T}_{qj}(t) = T_0.$$

Substituting this function into the budget constraint yields

$$w_{1j}(t)\bar{T}_{1j}(t) + w_{2j}(t)\bar{T}_{2j}(t) + c_j(t) + s_j(t) = \bar{y}_j(t)$$

$$\equiv (1 + r(t))k_j(t) + w_{1j}(t)T_0 + w_{2j}(t)T_0. \tag{9.6}$$

It should be remarked that $w_{1j}(t)T_0 + w_{2j}(t)T_0$ is the potential wage income of the family and $w_{1j}(t)\bar{T}_{1j}(t) + w_{2j}(t)\bar{T}_{2j}(t)$ is the opportunity cost of the leisure. The right-hand side is the potential disposable income, and the left-hand is the actual expenditure plus opportunity cost. At each point in time, a household decides the four variables subject to the disposable income. I assume that utility level $U_j(t)$ is dependent on $\bar{T}_{1j}(t)$, $\bar{T}_{2j}(t)$, $c_j(t)$, and $s_j(t)$ as follows:

$$U_j(t) = \bar{T}_{1j}^{\bar{\sigma}_{1j}}(t)\bar{T}_{2j}^{\bar{\sigma}_{2j}}(t)c_j^{\bar{\xi}_j}(t)s_j^{\bar{\lambda}_j}(t), \bar{\sigma}_{1j}, \bar{\sigma}_{2j}, \bar{\xi}_j, \bar{\lambda}_j > 0, \tag{9.7}$$

where $\bar{\sigma}_{1j}$, $\bar{\sigma}_{2j}$, $\bar{\xi}_j$, and $\bar{\lambda}_j$ are respectively propensities of a household in group j to use leisure time, to consume goods and services, and to hold wealth. There are various determinants for utility in the literature on family economics (Albanesi and Olivetti 2009; Patrick *et al.* 2009; Macro *et al.* 2022; Munir and Ameer 2022; Majekodunmi *et al.* 2023; Piao and Managi 2023). Here, for simplicity, I specify the utility function with the Cobb-Douglas form. Maximizing U_j subject to the budget constraints (9.6) yields

$$w_{1j}(t)\bar{T}_{1j}(t) = \sigma_{1j}\bar{y}_j(t), w_{2j}(t)\bar{T}_{2j}(t) = \sigma_{2j}\bar{y}_j(t), c_j(t) = \xi_j\bar{y}_j(t),$$

$$s_j(t) = \lambda_j\bar{y}_j(t), \tag{9.8}$$

where

$$\sigma_{1j} \equiv \bar{\sigma}_{1j}\rho_j, \sigma_{2j} \equiv \bar{\sigma}_{2j}\rho_j, \xi_j \equiv \bar{\xi}_j\rho_j, \lambda_j \equiv \bar{\lambda}_j\rho_j, \rho_j \equiv \frac{1}{\bar{\sigma}_{1j} + \bar{\sigma}_{2j} + \bar{\xi}_j + \bar{\lambda}_j}.$$

I see that the expenditure on each item is equal to the potential disposable income by the item's propensity to consume. From (9.4), I have

$$\frac{\bar{T}_{1j}(t)}{\bar{T}_{2j}(t)} = \frac{\sigma_{1j}h_{2j}}{\sigma_{2j}h_{1j}}.$$

The ratio of time at home between husband and wife is positively related to the ratio of men's and women's propensity to stay at home and negatively related to the ratio of men's and women's human capital.

According to the definitions of $s_j(t)$, group j's wealth accumulation is given by:

$$\dot{k}_j(t) = s_j(t) - k_j(t). \tag{9.9}$$

This equation simply means that the change in wealth is equal to the saving minus dissaving. As output is either consumed or saved, the sum of net savings and consumption equals output. That is

$$C(t) + S(t) - K(t) + \delta_k K(t) = F(t), \tag{9.10}$$

where $C(t)$ is the sum of consumption and $S(t) - K(t) + \delta_k K(t)$ is the sum of net savings of all the groups, and

$$C(t) = \sum_j c_j(t) N_j,\ S(t) - \delta K(t) = \sum_j \left(s_j(t) - \delta k_j(t)\right) N_j,$$

where $\delta \equiv 1 - \delta_k$. I have thus built the dynamic model. The dynamics consist of J-dimensional differential equations for k_j. To analyze the properties of the dynamic system, it is necessary to express the dynamics in terms of J variables at any point in time. The following lemma, which is proved in the appendix, shows that the dynamics are controlled by J-dimensional differential equations.

Lemma 9.1
The dynamics of the economic system is governed by the following J-dimensional differential equations:

$$\dot{k}_j(t) = \Phi_j(k_1(t), \cdots, k_n(t)), j = 1, \cdots, J, \tag{9.11}$$

where Φ_j are differentiable functions of $k_1(t), \cdots, k_J(t)$. Moreover, all the other variables can be determined as functions of $k_1(t), \cdots, k_J(t)$ at any point of time by the following procedure: $k(t)$ by (A9.6) $\rightarrow T_{qj}(t)$ by (A9.5) $\rightarrow \bar{T}_{qj}(t) = T_0 - T_{qj}(t)$ $\rightarrow N(t)$ by (9.1) $\rightarrow r(t)$ and $w_j(t)$ by (9.2) $\rightarrow \bar{y}_j(t)$ by (9.6) $\rightarrow c_j(t)$ and $s_j(t)$ by (9.8) $\rightarrow K(t) = k(t)N(t) \rightarrow F(K(t), N(t)) \rightarrow f(t) = F(t)/N(t) \rightarrow U_j(t)$ by (9.7).

This lemma is important as it enables us to follow the motion of the entire system over time with initial conditions. As it is difficult to find explicit conclusions about the dynamic behavior of the system, in the remainder of this chap. I am concerned with a few special cases of the general model.

9.2 The 3-Group Dynamic Economy

This section simulates the model when the economy consists of three different groups. For illustration, the production function takes on the Cobb-Douglas form, $f(k) = Ak^{1/3}$. As shown in (A9.6) in the appendix, $k(t)$ is determined as a function of $k_j(t)$, $j = 1, 2, 3$, by the following equation:

$$\Lambda(k) \equiv k - \varphi_1 k^{\frac{2}{3}} - \varphi_2 = 0, \tag{9.12}$$

in which

$$\varphi_1 \equiv \delta\left(\sum_{j=1}^{3} k_j N_j - \sum_{j=1}^{3} \bar{\xi}_j k_j\right)\left(\sum_{j=1}^{3} \bar{\xi}_j h_j^*\right)^{-1},$$

$$\varphi_2 \equiv A\left(\sum_{j=1}^{3} N_j k_j - \frac{1}{3}\sum_{j=1}^{3} \bar{\xi}_j k_j\right)\left(\sum_{j=1}^{3} \bar{\xi}_j h_j^*\right)^{-1},$$

$$h_j^* \equiv \left(h_{1j} + h_{2j}\right)\frac{2AT_0}{3}, \ \bar{\xi}_j \equiv N_j\left(\xi_j + \lambda_j\right).$$

Equation (9.13) has a unique solution for given $k_j(t)$:

$$k(t) = \varphi(k_1, k_2, k_3) \equiv \left(\frac{\varphi_1}{3} + \frac{2^{\frac{1}{3}}\varphi_1^2}{3\varphi_0} + \frac{\varphi_0}{3\sqrt{2}}\right)^3, \tag{9.13}$$

where

$$\varphi_0 = \left(2\varphi_1^3 + 27\varphi_2 + 3\sqrt{3}\sqrt{4\varphi_1^3\varphi_2 + 27\varphi_2^2}\right)^{1/3}.$$

According to (A9.1) and $f(k) = Ak^{1/3}$, I have

$$\bar{y}_j(t) = \left(\frac{A\varphi^{-2/3}}{3} + \delta\right)k_j + \frac{\left(h_{1j} + h_{2j}\right)T_0 2Ak^{1/3}}{3}, j = 1, 2, 3. \tag{9.14}$$

Insert $s_j = \lambda_j \bar{y}_j$ and (9.14) in (9.9):

$$\dot{k}_j = \lambda_j\left[\left(\frac{A\varphi^{-\frac{2}{3}}}{3} + \delta\right)k_j + \frac{\left(h_{1j} + h_{2j}\right)T_0 2Ak^{\frac{1}{3}}}{3}\right] - k_j,$$

$$j = 1, 2, 3. \tag{9.15}$$

The three differential equations contain three variables, $\{k_j(t)\}$. With proper initial conditions, $\{k_j(0)\}$, the differential equations determine values of $\{k_j(t)\}$ over time. According to Lemma 9.1, all the other variables are determined in the system. It is sufficient to examine the dynamic properties of the differential equations.

At equilibrium point I have $\lambda_j \bar{y}_j = k_j$. From $\lambda_j \bar{y}_j = k_j$ and (A9.1), I have

$$k_j = \frac{f_j(k)}{1/\lambda_j - f_\delta(k)}. \tag{9.16}$$

where

$$f_\delta(k) = \frac{Ak^{-2/3}}{3} + \delta > 0, f_j(k) = h_j^* k^{1/3}, h_j^* \equiv \frac{(h_{1j} + h_{2j})2AT_0}{3}.$$

From (9.13) and (9.16), I have

$$k - \varphi(k) = 0. \tag{9.17}$$

For a solution of (9.17) to be meaningful, it is necessary to require the work times to be non-negative and not greater than the time available. To simulate the model, I specify the available time $T_0 = 24$ and the other parameters as follows:

$$\begin{pmatrix} \alpha \\ A \\ \delta_k \end{pmatrix} = \begin{pmatrix} \frac{1}{3} \\ 0.9 \\ 0.05 \end{pmatrix}, \begin{pmatrix} h_{11}, h_{21} \\ h_{12}, h_{22} \\ h_{13}, h_{23} \end{pmatrix} = \begin{pmatrix} 2.5,1.5 \\ 2.0,1.2 \\ 1.5,1.0 \end{pmatrix}, \begin{pmatrix} N_1 \\ N_2 \\ N_3 \end{pmatrix} = \begin{pmatrix} 2 \\ 5 \\ 10 \end{pmatrix},$$

$$\begin{pmatrix} \xi_1 \\ \xi_2 \\ \xi_3 \end{pmatrix} = \begin{pmatrix} 0.15 \\ 0.175 \\ 0.2 \end{pmatrix}, \begin{pmatrix} \bar{\lambda}_1 \\ \bar{\lambda}_2 \\ \bar{\lambda}_3 \end{pmatrix} = \begin{pmatrix} 0.85 \\ 0.825 \\ 0.8 \end{pmatrix}, \begin{pmatrix} \bar{\sigma}_{11}, \bar{\sigma}_{21} \\ \bar{\sigma}_{12}, \bar{\sigma}_{22} \\ \bar{\sigma}_{13}, \bar{\sigma}_{23} \end{pmatrix} = \begin{pmatrix} 0.07,0.08 \\ 0.08,0.09 \\ 0.10,0.11 \end{pmatrix}. \tag{9.18}$$

Group 1 is called the rich class—with the highest levels of human capital for men and women and the highest propensity to own wealth. The population share of the rich class in the total population is only 2/17%. Group 2 is termed the middle class—the levels of the human capital of man and woman are lower than the corresponding levels of the rich class but higher than the other group. Its population share is 5/17%. Group 3 is called the working class. The human capital levels of this group are low and its propensity to save is not high. The share of the population is 10/17%. I specify that men's propensity to stay at home is lower than women's, but men's human capital is higher than women within the same group. The total productivity is specified at 0.9. It should be remarked that although the specified values are not based on empirical observations, the choice does not seem to be unrealistic. With regard to the preference parameters, what is important in this model is their relative values.

With the parameters specified in (9.18), I plot (3.17) as in Fig. 9.1. The simulation identifies the existence of a unique equilibrium point under (9.17).

Following Lemma 9.1, I now determine the equilibrium values of all the variables. The equilibrium values are as follows:

$$\begin{pmatrix} r \\ k \\ f \end{pmatrix} = \begin{pmatrix} 0.065 \\ 4.19 \\ 1.45 \end{pmatrix}, \begin{pmatrix} N \\ K \\ F \end{pmatrix} = \begin{pmatrix} 481.45 \\ 2996.82 \\ 698.38 \end{pmatrix}, \begin{pmatrix} w_{11} \\ w_{12} \\ w_{13} \end{pmatrix} = \begin{pmatrix} 2.42 \\ 1.45 \\ 1.93 \end{pmatrix},$$

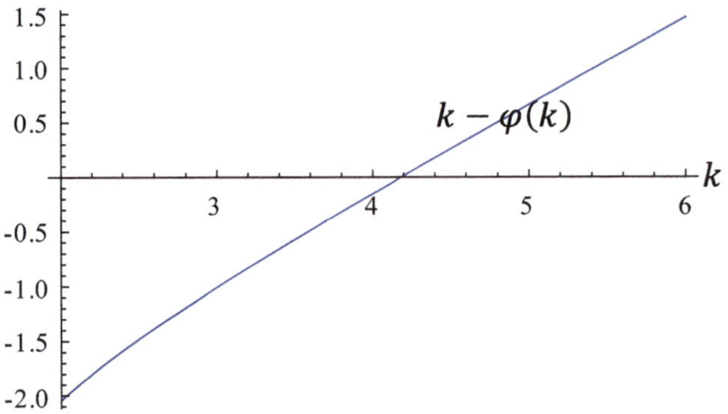

Fig. 9.1 The existence of a unique equilibrium point

$$\begin{pmatrix} w_{21} \\ w_{22} \\ w_{23} \end{pmatrix} = \begin{pmatrix} 1.16 \\ 1.45 \\ 0.97 \end{pmatrix}, \begin{pmatrix} k_1 \\ k_2 \\ k_3 \end{pmatrix} = \begin{pmatrix} 322.96 \\ 210.58 \\ 129.80 \end{pmatrix}, \begin{pmatrix} T_{11} \\ T_{12} \\ T_{13} \end{pmatrix} = \begin{pmatrix} 13.00 \\ 13.44 \\ 12.82 \end{pmatrix},$$

$$\begin{pmatrix} T_{21} \\ T_{22} \\ T_{23} \end{pmatrix} = \begin{pmatrix} 3.05 \\ 4.21 \\ 5.54 \end{pmatrix}, \begin{pmatrix} c_1 \\ c_2 \\ c_3 \end{pmatrix} = \begin{pmatrix} 56.99 \\ 44.67 \\ 32.45 \end{pmatrix}. \tag{9.19}$$

With the initial conditions, the motion of the system is plotted in Fig. 9.2. The system approaches the equilibrium point. The rate of interest falls, and the total capital is increased before they approach their equilibrium values. As the economic conditions are improved, the total labor supply falls, even though the total output changes slightly over the study period. The capital intensity and the wage rates are increased. The work times of both men and women from group 1 are reduced and the work times of men and women from the other two groups are increased. The wealth and consumption levels per household are increased.

9.3 A Rise in Human Capital of the Women in Group 1

There are studies on various aspects on differences in gender time distribution and household production (Bridgman *et al.* 2018; Boerma and Karabarbounis 2021; Giannola 2024). As I have explicitly provided the procedure to simulate the motion, it is straightforward to make a comparative dynamic analysis. First, I examine the case that all the parameters, the human capital level of group 1's women are the same as in (9.18). I increase.

$$h_{21} : 1.5 \text{ to } 2$$

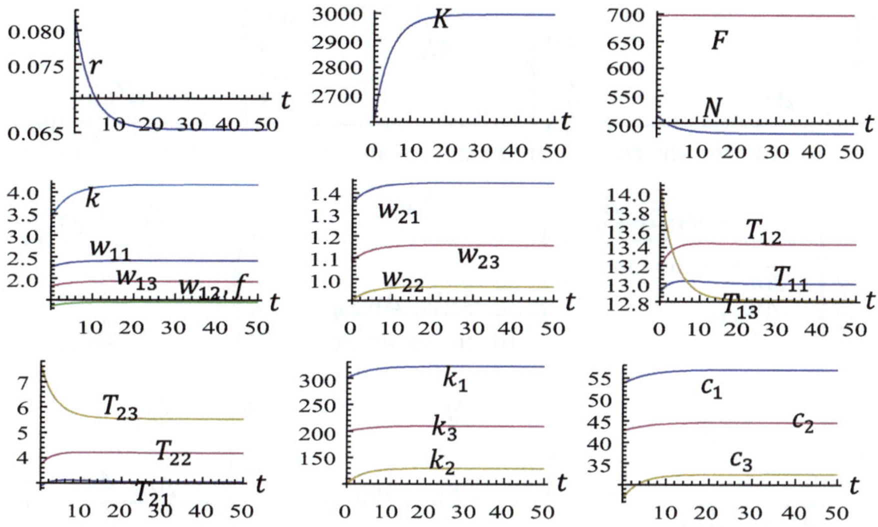

Fig. 9.2 The motion of the system

The result is illustrated in Fig. 9.3. As the human capital is increased, the rate of interest first rises over and then falls below the corresponding values before the changes. The total capital and output are increased. The labor force rises initially and then falls. This happens because as human capital of group 1's women is improved, the women's work time is increased (as her opportunity cost at home is increased). This causes the total labor input to rise. As the economic conditions are further improved, the work time of the women begins to fall. Finally, the total labor force rises over the corresponding equilibrium value before the change but not so much in comparison to the initial time. Similarly, the wage rates are increased; the wage rate of the group whose human capital is increased is increased most rapidly. The consumption level per household of group 1 is increased very much but the other two groups are changed only slightly. The analytical results imply that if the other conditions are not changed, as women's human capital is increased, their work time tends to be increased. The change in one group's women's education has a weak impact on the other groups' female labor participation. As mentioned in the previous chapter, there is a large number of empirical and theoretical literature on economic growth with time distribution between home and non-home economic and leisure activities. Based on studies of some Asian economies, for instance, Banerjee (1999) demonstrates that capital did not strongly affect the existing patriarchal traditions but had harnessed them to its benefit in these Asian countries; it is mainly due to the state interventions and women's own changing perceptions that gender relations in the household had been changed.

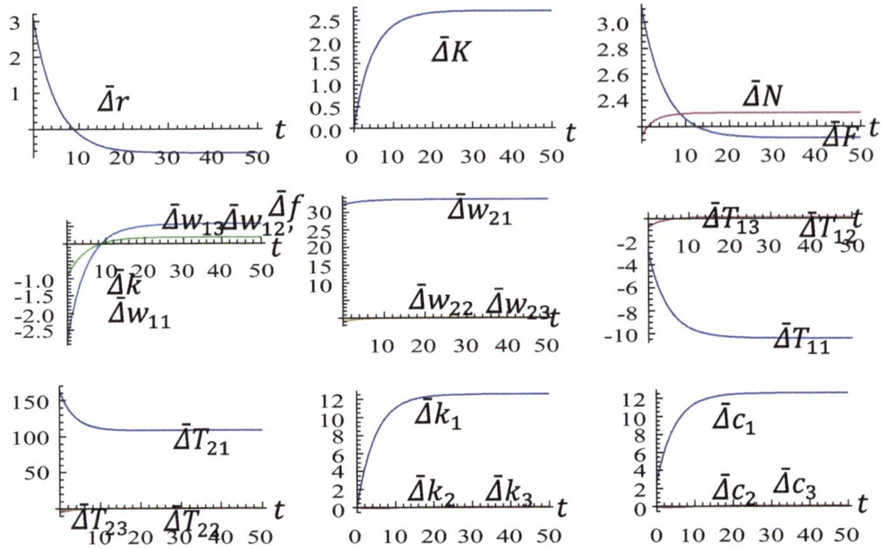

Fig. 9.3 The dynamic effects of a rise in human capital of group 1's wife

9.4 A Rise Group 1's Female Propensity to Stay at Home

I now increase the group 1's female propensity to stay at home in the following way:

$$\sigma_{21} : 0.08 \Rightarrow 0.1$$

.

The result is illustrated in Fig. 9.4. If the other conditions remain invariant and the woman from group 1 likes more to stay at home, the rate of interest falls initially, and then rises. The total capital, labor force, and national output are all reduced. The wage rates rise initially because the total labor force is reduced but shortly fall because the capital intensity falls as the society has less capital. As the wife reduces her work time, the husband increases his work; but the other groups' time distributions are slightly affected.

9.5 A Rise in Group 1's Propensity to Save

I now examine the household's propensity to save, increasing group 1's propensity to save:

$$\lambda_{10} : 0.85 \ \mathit{to} \ 0.88$$

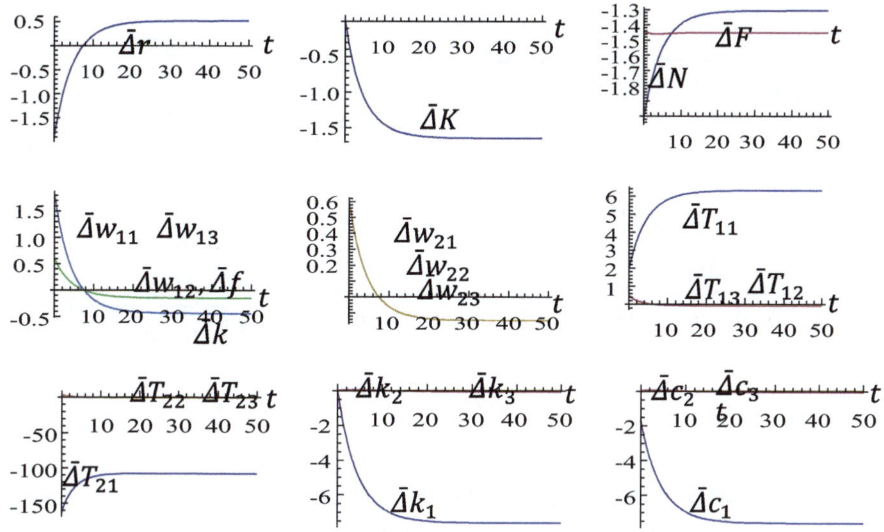

Fig. 9.4 The dynamic effects of a rise in the wife's propensity to use leisure

.

The result is illustrated in Fig. 9.5. As the propensity to save is increased, the rate of interest falls in the long term and the wage rate, total capital, and output level are increased, exactly as the standard Solow model predicts. Nevertheless, when examining the changes across households and genders, I see that the effects are different. Both man and woman from group 1 reduced their work times in the long term, but the workers from the other groups all increased their work hours. Moreover, group 1's wealth level and consumption per household are increased, but the corresponding variables of the other groups are only slightly increased.

9.6 Concluding Remarks

This chapter proposed a one-sector growth multi-group model with gender and endogenous labor supply to provide some insights into the dynamics of female labor participation, wealth, and income distribution in a competitive economy with capital accumulation as the main engine of economic growth. The model is influenced by many traditional ideas about growth in income and wealth distribution. The comparative dynamic analysis demonstrates that a rise in female education or propensity to work in one group will increase female labor participation of the group but has weak effects on the female labor participation of the other groups. It is straightforward to generalize the model by using more general production or utility functions. There are

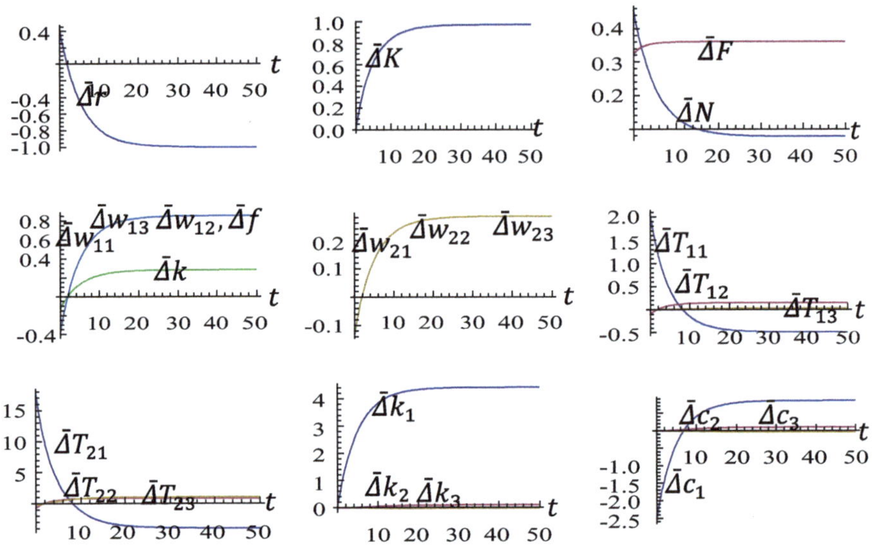

Fig. 9.5 The dynamic effects of a rise in group 1's propensity to save

some observed phenomena related to gender, human capital, and economic development that I should further examine in the research (Angelov *et al.* 2016; Deming 2017; Elsayed *et al.* 2017).

Appendix: Proving Lemma 9.1

I now prove Lemma 9.1. From the definition of $\bar{y}_j(t)$ and (9.1), I have

$$\bar{y}_j(t) = f_\delta(k)k_j + f_j(k), \quad \text{(A9.1)}$$

in which

$$f_\delta(k) \equiv f'^{(k)} + \delta > 0, f_j(k) \equiv \left[f(k) - kf'^{(k)}\right]\left(h_{1j} + h_{2j}\right)T_0 > 0,$$

$$\forall k > 0.$$

From $w_{qj}(t)\bar{T}_{1j}(t) = \sigma_{qj}\bar{y}_j(t)$, I have

$$\frac{\bar{T}_{2j}}{\bar{T}_{1j}} = \sigma_j, j = 1, \cdots, J,$$

$$\frac{\bar{T}_{1j}}{\bar{T}_{11}} = \bar{\sigma}_j \frac{\bar{y}_j}{\bar{y}_1}, j = 2, \cdots, J, \tag{A9.2}$$

where I use

$$\sigma_j \equiv \frac{h_{1j}\sigma_{2j}}{h_{2j}\sigma_{1j}}, \bar{\sigma}_j \equiv \frac{h_{11}\sigma_{1j}}{h_{1j}\sigma_{11}}.$$

From $T_{qj} = T_0 - \bar{T}_{qj}$, (A9.1) and (A9.2), I solve

$$T_{1j} = T_0 - \bar{T}_{11}f_j^*,$$

$$T_{2j} = \left(1 - \sigma_j\right)T_0 + \sigma_j f_j^* \bar{T}_{11}, \tag{A9.3}$$

where

$$f_j^*\left(k, k_1, k_j\right) \equiv \frac{\bar{\sigma}_j\left(f_\delta k_j + f_j\right)}{f_\delta k_1 + f_1}.$$

From (9.1) and $k = K/N$, I have

$$\sum_{j=1}^{J}\left(h_{1j}T_{1j} + h_{2j}T_{2j}\right)N_j = \frac{K}{k}. \tag{A9.4}$$

Solve (A9.3) and (A9.4) with T_{11} as the variable:

$$\bar{T}_{11} = \Omega_{11}(k, k_1, \ldots, k_J) \equiv \left[\frac{K}{k} - \sum_{j=1}^{J} T_0 N_j\left(h_{1j} + h_{2j}\left(1 - \sigma_j\right)\right)\right]$$
$$\left[\sum_{j=1}^{J} f_j^* N_j\left(\sigma_j h_{2j} - h_{1j}\right)\right]^{-1},$$

$$T_{1j} = \Omega_{1j}(k, k_1, \ldots, k_J) \equiv T_0 - \Omega_{11}f_j^*, j = 2, \ldots, J,$$

$$T_{2j} = \Omega_{2j}(k, k_1, \ldots, k_J) \equiv \left(1 - \sigma_j\right)T_0 + \sigma_j f_j^* \Omega_{11}. \tag{A9.5}$$

From the above equations, it is straightforward to show that the work times of all the groups are uniquely determined as functions of k, and $k_1, \cdots, k_J$.

From (9.10), I have

$$\sum_j \left(c_j + s_j\right)N_j = (f + \delta k)N.$$

Insert (A9.1), (9.1), and c_j and s_j in (9.8) in the above equation:

$$\Lambda(k, k_1, \ldots, k_J) \equiv \left(\frac{f}{k} + \delta\right)K - \sum_{j=1}^{J} N_j(\xi_j + \lambda_j)(f_\delta k_j + f_j) = 0, \quad \text{(A9.6)}$$

where $N = K/k$ is applied. I now show that for any given $k_j \geq 0$ for all j, $\Lambda(k) = 0$ has at least one positive solution. Note that $K > 0$ (when at least one $k_j > 0$) is a function of $k_1, \cdots, k_J$. According to the definitions of f_j and f_δ, and the properties of f, it is straightforward to check the following properties of $\Lambda(k)$:

$$\Lambda(k) \to +\infty \text{as } k \to 0,$$

$$\Lambda(k) \to -\infty \text{as } k \to +\infty,$$

where

$$\frac{f}{k} \to +\infty \text{as } k \to 0, \frac{f}{k} \to 0 \text{ as } k \to +\infty,$$

$$f' - \frac{f}{k} < 0, f' > 0, f'' < 0, \forall k > 0,$$

are applied. Hence, $\Lambda(k) = 0$ has at least one positive solution. The solution can be expressed as a function of $k_1, \cdots, k_J$. Take the derivative of $\Lambda(k)$ with respect to k:

$$\frac{d\Lambda}{dk} = \left(f' - \frac{f}{k}\right)\frac{K}{k} - \sum_j N_j(\xi_j + \lambda_j)\left(k_j - (h_{1j} + h_{2j})kT_0\right)f''.$$

As the sign of $d\Lambda/dk$ is ambiguous, the uniqueness of solution is not confirmed. As $k(t)$ is a function of $k_1, \cdots, k_J$ at any point of time, from (A9.1), it can be seen that $\bar{y}_j(t)$ are functions of $k_1, \cdots, k_J$. Hence, from (9.9), (A9.1) and $s_j = \lambda_j \bar{y}_j$, I get

$$\dot{k}_j(t) = \Phi_j(k_1(t), \cdots, k_J(t)) \equiv \lambda_j\left[f_\delta(k)k_j + f_j(k)\right] - k_j,$$

$$j = 1, \cdots, J. \quad \text{(A9.7)}$$

The lemma is confirmed.

Chapter 10
An Economic Growth Model with Endogenous Birth and Mortality Rates

Many modern economies consist of multiple races. Different races have different habits, customs, and attitudes to family and having children. Even if a society was fair and there was no racial discrimination, it is reasonable to consider that the cultural differences may result in differences in wealth and income and population. In order to explain consequences of racial differences in values and human capital, this chapter deals with dynamic interdependence between different races' birth rates, mortality rates, populations, wealth accumulation, and time distributions between work, leisure, and children caring. This chapter emphasizes the role of human capital, technological, and preference changes on the birth and mortality rates and time distributions. The basic economic structure is based on the Walrasian general equilibrium theory, and wealth accumulation is based on the Solow growth model. The wealth and income inequality is due to heterogeneity in households' preferences and human capital levels as well as the households' initial wealth. I also model gender differences in human capital, the propensity to use leisure time, and children caring efficiency. The chapter models the dynamics of racial differences in wealth, income, birth rates, mortality rates, and populations.

Although endogenous population dynamics are mostly neglected in the main streams of economic growth theory, interaction between economic growth and population change has been a challenging question in economics even since Malthus published his *An Essay on the Principle of Population* in 1798. This study is to examine dynamic interactions between wealth accumulation and population dynamics with endogenous birth rates and mortality rates in a multi-race neoclassical growth framework. There are many factors, such as changes in gender gap in wages (Galor and Weil 1996), labor market frictions (Adsera 2005), and age structure (Hock and Weil 2012), which influence fertility. Bosi and Seegmuller (2012) study heterogeneity of households in terms of capital endowments, mortality, and costs per surviving child. Varvarigos and Zakaria (2013) examine interactions between fertility choice and expenditures on health in the traditional overlapping-generations framework. Another determinant of population change is mortality rate (Robinson and

W. Zhang, *A Dynamic Economic Theory of Heterogenous Households*,
https://doi.org/10.1007/978-981-95-8918-0_10

Srinivasan 1997; Lancia and Prarolo 2012; Zhang 2014d, 2015b, 2015f, 2016a). One can find many studies on relations between economic growth models and endogenous longevity (Blackburn and Cipriani 2002; Chakraborty 2004; Hazan and Zoabi 2006; Balestra and Dottori 2012). There are many theoretical models on longevity (Boucekkine *et al.* 2002; Lee and Mason 2010; Ludwig *et al.* 2012).

This chapter is strongly influenced by the literature of the neoclassical growth theory and the literature of population growth and economic development. Its unique contribution is to model population growth of multiple races in the framework of the Solow growth model with endogenous wealth accumulation and gender time distribution between work, leisure, and children caring. It analyzes the link between wealth growth, economic growth, gender division of labor, and population growth. The birth rate and mortality rate dynamics are influenced by the Haavelmo population model and the Barro-Becker fertility choice model. It synthesizes these dynamic mechanisms in a compact framework (Zhang 2016c, 2020d). This chapter is based on Zhang (2021b) and is organized as follows. Section 10.1 introduces the basic model with wealth accumulation and population dynamics. Section 10.2 examines the dynamics of the system and its properties. Section 10.3 shows how the system reacts to a rise in the human capital of race 1's women. Section 10.4 shows the effects of a rise in race 1's mother spending time on per child fostering. Section 10.5 shows how a rise in the total factor productivity changes the dynamics of income and wealth distribution between the races. Section 10.6 shows how a fall in the propensity to have children shifts the path of economic development. Section 10.7 analyses what happens in the system when race 1's income has a stronger impact on the mortality rate. Section 10.8 examines the impact of a rise in woman's propensity to pursue leisure activities on the economic system. Section 10.9 studies the impact of a rise in race 1's propensity to save. Section 10.10 concludes the chapter. The appendix proves Lemma 10.1.

10.1 The Multi-Race Growth Model With Endogenous Time

The economy has one sector, producing a single commodity for consumption and investment. Capital depreciates at a constant exponential rate, 0.03 which is independent of the manner of use. Technology of the production sector is characterized by constant returns to scale. All markets are perfectly competitive. Factors are inelastically supplied, and the available factors are fully utilized at every moment. Savings are undertaken only by households. All earnings of firms are distributed in the form of payments to factors of production. Households own assets of the economy and distribute their incomes to consumption, fostering children, and wealth accumulation. The population of each gender is homogeneous. It is assumed that each family consists of husband, wife, and children. All the families are identical. Let subscripts $q = 1$ and $q = 2$ stand for man and woman respectively. The population is classified into J groups, each group with population, $2N_j(t)$. I use $N_j(t)$ to stand for the population of each gender in group j. Let (j, q) index a person of gender q in group j. Let $T_{jq}(t)$ and $\overline{T}_{jq}(t)$ stand for work time and time spent on taking care of children of (j, q) and $\bar{N}(t)$ for the flow of labor services used in time t for production. I have $\bar{N}(t)$ as follows:

$$\bar{N}(t) = \sum_{j=1}^{J} \left[h_{j1}T_{j1}(t) + h_{j2}T_{j2}(t)\right]N_j(t), \tag{10.1}$$

where h_{jq} is the level of human capital of person (j, q).

Production Sector

The production sector uses capital and labor as inputs. Let $K(t)$ stand for the capital stock at time. The production function is

$$F(t) = AK^{\alpha}(t)\bar{N}^{\beta}(t), \alpha, \beta > 0, \alpha + \beta = 1, \tag{10.2}$$

where $F(t)$ is the output level, and A, α, and β are parameters. Markets are competitive; thus labor and capital earn their marginal products. Profit is given by:

$$F(t) - (r(t) + \delta_k)K(t) - w(t)\bar{N}(t).$$

The marginal conditions are

$$r(t) + \delta_k = \frac{\alpha F(t)}{K(t)}, w(t) = \frac{\beta F(t)}{\bar{N}(t)}, w_{jq}(t) = h_{jq}w(t). \tag{10.3}$$

Consumer Behaviors

Households decide time distribution, consumption level of commodity, number of children, and amount of saving. To describe behavior of consumers, I denote per family wealth by $\bar{k}_j(t)$. Per family current income from the interest payment and the wage payments is

$$y_j(t) = r(t)\bar{k}_j(t) + \left[h_{j1}T_{j1}(t) + h_{j2}T_{j2}(t)\right]w(t).$$

I call $y_j(t)$ the current income in the sense that it comes from consumers' payment for efforts and consumers' current earnings from ownership of wealth. The total value of wealth that a family can sell to purchase goods and to save is equal to $\bar{k}_j(t)$. Here, it is assumed that selling and buying wealth can be conducted instantaneously without any transaction cost. The disposable income per family is given by:

$$\hat{y}_j(t) = y_j(t) + \bar{k}_j(t). \tag{10.4}$$

Let $n_j(t)$ and $p_{bj}(t)$ stand for the birth rate and the cost of birth. Children will have the same level of wealth as that of the parent. In addition to the time spent on children, the cost of the parent is given by:

$$p_{bj}(t) = n_j(t)\bar{k}_j(t). \tag{10.5}$$

Here, other possible costs such as purchases of goods and services are omitted. In the fertility choice model by Barro and Becker (1989), the cost also includes consumption of goods. I now introduce time spent on children. Becker (1981) emphasizes costs of the mother's time rearing children to adulthood. In some societies, women are the primary providers of fostering of children. The following relation between fertility rate and the parent's time on raising children is assumed:

$$\bar{T}_{jq}(t) = \theta_{jq} n_j(t), \theta_{jq} \geq 0, \tag{10.6}$$

where θ_{jq} is the time required for mother (father) on raising one child. The specified function form implies that if the parents want more children, they spend more time on fostering children. This requirement is strict as fostering of children tends to exhibit increasing return to scale. For instance, the time per child tends to fall as the family has more children. The constant return to scale is required because it makes the analysis mathematically tractable.

The household distributes the total available budget between saving, $s_j(t)$, consumption of goods, $c_j(t)$, and fostering of children, $p_{bj}(t)$. The budget constraint is

$$p_j(t)c_j(t) + s_j(t) + \bar{k}_j(t)n_j(t) = \hat{y}_j(t). \tag{10.7}$$

I consider that except work and fostering of children, parents also have their leisure. The leisure time of person (j, q) are denoted by $\tilde{T}_{jq}(t)$. Each person is faced with the following time constraint:

$$T_{jq}(t) + \bar{T}_{jq}(t) + \tilde{T}_{jq}(t) = T_0, \tag{10.8}$$

where T_0 is the total available time for leisure, work, and fostering of children. Substituting (10.8) into (10.7) yields

$$p(t)c_j(t) + s_j(t) + \bar{k}_j(t)n_j(t) + \bar{T}_{j1}(t)w_{j1}(t) + \bar{T}_{j2}(t)w_{j2}(t)$$

$$+\tilde{T}_{j1}(t)w_{j1}(t) + \tilde{T}_{j2}(t)\, w_{j2}(t) = \bar{y}_j(t), \tag{10.9}$$

where

$$\bar{y}_j(t) \equiv (1 + r(t))\bar{k}_j(t) + \big(w_{j1}(t) + w_{j2}(t)\big)T_0.$$

The right-hand side is the "potential" income that the family can obtain by spending all the available time on work. The left-hand side is the sum of the consumption cost, the saving, the opportunity cost of fostering of children, and opportunity cost of leisure. Insert (10.6) in (10.9):

$$c_j(t) + s_j(t) + \tilde{w}_j(t)n_j(t) + \tilde{T}_{j1}(t)w_{j1}(t) + \tilde{T}_{j2}(t)w_{j2}(t) = \bar{y}_j(t), \qquad (10.10)$$

where

$$\tilde{w}_j(t) \equiv \bar{k}_j(t) + h_j w(t), \; h_j \equiv \theta_{j1}h_{j1} + \theta_{j2}h_{j2}.$$

The variable $\tilde{w}_j(t)$ is the opportunity cost of fostering children. Like Barro and Becker (1989), it is assumed that the parents' utility is dependent on the number of children. It is assumed that the utility is dependent on $c_j(t)$, $s_j(t)$, $\tilde{T}_{jq}(t)$, and $n_j(t)$ as follows:

$$U_j(t) = c_j^{\xi_{j0}}(t)s_j^{\lambda_{j0}}(t)\tilde{T}_{j1}^{\sigma_{j01}}(t)\tilde{T}_{j2}^{\sigma_{j02}}(t)n_j^{\upsilon_{j0}}(t),$$

where ξ_{j0} is called the propensity to consume, λ_{j0} is the propensity to own wealth, σ_{j0q} is the gender $q's$ propensity to use leisure time, and υ_{j0} is the propensity to have children. In this chapter, the parents' utility is dependent only on the number of their children. According to Soares (2005) parents' utility depends not only on their surviving offspring but also on length of each surviving child's lifespan. The first-order condition of maximizing $U_j(t)$ subject to (10.10) yields

$$c_j(t) = \xi_j\bar{y}_j(t), \; s_j(t) = \lambda_j\bar{y}_j(t), \; \tilde{T}_{jq}(t) = \frac{\sigma_{jq}\bar{y}_j(t)}{w_{jq}(t)},$$

$$n_j(t) = \frac{\upsilon_j\bar{y}_j(t)}{\tilde{w}_j(t)}, \qquad (10.11)$$

where

$$\xi_j \equiv \rho_j\xi_{j0}, \; \lambda_j \equiv \rho_j\lambda_{j0}, \; \sigma_{jq} \equiv \rho_j\sigma_{jq0}, \; \upsilon_j \equiv \rho_j\upsilon_{j0},$$

$$\rho_j \equiv \frac{1}{\xi_{j0} + \lambda_{j0} + \sigma_{j10} + \sigma_{j20} + \upsilon_{j0}}.$$

Birth and Mortality Rates and Population Dynamics

The approach in this chapter to population dynamics is influenced by the Haavelmo model (Haavelmo 1954; Stutzer 1980) and the Ramsey model (Razin and Ben-Zion 1975; Yip and Zhang 1997; Chu *et al.* 2013). According to the definitions, the population change follows:

$$\dot{N}_j(t) = \big(n_j(t) - d_j(t)\big)N_j(t), \tag{10.12}$$

where $n_j(t)$ and $d_j(t)$ are respectively the birth rate and mortality rate. It should be noted that Tournemaine and Luangaram (2012) construct a model of population growth and economic development. They examine interactions among fertility, education, growth rates of technical progress, and income per capita growth. They use the following technology of production of children: $n(t) = bT_b^{\theta}(t)$,

where $T_b(t)$ is the time of rearing children and b and θ are parameters. In their model, the mortality rate is assumed to be constant. This chapter introduces endogenous mortality rates. In the Haavelmo model, the mortality rate is negatively related to per capita income. It is assumed that the mortality rate is negatively related to the disposable income in the following way:

$$d_j(t) = \frac{\bar{\upsilon}_j N_j^{b_j}(t)}{\bar{y}_j^{a_j}(t)}, \tag{10.13}$$

where $\bar{\upsilon}_j \geq 0$, $a_j \geq 0$. I call $\bar{\upsilon}_j$ the mortality rate parameter. As in the Haavelmo model, an improvement in living conditions implies that people live longer. The term $N_j^{b_j}(t)$ takes account of possible influences of the population on mortality. For instance, when the population is overpopulated, environment is deteriorated. It is possible to take account of this kind of environmental effect by the term. In this case, it is reasonable to require b_j to be positive. It should be noted that the sign of b_j is generally ambiguous in the sense that the population may also have a positive impact on mortality. Insert (10.10) and (10.13) in (10.12):

$$\dot{N}_j(t) = \left(\frac{\upsilon_j \bar{y}_j(t)}{\tilde{w}_j(t)} - \frac{\bar{\upsilon}_j N_j^{b_j}(t)}{\bar{y}_j^{a_j}(t)}\right)N_j(t). \tag{10.14}$$

The equation describes the population dynamics.

Wealth Dynamics

According to the definition of $s_j(t)$, the change in the household's wealth is given by:

$$\dot{\bar{k}}_j(t) = s_j(t) - \bar{k}_j(t) = \lambda_j \bar{y}_j(t) - \bar{k}_j(t). \tag{10.15}$$

Value of Physical Wealth and Capital
The value of physical capital is equal to the value of physical wealth:

$$\sum_{j=1}^{J} \bar{k}_j(t)N_j(t) = K(t). \tag{10.16}$$

Demand for and Supply of Goods
The national saving is the sum of the households' saving. As output of the capital goods sector is equal to the net savings and the depreciation of capital stock, it follows:

$$S(t) + C(t) - K(t) + \delta_k K(t) = F(t), \tag{10.17}$$

where $S(t) - K(t) + \delta_k K(t)$ is the sum of the net saving and depreciation and

$$S(t) = \sum_{j=1}^{J} s_j(t)N_j(t),\ C(t) = \sum_{j=1}^{J} c_j(t)N_j(t).$$

The dynamic model is complete. The model is structurally a unification of the Walrasian general equilibrium and neoclassical growth theory. If I neglect the wealth accumulation and capital depreciation (i.e., capital being constant), then the model with heterogeneous households and one sector belongs to the Walrasian general equilibrium theory. The Solow model and the Haavelmo model can be considered as special cases of the model.

10.2 The Dynamics and Its Properties

This section examines dynamics of the model. First, I introduce

$$z(t) \equiv \frac{r(t) + \delta_k}{w(t)}.$$

It is to show that the dynamics can be expressed by differential equations with $z(t)$, $\left(\bar{k}_j(t)\right)$, and $(N_j(t))$ as the variables.

Lemma 10.1
The dynamics of the economic system are governed by:

$$\dot{z}(t) = \Omega_1\left(z(t), \left\{\bar{k}_j(t)\right\}, \left(N_j(t)\right)\right),$$

$$\dot{\bar{k}}_j(t) = \Omega_j\big(z(t), \{\bar{k}_j(t)\}, (N_j(t))\big), j = 2, \ldots, J,$$

$$\dot{N}_j(t) = \Lambda_j\big(z(t), \{\bar{k}_j(t)\}, (N_j(t))\big), \ j = 1, \ldots, J, \tag{10.18}$$

where $\Omega_j(t)$ and $\Lambda_j(t)$ are functions of $z(t)$, $\big(\bar{k}_j(t)\big)$, and $(N_j(t))$ defined in the Appendix. Moreover, all the other variables are determined as functions of $z(t)$, $\big(\bar{k}_j(t)\big)$, and $(N_j(t))$: $r(t)$ and $w_{jq}(t)$ by (A10.2) $\rightarrow \bar{k}_1(t)$ by (A10.10) $\rightarrow \bar{N}(t)$ by (A10.6) $\rightarrow \bar{y}_j(t)$ by (A10.3) $\rightarrow c_j(t)$, $s_j(t)$, $\tilde{T}_{jq}(t)$, and $n_j(t)$ by (10.11) $\rightarrow \bar{T}_{jq}(t)$ by (10.6) $\rightarrow T_{jq}(t)$ by (A10.5) $\rightarrow K(t)$ by (A10.7) $\rightarrow F(t)$ by (10.2).

The differential equations system (10.17) has $2J$ variables. As demonstrated in the appendix, the expressions are complicated. It is difficult to explicitly interpret economic implications of the equations. The parameters are as follows:

$$\alpha = 0.25, A = 2, b_j = 1, T_0 = 24, \delta_k = 0.05,$$

$$\begin{pmatrix} a_1 \\ a_2 \\ a_3 \end{pmatrix} = \begin{pmatrix} 0.1 \\ 0.2 \\ 0.3 \end{pmatrix}, \begin{pmatrix} h_{11} \\ h_{21} \\ h_{31} \end{pmatrix} = \begin{pmatrix} 2 \\ 1.5 \\ 1 \end{pmatrix}, \begin{pmatrix} h_{12} \\ h_{22} \\ h_{32} \end{pmatrix} = \begin{pmatrix} 1.5 \\ 1 \\ 0.5 \end{pmatrix},$$

$$\begin{pmatrix} \xi_{10} \\ \xi_{20} \\ \xi_{30} \end{pmatrix} = \begin{pmatrix} 0.2 \\ 0.2 \\ 0.2 \end{pmatrix}, \begin{pmatrix} \lambda_{10} \\ \lambda_{20} \\ \lambda_{30} \end{pmatrix} = \begin{pmatrix} 0.6 \\ 0.55 \\ 0.5 \end{pmatrix}, \begin{pmatrix} v_{10} \\ v_{20} \\ v_{30} \end{pmatrix} = \begin{pmatrix} 1 \\ 1.2 \\ 1.5 \end{pmatrix},$$

$$\begin{pmatrix} \sigma_{110} \\ \sigma_{210} \\ \sigma_{310} \end{pmatrix} = \begin{pmatrix} 0.1 \\ 0.12 \\ 0.16 \end{pmatrix}, \begin{pmatrix} \sigma_{120} \\ \sigma_{220} \\ \sigma_{320} \end{pmatrix} = \begin{pmatrix} 0.13 \\ 0.14 \\ 0.8 \end{pmatrix}, \begin{pmatrix} \bar{v}_1 \\ \bar{v}_2 \\ \bar{v}_3 \end{pmatrix} = \begin{pmatrix} 0.02 \\ 0.03 \\ 0.035 \end{pmatrix},$$

$$\begin{pmatrix} \theta_{11} \\ \theta_{21} \\ \theta_{31} \end{pmatrix} = \begin{pmatrix} 0.1 \\ 0.2 \\ 0.1 \end{pmatrix}, \begin{pmatrix} \theta_{12} \\ \theta_{22} \\ \theta_{32} \end{pmatrix} = \begin{pmatrix} 0.5 \\ 0.3 \\ 0.2 \end{pmatrix}. \tag{10.19}$$

The mother spends longer hours on fostering children than the father. Person $(1, 2)$ spends long time on per child, and person $(1, 1)$ spends short time on per child. Race 1's human capital is higher than race 2's and race 2's human capital is higher than race 3's. The relative propensities are listed as follows:

$$\begin{pmatrix} v_1 \\ \lambda_1 \\ \xi_1 \\ \sigma_{11} \\ \sigma_{12} \end{pmatrix} = \begin{pmatrix} 0.493 \\ 0.296 \\ 0.099 \\ 0.049 \\ 0.064 \end{pmatrix}, \begin{pmatrix} v_2 \\ \lambda_2 \\ \xi_2 \\ \sigma_{21} \\ \sigma_{22} \end{pmatrix} = \begin{pmatrix} 0.543 \\ 0.249 \\ 0.091 \\ 0.054 \\ 0.063 \end{pmatrix}, \begin{pmatrix} v_3 \\ \lambda_3 \\ \xi_3 \\ \sigma_{31} \\ \sigma_{31} \end{pmatrix} = \begin{pmatrix} 0.591 \\ 0.197 \\ 0.079 \\ 0.063 \\ 0.071 \end{pmatrix}.$$

Race 1's propensity to have children is lower than race 2's and race 2's propensity to have children is lower than race 3's. Both man and woman of race 3 have the highest propensities to stay at home. Race 1 has the highest propensity to save. The father has lower propensity to pursue leisure activities than the mother. The total productivity factor is $A = 2$. Although the specified values are not based on empirical observations, the choice does not seem to be unrealistic. To follow the motion of the system, I specify the initial conditions:

$$z(0) = 0.36, \bar{k}_2(0) = 33, \bar{k}_3(0) = 15, N_1(0) = 88, N_2(0) = 79,$$

$$N_3(0) = 92.$$

The simulation result is plotted in Fig. 10.1. The population grows from its low initial condition. As the population rate rises, the mortality rate is also increasing. The labor force is increased, and the wage rates are reduced. The falling wage rates reduce the opportunity cost of fostering children, resulting in the rise in birth rate. The rise in birth rate is associated with rise in both man's and woman's time of fostering children. As the income falls, both men and women work longer hours. Their leisure hours are reduced. The national wealth and output are increased in association with rising labor force. Nevertheless, both consumption level and wealth per household are reduced. It should be mentioned that in a two-period overlapping-generations model Strulik (2008) takes account of subsistence consumption and infant survival. The model predicts an inverted U-shape relationship between fertility and income. As the family has higher incomes, it has more resources for children rearing. On the other hand, a higher income makes the parents devote more resources to children caring. Some studies confirm that there is a decline in the fertility rate along the process of economic development (Kirk 1996; Ehrlich and Lui 1997). Figure 10.1 shows that relations between consumption and birth rates vary for different groups in different stages of economic growth.

It is straightforward to confirm that all the variables become stationary in the long term. This implies the existence of an equilibrium point. The simulation confirms the existence of the following equilibrium point:

$$N_1 = 86.2, N_2 = 78.3, N_3 = 95.6, K = 9644.7, \bar{N} = 12025.7,$$

$$F = 22760.7, n_1 = d_1 = 1.63, n_2 = d_2 = 2.13, n_3 = d_3 = 2.94,$$

$$r = 0.54, w_{11} = 2.84, w_{12} = 2.13, w_{21} = 2.13, w_{22} = 1.42,$$

$$w_{31} = 1.42, w_{32} = 0.71, T_{11} = 20.03, \tilde{T}_{11} = 3.78, \bar{T}_{11} = 0.16,$$

$$T_{12} = 16.6, \tilde{T}_{12} = 6.58, \bar{T}_{12} = 0.62, T_{21} = 20.05, \tilde{T}_{21} = 3.52,$$

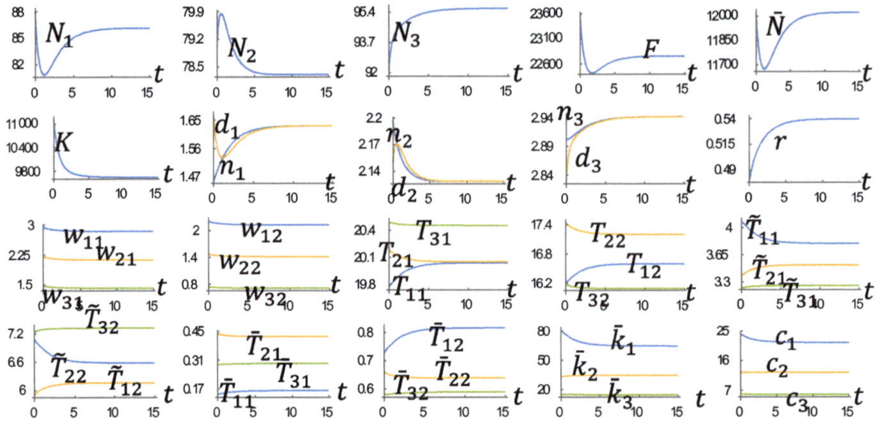

Fig. 10.1 The motion of the economic system

$$\bar{T}_{21} = 0.43, T_{22} = 17.2, \tilde{T}_{22} = 6.16, \bar{T}_{22} = 0.64, T_{31} = 20.45,$$

$$\tilde{T}_{31} = 3.25, \bar{T}_{31} = 0.29, T_{32} = 16.09, \tilde{T}_{32} = 7.32, \bar{T}_{32} = 0.59,$$

$$\bar{k}_1 = 64.69, \bar{k}_2 = 34.67, \bar{k}_3 = 14.44, c_1 = 21.56, c_2 = 12.5, c_3 = 5.77.$$

The populations of the three races are respectively $N_1 = 86.2$, $N_2 = 78.3$, and $N_3 = 95.6$. The population differences are due to the differences in human capital, the propensities to have children, and other factors. The following dynamic comparative statics demonstrates effects of some parameters on the population dynamics. The six eigenvalues are

$$-2.97, -2.13, -1.63, -0.68, -0.6, -0.54.$$

As the eigenvalues are negative, the unique equilibrium is locally stable. Hence, the system always approaches its equilibrium if it is not far from the equilibrium.

10.3 Human Capital of Race 1's Woman Being Improved

The traditional neoclassical approach holds that gender inequalities resulting from disparities in human capital will wither away as an economy experiences high growth (Beneria and Feldman 1992, Forsythe *et al.* 2000). According to Stotsky (2006: 18), "the neoclassical approach examines the simultaneous interaction of economic development and the reduction of gender inequalities. It sees the process of economic development leading to the reduction of these inequalities and also inequalities hindering economic development." This section examines how the following rise in the human capital of race 1's woman:

$$h_2 : 1.5 \Rightarrow 1.7.$$

The result is plotted in Fig. 10.2. The national labor force, national output, and national capital rise. The rate of interest falls. The wage rate of race 1's woman increases, and the wage rates of other groups are slightly affected. Race 1's population rises initially and falls slightly in the long term. The other two races' populations are slightly affected. Race 2's population rises initially and falls in the long term. Race 3's population is expanded. For race 1, the opportunity cost of child fostering is increased in association with the mother's wage rising. At the same time, the wage rate increased. The net result on the race's birth rate is that it rises initially and falls in the long term. The times that race 1's parents spend children caring change correspondingly. The mother from race 1 works more and the father works less. The father has more leisure time, and the mother has less. The family consumes more and has more wealth. The mortality rate falls in association with improved living conditions. With regard to the effects on the other two races, the change in race 1's human capital has little impact on their consumption and wealth levels, even though the birth and death rates are affected. It should be remarked that many studies demonstrate that life expectancy is increased with the aggregate human capital level (Blackburn and Cipriani 2002; Boucekkine *et al.* 2002). The result demonstrates the same trend if the mortality rate negatively related to the life expectancy is considered.

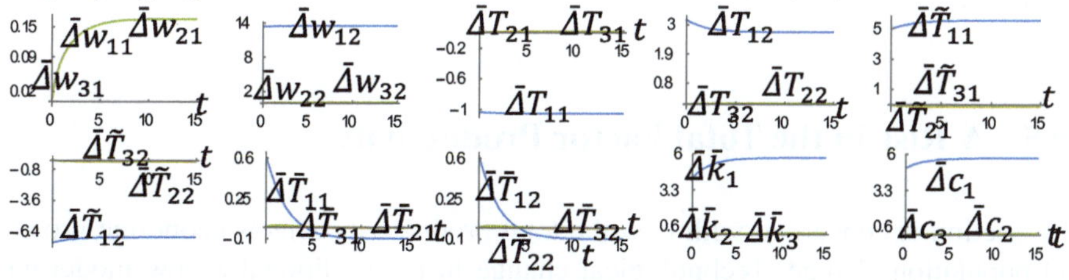

Fig. 10.2 Human capital of race 1's woman being improved

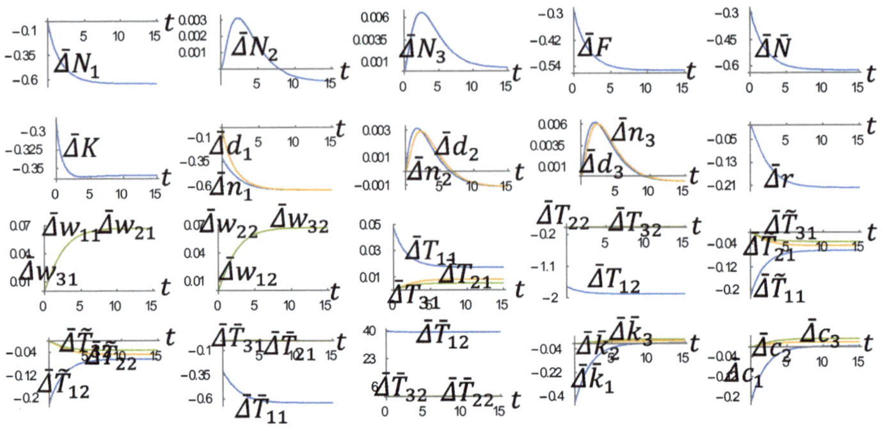

Fig. 10.3 Race 1's mother spending more time on per child fostering

10.4 Race 1's Mother Spending More Time on Per Child Fostering

There is a vast literature of empirical and theoretical literature on economic growth with time distribution. I consider that the mother spends more time on per child fostering. The parameter θ_{12} rises as follows:

$$\theta_{12} : 0.5 \Rightarrow 0.7.$$

The result is plotted in Fig. 10.3. Race 1's mother spends more time on children caring, and the father spends less time on children caring. Both the father and the mother spend less time on leisure. The mother works less hours, and the father works more hours. The other two races' time distributions are slightly affected. The national wealth, capital, and output are reduced. Race 1's population is reduced. Race 2's population rises initially and falls in the long term. Race 3's population is expanded.

10.5 A Rise in the Total Factor Productivity

This section is concerned with how the total productivity affects economic growth and population change. Technological change in the traditional Solow model has positive effects on the long-term economic growth. As the Solow model assumes a constant growth rate and constant return to scales, technological change has no impact on labor inputs and time distribution even in short terms. The total productivity rises as follows:

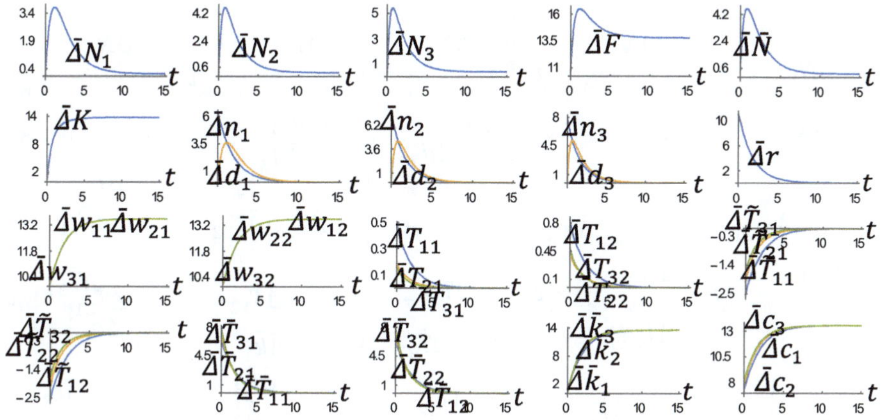

Fig. 10.4 A rise in the total productivity

$$A : 2 \Rightarrow 2.2.$$

The simulation results are plotted in Fig. 10.4. As the productivity is enhanced, the output level and wage rates are increased. The total capital and labor force are enhanced. The rate of interest is increased initially and is not affected in the long term. Each race's population rises. The birth and mortality rates are increased initially and not affected in the long term. The technological change results in the increases in the levels of consumption and wealth per household, and the opportunity cost of caring for children. It has no long-run impact on the time distributions.

10.6 A Fall in the Propensity to Have Children

Tournemaine and Luangaram (2012: 925) describe, "depending on the country, population growth may contribute, deter, or even have no impact on economic development. This ambiguous result is explained by the fact that the effects of population growth change over time. For example, a higher fertility rate can have a short-term negative effect caused by the cost of expenditures on children whereas it has a long-run positive effect through the larger labor force it generates." But it is argued that if a national economy has no economic activity characterized by increasing returns to scale, a rise in the population tends to reduce per person's living conditions. This section examines the effects of the following fall in race 1's propensity to have children:

$$\upsilon_{10} : 1 \Rightarrow 0.8.$$

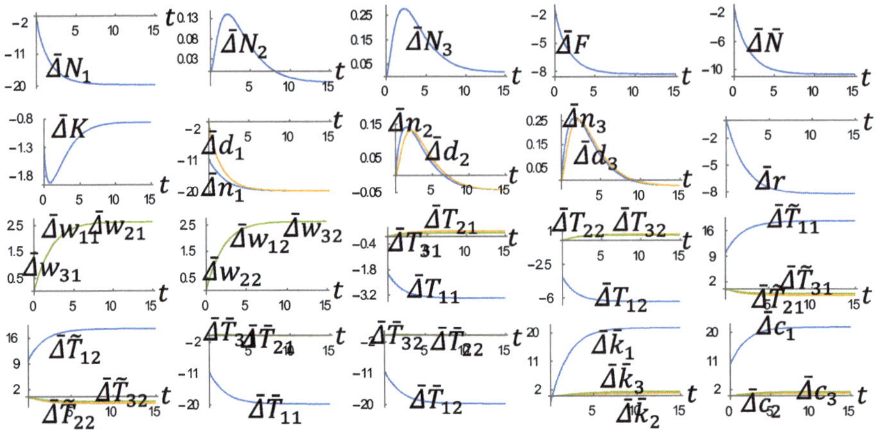

Fig. 10.5 A fall in race 1's propensity to have children

The simulation results are plotted in Fig. 10.5. As race has less interest in having children, the race's birth rate falls. Race 1 spends less time on fostering children, more time on leisure activities, and less time on working. The race's mortality rate also falls. Race 1's population is reduced. Race 2's population rises initially and falls in the long term. Race 3's population is increased. When the other conditions are kept constant, a rise in the propensity to have children has a great impact on the population growth. The capital, total labor input, and output level are all reduced. The wage rates are increased, and the rate of interest is reduced. The wealth and consumption levels increase.

10.7 Race 1's Income Having Stronger Impact on the Mortality Rate

I now examine what will happen to the economy when race 1's mortality rate is more negatively related to the disposable income:

$$a_1 : 0.01 \Rightarrow 0.02.$$

The result is plotted in Fig. 10.6. Race 1's population increases. Race 2's population rises initially and falls in the long term. Race 3's population rises initially and is not affected in the long term. The national labor force, capital and output are increased. Race 1's birth mortality rates are not affected in the long term. The other two races' birth mortality rates are slightly reduced in the long term. The wage rates are increased, and the rate of interest is reduced. The wealth and consumption levels increase. There are also slight changes in the time distributions.

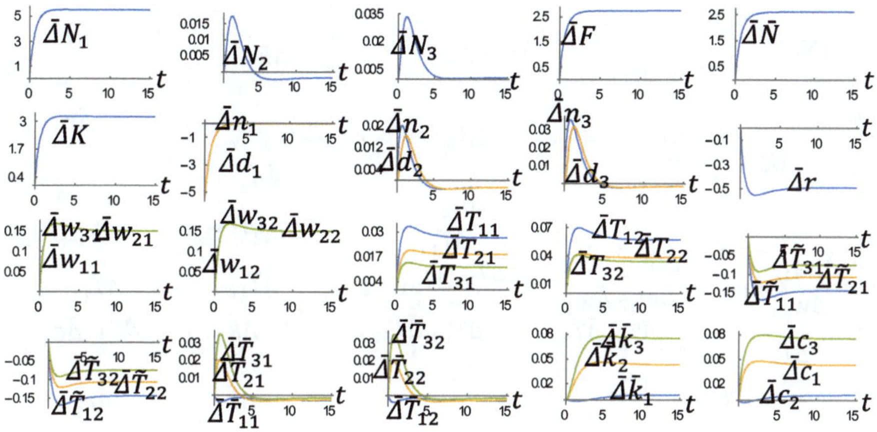

Fig. 10.6 Race 1's disposable income having stronger impact on the mortality rate

10.8 A Rise in Woman's Propensity to Pursue Leisure Activities

It is important to examine the economic consequences when woman strengthens her preference for pursuing leisure activities. This section deals with the effects when race 1's woman increases her propensity to pursue leisure:

$$\sigma_{02} : 0.13 \Rightarrow 0.15.$$

The simulation results are plotted in Fig. 10.7. An immediate consequence of the preference change is that the wife from race 1 spends more time on leisure and the husband has less leisure hours. The husband works more hours and the wife works less. Both the husband and wife reduce their time on fostering children. Race 1's birth and mortality rates are reduced. Race 1's population is reduced. The other two races' birth and mortality rates and populations are slightly affected. The national output, national labor force, and national capital are all reduced. The wage rates are reduced, and the rate of interest is increased. Race 1's representative household consumes less and has less wealth. The representative households of the other two races are slightly affected.

10.9 The Impact of Race 1's Propensity to Save

According to the Solow model, a rise in the propensity to save will increase per capita wealth but reduce per capita consumption level. The impact is different from the result in the Solow model in the long term. The (exogenous) population growth rate is not

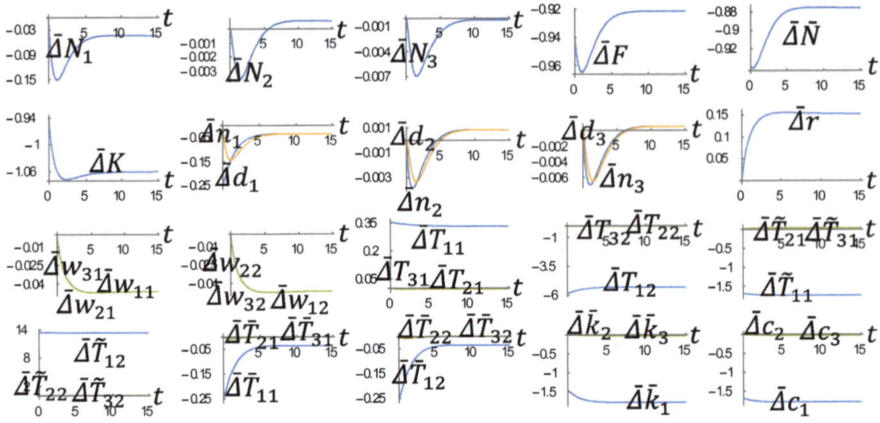

Fig. 10.7 A rise in woman's propensity to pursue leisure activities

affected by economic conditions in the traditional one-sector growth model. I now examine what will happen in our economy with endogenous birth rates and mortality rates when race 1's propensity to save is increased as follows:

$$\lambda_{10} : 0.6 \Rightarrow 0.62.$$

The simulation result is plotted in Fig. 10.8. Race 1's per household consumption level falls initially and rises in the long term. Race 1's per household wealth is increased. Both man and woman from race 1 work more hours initially and work less hours in the long term; they spend less hours on leisure initially and more hours in the long term; and they spend less hours on fostering of children. Race 1's population is reduced. Race 2's population rises initially and falls in the long term. Race 3's population is increased. The national labor supply and national output are reduced, while the national capital is augmented. The wage rates increase and the rate of interest is reduced. Races 2 and 3 consume more and own more wealth. Races 2 and 3 do not change time on fostering children; they increase work hours and reduce leisure hours. Race 1's change in the propensity to save not only affects the race's time distribution but also the other races' time distributions between leisure and work. The propensity to save directly affects capital accumulation. Changes in national capital stock affect marginal returns of work (i.e., wage rate). As the wage rates are affected, the other races' time distributions are affected.

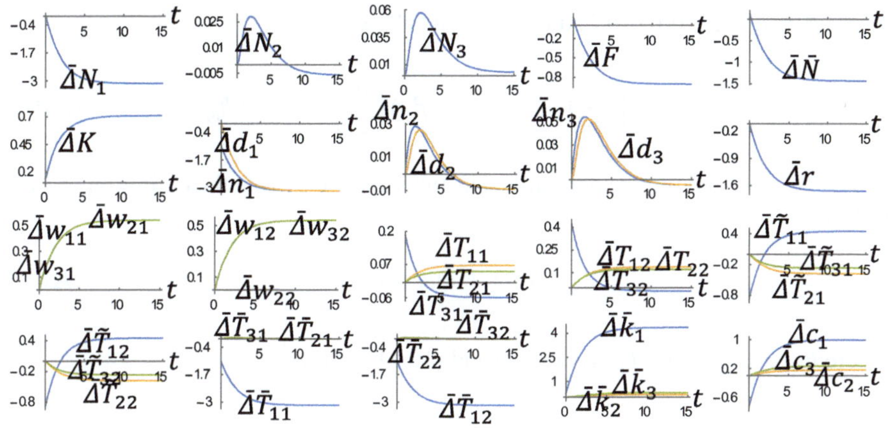

Fig. 10.8 The impact of race 1's propensity to save

10.10 Concluding Remarks

This chapter introduced endogenous population into a generalized Solow one sector growth model with multiple types of households. It dealt with a dynamic interdependence between different races' birth rates, mortality rates, populations, wealth accumulation, and time distributions between work, leisure, and children caring. It emphasized the role of human capital, technological, and preference changes in the birth and mortality rates and time distributions. The basic economic structure is based on the Walrasian general equilibrium theory and wealth accumulation is based on the Solow growth model. The wealth and income inequality are due to heterogeneity in households' preferences and human capital levels. It examined the effects of changes in the propensity to have children, the propensity to save, woman's propensity to use leisure, woman's human capital, and woman's emotional involvement in children caring. I can generalize and extend our model. In this chapter, children caring function exhibits constant return to scale in the parent's time spent on caring children. It is possible to generalize the model by applying more general assumptions about caring for children and mortality rate functions.

Appendix: Proving Lemma 10.1

I now show that the dynamics can be expressed by differential equations system. From (10.3), it follows:

$$z \equiv \frac{r + \delta_k}{w} = \frac{\tilde{\alpha}\bar{N}}{K}, \tag{A10.1}$$

where $\tilde{\alpha} \equiv \alpha/\beta$. From (10.2) and (10.3), it follows:

$$r = \alpha A\left(\frac{z}{\tilde{\alpha}_i}\right)^{\beta} - \delta_k, \; w = \beta A\left(\frac{\tilde{\alpha}}{z}\right)^{\alpha}, \; w_{jq} = h_{jq}\, w. \tag{A10.2}$$

Hence, r, w, and w_{jq} are determined as functions of z. From the definition of $\bar{y}$ and (10.3):

$$\bar{y}_j = (1 + r)\bar{k}_j + h_{j0}\, w, \tag{A10.3}$$

where $h_{j0} \equiv (h_{j1} + h_{j2})T_0$. By (10.8) and (10.11), I have

$$T_{jq} = T_0 - \bar{T}_{jq} - \tilde{T}_{jq} = T_0 - \left(\frac{\theta_{jq}\, \upsilon_j}{\tilde{w}_j} + \frac{\sigma_{jq}}{h_{jq}\, w}\right)\bar{y}_j. \tag{A10.4}$$

Insert (A10.3) in (A10.4):

$$T_{jq} = \chi_{jq} - \frac{\tilde{r}_{jq}\, \bar{k}_j + \bar{r}_q}{\tilde{w}_j} - r_{jq}\, \bar{k}_j, \tag{A10.5}$$

where

$$\chi_{jq} = \left(1 - \frac{(h_{j1} + h_{j2})\sigma_{jq}}{h_{jq}}\right)T_0, \; \tilde{r}_{jq} \equiv \theta_{jq}\upsilon_j(1 + r), \; \bar{r}_{jq} \equiv h_{j0}\, \theta_{jq}\upsilon_j w,$$

$$r_{jq} \equiv \frac{(1 + r)\sigma_{jq}}{h_{jq}\, w}.$$

Insert (A10.5) in (10.1):

$$\bar{N} = \sum\nolimits_{j=1}^{J}\left(\chi_j - \frac{\tilde{r}_j\bar{k}_j + \tilde{h}_{3j}}{\tilde{w}_j} - \tilde{r}_{0j}\bar{k}_j\right)N_j, \tag{A10.6}$$

where

$$\chi_j \equiv h_{j1}\chi_{j1} + h_{j2}\chi_{j2}, \; \tilde{r}_j \equiv h_{j1}\tilde{r}_{j1} + h_{j2}\tilde{r}_{j2}, \; \tilde{h}_{3j} \equiv h_{j1}\bar{r}_{j1} + h_{j2}\bar{r}_{j2},$$

$$\tilde{r}_{0j} \equiv h_{j1}r_{j1} + h_{j2}r_{j2}.$$

By the definition of z, it follows:

$$K = \frac{\tilde{\alpha}\bar{N}}{z}. \tag{A10.7}$$

Insert (A10.6) and (10.16) in (A10.7):

$$\left(z_1 + \frac{\tilde{r}_1}{\tilde{w}_1}\right)\bar{k}_1 + \frac{\tilde{h}_{31}}{\tilde{w}_1} = \phi_0\left(z, \left\{\bar{k}_j\right\}, (N_j)\right)$$

$$\equiv \chi_1 + \frac{1}{N_1}\sum_{j=2}^{J}\left(\chi_j - \frac{\tilde{r}_j\,\bar{k}_j + \tilde{h}_{3j}}{\tilde{w}_j} - z_j\,\bar{k}_j\right)N_j, \tag{A10.8}$$

where

$$z_j \equiv \tilde{r}_{0j} + \frac{z}{\tilde{\alpha}}.$$

Insert $\tilde{w}_1 = \bar{k}_1 + h_1\, w$ in (A10.8):

$$\bar{k}_1^2 + m_1\,\bar{k}_1 + m_2 = 0, \tag{A10.9}$$

where

$$m_1\left(z, \left\{\bar{k}_j\right\}, (N_j)\right) \equiv h_1\, w + \frac{\tilde{r}_1 - \phi_0}{z_1},$$

$$m_2\left(z, \left\{\bar{k}_j\right\}, (N_j)\right) \equiv \frac{\tilde{h}_{31} - h_1 w \phi_0}{z_1}.$$

Solve (A10.9):

$$\bar{k}_1 = \phi\left(z, \left\{\bar{k}_j\right\}, (N_j)\right) \equiv \frac{-m_1 \pm \sqrt{m_1^2 - 4m_2}}{2}. \tag{A10.10}$$

It is confirmed by the simulation that the following solution of (A10.10) has a meaningful solution:

$$\bar{k}_1 = \frac{-m_1 + \sqrt{m_1^2 - 4\,m_2}}{2}.$$

The following procedure shows how to express the variables as functions z, $\left\{\bar{k}_j\right\}$ and (N_j): r and w_{jq} by (A10.2) → $\bar{k}_1$ by (A10.10) → $\bar{N}$ by (A10.6) → $\bar{y}_j$ by (A10.3) → c_j, s_j, $\tilde{T}_{jq}$, and n_j by (10.11) → $\bar{T}_{jq}$ by (10.6) → T_{jq} by (A10.5) → K by (A10.7) → F by (10.2). From this procedure (10.15) and (10.14), it follows:

$$\dot{\bar{k}}_1 = \Omega_0\left(z, \left\{\bar{k}_j\right\}, (N_j)\right) \equiv s_1 - \bar{k}_1, \tag{A10.11}$$

$$\dot{\bar{k}}_j = \Omega_j\left(z, \left\{\bar{k}_j\right\}, (N_j)\right) \equiv s_j - \bar{k}_j, j = 2, \ldots, J,$$

$$\dot{N}_j = \Lambda_j\left(z, \left\{\bar{k}_j\right\}, (N_j)\right) \equiv \left(\frac{\upsilon_j \bar{y}_j}{\tilde{w}_j} - \frac{\bar{\upsilon}_j N_j^{b_j}}{\bar{y}_j^{a_j}}\right) N_j, j = 1, \ldots, J. \tag{A10.12}$$

Take derivatives of (A10.10) with respect to t:

$$\dot{\bar{k}}_1 = \frac{\partial \phi}{\partial z}\dot{z} + \sum_{j=2}^{J} \frac{\partial \phi}{\partial \bar{k}_j}\dot{\bar{k}}_j + \sum_{j=1}^{J} \frac{\partial \phi}{\partial N_j}\dot{N}_j. \tag{A10.13}$$

Insert (A10.12) in (A10.13):

$$\dot{\bar{k}}_1 = \frac{\partial \phi}{\partial z}\dot{z} + \sum_{j=2}^{J} \Omega_j \frac{\partial \phi}{\partial \bar{k}_j} + \sum_{j=1}^{J} \Lambda_j \frac{\partial \phi}{\partial N_j}. \tag{A10.14}$$

Equate the right-hand sides of (A10.11) and (A10.14):

$$\dot{z} = \Omega_1\left(z, \left\{\bar{k}_j\right\}, (N_j)\right)$$

$$\equiv \left(\Omega_0 - \sum_{j=2}^{J} \Omega_j \frac{\partial \phi}{\partial \bar{k}_j} - \sum_{j=1}^{J} \Lambda_j \frac{\partial \phi}{\partial N_j}\right)\left(\frac{\partial \phi}{\partial z}\right)^{-1}. \tag{A10.15}$$

In summary, the lemma is proved.

Chapter 11
Economic Growth with Social Status and Inequality

Since Veblen (1899) published the *Theory of the Leisure Class*, many economists have studied economic consequences of conspicuous consumption and social status. According to Veblen, people are interested in pursuing conspicuous consumption as it signals wealth and social status. Duesenberry (1949) held that people may try to improve social status by imitating the consumption standard of the social or classes above them. The purpose of this study is to introduce social status into a growth economic theory with heterogeneous households. In a recent study by Rege (2008), it is argued that people are concerned with social status because it serves as a signal of non-observable abilities. According to Rege (2008: 240), "By investing in social status a person can thus improve his chance of engaging in a complementary interaction with a high ability person. The idea that status can serve as a signal of abilities is not new and has been captured in several models. It has, for example, been demonstrated that workers can signal their ability to employers by undertaking some seemingly irrelevant but costly activity interpreted as status consumption (Frank 1985) or social culture (Fang 2001) and that people can 'burn money' on fashions to signal abilities in a 'dating game' (Pesendorfer)." Introduction of social status makes traditional growth models more robust in explaining economic growth processes (Cole *et al.* 1992; Konrad 1992; Fershtman *et al.* 1996; Rauscher 1997). This chapter is concerned with social status and growth with inequalities in income and wealth. The way that social status is integrated into our growth model is influenced by the literature that studies the macroeconomic effects of consumers' wealth-induced preferences for social status. In this literature social status is considered as functions of private wealth within neoclassical growth models (Zou 1994, 1995; Bakshi and Chen 1996; Gong and Zou 2001; Chang 2006; Chang and Tsai 2003; Corneo and Jeanne 2001a; Chang *et al.* 2004; Clemens 2004; Fisher and Hof 2005; Chen and Guo 2009, 2011). This chapter deals with social status within an integrated framework of the Walrasian general equilibrium and neoclassical growth theories. The two theories are the core models in the development of formal economic theories in modern times. This chapter develops a model to deal with interdependence

W. Zhang, *A Dynamic Economic Theory of Heterogenous Households*,
https://doi.org/10.1007/978-981-95-8918-0_11

between wealth and income distribution between heterogeneous groups with endogenous social status, based on Zhang (2012b, 2013d). This chapter is based on Zhang (2017d) and is organized as follows: Section 11.1 develops the growth model of wealth and income distribution among heterogeneous households with endogenous social status. Section 11.2 examines dynamic properties of the model and simulates the model with three groups. Section 11.3 analyzes how the system reacts to a rise in group 1's spirit of capitalism. Section 11.4 shows the effects of a rise in the total factor productivity of the capital goods sector on the income and wealth distribution. Section 11.5 demonstrates what happens in the economic dynamics when group 1's social status more strongly affects its propensity to save. Section 11.6 follows the shifts in the motion of the economic system when group 3's population rises. Section 11.7 analyzes the impact of a rise in the depreciation rate of physical capital. Section 11.8 shows the changes in social status and inequality when group 3's human capital rises. Section 11.9 shows what happens to the system when there is a rise in the output elasticity of capital of the capital goods sector. Section 11.10 concludes the chapter. The appendix proving Lemma 11.1.

11.1 The Basic Model with Social Status and Inequality

The economic system consists of capital goods and consumer goods sectors. The capital goods and consumer goods sectors are the same as in the Uzawa two sector model. Services are classified as consumer goods. Capital goods are used as inputs in the two sectors. Capital depreciates at a constant exponential rate δ_k $(0 < \delta_k < 1)$, which is independent of the manner of use. Households own assets of the economy and distribute their incomes to consume and save. Exchanges take place in perfectly competitive markets. Factor markets work well; factors are inelastically supplied, and the available factors are fully utilized at every moment. Savings are undertaken only by households. All earnings of firms are distributed in the form of payments to factors of production, labor, managerial skill and capital ownership. Each group has a fixed population, $\bar{N}_j$, $(j = 1, \ldots, J)$. It should be noted that in the Walrasian general equilibrium theory, $\bar{N}_j = 1$. Let prices be measured in terms of capital goods and the price of the commodity be unity. The wage rate of worker of type j and rate of interest are denoted by $w_j(t)$ and $r(t)$, respectively. Let $p(t)$ denote the price of consumer goods. The total capital stock $K(t)$ is allocated between the two sectors. Let subscript index, i and s stand for capital goods and consumer goods sectors, respectively. I use $N_m(t)$ and $K_m(t)$ to stand for the labor force and capital stocks employed by sector m. The total population $\bar{N}$ and total qualified labor supply N are:

$$\bar{N} = \sum_{j=1}^{J} \bar{N}_j, N = \sum_{j=1}^{J} h_j \bar{N}_j, \tag{11.1}$$

in which h_j is the human capital of group j. The assumption of labor force being fully employed implies

$$N_i(t) + N_s(t) = N. \tag{11.2}$$

Capital goods sector

Let $F_m(t)$ stand for the production function of sector m, $m = i, s$. The production function of capital goods sector is specified as follows:

$$F_i(t) = A_i K_i^{\alpha_i}(t) N_i^{\beta_i}(t), \alpha_i, \beta_i > 0, \alpha_i + \beta_i = 1, \tag{11.3}$$

where A_i, α_i, and β_i are positive parameters. The marginal conditions for the capital goods sector are given by

$$r(t) + \delta_k = \frac{\alpha_i F_i(t)}{K_i(t)}, \; w(t) = \frac{\beta_i F_i(t)}{N_i(t)}, \tag{11.4}$$

where $w(t)$ is the wage rate of per qualified labor input. The wage rate of ethnic group j is

$$w_j(t) = h_j w(t).$$

Consumer goods sector

The production function of consumer goods sector is

$$F_s(t) = A_s K_s^{\alpha_s}(t) N_s^{\beta_s}(t), \alpha_s + \beta_s = 1, \alpha_s, \beta_s > 0, \tag{11.5}$$

where A_s, α_s, and β_s are the technological parameter of the service sector. The marginal conditions are:

$$r(t) + \delta_k = \frac{\alpha_s p(t) F_s(t)}{K_s(t)}, \; w(t) = \frac{\beta_s p(t) F_s(t)}{N_s(t)}. \tag{11.6}$$

Current income and disposable income

Let $\bar{k}_j(t)$ stand for per capita wealth of group j. I have $\bar{k}_j(t) = \bar{K}_j(t)/\bar{N}_j$, where $\bar{K}_j(t)$ is the total wealth held by group j. Per capita current income from the interest payment $r(t)\bar{k}_j(t)$, and the wage payment $h_j w(t)$, is

$$y_j(t) = r(t)\bar{k}_j(t) + h_j w(t).$$

The per capita disposable income is the sum of the current disposable income and the value of wealth. That is

$$\hat{y}_j(t) = y_j(t) + \bar{k}_j(t). \tag{11.7}$$

Description of social status

First, I review a few approaches to social status in formal growth models. Following Zou (1994, 1995) and assuming that each household provides fixed labor supply and maximizing its lifetime utility U, Chen and Guo (2009) introduce social status as a function of wealth as follows:

$$U = \int_0^{\infty} \left[\frac{c^{1-\sigma}(t) - 1}{1 - o} + \beta \frac{k^{1-\sigma}(t) - 1}{1 - o} \right] e^{\rho t} dt,$$

where $c(t)$ and $k(t)$, are, respectively, the household's consumption and capital stock, ρ is the time discount rate, and β measures the degree for the spirit of capitalism. It should be noted that Kurz (1968) first uses both consumption flows and capital stocks as components of utility functions. In another study, Chen and Guo (2011) investigates effects of relative wealth-induced preferences for social status on equilibrium growth in a standard one-sector AK model. The model predicts that there is a positive output-growth effect in response to changes of the strength for social status. The utility is specified as follows:

$$U = \int_0^{\infty} \frac{\left[c(t)(k(t)/K(t))^{\beta} \right]^{1-\sigma} - 1}{1 - \sigma} e^{-\rho t} dt.$$

The household is assumed to derive utilities from the wealth-based social status which is represented by its physical-capital ownership $k(t)$ relative to the economy-wide level of physical-capital stock $K(t)$. They interpret $\beta > 0$ as the degree of the spirit of capitalism. In another research by Corneo and Jeanne (1999), the utility function is specified as

$$U = \int_0^{\infty} [u(c(t)) + v(t)] e^{\rho t} dt,$$

where $v(t)$ is a variable called an individual's social esteem or status utility.

Being inspired by the literature on economic growth with social status, I introduce the following social status function:

$$\omega_j\left(\left(\bar{k}_j(t)\right)\right) = \omega_{j0} + \omega_{jL} \bar{k}_j(t), \tag{11.8}$$

where ω_{j0} and ω_{jL} positive parameters. The specified form implies that social status is positively related to the household's wealth. This is a simplified form of possible social status functions as social status can be dependent on many other variables such as education, human capital, family heritage, human networks with celebrities, relative richness in the same group position, and the like.

Budget and utility function

The disposable income is used for saving and consumption. The representative household from group j would distribute the total available budget between savings $s_j(t)$ and consumer goods $c_j(t)$. The budget constraint is

$$p(t)c_j(t) + s_j(t) = \hat{y}_j(t). \tag{11.9}$$

At each point of time, consumers have two variables to decide. The utility level $U_j(t)$ is dependent on $c_j(t)$ and $s_j(t)$ as follows:

$$U_j(t) = c_j^{\xi_{j0}(\omega_j(t))}(t) s_j^{\lambda_{j0}(\omega_j(t))}(t),\ \xi_{j0}(\omega_j(t)),\ \lambda_{j0}(\omega_j(t)) > 0,$$

where $\xi_{j0}(\omega_j(t))$ is the propensity to consume consumer goods and $\lambda_{j0}(\omega_j(t))$ the propensity to save. The propensity to save and to consume are affected by social status function $\omega_j(t)$. It should be noted that although there are many heterogeneous-households growth models with endogenous wealth accumulation, the heterogeneity in these studies is by the differences in the initial endowments of wealth among different types of households rather than in preferences. Different households are essentially homogeneous in the sense that all the households have the same preference utility function in the approach.

Social status and propensities to save and to consume

Rather than using capital stock as a decision variable, I consider that it is through affecting the propensities to consume and to save that social status affects growth and inequality. It is assumed that the propensities to consume and to save are related to social status in the following way:

$$\xi_{j0}(\omega_j(t)) = \bar{\xi}_{j0} + \tilde{\xi}_{j0}\omega_j(t),\ \lambda_{j0}(\omega_j(t)) = \bar{\lambda}_{j0} + \tilde{\lambda}_{j0}\omega_j(t), \tag{11.10}$$

where $\bar{\xi}_{j0}$ and $\bar{\lambda}_{j0}$ are positive parameters, and $\tilde{\xi}_{j0}$ and $\tilde{\lambda}_{j0}$ are parameters which may be either positive, zero, or negative. The propensity to consume may be enhanced by social status, for instance, through the so-called conspicuous consumption. The propensity to save is influenced by social status as more wealth tends to enhance social status. The so-called spirit of capitalism affects the propensity to save. Although social status may interact with propensities through so many channels, this study accepts the above linear form for convenience of analysis.

Optimal household behavior

Maximizing the utility subject to (11.9) yields

$$p(t)c_j(t) = \xi_j\left(\left(\bar{k}_j(t)\right)\right)\hat{y}_j(t),\ s_j(t) = \lambda_j\left(\left(\bar{k}_j(t)\right)\right)\hat{y}_j(t), \tag{11.11}$$

where

$$\begin{aligned} \xi_j\left(\left(\bar{k}_j(t)\right)\right) &\equiv \rho_j\left(\left(\bar{k}_j(t)\right)\right)\xi_{j0}\left(\left(\bar{k}_j(t)\right)\right), \\ \lambda_j\left(\left(\bar{k}_j(t)\right)\right) &\equiv \rho_j\left(\left(\bar{k}_j(t)\right)\right)\lambda_{j0}\left(\left(\bar{k}_j(t)\right)\right), \\ \rho_j\left(\left(\bar{k}_j(t)\right)\right) &\equiv \frac{1}{\xi_{j0}\left(\left(\bar{k}_j(t)\right)\right)+\lambda_{j0}\left(\left(\bar{k}_j(t)\right)\right)}. \end{aligned}$$

Wealth accumulation
According to the definition of $s_j(t)$, the change in the household's wealth is given by

$$\dot{\bar{k}}_j(t) = s_j(t) - \bar{k}_j(t). \tag{11.12}$$

This equation simply states that the change in wealth is equal to saving minus dissaving.

Demand and supply of the two sectors
The demand and supply equilibrium for the consumer goods sector is

$$\sum_{j=1}^{J} c_j(t)\bar{N}_j = F_s(t). \tag{11.13}$$

As output of the capital goods sector is equal to the depreciation of capital stock and the net savings, it follows:

$$S(t) - K(t) + \delta_k K(t) = F_i(t), \tag{11.14}$$

where

$$S(t) \equiv \sum_{j=1}^{J} s_j(t)\bar{N}_j,\ K(t) = \sum_{j=1}^{J} \bar{k}_j(t)\bar{N}_j.$$

Capital being fully utilized
Total capital stock $K(t)$ is allocated to the two sectors:

$$K_i(t) + K_s(t) = K(t). \tag{11.15}$$

The model is complete. The model is structurally general in the sense that some well-known models in economics can be considered as its special cases. For instance, if the population is homogeneous, the model is structurally similar to the neoclassical growth model by Solow (1956) and Uzawa (1961). It is structurally similar to the Walrasian model if the wealth is fixed and depreciation is neglected. The new aspect of economic growth in this study is the interaction between social status and wealth accumulation (and other variables).

11.2 The Dynamics and Its Properties

As the dynamic system consists of any (finite) number of households, it should be nonlinear and highly dimensional with wealth accumulation. As it is difficult to get explicitly analytical properties of the nonlinear dynamic system, I conduct computer simulation to follow the motion of the dynamic system. The following lemma shows that the dimension of the dynamical system is the same as the number of groups. I also provide a computational procedure for calculating all the variables at any point in time. First, introduce a new variable $z(t)$:

$$z(t) \equiv \frac{r(t) + \delta_k}{w_j(t)/h_j}.$$

Lemma 11.1
The motion of the economic system is determined by J differential equations with $z(t)$ and $\{\bar{k}_j(t)\} \equiv (\bar{k}_2(t), \cdots, \bar{k}_J(t))$ as the variables:

$$\begin{aligned} \dot{z}(t) &= \Lambda_1\big(z(t), \{\bar{k}_j(t)\}\big), \\ \dot{\bar{k}}_j(t) &= \Lambda_j\big(z(t), \{\bar{k}_j(t)\}\big), j = 2, \ldots, J, \end{aligned} \tag{11.16}$$

in which $\Lambda_j(t)$ are unique functions of $z(t)$and $\{\bar{k}_j(t)\}$ defined in the Appendix. At any point in time the other variables are unique functions of $z(t)$and $(\bar{k}_j(t))$ determined by the following procedure: $r(t)$ and $w_j(t)$ by (A11.3) $\rightarrow$ $\bar{k}_1(t)$ by (A11.14) $\rightarrow$ $\xi_j(t)$ by (A11.13) $\rightarrow$ $N_s(t)$ by (A11.7)$\rightarrow$$N_i(t)$ by (A11.8) $\rightarrow$ $w(t) = w_1(t)/h_1$ $\rightarrow$ $\hat{y}_j(t)$ by (A11.5) $\rightarrow$ $K_s(t)$ and $K_i(t)$ by (A11.1) $\rightarrow$ $F_i(t)$ and $F_s(t)$ by the definitions $\rightarrow$ $p(t)$ by (A11.4) $\rightarrow$ $c_j(t)$ and $s_j(t)$ by (11.13) $\rightarrow$ $K(t) = K_i(t) + K_s(t)$.

It should be noted that as the expressions are: too complicated, it is difficult to provide a clear and simple analytical interpretation of the result. The lemma gives a computational procedure for following the motion of the economic system with any number of households. It is well known that calibration of general equilibrium involves solving high-dimensional nonlinear equations. As it is difficult to get an explicit analytical solution, the model is simulated. It should be noted that the procedure in the lemma is valid for any functional forms of

$$\xi_{0j}\big((\omega_j(t))\big) \text{ and } \lambda_{0j}\big((\omega_j(t))\big)$$

(if they satisfy mathematical properties such as existence of first derivatives).

The model is simulated for the three-group economy. The parameter values are as follows:

$$A_i = 1.3, A_s = 1, \alpha_i = 0.34, \alpha_s = 0.3, \delta_k = 0.05,$$

$$\begin{pmatrix} \bar{N}_1 \\ \bar{N}_2 \\ \bar{N}_3 \end{pmatrix} = \begin{pmatrix} 10 \\ 30 \\ 60 \end{pmatrix}, \begin{pmatrix} h_1 \\ h_2 \\ h_3 \end{pmatrix} = \begin{pmatrix} 4 \\ 2 \\ 1 \end{pmatrix}, \begin{pmatrix} \omega_{10} \\ \omega_{20} \\ \omega_{30} \end{pmatrix} = \begin{pmatrix} 0.01 \\ 0.01 \\ 0.01 \end{pmatrix}, \begin{pmatrix} \omega_{1L} \\ \omega_{2L} \\ \omega_{3L} \end{pmatrix} = \begin{pmatrix} 0.01 \\ 0.008 \\ 0.005 \end{pmatrix},$$

$$\begin{pmatrix} \bar{\lambda}_{10} \\ \bar{\lambda}_{20} \\ \vec{\lambda}_{30} \end{pmatrix} = \begin{pmatrix} 0.8 \\ 0.75 \\ 0.7 \end{pmatrix}, \begin{pmatrix} \tilde{\lambda}_{10} \\ \tilde{\lambda}_{20} \\ \tilde{\lambda}_{30} \end{pmatrix} = \begin{pmatrix} 0.1 \\ 0.1 \\ 0.1 \end{pmatrix}, \begin{pmatrix} \tilde{\xi}_{10} \\ \tilde{\xi}_{20} \\ \tilde{\xi}_{30} \end{pmatrix} = \begin{pmatrix} 0.12 \\ 0.18 \\ 0.2 \end{pmatrix},$$

$$\begin{pmatrix} \bar{\xi}_{10} \\ \bar{\xi}_{20} \\ \bar{\xi}_{30} \end{pmatrix} = \begin{pmatrix} 0.05 \\ 0.05 \\ 0.05 \end{pmatrix} \tag{11.17}$$

The population of group 3 is largest, while the population of group 2 is the next. The capital goods and consumer goods sector's total productivities are, respectively, 1.3 and 1. The depreciation rate of physical capital is specified at 0.05. In the literature of economic growth physical depreciation rates are often fixed near 0.05. In their empirical studies Nadiri and Prucha (1993) estimate the depreciation rate of physical capital 0.059. There are different empirical results in estimation of depreciation rates of physical capital and knowledge (Nadiri and Prucha 1993; Fraumeni 1997; Hall 2007). The parameter values related to reference changes relatively small. The initial conditions are: as follows:

$$z(0) = 0.06, \bar{k}_2(0) = 10, \bar{k}_3(0) = 4,$$

The motion of the variables is plotted in Fig. 11.1. In the figure, the national income is

$$Y(t) = F_i(t) + p(t) F_s(t).$$

Due to the fixed positions of the initial state, the national output and wealth/capital fall over time. The output level of the capital goods sector rises, and the output level of the consumer goods sector fall slightly overtime. The price of consumer goods decreases. The rate of interest falls in association with rising wage rates. Group 1'*s* per capita wealth, per capita consumption, social status and propensity to save are all reduced. The other two groups' per capita wealth levels, per capita consumption levels, social status and propensities to save are all enhanced. The wealth inequalities between group 1 and other two groups are reduced over time.

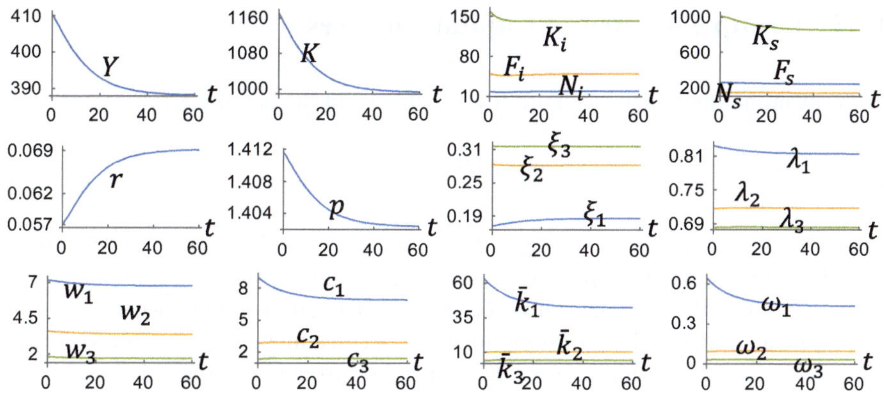

Fig. 11.1 The motion of the economic system

It is straightforward to confirm that all the variables become stationary in the long term. This implies the existence of an equilibrium point. I also simulate the model with other initial conditions which lead to the same equilibrium point. The existence of equilibrium is guaranteed with the specified parameter values. The equilibrium values in (11.18) are as follows:

$$Y = 388.1, \bar{K}_1 = 423.6, \bar{K}_2 = 312.3, \bar{K}_3 = 257.9, r = 0.069, p = 1.40,$$

$$w_1 = 6.74, w_2 = 3.37, w_3 = 1.69, F_i = 49.69, F_s = 241.3, N_i = 19.46,$$

$$N_s = 140.54, K_i = 141.8, K_s = 852.1, \omega_1 = 0.43, \omega_2 = 0.09,$$

$$\omega_3 = 0.03, \lambda_1 = 0.81, \lambda_2 = 0.72, \lambda_3 = 0.68, \xi_1 = 0.19, \xi_2 = 0.28,$$

$$\xi_3 = 0.32, \bar{k}_1 = 42.36, \bar{k}_2 = 10.41, \bar{k}_3 = 4.30, c_1 = 6.90, c_2 = 2.92,$$

$$c_3 = 1.41. \tag{11.18}$$

It is straightforward to calculate the three eigenvalues as follows:

$$\{-0.24, -0.18, -0.09\}.$$

The eigenvalues are real and negative. The equilibrium is locally stable. This guarantees the validity of exercising comparative dynamic analysis with the same initial conditions.

11.3 Group 1's Spirit of Capitalism Rises

I now examine the effects of the following change in the parameter:

$$\omega_{1L} : 0.01 \Rightarrow 0.012.$$

Group 1's spirit of capitalism rises. The simulation result is plotted in Fig. 11.2. The change has a strong impact on the national economy. As group 1 strengthens its spirit of capitalism, its social status is enhanced. The group's propensity to save and wealth are augmented. The consumption level of consumer goods is reduced initially and is augmented in the long term. The other two groups' wealth and consumption levels are increased. The price of consumer goods is increased. The rate of interest is reduced in tandem with rising wage rates. The national output and wealth are increased. Some of the labor force is shifted from the consumer goods sector to the capital goods sector. The output levels and capital input of the two sectors are increased. The inequality between group 1 and the other two groups are enlarged. This confirms that if the rich strengthen its spirit of capitalism, the inequality between the rich and the poor is enlarged. It should be noted that in their research on interaction between pecuniary emulation and inequality, Corneo and Jeanne (1999, 1667) conclude: "On the one hand, the presence of pecuniary emulation tends to underscore the conventional view that equality has a positive impact on growth. A more equal distribution of wealth, by reducing the distance between the wealth levels of classes, makes pecuniary emulation easier for the poor. Hence, equality strengthens the incentive to accumulate for status reasons and is beneficial for economic growth. This mechanism has already been put forward by Cole *et al.* (1992) and Fershtman *et al.* (1996) and is thoroughly investigated in our companion paper Corneo and Jeanne (1997a)." It is straightforward to show that in our model if ω_{3L} is increased, then economic growth is encouraged and inequality between group 1 and group 3 is reduced.

11.4 The Total Productivity of the Capital Goods Sector Rises

As the economy improves its technology, its productivity is enhanced. It is interesting to examine how technological changes affect the relationship between growth, social status, and inequality. The total productivity of the capital goods sector increases as follows:

$$A_i : 1.3 \Rightarrow 1.32.$$

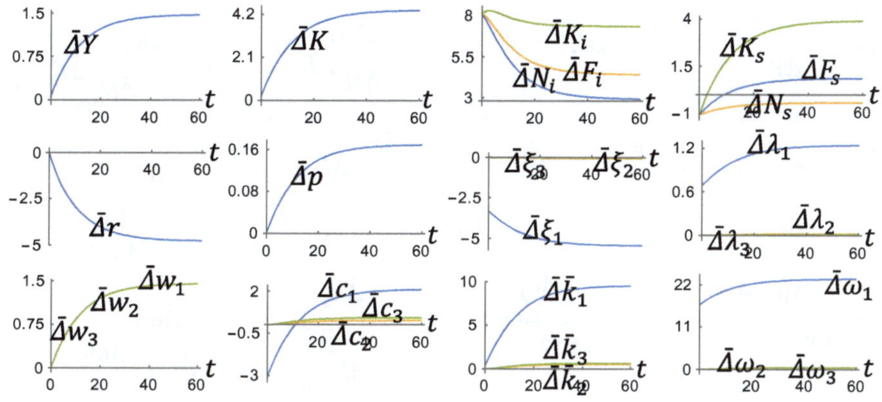

Fig. 11.2 Group 1's spirit of capitalism rises

The simulation result is plotted in Fig. 11.3. It is reasonable to expect that the technological improvement increases the national output and national wealth. As the technological change takes place in the capital goods sector, the price of consumer goods is enhanced. The rate of interest rises in the short term and falls in long term. The wage rates of all the groups increase. Although each group's social status is enhanced, group 1'*s* is enhanced more than group 2'*s* and group 2'*s* social status is enhanced more than group 3'*s* social status. As wealth is a linear function of social status, the change rate in wealth is the same as the change rate in social status. The consumption levels of the three groups' representative households fall initially and rise in the long term. The technological change enlarges the gaps in social status and wealth.

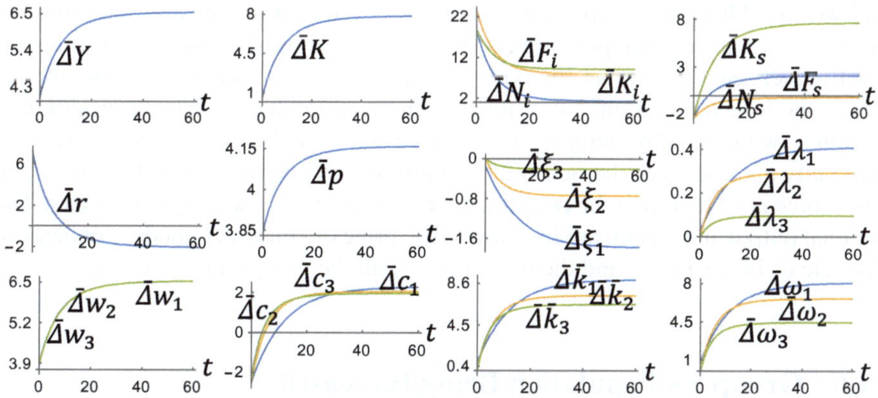

Fig. 11.3 The total productivity of the capital goods sector being enhanced

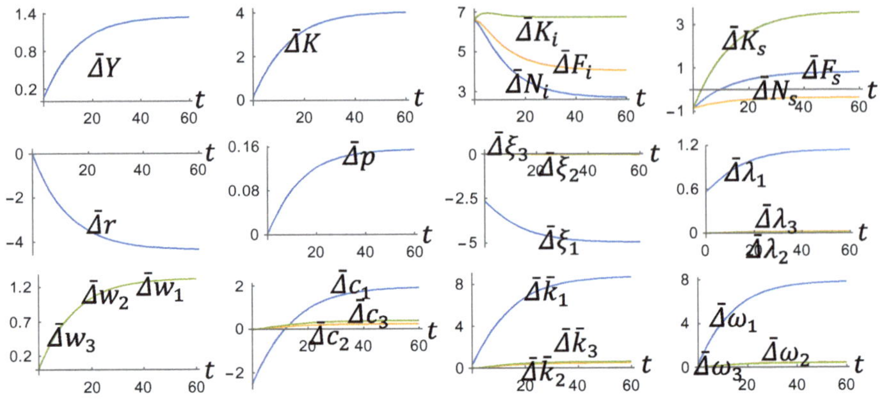

Fig. 11.4 Group 1's social status more strongly affecting its propensity to save

11.5 Group 1's Social Status More Strongly Affecting Its Propensity to Save

Group 1's propensity to save to be more strongly affected by its social status as follows:

$$\tilde{\lambda}_{10} : 0.1 \Rightarrow 0.12.$$

The simulation result is plotted in Fig. 11.4. The group's propensity to save is increased and the other two groups' preferences are slightly affected. Group 1's social status and wealth are increased more than the other two groups' social status and wealth. Although group 1's consumption is reduced in the short term and the other two groups' consumption levels are increased slightly, group 1's consumption level is increased more than the other two groups' in the long term. This implies that in the long term, group 1 consumes even more and has even more wealth than the other two groups by weighing more social status on the propensity to save. The inequality gaps between the rich and the other two groups are enlarged. Some of the labor force is shifted from the consumer goods sector to the capital goods sector. The national output and wealth are increased. The price of consumer goods is enhanced. The rate of interest falls, and the wage rates of all the groups are increased.

11.6 Group 3's Population Being Increased

I now examine what happens to the economic system when group 3's population increases as follows:

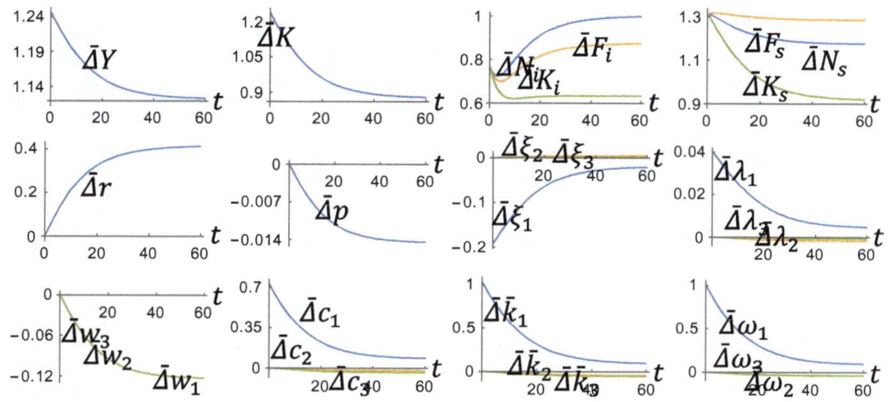

Fig. 11.5 Group 3's population being increased

$$N_3 : 60 \Rightarrow 62.$$

The simulation result is plotted in Fig. 11.5. As the population increases, it is reasonable to expect that the national output and national wealth increase. The output levels and two-factor input of the two sectors are augmented. The price of consumer goods is slightly affected. The rate of interest rises, and the wage rates of all the groups decrease. Group 1's social status, propensity to save, consumption level and wealth are all increased, while the other two groups' social status, propensity to save, consumption level and wealth are all slightly reduced. Group 3's population expansion enlarges gaps in social status and wealth between group 1 and the other two groups.

11.7 The Depreciation Rate of Physical Capital Rises

The impact of depreciations on economic growth is emphasized in literature of growth (Nadiri and Prucha 1993). I now examine what happens in the economic system when the depreciation rate rises as follows:

$$\delta_k : 0.05 \Rightarrow 0.055.$$

The simulation result is plotted in Fig. 11.6. As physical capital depreciates faster, the national output and wealth are reduced. The output level and two-factor input of the capital goods sector are augmented. The output level and two-factor input of the consumer goods sector are reduced. The price of consumer goods, the rate of interest falls, and the wage rates of all the groups are all reduced. All the groups' social status, propensities to save, consumption levels and wealth levels are all reduced. Group 1's

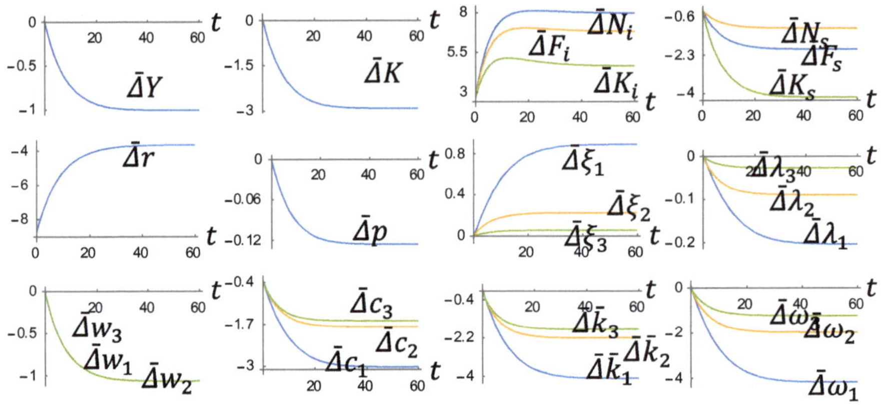

Fig. 11.6 The depreciation rate of physical capital rises

social status, propensities to save, consumption levels and wealth levels are reduced more than group 2's; group 2's propensities to save, consumption levels and wealth levels are reduced more than group 3's. This implies that faster capital depreciation reduces the inequalities.

11.8 Group 3's Human Capital Rises

I now examine what happens to the economic system when group 3's human capital is enhanced as follows:

$$h_3 : 1 \Rightarrow 1.5.$$

The simulation result is plotted in Fig. 11.7. The national output and national wealth are augmented. The output levels and two-factor input of the two sectors are augmented. The price of consumer goods is slightly affected. The rate of interest is reduced initially and enhanced in the long term. Group 3's wage rises and the other two groups' wage rates are slightly affected. Group 3's and group 1's social status, propensity to save, consumption level and wealth are all increased, while group 2's social status, propensity to save, consumption level and wealth are all slightly changed. The inequalities between group 1 and group 3 are reduced and the inequalities between group 2 and group 1 are enlarged.

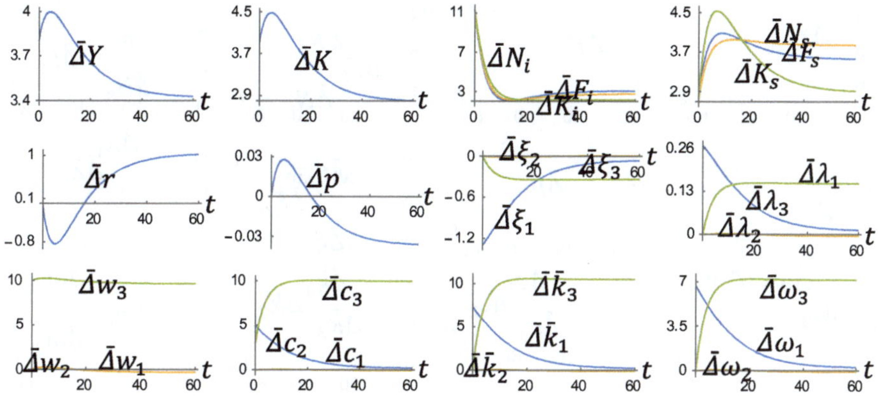

Fig. 11.7 Group 3's human capital rises

11.9 A Rise in the Output Elasticity of Capital of the Capital Goods Sector

I will now examine the following rise in the output elasticity of capital of the capital goods sector:

$$\alpha_i : 0.34 \Rightarrow 0.35.$$

A rise in the parameter implies that the share of capital contribution to the output is increased. The simulation result is plotted in Fig. 11.8. The national output and national wealth are augmented. The output levels and capital input of the two sectors are augmented. Initially, some of the labor force is shifted from the consumer goods sector to the capital goods sector; in the long term, some of the labor force is shifted from the capital goods sector to the consumer goods sector. In the long term, all the groups' social status, propensities to save, consumption levels, and wealth levels are increased. Figure 11.8 shows that these variables are increased differently. In the long term, the inequalities between group 1 and the other two groups are enlarged.

11.10 Concluding Remarks

This chapter dealt with interactions between social status, economic growth, and income and wealth distribution in an economic growth model of heterogeneous households with economic structure. The model emphasized the role of social status in economic structural change and wealth and income distribution. It is influenced by the ideas related to economic growth and social status in the literature of economic growth and is developed within the framework of an integrated Walrasian general

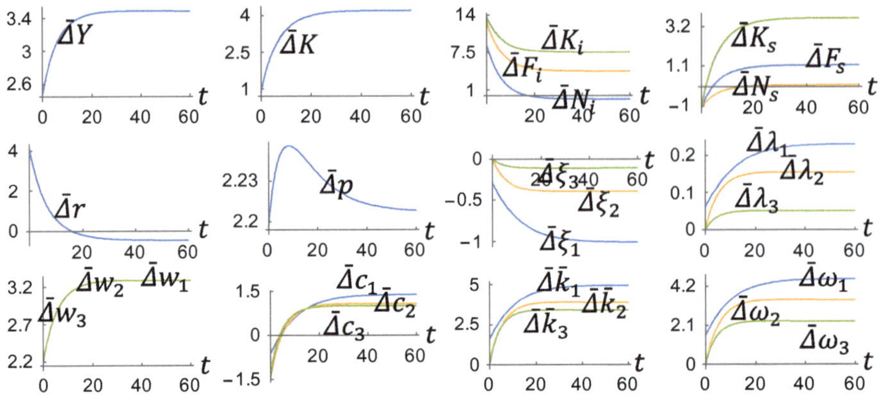

Fig. 11.8 A rise in the output elasticity of capital of the capital goods sector

equilibrium theory and neoclassical growth theory. The economic system consists of one capital goods sector, one consumer goods sector, and any number (of types) of households. The motion is described by a set of differential equations. This chapter examines how changes in different parameters affect inequalities and economic growth. The relations between inequality and economic growth are determined by many factors. They are expectably ambiguous or development-dependent in the sense that one may observe positive or negative relations according to the parameter value combinations and state of economic development. As the analytical framework is general, it is possible to generalize and extend the model in different aspects. One important direction is to introduce taxation into the general dynamic equilibrium model with social status, for instance, along the directions in the literature (Ng 1987; Ireland 1994, 1998; Bagwell and Bernheim 1996; Corneo and Jeanne 1997b; Rege 2008).

Appendix: Proving Lemma 11.1

By (11.4) and (11.6), it follows:

$$z \equiv \frac{r + \delta_k}{w} = \frac{N_i}{\bar{\beta}_i K_i} = \frac{N_s}{\bar{\beta}_s K_s}, \tag{A11.1}$$

where $\bar{\beta}_j \equiv \beta_m / \alpha_m$. From (A11.1) and (11.15):

$$\bar{\beta}_i K_i + \bar{\beta}_s K_s = \frac{N}{z}. \tag{A11.2}$$

Insert (A11.1) in (11.4):

$$r = \alpha_r z^{\beta_i} - \delta_k, \; w_j = \alpha_w h_j z^{-\alpha_i}, \tag{A11.3}$$

where

$$\alpha_r = \alpha_i A_i \bar{\beta}_i^{\beta_i}, \; \alpha_w = \beta_i A_i \bar{\beta}_i^{-\alpha_i}.$$

Hence, the rate of interest and the wage rates are determined as functions of z. From (11.5) and (11.6), I have

$$p = \frac{\bar{\beta}_s^{\alpha_s} z^{\alpha_s} w}{\beta_s A_s}, \tag{A11.4}$$

where $w = w_1/h_1$. From (A11.3) and the definitions of $\hat{y}_j$, I have

$$\hat{y}_j = (1 + r)\bar{k}_j + h_j w. \tag{A11.5}$$

Insert $pc_j = \xi_j \hat{y}_j$ in (11.13):

$$\sum_{j=1}^{J} \xi_j \bar{N}_j \hat{y}_j = pF_s. \tag{A11.6}$$

Substituting (A11.5) in (A11.6) yields

$$N_s = \sum_{j=1}^{J} \tilde{g}_j \bar{k}_j + \tilde{g}, \tag{A11.7}$$

where $pF_s = wN_s/\beta_s$ is applied and

$$\tilde{g}_j \equiv \beta_s \xi_j W \bar{N}_j, \; \tilde{g} \equiv \beta_s \sum_{j=1}^{J} h_j \xi_j \bar{N}_j, \; W \equiv \frac{1 + r}{w}.$$

From (11.2) and (A11.7),

$$N_i = N - N_s, \tag{A11.8}$$

From (A11.1) and (11.15),

$$\frac{N_i}{\bar{\beta}_i} + \frac{N_s}{\bar{\beta}_s} = zK. \tag{A11.9}$$

Insert (A11.8) in (A11.9):

$$\frac{\bar{\beta}N}{\bar{\beta}_i} + N_s = \bar{\beta}zK, \tag{A11.10}$$

where

$$\bar{\beta} \equiv \left(\frac{1}{\bar{\beta}_s} - \frac{1}{\bar{\beta}_i}\right)^{-1}.$$

From (A11.10) and

$$\sum_{j=1}^{J} \left(h_j + W\bar{k}_j\right)\bar{N}_j \xi_j = \frac{\bar{\beta}zK}{\beta_s} - \frac{\bar{\beta}N}{\beta_s \bar{\beta}_i}. \tag{A11.11}$$

Insert $K = \sum_{j=1}^{J} \bar{k}_j \bar{N}_j$ in (A11.11):

$$\left(h_1 + W\bar{k}_1\right)\xi_1 - W_0 \bar{k}_1 = \bar{W}, \tag{A11.12}$$

where

$$W_0(z) \equiv \frac{\bar{\beta}z}{\beta_s}, \ \bar{W}\left(z, \left\{\bar{k}_j\right\}\right)$$
$$\equiv \left(W_0 \sum_{j=2}^{J} \bar{k}_j \bar{N}_j - \sum_{j=2}^{J} \left(h_j + W\bar{k}_j\right)\bar{N}_j \xi_j - \frac{\bar{\beta}N}{\beta_s \bar{\beta}_i}\right)\frac{1}{\bar{N}_1}.$$

From the definitions of ξ_j, (11.10) and (11.11):

$$\xi_j = \frac{\bar{\omega}_{j0} + \bar{k}_j}{\tilde{\omega}_{j0} + \hat{\omega}_{j0}\bar{k}_j}, \tag{A11.13}$$

where

$$\bar{\omega}_{j0} \equiv \frac{\bar{\xi}_{j0} + \tilde{\xi}_{j0}\omega_{j0}}{\tilde{\xi}_{j0}\omega_{jL}}, \ \tilde{\omega}_{j0} \equiv \frac{\bar{\xi}_{j0} + \bar{\lambda}_{j0} + \left(\tilde{\xi}_{j0} + \tilde{\lambda}_{j0}\right)\omega_{j0}}{\tilde{\xi}_{j0}\omega_{jL}}, \ \hat{\omega}_{j0} \equiv \frac{\tilde{\xi}_{j0} + \tilde{\lambda}_{j0}}{\tilde{\xi}_{j0}}.$$

Insert (A11.13) for the case of $j = 1$ in (A11.12):

$$\bar{k}_1^2 + f\bar{k}_1 + f_0 = 0, \tag{A11.14}$$

where

$$f\left(z, \left\{\bar{k}_j\right\}\right) \equiv \frac{\bar{\omega}_{10} W + h_1 - \widetilde{\omega}_{10} W_0 - \hat{\omega}_{10} \bar{W}}{W - \hat{\omega}_{10} W_0},$$

$$f_0\left(z, \left\{\bar{k}_j\right\}\right) \equiv \frac{\bar{\omega}_{10} h_1 - \bar{W} \widetilde{\omega}_{10}}{W - \hat{\omega}_{10} W_0}.$$

Solve (A11.14)

$$\bar{k}_1 = \varphi\left(z, \left\{\bar{k}_j\right\}\right) = -\frac{f}{2} \pm \sqrt{\frac{f^2}{4} - f_0}. \quad \text{(A11.15)}$$

The problem has two solutions. I will determine meaningful solutions by simulation. In the simulation there is a unique meaningful solution:

$$\bar{k}_1 = \varphi\left(z, \left\{\bar{k}_j\right\}\right) = -\frac{f}{2} + \sqrt{\frac{f^2}{4} - f_0}.$$

It is straightforward to confirm that all the variables can be expressed as functions of z and $\left\{\bar{k}_j\right\}$ by the following procedure: r and w_j by (A11.3) $\rightarrow \bar{k}_1$ by (A11.14) $\rightarrow$ ξ_j by (A11.13) $\rightarrow N_s$ by (A11.7)$\rightarrow N_i$ by (A11.8)$\rightarrow w = w_1/h_1 \rightarrow \hat{y}_j$ by (A11.5) $\rightarrow K_s$, and K_i by (A11.1) $\rightarrow F_i$ and F_s by the definitions $\rightarrow p$ by (A11.4) $\rightarrow c_j$ and s_j by (11.13) $\rightarrow K = K_i + K_s$. From this procedure and (11.12), I have

$$\dot{\bar{k}}_1 = \Lambda_0\left(z, \left\{\bar{k}_j\right\}\right) \equiv \lambda_1 \hat{y}_1 - \bar{k}_1, \quad \text{(A11.16)}$$

$$\dot{\bar{k}}_j = \Lambda_j\left(z, \left\{\bar{k}_j\right\}\right) \equiv \lambda_j \hat{y}_j - \bar{k}_j, j = 2, \ldots, J. \quad \text{(A11.17)}$$

Taking derivatives of eq. (A11.14) with respect to t implies

$$\dot{\bar{k}}_1 = \frac{\partial \varphi}{\partial z} \dot{z} + \sum_{j=2}^{J} \Lambda_j \frac{\partial \varphi}{\partial \bar{k}_j}, \quad \text{(A11.18)}$$

where (A11.16) is applied. Equal (A11.17) and (A11.15):

$$\dot{z} = \left(\Lambda_0 - \sum_{j=2}^{J} \Lambda_j \frac{\partial \varphi}{\partial \bar{k}_j}\right) \left(\frac{\partial \varphi}{\partial z}\right)^{-1}. \quad \text{(A11.19)}$$

In summary, I proved the lemma.

Chapter 12
Income and Wealth Distribution in a Monetary Growth Model

> When I was young, I thought that money was the most important thing in life; now that I am old, I know it is.
>
> Oscar Wilde

Money was dominantly assumed neutral in the long term in neoclassical growth theory. Common sense tells us that this cannot be true in general as it is obvious that the fool uses money differently from the wise. It is still too early to fully model monetary processes of different agents. This chapter studies the relationship between money and economic growth still in neoclassical growth framework. From empirical as well as theoretical literatures on money and growth, it is known that the relationships are ambiguous in the sense that they can be positive, independent, negative, or situation-dependent, depending on countries or periods within the same country or analytical frameworks. This chapter readdresses issues related to the interdependence between economic growth and money. But different from the most formal models in the literature of money and growth, I study relationship between money and distribution between heterogeneous households. If money is not neutral, inflation policy affects economic growth. As households have various preferences for consumption and saving and varied levels of human capital, it is reasonable to expect that inflation policy should have different effects on income and wealth distribution between heterogenous groups. This chapter is an integration of the core ideas in Walrasian general equilibrium theory, neoclassical growth theory, and monetary growth theory.

In economic theory, modeling money involves intriguing and important questions. As far as this chapter is concerned, our model is much influenced by Tobin's seminal contribution in 1965 to growth with capital and money. Tobin (1965) introduces money into the Solow model which uses capital accumulation as the economic mechanism of growth (with exogenous technological change and exogeneous population). Withing similarly within an isolated economy like in the Solow model, Tobin introduces "outside money", which is the part of part of money stock issued by the government. Money is competitive with real capital in the portfolios of agents. As

W. Zhang, *A Dynamic Economic Theory of Heterogenous Households*,
https://doi.org/10.1007/978-981-95-8918-0_12

in the Solow model, household behavior is not based on utility-maximization. After Tobin published his important model, economists tried to deal with monetary growth problems with microeconomic foundation. One of these approaches is the so-called money in the utility (MIU) function approach. The earlier works are by Patinkin (1965), Sidrauski (1967), and Friedman (1969). The approach assumes that people hold money as it yields some services. Another reason is that it is an easy way to enter real balances directly into the utility function. There is an extensive literature on the approach and empirical studies on monetary issues (Wang and Yip 1992; Zhang 2012c; Akinsola 2017; Breuer et al. 2018). This study applies Zhang's MIU approach to determining money holdings by heterogenous households (Zhang 2013e). Like the Tobin model, this study is still based on neoclassical growth model. Rather than a single household, this study classifies the population into different types of households. The model in this chapter is Walrasian as the perfect competitive economy has a market equilibrium due to interdependence between profit-maximizing firms and utility-maximizing households for given levels of wealth money. It should be noted that this chapter is influenced by Zhang's two models (Zhang 2013e, 2013f). This chapter is based on Zhang (2020a) and is organized as follows. Section 12.1 develops the monetary growth model with endogenous wealth and capital with income and wealth distribution between heterogeneous groups. Section 12.2 analyzes properties of the model and identifies the existence of an equilibrium point. Section 12.3 shows the impact of a rise in the inflation policy on the economic equilibrium structure. Section 12.4 shows how a rise in group 1's propensity to hold money changes the economic equilibrium. Section 12.5 analyzes the impact of a rise in group 3's human capital. Section 12.6 shows how a rise in group 3's population changes each group's economic conditions in the long term. Section 12.7 studies the effects of a rise household 3's propensity to save. Section 12.8 analyzes the long-run economic structural change when group 3's propensity to use leisure time is increased. Section 12.9 analyzes the impact of a rise in the consumer good sector's total factor productivity. Section 12.10 concludes the chapter. The appendix proves Lemma 12.1.

12.1 The Monetary Growth Model with Multiple Groups

This section builds a Walrasian monetary general equilibrium growth model of endogenous wealth accumulation. The economy produces two goods: capital goods and consumer goods, correspondingly by capital good sector and consumer goods sector. I follow the Solow-Uzawa growth model in describing production sectors. The core model in the neoclassical growth theory was the Solow one-sector growth model (Takayama, 1985; Galor, 1992; Jensen et al., 2001; Jensen, 2003). There are two inputs—labor and capital. Capital depreciates at a constant exponential rate, δ_k. Let $r(t)$ represent the rate of interest. The households hold wealth and money and receive income from wages, and interest payments of wealth. All markets are perfectly competitive. Inputs are freely mobile between the two sectors. The population is classified into J groups, each group with fixed population, $\overline{N}_j, j = 1, \ldots, J$.

Group j distributes the available time T_0 between leisure $\overline{T}_j(t)$ and work $T_j(t)$. Let $N(t)$ for the flow of labor services used for production. I have

$$N(t) = \sum_{j=1}^{J} h_j T_j(t) \overline{N}_j, \tag{12.1}$$

where h_j are the levels of human capital of group j.

Capital Goods Sector

The capital good sector uses capital and labor as inputs. Subscript indexes, i and s, denote respectively the capital good and consumer good sectors. Let $K_m(t)$ and $N_m(t)$ represent the capital stock and labor force used by sector m, $m = i, s$, at time t. The output level of sector m is given by $F_m(t)$. The capital good sector's production function is taken on the Cobb-Douglas form:

$$F_i(t) = A_i K_i^{\alpha_i}(t) N_i^{\beta_i}(t), \alpha_i, \beta_i > 0, \alpha_i + \beta_i = 1, \tag{12.2}$$

where A_i, α_i, and β_i are parameters. All the markets are competitive. Input factors are paid according to their marginal products. Firms are faced with the wage rate $w(t)$ and the real rate of interest $r(t)$ determined in markets. The marginal conditions are

$$r(t) + \delta_k = \frac{\alpha_i F_i(t)}{K_i(t)}, w(t) = \frac{\beta_i F_i(t)}{N_i(t)}. \tag{12.3}$$

The wage rate of group j is

$$w_j(t) = h_j w(t). \tag{12.4}$$

Consumer Goods Sector

The production function is taken on the Cobb-Douglas form as

$$F_s(t) = A_s K_s^{\alpha_s}(t) N_s^{\beta_s}(t), \alpha_s, \beta_s > 0, \alpha_s + \beta_s = 1, \tag{12.5}$$

where A_s, α_s, and β_s are parameters. I use $p_s(t)$ to stand for the price of consumer good. The marginal conditions imply

$$r(t) + \delta_k = \frac{\alpha_s p_s(t) F_s(t)}{K_s(t)}, w(t) = \frac{\beta_s p_s(t) F_s(t)}{N_s(t)}. \tag{12.6}$$

Monetary Policy

Money is introduced by assuming that a central bank distributes at no cost to the population a per capita amount of fiat money, $M(t) > 0$. The scheme with which the money stock changes over time is known to all agents. The constant net growth rate of money stock is denoted by μ. It follows:

$$\dot{M}(t) = \mu M(t), \mu > 0. \tag{12.7}$$

Let $m(t)$ denote the real value of money per capita measured in units of the good output:

$$m(t) = \frac{M(t)}{P(t)}, \tag{12.8}$$

where $P(t)$ is the price of money. The government expenditure per household $\tau(t)$ is as follows:

$$\tau(t) = \frac{\dot{M}(t)}{P(t)} = \frac{\mu M(t)}{P(t)} = \mu m(t). \tag{12.9}$$

Each household gets $\mu m(t)$ units of paper money from the government. Let $m_j(t)$ denote the real money held by group j. As the money is held by households, it follows:

$$\sum_{j=1}^{J} m_j(t)\overline{N}_j = m(t)\overline{N}, \tag{12.10}$$

where

$$\overline{N} \equiv \sum_{j=1}^{J} \overline{N}_j.$$

Current Income and Disposable Income

Let $\pi(t)$ and $\bar{k}_j(t)$ respectively denote the inflation rate and wealth of group j. It follows:

$$\pi(t) = \frac{\dot{P}(t)}{P(t)}.$$

The current income of a household in group j is as follows:

$$y_j(t) = r(t)\bar{k}_j(t) + T_j(t)w_j(t) - \pi(t)m_j(t) + \tau(t),$$
$$j = 1, \ldots J, \tag{12.11}$$

where $r(t)\bar{k}_j(t)$ is the interest payment, $w_j(t)$ is the wage income, $\pi(t)m_j(t)$ is the real cost of holding money, and $\tau(t)$ is the real value of paper money from the government. The disposable income is given by

$$\hat{y}_j(t) = y_j(t) + a_j(t), \tag{12.12}$$

where $a_j(t) \equiv \bar{k}_j(t) + m_j(t)$ is the real wealth of group j. The total value of wealth that group j can sell to purchase goods and to save is $a_j(t)$. The time constraints imply

$$T_j(t) + \overline{T}_j(t) = T_0. \tag{12.13}$$

Insert (12.11) and (12.13) in (12.12):

$$\hat{y}_j(t) = \bar{y}_j(t) - \overline{T}_j(t)w_j(t) - (\pi(t) - 1)m_j(t), \tag{12.14}$$

where

$$\bar{y}_j(t) = (1 + r(t))\bar{k}_j(t) + T_0 w_j(t) + \tau(t).$$

A household in group j distributes the disposable income bewteen real money balances $m_j(t)$, saving $s_j(t)$, consumption of goods $c_j(t)$. The budget constraint is given by:

$$(1 + r(t))m_j(t) + c_j(t) + s_j(t) = \hat{y}_j(t). \tag{12.15}$$

From (12.14) and (12.15):

$$\overline{T}_j(t)w_j(t) + (\pi(t) + r(t))m_j(t) + p_s(t)c_j(t) + s_j(t) = \bar{y}_j(t). \tag{12.16}$$

The utility level of household j is represented by

$$U_j(t) = \overline{T}_j^{\sigma_{0j}}(t)m_j^{\varepsilon_{0j}}(t)c_j^{\xi_{0j}}(t)s_j^{\lambda_{0j}}(t),\ \sigma_{0j}, \varepsilon_{0j}, \xi_{0j}, \lambda_{0j} > 0,$$

in which ε_{0j}, ξ_{0j}, σ_{0j}, and λ_{0j} are called, respectively, propensities to hold money, to consume goods, to use leisure time, and to hold wealth (save). Maximizing $U_j(t)$ subject to (12.13) yields

$$\begin{aligned} &w_j(t)\overline{T}_j(t) = \sigma_j\bar{y}_j(t),\ (\pi(t) + r(t))m_j(t) = \varepsilon_j\bar{y}_j(t), \\ &p_s(t)c_j(t) = \xi_j\bar{y}_j(t),\ s_j(t) = \lambda_j\bar{y}_j(t), \end{aligned} \tag{12.17}$$

where

$$\sigma_j \equiv \rho_j\sigma_{0j},\ \varepsilon_j \equiv \rho_j\varepsilon_{0j},\ \xi_j \equiv \rho_j\xi_{0j},\ \lambda_j \equiv \rho_j\lambda_{0j},\ \rho_j$$

$$\equiv \frac{1}{\sigma_{0j} + \varepsilon_{0j} + \xi_{0j} + \lambda_{0j}}.$$

Households' Wealth Accumulation

According to the definition of $s_j(t)$, the wealth accumulation of household $j's$ wealth change is given by

$$\dot{a}_j(t) = s_j(t) - a_j(t). \tag{12.18}$$

The Relation Between Change in Money Stock, Inflation Policy, and Inflation Rate

According to the definitions and (12.7):

$$\dot{m}(t) = \frac{\dot{M}(t)}{M(t)} - \frac{\dot{P}(t)}{P(t)} = (\mu - \pi(t))m(t). \tag{12.19}$$

Full Employment of Input Factors
Capital stock is fully employed:

$$K_i(t) + K_s(t) = K(t). \tag{12.20}$$

The total physical wealth is owned by the households:

$$\sum_{j=1}^{J} \bar{k}_j(t)\bar{N}_j = K(t). \tag{12.21}$$

The labor is fully employed:

$$N_i(t) + N_s(t) = N(t). \tag{12.22}$$

Market Clearing in Consumer Goods Markets

The demand for consumer goods equals the supply:

$$\sum_{j=1}^{J} c_j(t)\overline{N}_j = F_s(t). \tag{12.23}$$

The model is complete. The model is structurally a unification of the Walrasian general equilibrium, neoclassical growth theory, and MIU approach in monetary economics with Zhang's approach to the group behavior. If wealth accumulation and monetary dynamics are omitted, then the model becomes a Walrasian general equilibrium model. If the population is homogenous and money is omitted, then the model is similar to the Uzawa model in the neoclassical growth theory. If the population is homogeneous, then the model is a monetary neoclassical growth model. Our model is deviated from the mainstreams in economic dynamics in how to model behavior of groups.

12.2 The Equilibrium Structure of the Dynamic Economy

The model is structurally complicated. It includes basic economic mechanisms of Walrasian general economic theory, monetary economics, and neoclassical growth theory. The model is high-dimensional and nonlinear. Introduce a variable:

$$z(t) \equiv \frac{r(t) + \delta_k}{w(t)}.$$

The following lemma is confirmed in the appendix.

Lemma 12.1
The dynamics of the monetary economy with $J-$ group households are described by the following $J+1$ nonlinear differential equations:

$$\dot{m}(t) = \Omega_0\left(\left\{\bar{k}_j(t)\right\}, z(t), m(t)\right),$$
$$\dot{z}(t) = \tilde{\Omega}_1\left(\left\{\bar{k}_j(t)\right\}, z(t), m(t)\right),$$
$$\dot{\bar{k}}_j(t) = \tilde{\Omega}_j\left(\left\{\bar{k}_j(t)\right\}, z(t), m(t)\right), j = 2, \ldots, J, \tag{12.24}$$

where Ω_0 and $\tilde{\Omega}_j$ are functions of $\left\{\bar{k}_j(t)\right\} = \left(\bar{k}_2(t), \ldots, \bar{k}_J(t)\right)$, $z(t)$, and$m(t)$ defined in the Appendix. The rest variables are given as functions of $\left\{\bar{k}_j(t)\right\}$, $z(t)$, and$m(t)$ by the following procedure: $r(t)$ with (A12.2) $\rightarrow$ $w(t)$ by (A12.3) $\rightarrow$ $w_j(t)$ by (12.4) $\rightarrow$ $p_s(t)$ by (A12.4) $\rightarrow$ $\bar{k}_1(t)$ by (A12.15) $\rightarrow$ $\pi(t)$ by (A12.16) $\rightarrow$ $m_j(t)$ by (A12.17) $\rightarrow$ $a_j(t) = \bar{k}_j(t) + m_j(t)$ $\rightarrow$ $\bar{y}_j(t)$ by (A12.8) $\rightarrow$ $\overline{T}_j(t)$, $c_j(t)$, and $s_j(t)$ by (A12.17) $\rightarrow$ $K(t)$ by (A12.11) $\rightarrow$ $K_i(t)$ and $K_s(t)$ by (A12.6) $\rightarrow$ $N_i(t)$ and $N_s(t)$ by (A1) $\rightarrow$ $F_i(t)$ by (12.2) $\rightarrow$ $F_s(t)$ by (12.5) $\rightarrow$ $m(t)$ by (12.7) $\rightarrow$ $P(t)$ by (12.8) $\rightarrow$ $Y(t) = F_j(t) + p_s(t)F_s(t)$.

For simulation, I choose $J = 3$ and specify the parameter values:

$$\bar{N}_1 = 50,\ \bar{N}_2 = 300,\ \bar{N}_3 = 200,\ h_1 = 5,\ h_2 = 3,\ h_3 = 2,\ A_i = 1.3,$$
$$A_s = 1, \alpha_i = 0.29,\ \alpha_s = 0.32,\ \lambda_{01} = 0.78,\ \xi_{01} = 0.12,\ \varepsilon_{01} = 0.02,$$
$$\sigma_{01} = 0.2, \lambda_{02} = 0.75,\ \xi_{02} = 0.16, \varepsilon_{02} = 0.03,\ \sigma_{02} = 0.18,\ \lambda_{03} = 0.7,$$

$$\xi_{03} = 0.18, \varepsilon_{03} = 0.04, \ \sigma_{01} = 0.15, \ \mu = 0.03, \ T_0 = 1,$$
$$\delta_k = 0.05. \tag{12.25}$$

The three populations are respectively 50, 300, and 200. The levels of human capital are correspondingly 5, 3, and 2. Group 1 (12.3) has the smallest (largest) population size and highest (lowest) human capital. The inflation policy is fixed at 3%. The output elasticities of capital of the capital goods and consumer good sectors are respectively 0.29 and 0.32. The three groups have different preferences. As the genuine dynamics is complicated, I am concerned with the equilibrium structure. The system has an equilibrium point as follows:

$$Y = 1560.7, F_i = 743.6, F_s = 646.8, w = 1.19, w_1 = 6,$$
$$w_2 = 3.58, w_3 = 2.38, r = 0.15, m = 1.26, \pi = 0.03, p_s = 1.26,$$
$$N = 980.5, N_i = 442.7, N_s = 465.9, K = 2370.2, K_i = 1071.2,$$
$$K_s = 1299, \bar{k}_1 = 10.1, \bar{k}_2 = 4.73, \bar{k}_3 = 2.24, T_1 = 0.37, T_2 = 0.59,$$
$$T_3 = 0.71, c_1 = 1.81, c_2 = 1.29, c_3 = 0.84, m_1 = 1.66, m_2 = 1.34,$$
$$m_3 = 1.03, a_1 = 11.73, a_2 = 6.07, a_3 = 3.27, U_1 = 6.59.73,$$
$$U_2 = 3.46, U_3 = 1.85. \tag{12.26}$$

Group 1 has highest wage rate, money holding, physical wealth, wealth, consumption, utility level, group 2's corresponding variables are next, and group 3's corresponding variables are lowest. A household in group 2 works more than group 1 and less than group 3. The equilibrium inflation rate is equal to the inflation policy.

12.3 A Rise in the Inflation Policy

This section analyzes how the economic equilibrium is affected when the inflation policy is increased as follows:

$$\mu : 0.03 \Rightarrow 0.035.$$

The result is listed in (12.27). Money is not neutral in the long term. A rise in inflation increases cost of holding money. All the households hold less (real) money and have more wealth. As inflation is increased, the households tend to hold more real wealth $\bar{k}_j$. The national real money is decreased. The total physical capital stock is increased. Each sector employs more capital. The wage rates are increased. The households work less hours as net results of rises in the wage rates and wealth. The national labor supply is reduced. They consume more consumer goods and have higher levels of utility. The rate of interest falls. The capital good sector produces less. The consumer good sector produces more in association with falling price.

$$\begin{aligned}
&\overline{\Delta}Y = 0.17, \overline{\Delta}F_i = -0.68, \overline{\Delta}F_s = 0.98, \overline{\Delta}w = \overline{\Delta}w_1 = \overline{\Delta}w_2 = \overline{\Delta}w_3 = 0.47,\\
&\overline{\Delta}r = -1.53, \overline{\Delta}m = -0.48, \overline{\Delta}\pi = 16.7, \overline{\Delta}p_s = -0.05, \overline{\Delta}N = -0.32,\\
&\overline{\Delta}N_i = -1.14, \overline{\Delta}N_s = 0.46, \overline{\Delta}K = 1.37, \overline{\Delta}K_i = 0.48, \overline{\Delta}K_s = 2.11,\\
&\overline{\Delta}k_1 = 0.89, \overline{\Delta}k_2 = 1.38, \overline{\Delta}k_3 = 1.9, \overline{\Delta}T_1 = -0.3, \overline{\Delta}T_2 = -0.33,\\
&\overline{\Delta}T_3 = -0.31, \overline{\Delta}c_1 = 0.65, \overline{\Delta}c_2 = 0.96, \overline{\Delta}c_3 = 1.22, \overline{\Delta}m_1 = -0.82,\\
&\overline{\Delta}m_2 = -0.52, \overline{\Delta}m_3 = -0.26, \overline{\Delta}a_1 = 0.65, \overline{\Delta}a_2 = 0.96,\\
&\overline{\Delta}a_3 = 1.22, \overline{\Delta}U_1 = 0.61, \overline{\Delta}U_2 = 0.94, \overline{\Delta}U_3 = 1.18. \qquad (12.27)
\end{aligned}$$

The results are similar to those obtained through the Tobin model (Tobin, 1956) which is a monetary neoclassical growth model identical to the Solow model when inflation policy is zero. Although the Tobin model is not based on utility-maximization like our model, demand and supply are similar to our model. The Tobin model predicts that the long-term capital and consumption are positively related to inflation policy. In Tobin's approach, money and capital are substitutes. Portfolio choice between money and capital is affected by inflation policy. A higher inflation reduces the rate of return of money, which would increase capital in the economy. More capital enhances output. Hence the consumption increase. It should be noted that in the literature of monetary economic growth, different approaches provide opposite relationships between money and growth. Sidrauski (1967) applied the Ramsey approach and got the superneutrality of money. Stockman (1981) introduced money in the expenditure function and got the anti-Tobin effects.

12.4 Group 1 Increases the Propensity to Hold Money

This section analyzes the economic equilibrium is affected when group 1 increases the propensity to hold money as follows:

$$\varepsilon_{01} : 0.02 \Rightarrow 0.023.$$

The result is listed in (12.28). Group 1 has more money, while each household in the other two groups has less money. Group 1 has more money, while each household in the other two groups has less money. Group 1 holds less physical capital and wealth, consumes less consumer goods, and works more hours, while each household from the other two groups holds more physical capital and wealth, consumes more consumer goods, and works less hours. Group 1's utility is lowered, while each household from the other two groups has higher utility. The wage rate is reduced in association in rises in the rate of interest. The national money is increased. The total labor supply is enhanced, but national physical capital is reduced. Each sector employs more labor but less capital. The national output is slightly augmented. The capital good sector produces more, while the consumer goods sector produces less in association with rises in the price.

$$\begin{aligned}
\bar{\Delta}Y &= 0.004,\ \bar{\Delta}F_i = 0.42,\ \bar{\Delta}F_s = -0.41,\ \bar{\Delta}w = \bar{\Delta}w_1 = \bar{\Delta}w_2 = \bar{\Delta}w_3 \\
&= -0.4,\ \bar{\Delta}r = 1.3,\ \bar{\Delta}m = 0.32,\ \bar{\Delta}\pi = 0,\ \bar{\Delta}p_s = 0.04,\ \bar{\Delta}N = 0.41, \\
\bar{\Delta}N_i &= 0.82,\ \bar{\Delta}N_s = 0.03,\ \bar{\Delta}K = -0.98,\ \bar{\Delta}K_i = -0.55,\ \bar{\Delta}K_s = -1.33, \\
\bar{\Delta}\bar{k}_1 &= -7.12,\ \bar{\Delta}\bar{k}_2 = 0.63,\ \bar{\Delta}\bar{k}_3 = 0.82,\ \bar{\Delta}T_1 = 7.83,\ \bar{\Delta}T_2 = -0.5, \\
\bar{\Delta}T_3 &= -0.3,\ \bar{\Delta}c_1 = -4.97,\ \bar{\Delta}c_2 = 0.33,\ \bar{\Delta}c_3 = 0.33,\ \bar{\Delta}m_1 = 8.12, \\
\bar{\Delta}m_2 &= -0.75,\ \bar{\Delta}m_3 = -0.75,\ \bar{\Delta}a_1 = -4.97,\ \bar{\Delta}a_2 = 0.33, \\
\bar{\Delta}a_3 &= 0.33,\ \bar{\Delta}U_1 = -5.28,\ \bar{\Delta}U_2 = 0.41,\ U_3 = 0.36. \qquad (12.28)
\end{aligned}$$

12.5 Group 3's Human Capital Is Enhanced

This section analyzes how the economic equilibrium is affected when group 3's human capital is enhanced as follows:

$$h_3 : 2 \Rightarrow 2.2.$$

The result is listed in (12.29). Group 3's wage rate is enhanced, while the other two groups' wage rates are reduced. Group 3 has more money, owns more physical capital, has more wealth, while each household from the other groups has less money, but owns more physical capital and has more wealth. All the households consume more consumer goods, enjoy more leisure hours, and have higher utilities. The national money is enhanced, and rate of interest is increased. The total labor supply and national physical capital are augmented. Each sector employs more labor but less labor force. The national output is augmented. The two sectors both produce more. The price of consumer goods rises slightly.

$$\begin{aligned}
&\overline{\Delta}Y = 2.67, \overline{\Delta}F_i = 2.56, \overline{\Delta}F_s = 2.74, \overline{\Delta}w = \overline{\Delta}w_1 = \overline{\Delta}w_2 = -0.19, \\
&\overline{\Delta}w_3 = 9.79, \overline{\Delta}r = 0.62, \overline{\Delta}m = 2.59, \overline{\Delta}\pi = 0, \overline{\Delta}p_s = 0.02, \\
&\overline{\Delta}N = 2.86, \overline{\Delta}N_i = 2.76, \overline{\Delta}N_s = 2.96, \overline{\Delta}K = 2.2, \overline{\Delta}K_i = 2.09, \\
&\overline{\Delta}K_s = 2.29, \overline{\Delta}\bar{k}_1 = 0.24, \overline{\Delta}\bar{k}_2 = 0.33, \overline{\Delta}\bar{k}_3 = 10.31, \overline{\Delta}T_1 = -0.58, \\
&\overline{\Delta}T_2 = -0.26, \overline{\Delta}T_3 = -0.1, \overline{\Delta}c_1 = 0.15, \overline{\Delta}c_2 = 0.18, \overline{\Delta}c_3 = 10.05, \\
&\overline{\Delta}m_1 = -0.37, \overline{\Delta}m_2 = -0.33, \overline{\Delta}m_3 = 9.49, \overline{\Delta}a_1 = 0.15, \overline{\Delta}a_2 = 0.18, \\
&\overline{\Delta}a_3 = 10.05, \overline{\Delta}U_1 = 0.21, \overline{\Delta}U_2 = 0.22, \overline{\Delta}U_3 = 9.23. \qquad (12.29)
\end{aligned}$$

12.6 Group 3's Population Enlarged

This section studies how the economic equilibrium is affected when group 3's population is enlarged as follows:

$$\overline{N}_3 : 2 \Rightarrow 2.2.$$

The result is listed in (12.30). The wage rate is reduced, and the rate of interest is enhanced. Each household holds less money, owns more physical capital and has more wealth. All the households consume more, work less, and enjoy higher levels of utility. The national money per household is reduced and rate of interest is increased. The total labor supply and national physical capital are augmented. Each sector employs more labor and capital. The national output is augmented. The two sectors both produce more. The price of consumer goods rises slightly.

$$\begin{aligned}
&\overline{\Delta}Y = 1.34, \overline{\Delta}F_i = 1.28, \overline{\Delta}F_s = 1.37, \overline{\Delta}w = \overline{\Delta}w_1 = \overline{\Delta}w_2 = \overline{\Delta}w_3 = -0.1,\\
&\overline{\Delta}r = 0.32, \overline{\Delta}m = -0.51, \overline{\Delta}\pi = 0, \overline{\Delta}p_s = 0.01, \overline{\Delta}N = 1.43, \overline{\Delta}N_i = 1.38,\\
&\overline{\Delta}N_s = 1.48, \overline{\Delta}K = 1.1, \overline{\Delta}K_i = 1.04, \overline{\Delta}K_s = 1.14, \overline{\Delta}\bar{k}_1 = 0.11,\\
&\overline{\Delta}\bar{k}_2 = 01.5, \overline{\Delta}\bar{k}_3 = 01.9, \overline{\Delta}T_1 = -0.28, \overline{\Delta}T_2 = -0.12, \overline{\Delta}T_3 = -0.07,\\
&\overline{\Delta}c_1 = 0.07, \overline{\Delta}c_2 = 0.07, \overline{\Delta}c_3 = 0.07, \overline{\Delta}m_1 = -0.2, \overline{\Delta}m_2 = -0.19,\\
&\overline{\Delta}m_3 = -0.19, \overline{\Delta}a_1 = 0.07, \overline{\Delta}a_2 = 0.07, \overline{\Delta}a_3 = 0.07, \overline{\Delta}U_1 = 0.1,\\
&\overline{\Delta}U_2 = 0.09, \overline{\Delta}U_3 = 0.08.
\end{aligned} \tag{12.30}$$

12.7 Group 3's Propensity to Save Increases

I now analyze how the economic equilibrium is affected when group 3's propensity to save is enhanced as follows:

$$\lambda_{03} : 0.7 \Rightarrow 0.71.$$

The result is listed in (12.31). Group 3 has more wealth and has more physical capital, while each household from the other groups has less wealth and has less physical capital. All the households hold more money. Group 3 has more leisure time and consumes more goods, while each household from the other groups has less leisure time and consumes less. Group 3 enjoys higher utility, while each household from the other groups has lower utility. The national money is enhanced, and rate of interest is reduced. The total labor supply and national physical capital are augmented. Each sector employs more labor and capital. The national output is augmented. The two sectors both produce more. The price of consumer goods decreases slightly.

$$\begin{aligned}
&\bar{\Delta}Y = 0.14,\ \bar{\Delta}F_i = 0.28,\ \bar{\Delta}F_s = 0.02,\ \bar{\Delta}w = \bar{\Delta}w_1 = \bar{\Delta}w_2 = \bar{\Delta}w_3 = 0.08,\\
&\bar{\Delta}r = -0.26, \bar{\Delta}m = 0.24, \bar{\Delta}\pi = 0, \bar{\Delta}p_s = -0.01, \bar{\Delta}N = 0.06, \bar{\Delta}N_i = 0.2,\\
&\bar{\Delta}N_s = -0.07,\ \bar{\Delta}K = 0.33,\ \bar{\Delta}K_i = 0.48,\ \bar{\Delta}K_s = 0.2,\ \bar{\Delta}\bar{k}_1 = -0.09,\\
&\bar{\Delta}\bar{k}_2 = -0.12, \bar{\Delta}\bar{k}_3 = 2.22,\ \bar{\Delta}T_1 = 0.23,\ \bar{\Delta}T_2 = 0.1,\ \bar{\Delta}T_3 = -0.06,\\
&\bar{\Delta}c_1 = -0.05,\ \bar{\Delta}c_2 = 0.06, \bar{\Delta}c_3 = 0.23,\ \bar{\Delta}m_1 = 0.16,\ \bar{\Delta}m_2 = 0.15,\\
&\bar{\Delta}m_3 = 0.45, \bar{\Delta}a_1 = -0.05,\ \bar{\Delta}a_2 = -0.06, \bar{\Delta}a_3 = 1.66,\\
&\bar{\Delta}U_1 = -0.08,\ \bar{\Delta}U_2 = -0.08,\ \bar{\Delta}U_3 = 2.47.\ \ (12.31)
\end{aligned} \tag{12.31}$$

12.8 Group 3's Propensity to Use Leisure Time Is Increased

I now analyze how the economic equilibrium is affected when group 3's propensity to use leisure time is enhanced as follows:

$$\sigma_{03} : 0.15 \Rightarrow 0.16.$$

The result is listed in (12.32). Group 3 has more leisure time, while each household from the other groups work more. Group 3 holds less money, while each household from the other groups holds more. All the households have less wealth and less physical capital. The wage rate increases slightly. All the households have lower utility levels. The national money is reduced. The rate of interest is reduced. The total labor supply and national physical capital are reduced. Each sector employs less labor and capital. The national output is reduced. The two sectors both produce less. The price of consumer goods falls slightly.

$$\begin{aligned}
&\overline{\Delta}Y = -0.51, \overline{\Delta}F_i = -0.49, \overline{\Delta}F_s = -0.53, \overline{\Delta}w = \overline{\Delta}w_1 = \overline{\Delta}w_2 = \overline{\Delta}w_3\\
&\qquad = 0.04, \overline{\Delta}r = -0.12, \overline{\Delta}m = -0.5, \overline{\Delta}\pi = 0, \overline{\Delta}p_s = -0.004,\\
&\overline{\Delta}N = -0.55, \overline{\Delta}N_i = -0.53, \overline{\Delta}N_s = -0.57, \overline{\Delta}K = -0.42,\\
&\overline{\Delta}K_i = -0.4, \overline{\Delta}K_s = -0.44, \overline{\Delta}\bar{k}_1 = -0.05, \overline{\Delta}\bar{k}_2 = -0.07,\\
&\overline{\Delta}\bar{k}_3 = -1.98, \overline{\Delta}T_1 = 0.11, \overline{\Delta}T_2 = 0.05, \overline{\Delta}T_3 = -1.9, \overline{\Delta}c_1 = -0.03,\\
&\overline{\Delta}c_2 = -0.04, \overline{\Delta}c_3 = -1.93, \overline{\Delta}m_1 = 0.07, \overline{\Delta}m_2 = 0.07,\\
&\overline{\Delta}m_3 = -1.83, \overline{\Delta}a_1 = -0.03, \overline{\Delta}a_2 = -0.04, \overline{\Delta}a_3 = -1.93,\\
&\overline{\Delta}U_1 = -0.04, \overline{\Delta}U_2 = -0.04, \overline{\Delta}U_3 = -2.27.
\end{aligned} \tag{12.32}$$

12.9 The Consumer Good Sector's Total Productivity Is Enhanced

This section shows how the economic equilibrium is affected when the consumer good sector's total productivity factor is enhanced as follows:

$$A_s : 1 \Rightarrow 1.05.$$

The result is listed in (12.33). All the households have more money and have less wealth and less physical capital. They all work more hours and consume less consumer goods. Their utility levels are lowered. The wage rate is slightly increased. The national money is augmented. The rate of interest is reduced. The total labor supply is increased, while the national physical capital is reduced. The capital good sector employs more input, while the consumer good sector employs less input. The capital good sector produces more, while the consumer good sector produces less. The price of consumer goods falls.

$$\begin{aligned}
&\overline{\Delta}Y = 0.02, \overline{\Delta}F_i = 5.33, \overline{\Delta}F_s = -0.04, \overline{\Delta}w = \overline{\Delta}w_1 = \overline{\Delta}w_2 = \overline{\Delta}w_3 = 0.06,\\
&\overline{\Delta}r = -0.19, \overline{\Delta}m = 0.11, \overline{\Delta}\pi = 0, \overline{\Delta}p_s = -4.77, \overline{\Delta}N = 0.07, \overline{\Delta}N_i = 5.27,\\
&\overline{\Delta}N_s = -4.86, \overline{\Delta}K = -0.09, \overline{\Delta}K_i = 5.47, \overline{\Delta}K_s = -4.68, \overline{\Delta}\overline{k}_1 = -0.06,\\
&\overline{\Delta}\overline{k}_2 = -0.09, \overline{\Delta}\overline{k}_3 = -0.12, \overline{\Delta}T_1 = 0.16, \overline{\Delta}T_2 = 0.07, \overline{\Delta}T_3 = 0.04,\\
&\overline{\Delta}c_1 = -0.04, \overline{\Delta}c_2 = -0.05, \overline{\Delta}c_3 = -0.04, \overline{\Delta}m_1 = 0.12,\\
&\overline{\Delta}m_2 = 0.11, \overline{\Delta}m_3 = 0.11, \overline{\Delta}a_1 = -0.04, \overline{\Delta}a_2 = -0.05,\\
&\overline{\Delta}a_3 = -0.04, \overline{\Delta}U_1 = -0.06, \overline{\Delta}U_2 = -0.06, \overline{\Delta}U_3 = -0.05.
\end{aligned} \tag{12.33}$$

12.10 Concluding Remarks

This chapter proposed a dynamic equilibrium growth model to examine the relationship between economic growth and money growth by integrating the Walrasian general equilibrium theory, neoclassical growth theory, and MIU approach in monetary economics with the concept of disposable income and utility function. It provides some insights into complexity of monetary economic growth. Traditional theories which have been empirically tested based don't give any convergent conclusions on the role of money in economic growth. The theoretical model in this chapter is based on multiple forces of economic growth well accepted in the literature of economic growth. It provides some insights into situation-dependent conclusions in the literature of empirical studies on the role of government's monetary policy. It can be extended in different ways. It is important to use more general forms of production functions and utility functions. The government's monetary policy is oversimplified. Growth money is an endogenous variable of social and economic changes. For instance, it is possible to replace the fixed money growth rate policy with the Taylor rule. Issues related to government debts are a main concern in the literature. It is conceptually not difficult to examine interdependence between money growth and national debts on the basis of our model.

Appendix: Proving Lemma 12.1

With (12.3) and (12.6), it follows:

$$z \equiv \frac{r+\delta_k}{w} = \frac{\tilde{\alpha}_i N_i}{K_i} = \frac{\tilde{\alpha}_s N_s}{K_s}, \tag{A12.1}$$

where time index is omitted and $\tilde{\alpha}_j \equiv \alpha_j/\beta_j,\ j = i, s$. From (12.2) and (12.3):

$$r(z) = \frac{\alpha_i A_i z^{\beta_i}}{\tilde{\alpha}_i^{\beta_i}} - \delta_k. \tag{A12.2}$$

where (A1) is applied. Equation (A12.1) also implies

$$w(z) = \frac{r+\delta_k}{z}. \tag{A12.3}$$

From (12.5), (12.6), and (A12.1), it follows:

$$p_s(z) = \frac{z^{\alpha_s} w}{A_s \beta_s \tilde{\alpha}_s^{\alpha_s}}. \tag{A12.4}$$

Insert (A12.1) in (12.22):

$$\left(\frac{K_i}{\tilde{\alpha}_i} + \frac{K_s}{\tilde{\alpha}_s}\right) z = N. \tag{A12.5}$$

Solve (A12.5) and (12.20)

$$K_i = \frac{\tilde{\alpha} N}{z} - \frac{\tilde{\alpha} K}{\tilde{\alpha}_s},\ K_s = \frac{\tilde{\alpha} K}{\tilde{\alpha}_i} - \frac{\tilde{\alpha} N}{z}, \tag{A12.6}$$

where

$$\tilde{\alpha} \equiv \left(\frac{1}{\tilde{\alpha}_i} - \frac{1}{\tilde{\alpha}_s}\right)^{-1}.$$

By (A12.6) and (A12.1), I have

$$N_i = \left(N - \frac{zK}{\tilde{\alpha}_s}\right)\frac{\tilde{\alpha}}{\tilde{\alpha}_i}, N_s = \left(\frac{zK}{\tilde{\alpha}_i} - N\right)\frac{\tilde{\alpha}}{\tilde{\alpha}_s}. \tag{A12.7}$$

From (12.14), (12.9), and (12.4), I have

$$\bar{y}_j = R\bar{k}_j + T_0 h_j w + \mu m. \tag{A12.8}$$

where $R \equiv 1 + r$. Insert (12.17) in (A12.8):

$$\overline{T}_j = \frac{R\sigma_j\bar{k}_j}{w_j} + \sigma_j T_0 + \frac{\sigma_j \mu m}{w_j}. \tag{A12.9}$$

By (A12.9) and (12.13):

$$T_j = \left(1 - \sigma_j\right)T_0 - \frac{R\sigma_j\bar{k}_j}{w_j} - \frac{\sigma_j \mu m}{w_j}. \tag{A12.10}$$

From (A12.10) and (12.1), I have

$$N = \sigma_0 - \overline{\sigma}m - \sum_{j=1}^{J}\overline{\sigma}_j\bar{k}_j, \tag{A12.11}$$

where

$$\sigma_0 \equiv T_0\sum_{j=1}^{J}\left(1 - \sigma_j\right)h_j\overline{N}_j, \overline{\sigma}_j \equiv \frac{R\sigma_j\overline{N}_j}{w}, \overline{\sigma} \equiv \frac{\mu}{w}\sum_{j=1}^{J}\sigma_j\overline{N}_j.$$

Insert (12.17) in (12.23):

$$\sum_{j=1}^{J}\xi_j\overline{N}_j\bar{y}_j = \frac{wN_s}{\beta_s}, \tag{A12.12}$$

where (12.6) is applied. Insert (A12.8) and (A12.7) in (A12.12):

$$\sum_{j=1}^{J}\overline{\xi}_j\bar{k}_j + h + \overline{\xi}m = \frac{zK}{\tilde{\alpha}_i} - N. \tag{A12.13}$$

where

$$\overline{\xi}_j \equiv \frac{\alpha_s R \xi_j \overline{N}_j}{\tilde{\alpha} w}, h \equiv \frac{\alpha_s T_0}{\tilde{\alpha}} \sum_{j=1}^{J} \xi_j \overline{N}_j h_j, \overline{\xi} \equiv \frac{\alpha_s \mu m}{\tilde{\alpha} w} \sum_{j=1}^{J} \xi_j \overline{N}_j.$$

Substituting (A12.11) and (12.21) into (A12.13) yields

$$\sum_{j=1}^{J} \left(\overline{\xi}_j - \frac{z\overline{N}_j}{\tilde{\alpha}_i} - \overline{\sigma}_j \right) \overline{k}_j + h + \sigma_0 + \left(\overline{\xi} - \overline{\sigma} \right) m = 0. \tag{A12.14}$$

Solving (A12.14) with $\overline{k}_1$ as the variable, I have

$$\overline{k}_1 = \Lambda\left(\left\{ \overline{k}_j \right\}, z, m \right) \equiv \left(\sum_{j=2}^{J} \left(\overline{\xi}_j - \frac{z\overline{N}_j}{\tilde{\alpha}_i} - \overline{\sigma}_j \right) \overline{k}_j + h + \sigma_0 + \left(\overline{\xi} - \overline{\sigma} \right) m \right) \left(\frac{z\overline{N}_1}{\tilde{\alpha}_i} + \overline{\sigma}_1 - \overline{\xi}_1 \right)^{-1}. \tag{A12.15}$$

Insert (A12.8) in (A12.14):

$$\pi = \tilde{\Lambda}\left(\left\{ \overline{k}_j \right\}, z, m \right) \equiv \frac{R}{m\overline{N}} \sum_{j=2}^{J} \varepsilon_j \overline{N}_j \overline{k}_j + \overline{r}, \tag{A12.16}$$

where

$$\overline{r}(z) \equiv \frac{w T_0}{m\overline{N}} \sum_{j=1}^{J} \varepsilon_j h_j \overline{N}_j + \frac{\mu}{\overline{N}} \sum_{j=1}^{J} \varepsilon_j \overline{N}_j - r.$$

By (12.17), (A12.15), and (A12.16):

$$m_j = \Lambda_j\left(\left\{ \bar{k}_j \right\},\ z,\ m \right) \equiv \frac{\varepsilon_j \left(R\bar{k}_j + T_0\, h_j w + \mu m \right)}{\pi + r}, \tag{A12.17}$$

where (A12.14) is applied. It is straightforward to check that all the variables can be expressed as functions of $\left\{ \overline{k}_j \right\}$, z, and m at any point in time as follows: r with (A12.2) $\rightarrow$ w by (A12.3) $\rightarrow$ w_j by (12.4) $\rightarrow$ p_s by (A12.4) $\rightarrow$ $\overline{k}_1$ by (A12.15) $\rightarrow$ π by (A12.16) $\rightarrow$ m_j by (A12.17) $\rightarrow$ $a_j = \overline{k}_j + m_j \rightarrow \overline{y}_j$ by (A12.8) $\rightarrow$ $\overline{T}_j$ c_j, and s_j by (12.17) $\rightarrow$ K by (A12.11) $\rightarrow$ K by (12.21) $\rightarrow$ K_i and K_s by (A12.6) $\rightarrow$ N_i and N_s by (A12.1) $\rightarrow$ F_i by (12.2) $\rightarrow$ F_s by (12.5) $\rightarrow$ m by (12.7) $\rightarrow$ P by (12.8) $\rightarrow$ $Y = F_j + p_s F_s$. From this procedure, (12.18) and (12.19), I get

$$\dot{\bar{k}}_j + \dot{m}_j = \Omega_j\left(\left\{\bar{k}_j\right\},\ z,\ m\right) \equiv s_j - a_j, \tag{A12.18}$$

$$\dot{m} = \Omega_0\left(\left\{\bar{k}_j\right\},\ z,\ m\right) \equiv (\mu - \pi)m. \tag{A12.19}$$

Take derivative of (A12.17) in time:

$$\dot{m}_j = \sum_{j=2}^{J} \frac{\partial \Lambda_j}{\partial \bar{k}_q}\dot{\bar{k}}_q + \frac{\partial \Lambda_j}{\partial z}\dot{z} + \Omega_0 \frac{\partial \Lambda_j}{\partial m}. \tag{A12.20}$$

in which (A12.18) and (A12.19) are applied. From (A12.15), it follows:

$$\dot{\bar{k}}_1 = \sum_{j=2}^{J} \frac{\partial \Lambda}{\partial \bar{k}_j}\dot{\bar{k}}_j + \frac{\partial \Lambda}{\partial z}\dot{z} + \Omega_0 \frac{\partial \Lambda}{\partial m}. \tag{A12.21}$$

Insert (A12.20) and (A12.21) in (A12.18)

$$\sum_{q=2}^{J} \left(\frac{\partial \Lambda}{\partial \bar{k}_q} + \frac{\partial \Lambda_1}{\partial \bar{k}_q}\right)\dot{\bar{k}}_q + \left(\frac{\partial \Lambda}{\partial z} + \frac{\partial \Lambda_1}{\partial z}\right)\dot{z} = \Omega_1 - \Omega_0 \frac{\partial \Lambda}{\partial m} - \Omega_0 \frac{\partial \Lambda_1}{\partial m},$$

$$\dot{\bar{k}}_j + \sum_{j=2}^{J} \frac{\partial \Lambda_j}{\partial \bar{k}_q}\dot{\bar{k}}_q + \frac{\partial \Lambda_j}{\partial z}\dot{z} = \Omega_j - \Omega_0 \frac{\partial \Lambda_j}{\partial m}. \tag{A12.22}$$

Equation (A.12.22) is linear in $\left\{\dot{\bar{k}}_j\right\}$ and $\dot{z}$. It is straightforward to solve the linear equations. As it is tedious to give the explicit expressions, I express the solution of (A.12.22) in the form of differential equations as follows:

$$\dot{z} = \tilde{\Omega}_1\left(\left\{\bar{k}_j\right\},\ z,\ m\right),$$
$$\dot{\bar{k}}_j = \tilde{\Omega}_j\left(\left\{\bar{k}_j\right\},\ z,\ m\right),\quad j = 2,\ \ldots,\ J. \tag{A12.23}$$

Differential equations (A.12.19) and (A.12.23) have $J + 1$ equations and contain the same number of variables $\left\{\bar{k}_j\right\}$, z, and m. The lemma is confirmed.

Chapter 13
Global Trade and Business Cycles with Endogenous Human Capital

> In order to get beyond racism, we must first take account of race. There is no other way. And in order to treat some persons equally, we must treat them differently.
>
> Harry A. Blackmun (1908–1999)

There are different ideas and theories to explain well-observed business cycles and economic oscillations. The two contemporary theories of business cycles are the Keynesian economics and the real business-cycle theory. The Keynesian economic business cycle theory considers demand changes as the main sources of business cycles. The real business-cycle theory explains business-cycle fluctuations by real shocks. Different from other influential business-cycle theories, the real business-cycle theory considers business cycles as the efficient response to exogenous changes in the real economic variables. The purpose of this study is to demonstrate existence of business cycles in the dynamic growth model of heterogeneous households with wealth accumulation and human capital accumulation in a multi-country global economy proposed by Zhang (2015a). It shows how fluctuations in one country cause business cycles not only in the national economy but also in all the countries in the global economy with free trade. It should be noted that modern nonlinear dynamic economic theory shows that business cycles may occur in a dynamic system with or without any exogenous influences (Zhang 1991, 2005c, 2006b, 2023, 2024b; Lorenz 1993; Flaschel et al. 1997; Chiarella and Flaschel 2000; Boldrin et al. 2001a; Shone 2002; Gandolfo 2005; Puu 2011; Tian 2015). Different studies explain economic business cycles from different perspectives. Lucas (1977) demonstrates how some shocks affect all sectors in an economy. In the neoclassical growth model by Chatterjee and Ravikumar (1992), seasonal perturbations to taste and technology cause business cycles. Gabaix (2011) shows that uncorrelated sectoral shocks are determinants of aggregate fluctuations (Giovanni et al. 2014; Stella 2015). This chapter identifies economic fluctuations due to exogenous shocks in preferences and technologies.

W. Zhang, *A Dynamic Economic Theory of Heterogenous Households*,
https://doi.org/10.1007/978-981-95-8918-0_13

It has been reported that the richest 1% of the world population own almost half of the world's wealth. Moreover, it does seem that inequality be enlarged in the near future in tandem with rapid economic globalization. There is a need-to-know determinants of inequality and dynamics of inequality. This need is emphasized by Forbes (2000) as follows: "careful reassessment of the relationship between these two variables (growth rate and income inequality) needs further theoretical and empirical work evaluating the channels through which inequality, growth, and any other variables are related." Zhang (2015a) has recently built a model to insights into the well-reported phenomena that the richest 1% of the world population owns almost half of the world's wealth. The study is primarily concerned with dynamic interdependence between time distribution between work and leisure, wealth and physical capital accumulation, human capital accumulation, and trade patterns in a multi-country neoclassical growth theory framework.

Zhang's model is built for any number of national economies. The study is concerned with not only inequalities in income, wealth, and economic structures between (any number of) countries, but also differences in human capital between countries. It is significant to examine dynamic interdependence between economic growth and human capital. The main force of economic growth is capital accumulation in the neoclassical growth theory. But the dynamics of this single variable fail to properly explain why countries grow differently. The dynamics of human capital are considered another key determinant of economic growth. Zhang (2015a) integrated the approaches in the neoclassical growth theory and the growth theory with human capital to explain the dynamics of global growth and inequalities in income and wealth. This chapter generalizes Zhang's model by allowing all the time-dependent parameters to be time-dependent. By the generalization, this chapter is able to examine effects of exogenous fluctuations in any parameter on the motion of the system. This chapter is based on Zhang (2020d) and is organized as follows. Section 13.1 defines the neoclassical growth model of a multi-country economy with capital accumulation and human capital accumulation. Section 13.2 shows that the dynamics of the economy can be described by a set of dimensional differential equations. Section 13.3 studies how exogenous oscillations in the efficiency of applying human capital by country 1's rich group affect the global economic structure and income and wealth distribution. Section 13.4 shows the processes that fluctuate in country 1's total factor productivity affect the dynamic system. Section 13.5 shows the effects that the propensity to save of country 1's group 1 periodically oscillates. Section 13.6 follows the changes in the system when the return to scale in human capital accumulation of country 1's group 1 periodically oscillates. Section 13.7 analyzes the impact on the dynamics when there are exogenous fluctuations in country 1's depreciation of physical capital. Section 13.8 plots what happens in the system when there are fluctuations in the depreciation of human capital of country 1's group 1. Section 13.9 concludes the chapter. The appendix proves Lemma 13.1.

13.1 The Multi-Country Growth Model with Exogenous Shocks

All the economy can produce a homogenous tradable commodity. Most aspects of production sectors in the model are similar to the neoclassical one-sector growth model (Zhang 2003c, 2013a). Households own assets of the economy and distribute their incomes to consume and save. Production sectors or firms use capital and labor. Exchanges take place in perfectly competitive markets. Production sectors sell their product to households or to other sectors and households sell their labor and assets to production sectors. Factor markets work well; factors are inelastically supplied and the available factors are fully utilized at every moment. Savings are undertaken only by households, which implies that all earnings of firms are distributed in the form of payments to factors of production. All savings volunteered by households are absorbed by firms. Commodities are traded without any barriers such as transport costs or tariffs. There is no migration between the countries. Let prices be measured in terms of the commodity and the price of the commodity be unity. It is assumed that the population of country j can be classified into Q_j groups, indexed by q, according to their preferences, wealth, human capital, and social status. The total number of types of households Q in the world economy is given by

$$Q = \sum_{j=1}^{J} Q_j.$$

A group q in country j is indexed by (j, q). I introduce

$$Q^* \equiv \{(j, q) | j = 1, \ldots, J, q = 1, \ldots, Q_j\}.$$

Let the population of group q in country j be $N_{jq}(t)$ in time t. Let $T_{jq}(t)$ stand for the work time of a typical worker in group (j, q). The variable $N_j(t)$ represents the total qualified labor force in country j. A worker's labor force is $T_{jq}(t)H_{jq}^{m_{jq}(t)}(t)$, where $m_{jq}(t)$ is a time-dependent parameter measuring utilization efficiency of human capital by group (j, q). The labor input is the work time by the effective human capital. A group's labor input is the group's population by each member the labor force, that is, $T_j(t)H_j^{m_j(t)}(t)N_{jq}(t)$. As the total qualified labor force is the sum of all the groups' labor forces, country j 's total labor force $N_j(t)$ is as follows:

$$N_j(t) = \sum_{q=1}^{Q_j} T_{jq}(t)H_{jq}^{m_{jq}(t)}(t)N_{jq}(t), \; q = 1, \ldots, Q. \tag{13.1}$$

where $H_{jq}(t)$ is the level of human capital of group (j, q). The wage and interest rates are denoted by $w_{jq}(t)$ and $r_j(t)$, respectively, in the j th country. In the free trade system, the interest rate is identical throughout the world economy, i.e., $r(t) = r_j(t)$.

Production Sectors

The production sector employs two input factors, capital $K_j(t)$ and labor force $N_j(t)$. Country j' s production function $F_j(t)$ is specified as follows:

$$F_j(t) = A_j(t)K_j^{\alpha_j(t)}(t)N_j^{\beta_j(t)}(t), \alpha_j(t), \beta_j(t) > 0,$$
$$\alpha_j(t) + \beta_j(t) = 1, \tag{13.2}$$

where $A_j(t)$, $\alpha_j(t)$, and $\beta_j(t)$ are positive parameters. The profits are:

$$F_j(t) - \left(r(t) + \delta_{kj}(t)\right)K_j(t) - w(t)N_j(t).$$

The marginal conditions for maximizing the profits are:

$$r(t) + \delta_{kj}(t) = \frac{\alpha_j(t)F_j(t)}{K_j(t)}, w(t) = \frac{\beta_j(t)F_j(t)}{N_j(t)}. \tag{13.3}$$

The Current Income and Disposable Income

The wage rate of group (j, q) is:

$$w_{jq}(t) = w_j(t)H_{jq}^{m_{jq}(t)}(t), (j, q) \in Q^*. \tag{13.4}$$

The per capita current income from the interest payment $r(t)\bar{k}_{jq}(t)$ and the wage payment $T_{jq}(t)w_{jq}(t)$ is:

$$y_{jq}(t) = r(t)\bar{k}_{jq}(t) + T_{jq}(t)w_{jq}(t).$$

The total value of wealth that consumers can use is $\bar{k}_{jq}(t)$. Here, it is assumed that selling and buying wealth can be conducted instantaneously without any transaction cost. The per capita disposable income is given by:

$$\hat{y}_{jq}(t) = y_{jq}(t) + \bar{k}_{jq}(t) = (1 + r(t))\bar{k}_{jq}(t) + W_{jq}(t). \tag{13.5}$$

where $W_{jq}(t) \equiv T_{jq}(t)w_{jq}(t)$ is the wage income.

Budgets and Time Constrain

The typical consumer distributes the total available budget between saving $s_{jq}(t)$, consumption of goods $c_{jq}(t)$. The budget constraint is

$$c_{jq}(t) + s_{jq}(t) = \hat{y}_{jq}(t) = (1 + r(t))\bar{k}_{jq}(t) + w_{jq}(t)T_{jq}(t), \tag{13.6}$$

The time constraint for everyone:

$$T_{jq}(t) + \overline{T}_{jq}(t) = T_0, \tag{13.7}$$

where $\overline{T}_j(t)$ is the leisure time of the representative household and T_0 is the total available time. Insert (13.7) in (13.6):

$$w_{jq}(t)\overline{T}_{jq}(t) + c_{jq}(t) + s_{jq}(t) = \overline{y}_{jq}(t)$$
$$\equiv (1 + r(t))\overline{k}_{jq}(t) + T_0 w_{jq}(t). \tag{13.8}$$

Utility Function and Behavior of Households

The variable $\overline{y}_{jq}(t)$ is the disposable income when the household spends all the available time on work. The representative consumer's utility function is specified as a function $\overline{T}_{jq}(t)$, $c_{jq}(t)$, and $s_{jq}(t)$ as follows:

$$U_{jq}(t) = \overline{T}_{jq}^{\sigma_{jq0}(t)}(t) c^{\xi_{jq0}(t)}(t) s^{\lambda_{jq0}(t)}(t),$$
$$\sigma_{jq0}(t), \xi_{jq0}(t), \lambda_{jq0}(t) > 0, \tag{13.9}$$

where $\sigma_{jq0}(t)$ is the propensity to use leisure time, $\xi_{jq0}(t)$ is the propensity to consume, and $\lambda_{jq0}(t)$ the propensity to own wealth. Maximizing $U_{jq}(t)$ subject to (13.8) yields:

$$\overline{T}_{jq}(t) = \frac{\sigma_{jq}(t)\overline{y}_{jq}(t)}{w_{jq}(t)}, \; c_{jq}(t) = \xi_{jq}(t)\overline{y}_{jq}(t),$$
$$s_{jq}(t) = \lambda_{jq}(t)\overline{y}_{jq}(t), \tag{13.10}$$

where

$$\sigma_{jq0}(t) \equiv \rho_{jq}(t)\sigma_{jq0}(t), \; \xi_{jq0}(t) \equiv \rho_{jq}(t)\xi_{jq0}(t), \; \lambda_{jq0}(t)$$
$$\equiv \rho_{jq}(t)\lambda_{jq0}(t), \; \rho_{jq}(t) \equiv \frac{1}{\sigma_{jq0}(t) + \xi_{jq0}(t) + \lambda_{jq0}(t)}.$$

Change in the Household Wealth

According to the definitions of $s_{jq}(t)$, the wealth accumulation of the representative household (j, q) is given by:

$$\dot{\overline{k}}_{jq}(t) = s_{jq}(t) - \overline{k}_{jq}(t). \tag{13.11}$$

This equation simply states that the change in wealth is equal to saving minus dissaving.

Dynamics of Human Capital

This chapter applies Arrow's idea of "learning by producing" by Arrow (1962) to model human capital accumulation. The basic idea is that people accumulate more skills and have more ideas when they are engaged in economic production. The human capital accumulation is specified as follows:

$$\dot{H}_{jq}(t) = \frac{\tilde{\upsilon}_{jq}(t) c_{jq}^{a_{jq}(t)}(t) \overline{k}_{jq}^{\upsilon_{jq}(t)}(t) T_{jq}^{\theta_{jq}(t)}(t)}{H_{jq}^{\pi_{jq}}(t)} - \delta_{jq}(t) H_{jq}(t), \tag{13.12}$$

where $\delta_{jq}(t)$ is the depreciation rates of human capital, $0 < \delta_{jq}(t) < 1$. In (13.12), $\tilde{\upsilon}_{jq}(t)$, $a_{jq}(t)$, $\upsilon_{jq}(t)$, and $\theta_{jq}(t)$ are non-negative parameters, and $\pi_{jq}(t)$ is a parameter. The item $c_{jq}^{a_{jq}}$ implies a positive relation between human capital accumulation and consumption. The item $\overline{k}_{jq}^{\upsilon_{jq}}$ implies a positive relation between wealth and human capital accumulation. It can be interpreted that more wealth means, for instance, a higher social status. More wealth may also help one to maintain professional reputation. More work accumulates more human capital. The term $H_{jq}^{\pi_{jq}}$ implies that more human capital makes it easier (more difficult) to accumulate knowledge in the case of $\pi_{jq} < 0$ ($\pi_{jq} > 0$).

Demand of and Supply for Capital Goods

The global capital employed is equal to the global wealth. This implies:

$$K(t) = \sum_{j=1}^{J} K_j(t) = \sum_{j=1}^{J} \overline{K}_j(t) = \sum_{j=1}^{J} \sum_{q=1}^{Q_j} \overline{k}_{jq}(t) N_{jq}, \tag{13.13}$$

where $\overline{K}_j(t)$ is the value of wealth owned by country j:

$$\overline{K}_j(t) = \sum_{q=1}^{Q_j} \overline{k}_{jq}(t) N_{jq}. \tag{13.14}$$

The world production is equal to the world consumption and world net saving:

$$C(t) + S(t) - K(t) + \sum_{j=1}^{J} \delta_{kj} K_j(t) = F(t), \tag{13.15}$$

where

$$C(t) \equiv \sum_{j=1}^{J} \sum_{q=1}^{Q_j} c_{jq}(t) N_{jq}, \; S(t) \equiv \sum_{j=1}^{J} \sum_{q=1}^{Q_j} s_{jq}(t) N_{jq}, \; F(t) \equiv \sum_{j=1}^{J} F_j(t).$$

The model is complete. The model explains endogenous capital accumulation, human capital accumulation, labor supply, the international distribution of capital. The domestic markets of each country are perfectly competitive, international product and capital markets are freely mobile and labor is internationally immobile. The model is structurally general in the sense that some well-known models in theoretical economics can be considered as its special cases. For instance, if all the parameters are time-independent, the wealth and human capital are constant, the number of types of households is equal to the population, then the model is a Walrasian general equilibrium model.

13.2 The Dynamics and Its Properties

As the system has many variables and these variables are nonlinearly interrelated with differential equations, consists of any number of types of households, its dynamics is highly dimensional. The following lemma shows a computational procedure to follow the motion of the economic system. Introduce a variable:

$$z_1(t) \equiv \frac{r(t) + \delta_{k1}(t)}{w_1(t)}.$$

Lemma 13.1
The dynamics of the economy is governed by the following $2J$ dimensional differential equations system with $z(t)$, $\left\{\bar{k}_j(t)\right\}$, $\left(H_j(t)\right)$, and t where.

$$\left\{\bar{k}_j(t)\right\} \equiv \left(\bar{k}_2(t), \ldots, \bar{k}_J(t)\right), \left(H_j(t)\right) \equiv (H_1(t), \ldots, H_J(t)),$$

as the variables:

$$\dot{z}(t) = \Lambda_1\left(z(t), \left(H_j(t)\right), \left\{\bar{k}_j(t)\right\}, t\right),$$
$$\dot{\bar{k}}_j(t) = \Lambda_j\left(z(t), \left(H_j(t)\right), \left\{\bar{k}_j(t)\right\}, t\right), j = 2, \ldots, J,$$
$$\dot{H}_j(t) = \Omega_j\left(z(t), \left(H_j(t)\right), \left\{\bar{k}_j(t)\right\}, t\right), j = 1, \ldots, J,$$

in which Λ_j and Ω_j defined in the appendix are unique functions of $z(t)$, $\left\{\bar{k}_j(t)\right\}$, $\left(H_j(t)\right)$, and t at any point in time. For given $z(t)$, $\left\{\bar{k}_j(t)\right\}$, and $\left(H_j(t)\right)$, the other variables are uniquely determined at any point in time by the following procedure: $r(t)$ and $w(t)$ by (A13.3) $\rightarrow$ $w_j(t)$ by (A13.4) $\rightarrow$ $p(t)$ by (A13.5) $\rightarrow$ $\bar{k}_1(t)$ by (A18) $\rightarrow$ $N_i(t)$ by (A13.12) $\rightarrow$ $N(t)$ by (A13.11) $\rightarrow$ $N_s(t)$ by (A13.8) $\rightarrow$ $\bar{y}_j(t)$ by (A13.6)

$\rightarrow K_i(t)$ and $K_s(t)$ by (A13.1) $\rightarrow F_i(t)$ and $F_s(t)$ by the definitions $\rightarrow \overline{T}_j(t)$, $c_j(t)$, and $s_j(t)$ by (13.15) $\rightarrow K(t)$ by (13.4).

Following the lemma, I can simulate the dynamic equations with any number of types of households. Following Zhang (2015a), I first consider all the parameters time independent. The rest of this section is based on Zhang's simulation results. This chapter considers the world consists of three national economies, i.e., $J = 3$. The population and human capital utilization efficiency of the three economies are specified as follows:

$$N_{j1} = 1, N_{j2} = 69, N_{j3} = 20, T_0 = 24, j = 1, 2, 3$$
$$\begin{pmatrix} m_{11} \\ m_{21} \\ m_{31} \end{pmatrix} = \begin{pmatrix} 0.8 \\ 0.7 \\ 0.65 \end{pmatrix}, \begin{pmatrix} m_{12} \\ m_{22} \\ m_{32} \end{pmatrix} = \begin{pmatrix} 0.2 \\ 0.15 \\ 0.18 \end{pmatrix}, \begin{pmatrix} m_{13} \\ m_{23} \\ m_{33} \end{pmatrix} = \begin{pmatrix} 0.15 \\ 0.18 \\ 0.15 \end{pmatrix},$$
$$\begin{pmatrix} A_1 \\ A_2 \\ A_3 \end{pmatrix} = \begin{pmatrix} 1 \\ 0.8 \\ 0.75 \end{pmatrix}, \begin{pmatrix} \alpha_1 \\ \alpha_2 \\ a_3 \end{pmatrix} = \begin{pmatrix} 0.31 \\ 0.3 \\ 0.3 \end{pmatrix}. \tag{13.16}$$

The household preferences of the three economies are:

$$\begin{pmatrix} \lambda_{110} \\ \lambda_{210} \\ \lambda_{310} \end{pmatrix} = \begin{pmatrix} 0.94 \\ 0.9 \\ 0.85 \end{pmatrix}, \begin{pmatrix} \sigma_{110} \\ \sigma_{210} \\ \sigma_{310} \end{pmatrix} = \begin{pmatrix} 0.4 \\ 0.25 \\ 0.25 \end{pmatrix}, \begin{pmatrix} \xi_{110} \\ \xi_{210} \\ \xi_{310} \end{pmatrix} = \begin{pmatrix} 0.07 \\ 0.07 \\ 0.07 \end{pmatrix},$$
$$\begin{pmatrix} \lambda_{120} \\ \lambda_{220} \\ \lambda_{320} \end{pmatrix} = \begin{pmatrix} 0.65 \\ 0.63 \\ 0.55 \end{pmatrix}, \begin{pmatrix} \sigma_{120} \\ \sigma_{220} \\ \sigma_{320} \end{pmatrix} = \begin{pmatrix} 0.2 \\ 0.2 \\ 0.2 \end{pmatrix}, \begin{pmatrix} \xi_{120} \\ \xi_{220} \\ \xi_{320} \end{pmatrix} = \begin{pmatrix} 0.18 \\ 0.18 \\ 0.18 \end{pmatrix}, \tag{13.17}$$
$$\begin{pmatrix} \lambda_{130} \\ \lambda_{230} \\ \lambda_{330} \end{pmatrix} = \begin{pmatrix} 0.6 \\ 0.58 \\ 0.5 \end{pmatrix}, \begin{pmatrix} \sigma_{130} \\ \sigma_{230} \\ \sigma_{330} \end{pmatrix} = \begin{pmatrix} 0.2 \\ 0.2 \\ 0.2 \end{pmatrix}, \begin{pmatrix} \xi_{130} \\ \xi_{230} \\ \xi_{330} \end{pmatrix} = \begin{pmatrix} 0.2 \\ 0.2 \\ 0.2 \end{pmatrix}.$$

The parameters in the human capital accumulation equations are specified as follows:

$$\begin{pmatrix} \tilde{v}_{11} \\ \tilde{v}_{12} \\ \tilde{v}_{13} \\ \tilde{v}_{21} \\ \tilde{v}_{22} \\ \tilde{v}_{23} \\ \tilde{v}_{31} \\ \tilde{v}_{32} \\ \tilde{v}_{33} \end{pmatrix} = \begin{pmatrix} 0.8 \\ 0.4 \\ 0.1 \\ 0.7 \\ 0.35 \\ 0.1 \\ 0.6 \\ 0.3 \\ 0.3 \end{pmatrix}, \begin{pmatrix} a_{11} \\ a_{12} \\ a_{13} \\ a_{21} \\ a_{22} \\ a_{23} \\ a_{31} \\ a_{32} \\ a_{33} \end{pmatrix} = \begin{pmatrix} 0.3 \\ 0.2 \\ 0.1 \\ 0.3 \\ 0.2 \\ 0.1 \\ 0.3 \\ 0.2 \\ 0.2 \end{pmatrix}, \begin{pmatrix} v_{11} \\ v_{12} \\ v_{13} \\ v_{21} \\ v_{22} \\ v_{23} \\ v_{31} \\ v_{32} \\ v_{33} \end{pmatrix} = \begin{pmatrix} 0.2 \\ 0.1 \\ 0.1 \\ 0.2 \\ 0.1 \\ 0.1 \\ 0.2 \\ 0.1 \\ 0.1 \end{pmatrix},$$
$$\begin{pmatrix} \theta_{11} \\ \theta_{12} \\ \theta_{13} \\ \theta_{21} \\ \theta_{22} \\ \theta_{23} \\ \theta_{31} \\ \theta_{32} \\ \theta_{33} \end{pmatrix} = \begin{pmatrix} 0.2 \\ 0.1 \\ 0.1 \\ 0.2 \\ 0.1 \\ 0.1 \\ 0.2 \\ 0.1 \\ 0.1 \end{pmatrix}, \begin{pmatrix} \pi_{11} \\ \pi_{12} \\ \pi_{13} \\ \pi_{21} \\ \pi_{22} \\ \pi_{23} \\ \pi_{31} \\ \pi_{32} \\ \pi_{33} \end{pmatrix} = \begin{pmatrix} 0.1 \\ 0.2 \\ 0.4 \\ 0.12 \\ 0.2 \\ 0.4 \\ 0.15 \\ 0.2 \\ 0.2 \end{pmatrix}. \quad (13.18)$$

I specify:

$$\delta_{j1} = 0.04, \delta_{j2} = \delta_{j3} = 0.06, j = 1, 2, 3.$$

The initial conditions are as follows:

$$\begin{aligned} &z_1(0) = 0.059, \bar{k}_{12}(0) = 100, \bar{k}_{13}(0) = 60, \bar{k}_{21}(0) = 3860, \\ &\bar{k}_{22}(0) = 57, \bar{k}_{23}(0) = 42, \bar{k}_{31}(0) = 164, \bar{k}_{32}(0) = 47, \\ &\bar{k}_{33}(0) = 31, H_{11}(0) = 612, H_{12}(0) = 14, H_{13}(0) = 3, \\ &H_{21}(0) = 322, H_{22}(0) = 11, H_{23}(0) = 3.2, H_{31}(0) = 182, \\ &H_{32}(0) = 11, H_{33}(0) = 3. \end{aligned}$$

In Fig. 13.1, the national output Y, the share of each group's wealth in the national wealth θ_{jw}, and the ratio between group 1's and another group's wealth ϕ_j are respectively defined as:

$$\phi_j(t) \equiv \frac{\sum_{l=1}^{3} \overline{K}_{jl}(t)}{K(t)} 100, \phi_{jq}(t) \equiv \frac{\overline{K}_{jq}(t)}{\overline{K}_j(t)} 100, \tilde{\phi}_{jq}(t) \equiv \frac{\bar{k}_{j1}(t)}{\bar{k}_{jq}(t)} 100,$$
$$j = 1, 2, 3, q = 1, 2, 3.$$

Figure 13.2 describes the motion of the variables.

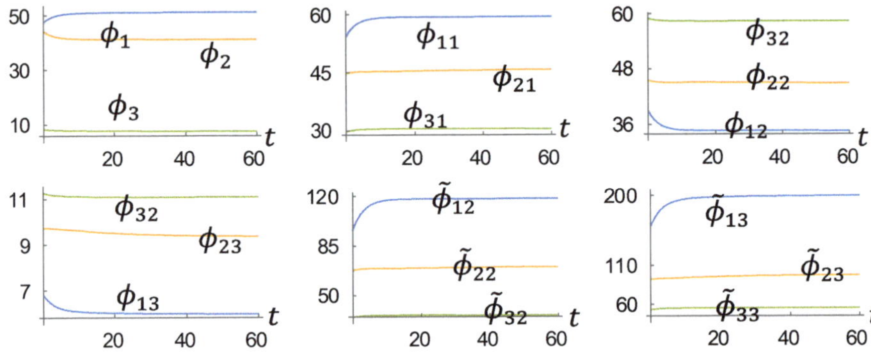

Fig. 13.1 Global and national wealth distributions over time

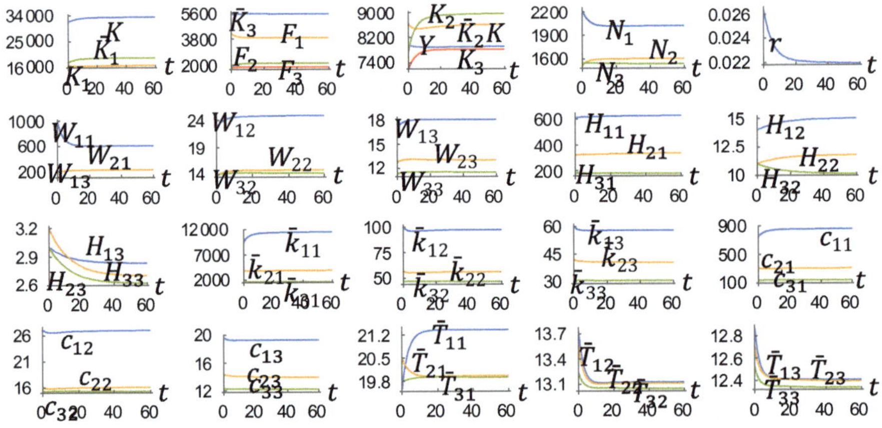

Fig. 13.2 The motion of the economic system

Zhang (2015a) identified the existence of a unique equilibrium. The equilibrium values are listed in (13.19).

$$\phi_1 = 51.2, \phi_2 = 41.1, \phi_3 = 7.66, \phi_{11} = 59.5, \phi_{21} = 34.6,$$
$$\phi_{31} = 5.95, \phi_{12} = 45.9, \phi_{22} = 44.8, \phi_{32} = 9.3, \phi_{13} = 20.5,$$
$$\phi_{23} = 58.4, \phi_{33} = 11.1, \tilde{\phi}_{12} = 119, \tilde{\phi}_{13} = 200, \tilde{\phi}_{22} = 71,$$
$$\tilde{\phi}_{23} = 98, \tilde{\phi}_{32} = 36, \tilde{\phi}_{33} = 55, Y = 7923.9, K = 33633.6, r = 0.022,$$
$$F_1 = 3896.8, F_2 = 2149.4, F_3 = 1877.6, N_1 = 2020.3, N_2 = 1602.9,$$
$$N_3 = 1534.8, K_1 = 16816.2, K_2 = 8976.2, K_3 = 7841.2,$$
$$\overline{K}_1 = 19483, \overline{K}_2 = 8648, \overline{K}_3 = 5502.3,$$

$$\begin{pmatrix} W_{11} \\ W_{12} \\ W_{13} \\ W_{21} \\ W_{22} \\ W_{23} \\ W_{31} \\ W_{32} \\ W_{33} \end{pmatrix} = \begin{pmatrix} 610 \\ 24.9 \\ 18.04 \\ 222 \\ 14.81 \\ 13.03 \\ 101.5 \\ 14.23 \\ 11.54 \end{pmatrix}, \begin{pmatrix} H_{11} \\ H_{12} \\ H_{13} \\ H_{21} \\ H_{22} \\ H_{23} \\ H_{31} \\ H_{32} \\ H_{33} \end{pmatrix} = \begin{pmatrix} 629.7 \\ 15.05 \\ 2.83 \\ 336.7 \\ 11.78 \\ 2.7 \\ 177.1 \\ 10.1 \\ 2.62 \end{pmatrix}, \begin{pmatrix} \bar{k}_{11} \\ \bar{k}_{12} \\ \bar{k}_{13} \\ \bar{k}_{21} \\ \bar{k}_{22} \\ \bar{k}_{23} \\ \bar{k}_{31} \\ \bar{k}_{32} \\ \bar{k}_{33} \end{pmatrix} = \begin{pmatrix} 11590 \\ 97.61 \\ 57.91 \\ 3968.3 \\ 56.13 \\ 40.35 \\ 1676.7 \\ 46.6 \\ 30.52 \end{pmatrix}, \begin{pmatrix} c_{11} \\ c_{12} \\ c_{13} \\ c_{21} \\ c_{22} \\ c_{23} \\ c_{31} \\ c_{32} \\ c_{33} \end{pmatrix} = \begin{pmatrix} 863.1 \\ 27.03 \\ 19.3 \\ 308.6 \\ 16.04 \\ 13.91 \\ 138.1 \\ 15.25 \\ 12.21 \end{pmatrix}, \begin{pmatrix} \bar{T}_{11} \\ \bar{T}_{12} \\ \bar{T}_{13} \\ \bar{T}_{21} \\ \bar{T}_{22} \\ \bar{T}_{23} \\ \bar{T}_{31} \\ \bar{T}_{32} \\ \bar{T}_{33} \end{pmatrix} = \begin{pmatrix} 21.35 \\ 13.12 \\ 12.41 \\ 19.98 \\ 13.11 \\ 12.39 \\ 19.91 \\ 13.04 \\ 12.34 \end{pmatrix}. \quad (13.19)$$

It is straightforward to calculate the eigenvalues as follows:

$$-0.65 \pm 0.23i, -0.43, 0.69 - 0.4, -0.397, -0.388, -0.36,$$
$$-0.25, -0.25, -0.08, -0.08, -0.08, -0.069, -0.069, -0.034,$$
$$-0.032, -0.022.$$

As the real parts of all the eigenvalues are negative, the equilibrium point is locally stable.

13.3 Exogenous Oscillations in the Efficiency of Applying Human Capital by Country 1's Rich Group

This section examines the effects of the following exogenous oscillations in the efficiency of applying human capital by country 1's rich:

$$m_{11}(t) = 0.8 + 0.01\sin(t).$$

The simulation results are plotted in Fig. 13.3. As the efficiency of applying human capital by country 1's rich fluctuate, the macroeconomic and microeconomic variables fluctuate around their long-term trend values.

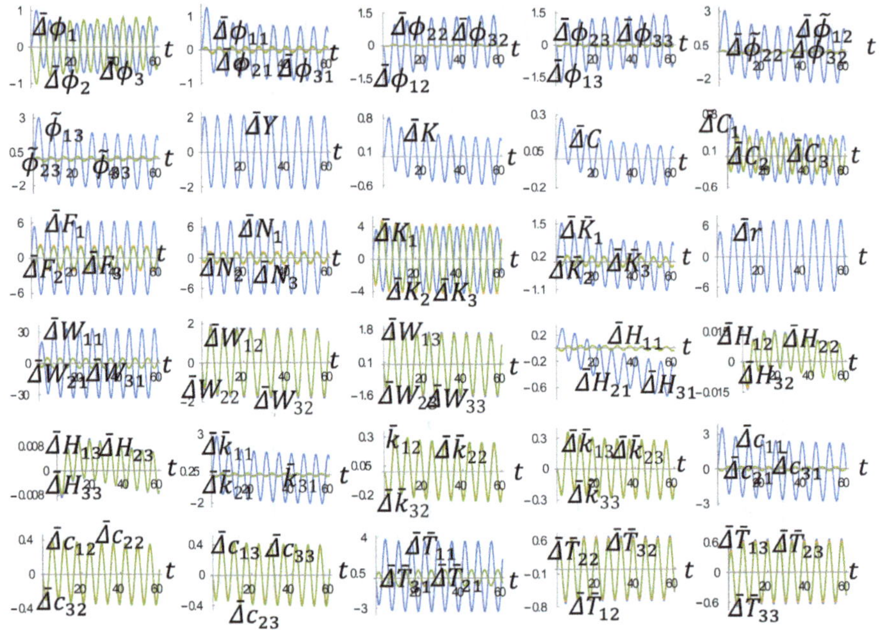

Fig. 13.3 Fluctuations in the efficiency of applying human capital by country 1's rich group

13.4 Fluctuations in Country 1's Total Factor Productivity

Another important question is what will happen to different people and the national economy if the total productivity is oscillatory. This section examines the effects of the following exogenous oscillations in country 1's total productivity:

$$A_1(t) = 1 + 0.05\sin(t).$$

The simulation results are plotted in Fig. 13.4.

13.5 The Propensity to Save of Country 1's Group1 Periodically Oscillating

I now periodically oscillate the propensity to save of country 1's group1 as follows:

$$\lambda_{110}(t) = 0.94 + 0.005\sin(t).$$

The simulation results are plotted in Fig. 13.5.

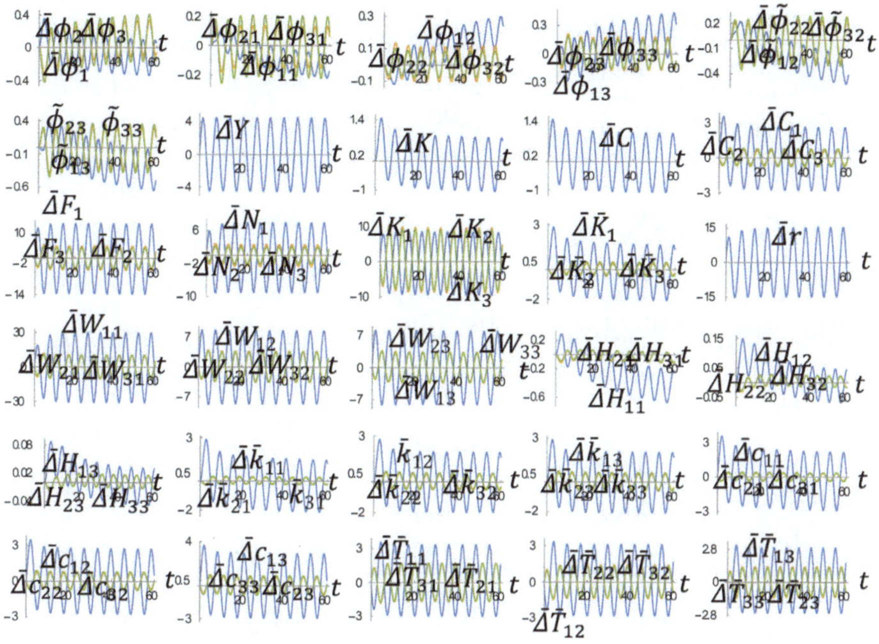

Fig. 13.4 Fluctuations in country 1's total factor productivity

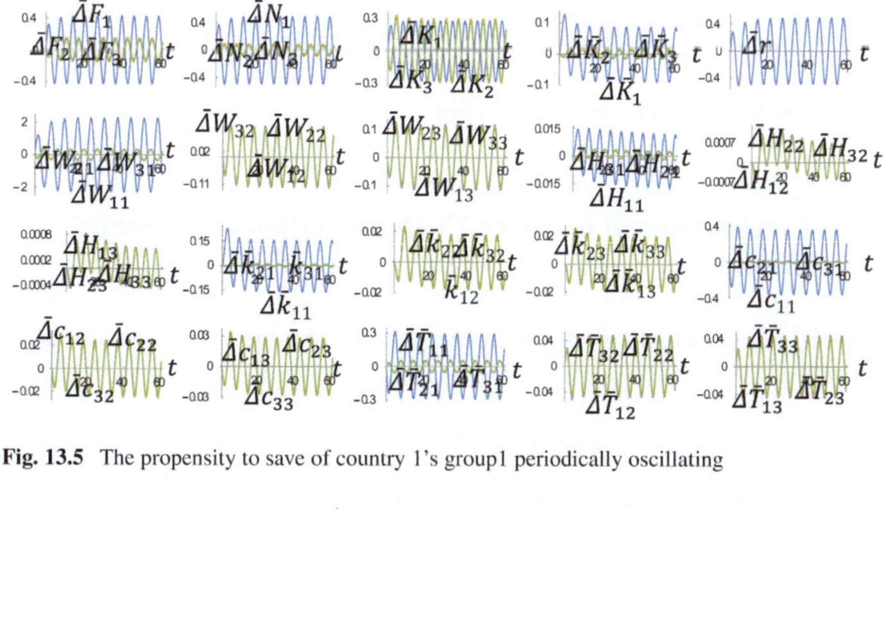

Fig. 13.5 The propensity to save of country 1's group1 periodically oscillating

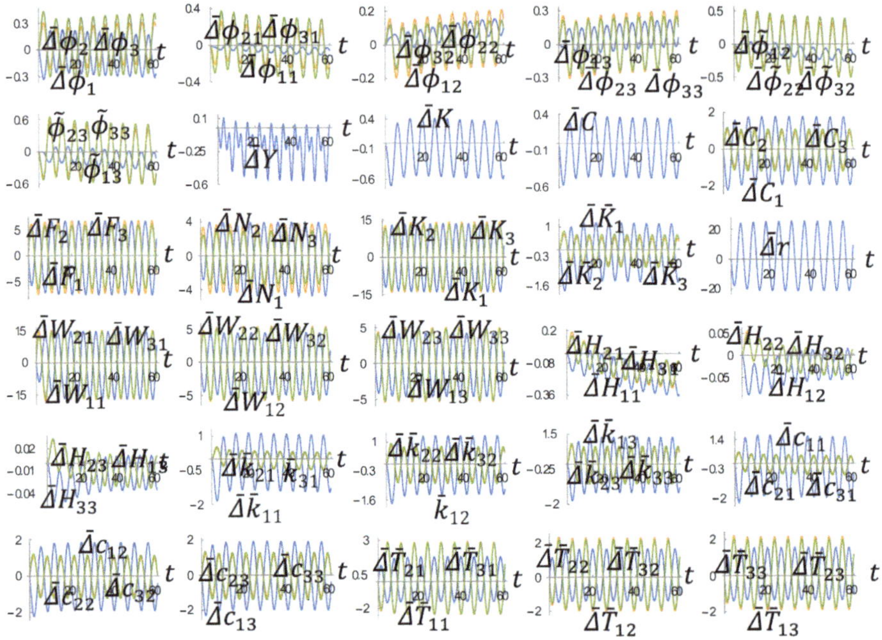

Fig. 13.6 Fluctuations in the return to scale in human capital accumulation

13.6 Fluctuations in the Return to Scale in Human Capital Accumulation

This section periodically oscillates the return to scale in human capital accumulation of country 1's group1 as follows:

$$\pi_{11}(t) = 0.1 + 0.03\sin(t).$$

The simulation results are plotted in Fig. 13.6.

13.7 Fluctuations in Country 1's Depreciation of Physical Capital

This section periodically oscillates country 1's depreciation of physical capital as follows:

$$\delta_{k1}(t) = 0.05 + 0.01\sin(t).$$

The simulation results are plotted in Fig. 13.7.

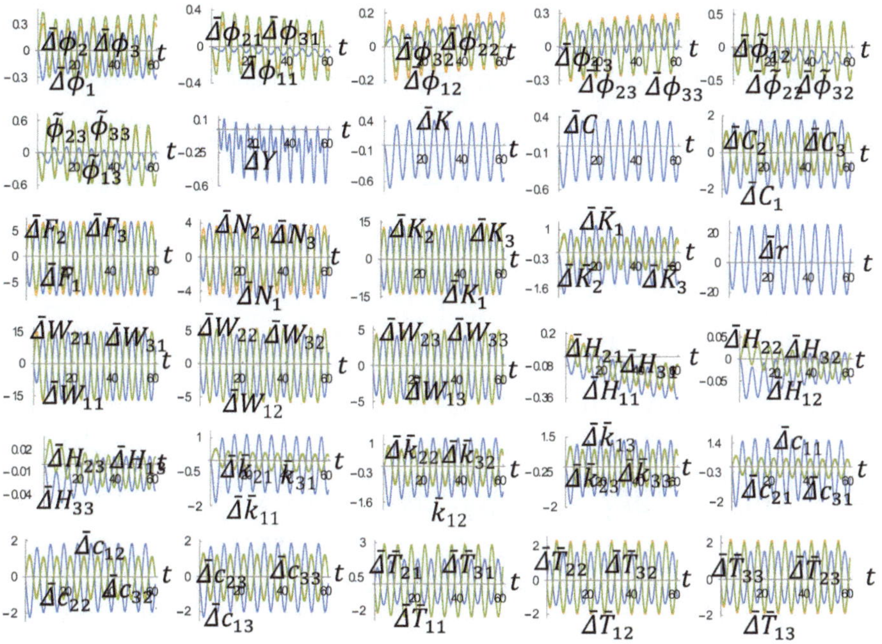

Fig. 13.7 Fluctuations in country 1's depreciation of physical capital

13.8 Fluctuations in the Depreciation of Human Capital of Country 1's Group 1

This section periodically oscillates the depreciation of human capital of country 1's group 1 as follows:

$$\delta_{11}(t) = 0.04 + 0.005 \sin(t).$$

The simulation results are plotted in Fig. 13.8.

13.9 Concluding Remarks

This chapter generalized the dynamic economic model of heterogeneous households built by Zhang (2015a). The original model provided insights into the economic mechanisms of how the richest one per cent of the global population own 50% of the global wealth. It explained inequality in a purely competitive economic environment with endogenous wealth and human capital accumulation. This chapter simulated a case with three countries and each country with three groups of the population. It demonstrated the existence of an equilibrium point at which the rich 1% own more

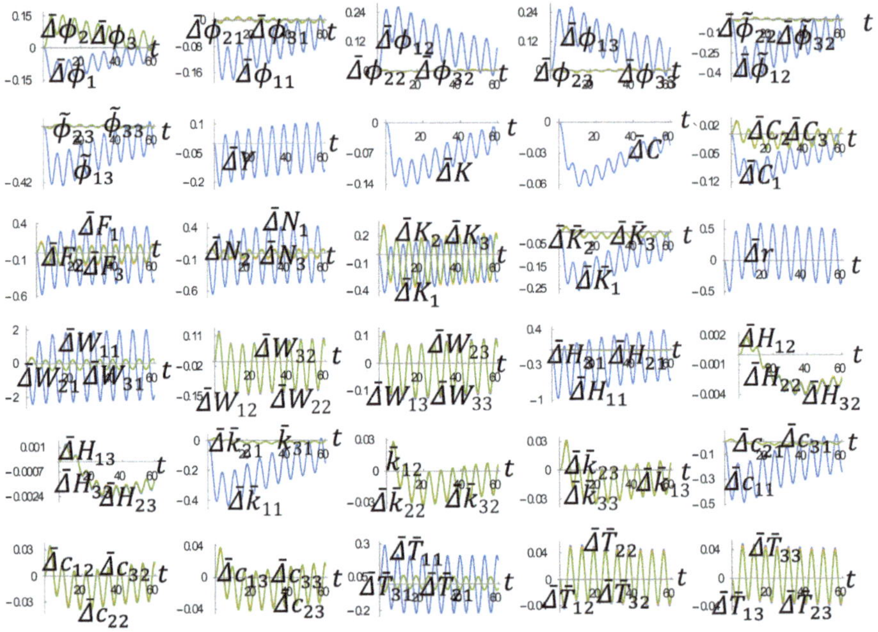

Fig. 13.8 Fluctuations in country 1's depreciation of human capital

than half of the global wealth. This chapter generalized Zhang's model by making all the time-independent parameters as time-dependent parameters. It demonstrated how the system reacts to different exogenous periodic perturbations. Many limitations of the model in this chapter become apparent in light of issues often addressed in the literature of growth theory (Batabyal and Nijkamp 2013; Akcigit and Ker 2018; Diebolt and Hippe 2019; Fonseca et al. 2019; Liao et al. 2019; Beenstock 2021; Chen et al. 2022; Bacolod et al. 2023). The model can be generalized to provide insights into other aspects of economic complexity.

Appendix: Proving Lemma 13.1

By (13.3), I obtain:

$$z_j \equiv \frac{r + \delta_{kj}}{w_j} = \frac{N_j}{\overline{\beta}_j K_j}, \tag{A13.1}$$

where $\overline{\beta}_q \equiv \beta_q / \alpha_q$. From (A13.1) and (13.3), it follows:

$$r = \alpha_{rj} z_j^{\beta_j} - \delta_{kj}, \; w_j = \alpha_{wj} z_j^{-\alpha_j}, \tag{A13.2}$$

where

$$\alpha_{rj} = \alpha_j A_j \overline{\beta}_j^{\beta_j}, \alpha_{wj} = \beta_j A_j \overline{\beta}_j^{-\alpha_j}.$$

From (A13.2):

$$z_j(z_1, t) = \left(\frac{\alpha_{r1} z_1^{\beta_1} - \delta_{k1} + \delta_{kj}}{\alpha_{rj}} \right)^{1/\beta_j}. \tag{A13.3}$$

Hence, I have:

$$w_{jq}\left(z_1, H_{jq}, t\right) = H_{jq}^{m_{jq}} w_j. \tag{A13.4}$$

The rate of interest and the wage rates are determined as functions of z_1 and $\left(H_{jq}\right)$. From (A13.4) and the definitions of $\overline{y}_j$, it follows:

$$\overline{y}_{jq}\left(z_1, \overline{k}_{jq} H_{jq}, t\right) = (1 + r)\overline{k}_{jq} + T_0 w_{jq}. \tag{A13.5}$$

Inserting $w_j \overline{T}_j = \sigma_j \overline{y}_j$ in (13.7) yields:

$$T_{jq} = T_0 - \frac{\sigma_{jq} \overline{y}_{jq}}{w_{jq}}. \tag{A13.6}$$

Insert (A13.5) in (A13.6):

$$T_{jq} = \left(1 - \sigma_{jq}\right) T_0 - \frac{(1 + r)\sigma_{jq} \overline{k}_{jq}}{w_{jq}}. \tag{A13.7}$$

Insert (A13.7) in (13.1):

$$N_j = n_j - \sum_{q=1}^{Q_j} n_{jq} \overline{k}_{jq}, \tag{A13.8}$$

where

$$n_j \equiv T_0 \sum_{q=1}^{Q_j} \left(1 - \sigma_{jq}\right) N_{jq} H_{jq}^{m_{jq}}, n_{jq} \equiv \left(\frac{1 + r}{w_j} \right) \sigma_{jq} N_{jq}.$$

By (A13.8) and (A13.1):

$$K_j = \frac{n_j}{\bar{\beta}_j z_j} - \frac{1}{\bar{\beta}_j z_j} \sum_{q=1}^{Q_j} n_{jq} \bar{k}_{jq}. \tag{A13.9}$$

Insert (A13.9) in (13.13):

$$\sum_{j=1}^{J} \frac{n_j}{\bar{\beta}_j z_j} = \sum_{j=1}^{J} \sum_{q=1}^{Q_j} \phi_{jq} \bar{k}_{jq}, \tag{A13.10}$$

where

$$\phi_{jq}\left(z_1, (H_{jq}), t\right) = \frac{n_{jq}}{\bar{\beta}_j z_j} + N_{jq}.$$

Solve (A13.10) with regard to $\bar{k}_{11}$:

$$\begin{aligned} \bar{k}_{11} &\equiv \phi\left(z_1, (H_{jq}), \{\bar{k}_{jq}\}, t\right) \\ &\equiv \left(\sum_{j=1}^{J} \frac{n_j}{\bar{\beta}_j z_j} - \sum_{j=2}^{J} \sum_{q=2}^{Q_j} \phi_{jq} \bar{k}_{jq} - \sum_{q=2}^{Q_j} \phi_{1q} \bar{k}_{1q} \right) \frac{1}{\phi_{11}}, \end{aligned} \tag{A13.11}$$

where

$$\left\{\bar{k}_{jq}\right\} \equiv \left(\bar{k}_{12}, \bar{k}_{1Q_1}, \bar{k}_{21}, \bar{k}_{JQ_J}\right).$$

It is straightforward to confirm that all the variables can be expressed as functions of z_{11}, $\left\{\bar{k}_{jq}\right\}$ and (H_{jq}) by the following procedure: r and w_j by (A13.2) → w_{jq} by (A13.4) → $\bar{k}_{11}$ by (A13.11) → N_j by (A13.8) → K_j by (A13.1) → $\overline{K}_j$ by (13.14) → $\bar{y}_{jq}$ by (A13.5) → F_j by (13.2) → $\overline{T}_{jq}$, c_{jq}, and s_{jq} by (13.10) → K by (13.13). From this procedure, (A13.11), (13.11), and (13.12), I have:

$$\dot{\bar{k}}_{11} = \bar{\Omega}\left(z_1, \{\bar{k}_{jq}\}, (H_{jq}), t\right) \equiv \lambda_{11} \bar{y}_{11} - \phi, \tag{A13.12}$$

$$\begin{aligned} \dot{\bar{k}}_{jq} &= \Lambda_{jq}\left(z_1, \{\bar{k}_{jq}\}, (H_{jq}), t\right) \equiv \lambda_{jq} \bar{y}_{jq} - \bar{k}_{jq}, \\ \dot{H}_{jq} &= \Omega_{jq}\left(z_1, \{\bar{k}_{jq}\}, (H_{jq}), t\right). \end{aligned} \tag{A13.13}$$

Taking derivatives of equation (A13.11) with respect to t and combining with (A13.13), I get:

$$\dot{\bar{k}}_{11} = \frac{\partial \phi}{\partial t} + \frac{\partial \phi}{\partial z_1} \dot{z}_1 + \sum_{q=2}^{Q_1} \Lambda_{1q} \frac{\partial \phi}{\partial \bar{k}_{1q}}$$

$$+\sum_{j=2}^{J}\sum_{q=1}^{Q_j}\Lambda_{jq}\frac{\partial\phi}{\partial\bar{k}_{jq}}+\sum_{j=1}^{J}\sum_{q=1}^{Q_j}\Omega_{jq}\frac{\partial\phi}{\partial H_{jq}}. \tag{A13.14}$$

Equaling the right-hand sizes of equations (A13.14) and (A13.12), I get:

$$\dot{z}_1 = \Lambda_{11}\left(z_1, \left\{\bar{k}_{jq}\right\}, (H_{jq}), t\right)$$
$$\equiv \left[\overline{\Omega} - \frac{\partial\phi}{\partial t} - \sum_{q=2}^{Q_1}\Lambda_{1q}\frac{\partial\phi}{\partial\bar{k}_{1q}} - \sum_{j=2}^{J}\sum_{q=1}^{Q_j}\Lambda_{jq}\frac{\partial\phi}{\partial\bar{k}_{jq}} - \sum_{j=1}^{J}\sum_{q=1}^{Q_j}\Omega_{jq}\frac{\partial\phi}{\partial H_{jq}}\right]\left(\frac{\partial\phi}{\partial z_1}\right)^{-1}. \tag{A13.15}$$

In summary, the lemma is confirmed.

Chapter 14
Growth and Inequality in an Economy with Perfect and Monopolistic Competition

> Madness is rare in individuals – but in groups, parties, nations, and ages, it is the rule.
>
> Friedrich Nietzsche

Economic reality of modern economies is characterized by co-existence of markets with perfect competition, monopolistic competition, monopoly (state planning), and different types of games. In modern growth theory, there are two main approaches with (proper) microeconomic foundations. Traditional neoclassical growth theory is mostly concerned with capital accumulation with economic structure but a homogeneous population (which implies no insight into income and wealth distribution among households). New dynamic economic theory is mainly concerned with perfect and monopolistic competition and knowledge creation and utilization without a proper mechanism for dealing with wealth accumulation. The two approaches failed to deal with economic growth with heterogeneous households. Economic dynamic theory lacks proper modeling frameworks for explaining dynamic issues related to income and wealth distributions, even though Walrasian theory provides a rational explanation about distribution of income and wealth in a static world. It is a great challenge to create a theory which includes the basic mechanisms in these approaches in a single framework with microeconomic foundation. The unique contribution to the literature of economic growth of this chapter is integrating the basic economic mechanisms in the Walrasian general equilibrium model, the Solow one-sector growth model, and the Dixit-Stiglitz model.

Modeling of monopolistic competition has recently become very popular in building macroeconomic models on the basis of microeconomic foundation. The ideas and modeling strategies in the literature of new economic theory enable economists to explain many well observed but not properly modeled phenomena. The theory of monopolistic competition has been applied to different issues of economics related to economic structures, economic growth, economic geography, international trade, and innovation and technological diffusion (Dixit and Stiglitz 1977; Krugman 1979, 1980; Lancaster 1980; Waterson 1984; Grossman and Helpman 1991; Benassy

W. Zhang, *A Dynamic Economic Theory of Heterogenous Households*,
https://doi.org/10.1007/978-981-95-8918-0_14

1996; Bertoletti and Etro 2015; Bachmann and Frings 2017; Behrens and Murata 2007, 2017; Nocco et al. 2017; Parenti et al. 2017; Kuwahara 2019; Zhang 2020c, 2020d, 2020e, 2020f; Buccella et al. 2021; Colombo and Lambertini 2023; Kyle and Lee 2023). Although macroeconomics based on monopolistic competition theory has provided many important insights into contemporary economic complexity, as far as economic dynamics is concerned, the approach has not succeeded in modeling wealth accumulation with heterogeneous households. Issues related to income and wealth distribution are important for understanding many problems of political economy in modern world. This chapter integrates neoclassical growth theory and Walrasian general equilibrium theory with monopolistic competition. It applies the main economic growth mechanism in neoclassical growth theory to model wealth accumulation and the general equilibrium economic principle to model income and wealth distribution. Perfect competition and monopolistic competition co-exist in the economic system.

Coexistence of perfect competition and monopolistic competition in macroeconomic dynamics with wealth accumulation is introduced by, for instance, Romer (1990). The economy has two sectors. The final goods sector is characterized by perfect competition and produces a single globally homogenous capital goods with identical firms. The middle goods sector is characterized by monopolistic competition and produces a variety of different goods with different firms. I model production and consumption of middle goods by following analytical framework for monopolistic competition by Dixit and Stiglitz (1977). Dixit and Stiglitz emphasize diversity of consumption-on-consumption structure. I base Solow's one-sector growth model to describe the final goods sector. The market mechanism of perfect competitive markets is based on traditional neoclassical growth theory. Another important issue of this research is related to dynamics of income and wealth distribution. Macroeconomics lacks a proper framework for analyzing issues related to growth and income and wealth distribution between heterogeneous households. This chapter deals with growth and inequality with perfect and monopolistic competition within an integrated framework of Walrasian general equilibrium theory. The model also studies dynamic interdependence between endogenous labor supply, economic growth, and profit sharing. This chapter makes an extension of Zhang's 2018 model with homogeneous population (Zhang 2018c) by introducing heterogenous households. This chapter is based on Zhang (2019a) and is organized as follows. Section 14.1 constructs the growth model of heterogenous households under perfect competition and monopolistic competition. Section 14.2 analyzes properties of the economy and simulates the economic system. Section 14.3 shows how the economic system reacts to a rise in the elasticity of substitution between two varieties. Section 14.4 shows the effects of a rise in the fixed labor cost of the middle goods firm on the income and wealth distribution and economic growth. Section 14.5 follows the dynamics of the changes caused by a rise in variety of middle goods. Section 14.6 studies the impact of a rise in the total productivity of the final goods sector on the motion of the economic system. Section 14.7 studies how the income and wealth distribution and national growth are affected owing to a rise in group 1's propensity to consume middle goods. Section 14.8 follows the changes caused by a rise group 1's propensity to save. Section 14.9 studies how the system is affected then there is a rise in group 3's human capital. Section 14.10 examines the effects of a rise in group 3's population. Section 14.11 shows how a shift in the profit distribution affects the growth and income and wealth distribution. Section 14.12 concludes the chapter. The appendix proves Lemma 14.1.

14.1 Modeling Returns to Scale and Growth with Heterogenous Households

This section builds a model of heterogeneous households to analyze economic growth with endogenous capital accumulation under perfect competition and monopolistic competition. I base Walrasian general theory on determination of price equilibrium in an economy with heterogeneous households, and base Solow's one-sector growth model to describe the final goods sector with perfect competition. The description of imperfect competition is based on the approach developed by Dixit and Stiglitz. The approaches are integrated by applying my utility function and concept of disposable income.

Total Labor Force

The population is classified into J groups according to human capital and preference. Let subscripts j stand for group j , j $= 1, ..., $ J. Let $T_j(t)$ stand for the work time of household j and $N(t)$ the flow of labor services used at time t for production. I have $N(t)$ as follows:

$$N(t) = \sum_{j=1}^{J} h_j T_j(t) \overline{N}_j, \tag{14.1}$$

where $\overline{N}_j$ and h_j are respectively the population and the level of human capital of group j. In this study for simplicity of analysis $\overline{N}_j$ and h_j are assumed fixed.

Final Goods Sector

The final goods sector is almost the same as the industrial sector in the Solow model. Let $F(t)$, $K(t)$, and $\tilde{N}(t)$ stand for, respectively, output of the final goods sector, capital input, and labor input. The production function is as follows:

$$F(t) = AK^{\alpha}(t)\tilde{N}^{\beta}(t), 0 < \alpha, \beta < 1, \alpha + \beta = 1, \tag{14.2}$$

in which A, α, and β are coefficients. Capital goods are used as a medium of exchange. It is taken as numeraire. Physical capital depreciates at a constant exponential rate δ_k. Let $w(t)$ and $r(t)$ stand for, respectively, the wage rate and the rate of interest. I have the profit of the final goods sector as follows:

$$\pi_0(t) = F(t) - (r(t) + \delta_k)K(t) - w(t)\tilde{N}(t).$$

Maximizing profit implies the following marginal conditions:

$$R(t) = \frac{\alpha F(t)}{K(t)}, w(t) = \frac{\beta F(t)}{\tilde{N}(t)}, w_j(t) = h_j w(t), \tag{14.3}$$

where $w_j(t)$ stand for the wage rate of the representative household in group j and $R_\delta(t) \equiv r(t) + \delta_k$. From (14.3), I have:

$$\frac{w_j(t)}{w_m(t)} = \frac{h_j}{h_m}.$$

This relation is due to assumption that there is no discrimination in the sense that anyone is paid per unit of time according to one's work efficiency.

Disposable Income and Profit Share

Let $\overline{k}_j(t)$ represent group $j's$ household wealth. As in Zhang (2018c), it is assumed that the total profit of all the firms of the middle goods sector is shared among the households. I use $\pi_j(t)$ to stand for the profit shared by the representative household in group j. The current income of the representative: household in group j :

$$y_j(t) = r(t)\overline{k}_j(t) + h_j T_j(t) w(t) + \pi_j(t). \tag{14.4}$$

The household disposable income $\hat{y}_j(t)$ is the sum of the current disposable income and the value of wealth:

$$\hat{y}_j(t) = y_j(t) + \overline{k}_j(t). \tag{14.5}$$

The concept of disposable income in our approach is different from the traditional concept of disposable income which is equal to the current income in our approach. Our disposable income is the sum of the value of what one earns currently and the value of what one owns. The possible transaction costs in terms of money and time are omitted. This implies, for instance, one can sell one's assets to purchase middle goods for consumption.

Budgets and Composite Good for Aggregating Middle Goods

The representative household spends the disposable income on saving $s_j(t)$, on consuming final goods $d_j(t)$, and on consuming middle goods $\tilde{c}_j(\varepsilon, t)$. Here, $\tilde{c}_j(\varepsilon, t)$ stands for the amount of variety ε that is consumed by group $j's$ representative household. Let variety ε distribute within the range from 0 to n, $\varepsilon \in [0, n]$. I follow Dixit and Stiglitz (1977) in describing consumption of middle goods. The composite good for each group is introduced as follows:

$$c_j(t) = \left(\int_0^n \tilde{c}_j^{\overline{\theta}}(\varepsilon, t) d\varepsilon \right)^{1/\overline{\theta}}, 1 > \overline{\theta}_j > 0, \tag{14.6}$$

where $\overline{\theta}$ is a positive parameter. The above function of constant elasticity of substation is widely applied in the recent literature of monopolistic competition (Spence 1976; Tirole 1988).

Let the price of $\tilde{c}_j(\varepsilon, t)$ be denoted by $\tilde{p}(\varepsilon, t)$. The disposable income is spent on saving, consuming final goods, and consuming middle goods. I have the budget constraint as follows:

$$d_j(t) + \int_0^n \tilde{p}(\varepsilon, t)\tilde{c}_j(\varepsilon, t)d\varepsilon + s_j(t) = \hat{y}_j(t). \tag{14.7}$$

$\overline{T}_j(t)$ denotes the leisure time at time t and T_0 (fixed) denotes the available time for work and leisure . The time constraint is expressed by

$$T_j(t) + \overline{T}_j(t) = T_0.$$

Insert the above equation in (14.4):

$$\hat{y}_j(t) = R(t)\overline{k}_j(t) - h_j\overline{T}_j(t)w(t) + W_j(t), \tag{14.8}$$

where (14.5) is applied and

$$R(t) \equiv 1 + r(t),\ W_j(t) \equiv h_jT_0w(t) + \pi_j(t)$$

Substituting (14.8) into (14.7) yields

$$h_j\overline{T}_j(t)w(t) + d_j(t) + \int_0^n \tilde{p}(\varepsilon, t)\tilde{c}_j(\varepsilon, t)d\varepsilon + s_j(t) = \overline{y}_j(t), \tag{14.9}$$

where

$$\overline{y}_j(t) \equiv R(t)\overline{k}_j(t) + W_j(t).$$

Utility Functions and Optimal Behavior

The utility level $U_j(t)$ is dependent on $\overline{T}_j(t)$, $d_j(t)$, $c_j(t)$ and $s_j(t)$ as follows:

$$U_j(t) = \overline{T}_j^{\sigma_{0j}}(t)c_j^{\chi_{0j}}(t)d_j^{\xi_{0j}}(t)s_j^{\lambda_{0j}}(t),\ \sigma_{0j}, \xi_{0j}, \lambda_{0j}, \chi_{0j} > 0, \tag{14.10}$$

where σ_{0j} is the propensity to use leisure time, ξ_{0j} is the propensity to consume final good, χ_{0j} is the propensity to consume intermediates, and λ_{0j} is the propensity to save. Many research papers with formal modeling have been published on dynamic interdependence between economic growth and time allocation. In the literature of economic development, reallocation of labor from households to the market in association of economic growth are modeling in different approaches (Becker 1965, 1976; Goodfriend and McDermott 1995; Kelly 1997; Edmonds and Pavcnik 2006; Ferber and Green 2007).

The problem is to maximize utility (14.10) subject to budget constraint (14.9). I apply the two-stage method to solve the optimization problem (Dixit-Stiglitz 1977). In the first stage, it is considered that there is a price $p(t)$ for $c_j(t)$. The budget for the question is

$$h_j w(t)\overline{T}_j(t) + d_j(t) + p(t)c_j(t) + s_j(t) = \overline{y}_j(t). \tag{14.11}$$

It is straightforward to show that the optimal solution is given by:

$$h_j w(t)\overline{T}_j(t) = \sigma_j \overline{y}_j(t),\ d_j(t) = \xi_j \overline{y}_j(t),\ p(t)c_j(t) = \chi_j \overline{y}_j(t),$$
$$s_j(t) = \lambda_j \overline{y}_j(t), \tag{14.12}$$

where

$$\sigma_j \equiv \rho_j \sigma_{0j},\ \xi_j \equiv \rho_j \xi_{0j},\ \chi_j \equiv \rho_j \chi_{0j},\ \lambda_j \equiv \rho_j \lambda_{0j},$$
$$\rho_j \equiv \frac{1}{\sigma_{0j} + \xi_{0j} + \chi_{0j} + \lambda_{0j}}.$$

The second-stage maximization is formed as follows: maximize $c_j(t)$ by choosing $\tilde{c}_j(\epsilon, t)$ subject to:

$$\int_0^n \tilde{p}(\varepsilon, t)\tilde{c}_j(\varepsilon, t)d\varepsilon = p(t)c_j(t). \tag{14.13}$$

Introduce the following Langrangian function:

$$\mathcal{L}_j(t) \equiv \left(\int_0^n \tilde{c}_j^{\bar{\theta}}(\varepsilon,\ t)\ d\varepsilon\right)^{\frac{1}{\bar{\theta}}}$$
$$+ \hbar_j(t)\left\{p(t)c_j(t) - \int_0^n \tilde{p}(\varepsilon,\ t)\ \tilde{c}_j(\varepsilon,\ t)d\varepsilon\right\}, \tag{14.14}$$

where $\hbar_j(t)$ is the Lagrangian multiplier. From (14.12), I get the following first-order conditions:

$$\frac{\partial \mathcal{L}_j(t)}{\partial \tilde{c}_j(\varepsilon,\ t)} = c_j^{1-\bar{\theta}}(t)\tilde{c}_j^{\bar{\theta}-1}(\varepsilon,\ t) - \hbar_j(t)\tilde{p}(\varepsilon,\ t) = 0\,,$$

$$\frac{\partial \mathcal{L}_j(t)}{\partial \hbar_j(t)} = p(t)c_j(t) - \int_0^n \tilde{p}(\varepsilon,\ t)\tilde{c}_j(\varepsilon,\ t)\, d\varepsilon = 0. \tag{14.15}$$

From the first equations in (14.15), it follows:

$$c_j^{1-\overline{\theta}}(t)\tilde{c}_j^{\overline{\theta}-1}(\varepsilon, t) = \hbar_j(t)\tilde{p}(\varepsilon, t). \tag{14.16}$$

From (14.16):

$$\frac{\tilde{c}_j(\varepsilon, t)}{\tilde{c}_j(\mu, t)} = \left(\frac{\tilde{p}(\varepsilon, t)}{\tilde{p}(\mu, t)}\right)^{1/(\overline{\theta}-1)} = \left(\frac{\tilde{p}(\varepsilon, t)}{\tilde{p}(\mu, t)}\right)^{-\omega}, \overline{\theta} = 1 - \frac{1}{\omega}. \tag{14.17}$$

where ω_j is the elasticity of substitution between any two varieties:

$$\frac{\left(\tilde{p}(\varepsilon, t)/\tilde{p}(\mu, t)\right)}{\left(\tilde{c}_j(\varepsilon, t)/\tilde{c}_j(\mu, t)\right)} \frac{d\left(\tilde{c}_j(\varepsilon, t)/\tilde{c}_j(\mu, t)\right)}{d\left(\tilde{p}(\varepsilon, t)/\tilde{p}(\mu, t)\right)} = \omega.$$

From (14.15), I solve:

$$\tilde{c}_j(\varepsilon, t)\tilde{p}(\varepsilon, t) = \left(\frac{\tilde{p}(\varepsilon, t)}{\tilde{p}(\mu, t)}\right)^{\gamma} \tilde{p}(\varepsilon, t)\tilde{c}_j(\mu, t).$$

where $\gamma \equiv 1/\left(\overline{\theta} - 1\right)$. From the above equations, it follows:

$$\begin{aligned} p(t)c_j(t) = \chi_j\overline{y}_j(t) &= \int_0^n \tilde{p}(\varepsilon, t)\tilde{c}_j(\varepsilon, t)d\varepsilon \\ &= \frac{\tilde{c}_j(\gamma, t)}{\tilde{p}^{\gamma}(\gamma, t)} \int_0^n \tilde{p}^{\overline{\theta}\gamma}(\varepsilon, t)d\varepsilon = \frac{\tilde{c}_j(\gamma, t)P_j(t)}{\tilde{p}^{\gamma}(\gamma, t)}, \end{aligned} \tag{14.18}$$

where

$$P_j(t) \equiv \int_0^n \tilde{p}^{\overline{\theta}\gamma}(\varepsilon, t)d\varepsilon.$$

Hence, I have:

$$\tilde{c}_j(\varepsilon, t) = \chi_j\overline{y}_j(t)\tilde{p}^{\gamma}(\varepsilon, t)P_j^{-1}(t). \tag{14.19}$$

From (14.19):

$$p(t) = \frac{\chi_j \bar{y}_j(t)}{c_j(t)} = \left(\int_0^n \tilde{c}_j^{\bar{\theta}}(\varepsilon, t) d\varepsilon \right)^{-\frac{1}{\theta}} \chi_j \bar{y}_j(t) = P_j(t)^{\frac{1}{\theta_Y}}. \tag{14.20}$$

The value share of variety ε in the total value of intermediates for consumption is

$$\varphi(\varepsilon, t) = \frac{\tilde{p}(\varepsilon, t)\tilde{c}(\varepsilon, t)}{\bar{y}(t)}, \tag{14.21}$$

where

$$\bar{y}(t) \equiv \sum_{j=1}^{J} \overline{N}_j \int_0^n \tilde{p}(\varepsilon, t)\tilde{c}_j(\varepsilon, t) d\varepsilon, \tilde{c}(\varepsilon, t) \equiv \sum_{j=1}^{J} \tilde{c}_j(\varepsilon, t)\overline{N}_j.$$

Household's Wealth Accumulation

The change in the household's wealth saving minus dissaving:

$$\dot{k}_j(t) = s_j(t) - \bar{k}_j(t). \tag{14.22}$$

Middle Goods Sector

Markets of middle goods are characterized of monopolistic competition. No firm in the middle goods sector can produce a product with an attribute that is very close to any given attribute of any other product. They are assumed to act atomistically in that no firm take account of possible impacts of its decisions on any other firm. Let $x(\varepsilon, t)$ stand for the output level of the producer of variety ε. The condition that demand equals supply are as follows:

$$\sum_{j=1}^{J} \tilde{c}_j(\varepsilon, t)\overline{N}_j = x(\varepsilon, t). \tag{14.23}$$

All middle goods are produced with the same cost function. The labor force used in producing each good is linearly related to output as follows:

$$l(\varepsilon, t) = \tilde{\alpha} + \tilde{\beta} x(\varepsilon, t), \tag{14.24}$$

where $l(\varepsilon, t)$ is labor force used in producing good ε, $\tilde{\alpha}$ is a fixed cost, and $\tilde{\beta}$ is a positive coefficient. The total labor force $N_x(t)$ used by the middle goods sector is the sum of labor force used by all the firms:

$$N_x(t) = \int_0^n l(\varepsilon, t) d\varepsilon. \tag{14.25}$$

The producer of variety ε has the following profit:

$$\overline{\pi}(\varepsilon, t) = \tilde{p}(\varepsilon, t)x(\varepsilon, t) - \big(\tilde{\alpha} + \tilde{\beta}x(\varepsilon, t)\big)w(t). \tag{14.26}$$

The symmetry of the problem implies that all immediate firms will produce the same quantity at the same price. I thus can use the shorthand notation:

$$x(t) = x_j(\varepsilon, t), \pi(t) = \overline{\pi}(\varepsilon, t), \tilde{p}(t) = \tilde{p}(\varepsilon, t) \text{ for all } \varepsilon.$$

From (14.23) and (14.26), it follows:

$$\overline{\pi}(t) = \big(\tilde{p}(t) - \tilde{\beta}w(t)\big)\sum_{j=1}^{J}\tilde{c}_j(\varepsilon, t)\overline{N}_j - \tilde{\alpha}w(t). \tag{14.27}$$

Insert (14.19) in (14.27):

$$\overline{\pi}(t) = \big(\tilde{p}(t) - \tilde{\beta}w(t)\big)\tilde{p}^{\gamma}(t)M(t) - \tilde{\alpha}w(t), \tag{14.28}$$

where

$$M(t) \equiv P_j^{-1}(t)\sum_{j=1}^{J}\chi_j\overline{y}_j(t)\overline{N}_j.$$

The first-order condition (i.e., $\partial\overline{\pi}/\partial\tilde{p} = 0$) implies the following fixed-markup pricing rule:

$$\tilde{p}(t) = \frac{\tilde{\beta}w(t)}{\overline{\theta}}. \tag{14.29}$$

Insert (14.26) in (14.25):

$$\overline{\pi}(t) = \vartheta w^{1+\gamma}(t)M(t) - \tilde{\alpha}w(t), \tag{14.30}$$

where

$$\vartheta \equiv \left(\frac{1}{\overline{\theta}} - 1\right)\tilde{\beta}\left(\frac{\tilde{\beta}}{\overline{\theta}}\right)^{\gamma}.$$

It should be noted that (14.26) is obtained under the consideration that a firm's action has negligible effect on $M(t)$. By the definitions, the profit share of the representative household is as follows:

$$\pi_j(t) = \frac{\mu_j n\overline{\pi}(t)}{\overline{N}_j}, \tag{14.31}$$

where $n\overline{\pi}(t)$ is the total profit of the middle goods sector and share distribution is specified as follows:

$$\sum_{j=1}^{J} \mu_j = 1, \mu_j \geq 0.$$

It should be noted that there are different ways to deal with behavior of firms of middle goods. For instance, as in Krugman (1980), I might require $\overline{\pi}(t) = 0$ as an equilibrium condition of free entry and exit. It is reasonable to assume that $\overline{\pi}(t)$ is positive and is invested as R&D activities so that the number of firms becomes endogenous. Another condition is that the profit is shared between households and firms.

Demand and Supply of Final Goods

Capital goods are the same as the commodity in the Solow model, which can be invested in as capital goods and consumed as consumer goods. As change in capital stock is equal to the output of the final good sector minus the total consumption and depreciations of capital stock, it follows:

$$\dot{K}(t) = F(t) - d(t)\overline{N} - \delta_k K(t), \tag{14.32}$$

in which $F(t)$ is the output of capital goods, $d(t)\overline{N}$ is the consumption of capital goods, and $\delta_k K(t)$ is the total depreciation of physical capital.

National Wealth

The national wealth $\overline{K}(t)$ is equal to the sum of wealth values of all the households in the economy:

$$\overline{K}(t) = \sum_{j=1}^{J} \overline{k}_j(t)\overline{N}_j. \tag{14.33}$$

As the national capital stock is fully employed, $\overline{K}(t) = K(t)$.

Labor and Capital Are Fully Employed

The labor force is fully employed:

$$\tilde{N}(t) + N_x(t) = \mathrm{N}(t), \tag{14.34}$$

where $N_x(t)$ is the labor force employed by the middle goods sector:

$$N_x(t) = nl(t).$$

The model is complete. It is based on Walrasian general equilibrium theory, the Solow model, and the Dixit-Stiglitz model.

14.2 The Dynamic Properties of the Model

The previous section constructed a growth model of heterogenous households by integrating Walrasian general equilibrium theory, the Solow one-sector growth model with endogenous capital accumulation, and the Dixit-Stiglitz model with monopolistic competition. The economy is characterized by the neoclassical growth mechanism with perfect competition and monopolistic competition. I introduce a variable as follows:

$$z(t) \equiv \frac{r(t) + \delta_k}{w(t)},$$
$$\left\{\overline{k}_j(t)\right\} \equiv \left(\overline{k}_2(t), \ldots, \overline{k}_J(t)\right).$$

The following lemma gives a computational program for following the movement of the economic system.

Lemma 14.1
The following differential equations determine the motion of the economic system:

$$\dot{z}(t) = \Phi_1\left(z(t), \left\{\overline{k}_j(t)\right\}, \overline{k}_3(t)\right),$$
$$\dot{\overline{k}}_2(t) = \Phi_2\left(z(t), \overline{k}_2(t), \overline{k}_3(t)\right),$$
$$\dot{\overline{k}}_3(t) = \Phi_3\left(z(t), \overline{k}_2(t), \overline{k}_3(t)\right), \tag{14.35}$$

where Φ_j are functions of $z(t)$ and $\left\{\overline{k}_j(t)\right\}$ defined in the appendix. Moreover, all the variables can be expressed as functions of $z(t)$ and $\left\{\overline{k}_j(t)\right\}$ by the following procedure: $r(t)$ and $w(t)$ by (A14.3) $\rightarrow \overline{k}_1(t)$ by (A14.18) $\rightarrow \tilde{p}(t)$ by (14.29) $\rightarrow \overline{y}_j(t)$ by (A14.8) $\rightarrow \overline{T}_j(t)$, $d_j(t)$, $s_j(t)$ by (14.12) $\rightarrow K(t)$ by (14.31) $\rightarrow \tilde{N}(t)$ by (A14.1) $\rightarrow \pi_j(t)$ by (A14.6) $\rightarrow x(t)$ by (A14.9) $\rightarrow N_x(t)$ by (A14.9) $\rightarrow N(t)$ by (14.34) $\rightarrow$ $F(t)$ by (A14.2) $\rightarrow \tilde{c}_j(t)$ by (14.19) $\rightarrow p(t)$ by (14.20) $\rightarrow l(t)$ by (14.24) $\rightarrow \varphi(t)$ by (14.21) $\rightarrow \overline{\pi}(t)$ by (14.26) $\rightarrow U_j(t)$ by (14.10).

The lemma is proved in the appendix. As the expressions are complicated, I show the dynamic behavior of the system by simulation for an economy with three groups. The parameters are as follows:

$$T_0 = 24, \overline{\theta} = 0.4, \delta_k = 0.05, A = 1.4, n = 200, \alpha = 0.35, \tilde{\alpha} = 0.01,$$
$$\tilde{\beta} = 0.05, \overline{N}_1 = 10, \overline{N}_2 = 40, \overline{N}_3 = 100, h_1 = 4, h_2 = 1.5, h_3 = 1,$$
$$\mu_1 = 0.3, \mu_2 = 0.3, \mu_3 = 0.4, \lambda_{01} = 0.7, \chi_{01} = 0.1, \xi_{01} = 0.2,$$
$$\sigma_{01} = 0.2, \lambda_{02} = 0.65, \chi_{02} = 0.1, \xi_{02} = 0.2, \sigma_{02} = 0.25, \lambda_{03} = 0.6,$$
$$\chi_{03} = 0.15, \xi_{03} = 0.25, \sigma_{03} = 0.3.$$

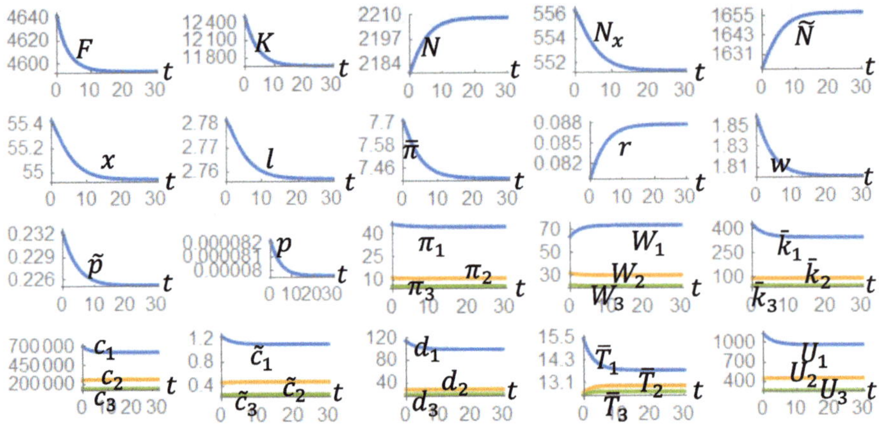

Fig. 14.1 The motion of the economic system

The fixed available time is 24 and depreciation rate of physical capital is 5 percent. The three groups' populations are respectively 10, 40, and 100. Group 1 has higher human capital than group 2, and group 2 than group 3. The number of varieties of middle goods is 200. The initial condition is as follows:

$$z_1(0) = 0.07, \bar{k}_2(0) = 90, \bar{k}_2(0) = 46.$$

The simulation result is plotted in Fig. 14.1. From the initial state, the national and final goods sector's output falls. The national labor supply rises over time. The middle goods sector employs less labor force, while the final goods sector employs more. Each firm of the middle goods produces less and employs less. The rate of interest rises, while the wage rate rises. The changes in the other variables over time are given in the figure.

The simulation shows that the economy becomes stationary in the long term. The equilibrium points are as follows:

$$\begin{aligned}
&F = 4593, K = 11666, N = 2208, N_x = 551, \tilde{N} = 1657, x = 55,\\
&l = 2.76, \bar{\pi} = 7.41, r = 0.088, w = 1.8, \tilde{p} = 0.23, p = 0.00008,\\
&\pi_1 = 44.44, \pi_2 = 11.1, \pi_3 = 5.93, W_1 = 73.8, W_2 = 29.9,\\
&W_3 = 20.5, \bar{k}_1 = 347, \bar{k}_2 = 90.96, \bar{k}_3 = 45.6, c_1 = 622588,\\
&c_2 = 263598, c_3 = 143082, \tilde{c}_1 = 1.1, \tilde{c}_2 = 0.47, \tilde{c}_3 = 0.25, d_1 = 99,\\
&d_2 = 28, d_3 = 19, \overline{T}_1 = 13.9, \overline{T}_2 = 12.9, \overline{T}_3 = 12.6, U_1 = 965,\\
&U_2 = 450, U_3 = 262,
\end{aligned}$$

The eigenvalue at the equilibrium point is:

$$-0.468, -0.395, -0.265.$$

This implies that the equilibrium point is locally stable.

14.3 The Elasticity of Substitution Between Two Varieties Rises

This section studies what happens to the economy when the elasticity of substitution between two varieties is increased as follows:

$$\overline{\theta} = 0.4 \Rightarrow 0.42.$$

The simulation result is plotted in Fig. 14.1. The figure shows that a rise in $\overline{\theta}$. implies a fall in the price of middle goods and rise in the output of each firm in the middle goods sector. The profit of each firm and profits shared by each household fell. All the households increase work hours, and the total labor supply is increased. The labor forces employed by the middle goods sector and by each firm rise and the labor force employed by the final goods sector rises. The output of the final goods sector and national wealth are reduced. The rate of interest rises and the wage rate falls. The aggregated good price rises and its consumption levels by the three groups fall. The wage incomes of the three groups are enhanced. The household has lower level of wealth and consumes less final goods. The utility levels of the three groups are all reduced (Fig.14.2).

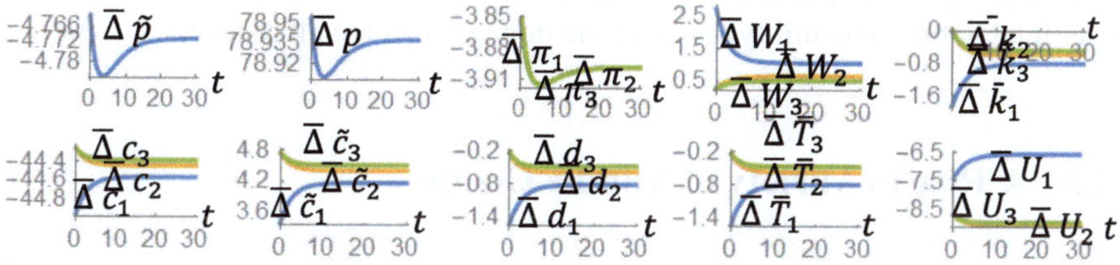

Fig. 14.2 The elasticity of substitution between two varieties rises

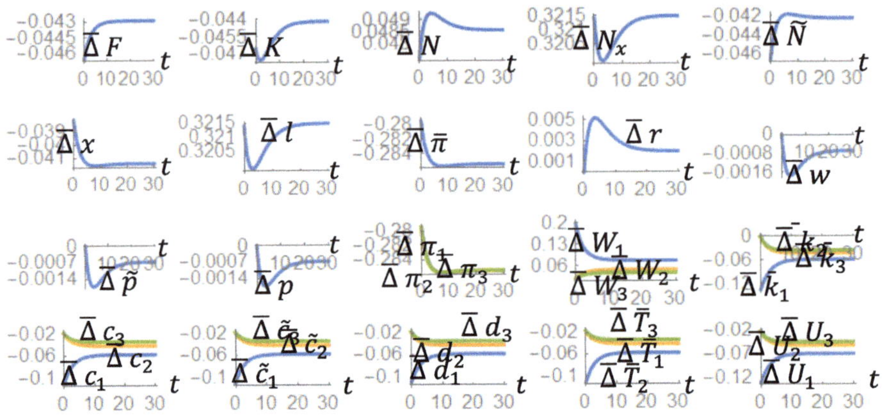

Fig. 14.3 Fixed labor cost of the middle goods firm is increased

14.4 The Fixed Labor Cost of the Middle Goods Firm Is Increased

I am now studying the impact that the fixed labor cost of the middle goods firm is increased as follows:

$$\tilde{\alpha} : 0.01 \Rightarrow 0.02.$$

The simulation result is plotted in Fig. 14.3. Each firm in the middle goods sector produces less in association in fall of the price of middle goods. The profits of each firm and profit shared by each household decrease. All the households increase work hours, and the total labor supply is increased. The labor force employed by the middle goods sector rises. The labor force by each firm rises. The labor force employed by the final goods sector falls. The output of the final goods sector and national wealth are reduced. The rate of interest rises and the wage rate falls. The aggregated good price rises and its consumption levels by the three groups fall. The wage incomes of the three groups are enhanced. The household has lower level of wealth and consumes fewer final goods. The utility levels of the three groups are all reduced.

14.5 A Rise in Variety of Middle Goods

This section now examines the impact of the following rise in variety of middle goods on the economy:

$$n : 200 \Rightarrow 210.$$

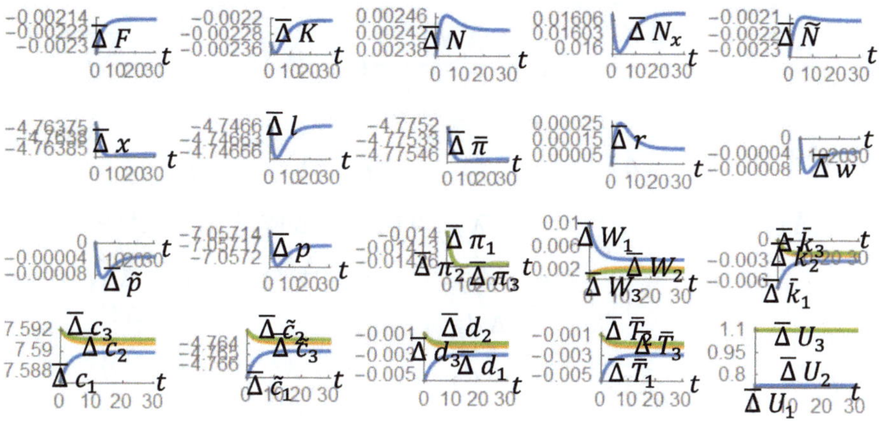

Fig. 14.4 A rise in variety of middle goods

This may happen, for instance, due to (exogenous) innovation and introduction of new products. The simulation result is plotted in Fig. 14.4. Macroeconomic variables are slightly affected. The consumption levels of each firm's product and each firm's production activities are strongly affected. The household utility levels are enhanced (due to the effect of love of variety).

14.6 The Total Factor Productivity of the Final Goods Sector Is Increased

This section studies the impact that the total factor productivity of the final goods sector is increased as follows:

$$A : 1.4 \Rightarrow 1.5.$$

The simulation result is plotted in Fig. 14.5. The output level of the final goods sector is enhanced. The national wealth is augmented. The representative household of group 1 increases work time initially and does not change time distribution in the long term. The households of the other groups reduce work hours initially and do not change time distribution in the long term. The total labor rises initially and does not change in the long term. The labor force employed by the middle goods sector falls initially and does not change in the long term. The labor force employed by the final goods sector rises initially and does not change in the long term. Each firm produces less output and employs less labor force initially, and the variables are not changed in the long term. The profits of each firm and profit shared by each household rise. The rate of interest is increased and is not changed in the long term. The wage rate is enhanced. The prices of middle goods and aggregate goods are

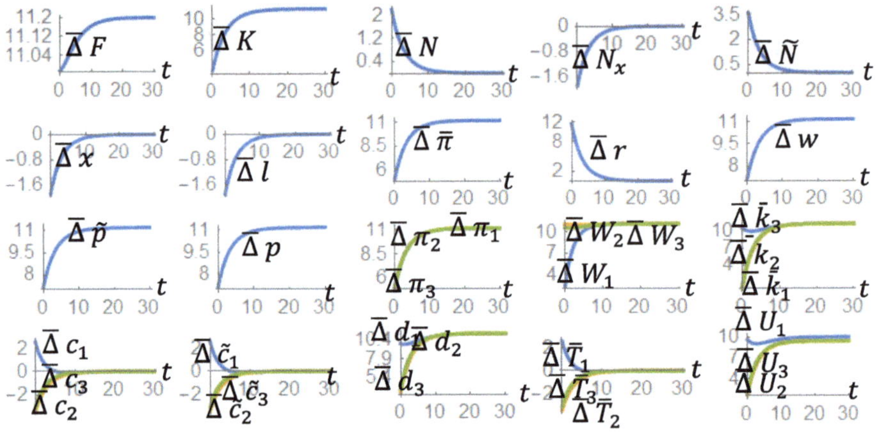

Fig. 14.5 The total productivity of the final goods sector rises

increased. Each household gets more wage income and owns more wealth. All the households consume more final goods. Their utility levels are enhanced.

14.7 Group 1's Propensity to Consume Middle Goods Is Enhanced

I now examine the impact that the following rise in group 1's propensity to consume middle goods:

$$\chi_{01} = 0.1 \Rightarrow 0.12.$$

The simulation result is plotted in Fig. 14.6. The national wealth and output level of final goods sector are reduced. Group 1's work hours are increased, while the other two groups' work hours are reduced. The national labor force is increased. The middle goods sector employs more labor force, while the final goods sector employs less labor force. Each firm's profit is increased and each household gets more profit. The rate of interest rises, while the wage rate falls. Group 1 gets more wage income, while the other two groups less. The household of group 1 has less wealth, while the households in the other two groups get more. Each firm produces more and employs more labor force. The prices of middle goods have fallen. The household of group consumes more middle goods and less final goods, while the households in the other groups slightly change their consumption levels.

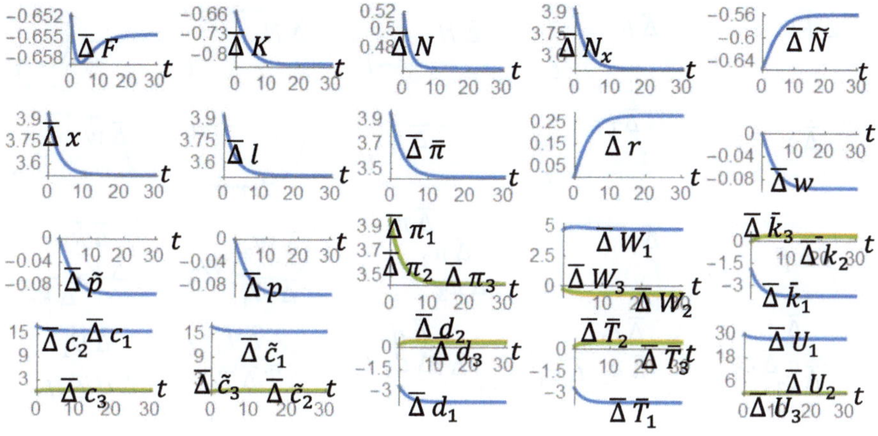

Fig. 14.6 Group 1's propensity to consume middle goods falls

14.8 Group 1's Propensity to Save Is Enhanced

I will study what will happen to the economy if group 1's propensity to save is increased as follows:

$$\lambda_{01} = 0.7 \Rightarrow 0.72.$$

The simulation result is plotted in Fig. 14.7. The national capital increases and the rate of interest decreases. The wage rate is enhanced. All the households get more wage incomes. The household from group 1 works more hours initially and less hours in the long term. The households from the other two groups work more hours. The firm gets less profits initially but more in the long term. Each household shares less profits initially but more in the long term. The prices of middle goods are augmented. The household of group 1 has higher utility levels, while the households from the other groups have almost the same levels.

14.9 Group 3 Enhances Human Capital

This section deals with the impact that the following rise in group 1's human capital on the economy:

$$h_3 = 1 \Rightarrow 1.2.$$

The simulation result is plotted in Fig. 14.8. The national labor force is augmented. The national capital and output of the final goods sector are augmented. The final

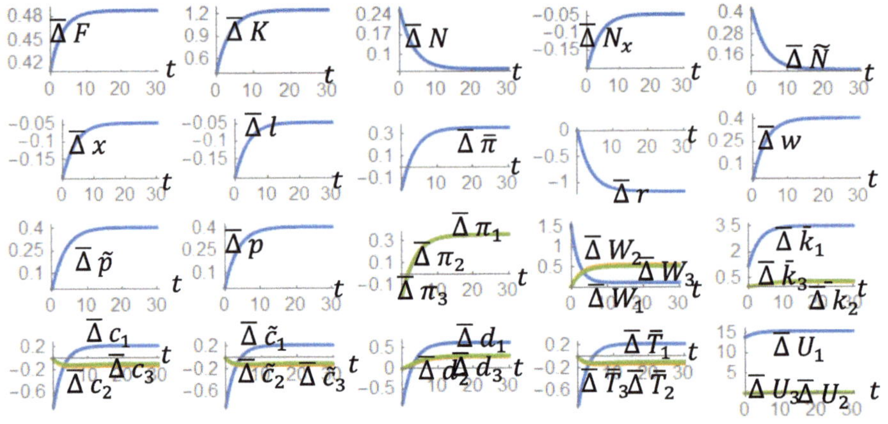

Fig. 14.7 Group 1's propensity to save is enhanced

goods and middle goods sectors employ more labor force. Each firm has more profits, employs more labor force, and produces more. The rate of interest falls initially and rises in the long term. The wage rate rises initially and falls in the long term. The household gets more wage income. In the long term the households of the other two groups get almost the same wage incomes. In long term the household from group 3 consumes more and has higher utility level.

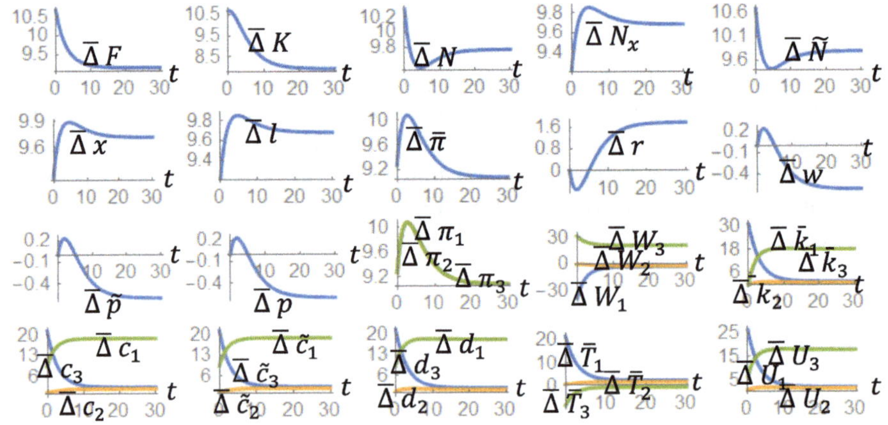

Fig. 14.8 Group 3 enhances human capital

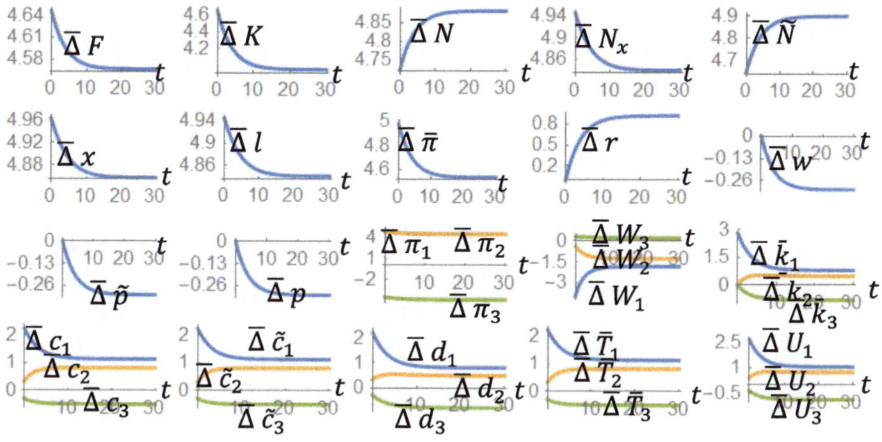

Fig. 14.9 Group 3's population is increased

14.10 Group 3's Population Is Increased

This section deals with the impact that the following rise in group's population has on the economy:

$$\overline{N}_3 = 100 \Rightarrow 110.$$

The simulation result is plotted in Fig. 14.9. The national capital and output of the final goods sector are increased. The rate of interest is reduced, and the wage rate is enhanced. All the households get more wage incomes. The household from group 3 works more hours. The households from the other two groups work less hours. The firm gets more profits. Each household of group 2 shares less profit. Each household of the other two groups shares more profit. The prices of middle goods are reduced. The household of group 3 consumes less goods and has less wealth, while the households from the other groups consume more goods and have more wealth. The household of group 3 has lower utility level, while the households from the other groups have higher utility levels. It is concluded that a population expansion of a poor group enlarges the national economy, benefits the individuals of the other groups, and deteriorates the poor household's living conditions.

14.11 The Profit Distribution Is Shifted

I now deal with the impact that the following changes in the profit distribution on the economy:

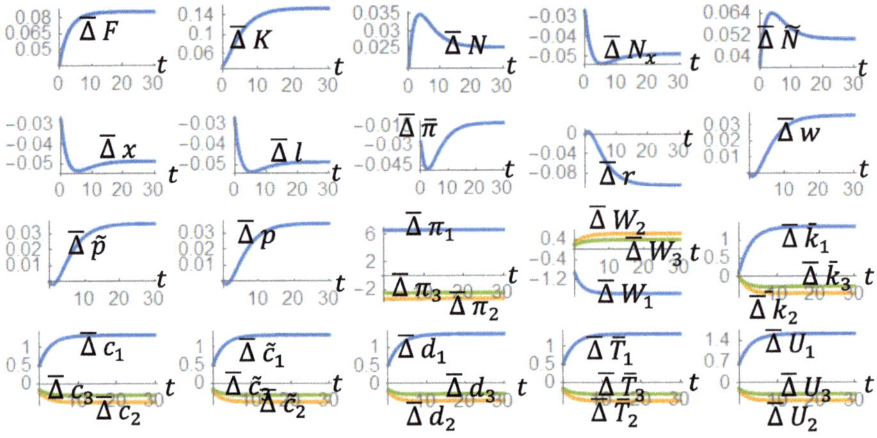

Fig. 14.10 The profit distribution is shifted

$$\mu 1 = 0.3 \Rightarrow 0.32;\ \mu 2 = 0.3 \Rightarrow 0.29;\ \mu 3 = 0.4 \Rightarrow 0.39.$$

It is assumed that the profit share of group 1 is increased, while the other two groups' are reduced. The simulation result is plotted in Fig. 14.10. The national capital and output of the final goods sector are increased. The rate of interest is reduced, and the wage rate is enhanced. The household from group 1 has more leisure time, while the households of the other groups work more hours. The household from group 1 has less wage income, while the households of the other groups receive more wage income. and work more hours. The firm's profit has changed slightly. Each household of group 1 has more profit, while each household of the other two groups receives less profit. The prices of middle goods are slightly increased. Each household of group 1 enjoy more leisure time, while each household of the other two groups works more hours. The household of group 1 consumes more goods and has more wealth, while the households from the other groups consume less goods and have less wealth. The household of group 1 has higher utility level, while the households from the other groups have lower utility levels.

14.12 Concluding Remarks

This chapter proposed an economic growth model with income and wealth distribution on the basis of Walrasian general equilibrium theory, neoclassical growth theory, and Dixit-Stiglitz monopolistic competitive theory. It made a unique contribution to the literature of economic growth with perfect competition and monopolistic competition by integrating the basic economic mechanism in the Walrasian general equilibrium model, the Solow one-sector growth model, and the Dixit-Stiglitz model. The final goods sector in our approach is based on Solow's one-sector growth model. The issues of distribution are referred to the Arrow-Debreu theory. The market mechanism of perfect competitive markets is based on traditional neoclassical growth theory. I described imperfect competition on the approach basically developed by Dixit and Stiglitz (1977). This chapter deviates from the Dixit-Stiglitz by assuming that non-zero profits are distributed to households. As there are a large number of publications in each of the three theories and the model integrated these basic models within a comprehensive framework, it is straightforward to extend and generalize the model in different ways on the basis of the literature. For instance, the distribution of profits is only a limited case of profit distribution. Profits may be shared by different agents for different uses. It can also be used for innovation. Also, much attention has been paid in economic geography to issues related to tax competition between regions (Andersson and Forslid 2003; Baldwin and Krugman 2004; Bayindir-Upmann and Ziad 2005; Kim et al. 2005; Pflüger 2004; Wang 2012; Naito and Ornori 2017; Veld et al. 2020). As I generalized the key models in new economic geography, it is straightforward to deal with the issues about regional tax competition with multiple regions (Andersson and Forslid 2003; Baldwin and Krugman 2004; Bayindir-Upmann and Ziad 2005; Borck and Pflüger 2006; Naito and Ornori 2017; Zhang 2019b, 2020g).

Appendix: Proving Lemma 14.1

From (14.2), I get:

$$z \equiv \frac{r+\delta_k}{w} = \frac{\overline{\beta}\tilde{N}}{K}, \tag{A14.1}$$

where $\overline{\beta} \equiv \alpha/\beta$. From (A14.1) and (14.2), it follows:

$$F = AK\left(\frac{z}{\overline{\beta}}\right)^{\beta}. \tag{A14.2}$$

From (14.3), it follows:

$$r = \alpha A\left(\frac{z}{\overline{\beta}}\right)^{\beta} - \delta_k,\ w = \frac{r+\delta_k}{z}. \tag{A14.3}$$

Insert (14.27) and (14.31) in the concept of $\hat{y}_j$:

$$\overline{y}_j = R\overline{k}_j + h_j T_0 w + \pi_j. \tag{A14.4}$$

From the definition of M :

$$M = \frac{1}{n\tilde{p}^{\overline{\theta}\gamma}} \sum_{j=1}^{J} \chi_j \overline{N}_j \overline{y}_j, \tag{A14.5}$$

where $P_j = n\tilde{p}^{\overline{\theta}\gamma}$ is applied. From (A14.5), (14.30), and (14.31), it follows:

$$\pi_j = \overline{\mu}_j \sum_{q=1}^{J} \chi_q \overline{N}_q \overline{y}_q - \frac{\mu_j \tilde{\alpha} n w}{\overline{N}_j}, \tag{A14.6}$$

where (14.29) is applied and

$$\overline{\mu}_j \equiv \frac{\mu_j \vartheta}{\left(\tilde{\beta}/\overline{\theta}\right)^{\overline{\theta}\gamma} \overline{N}_j}.$$

Insert (A14.6) in (A14.4):

$$\overline{y}_j - \overline{\mu}_j \sum_{q=1}^{J} \chi_q \overline{N}_q \overline{y}_q = R\overline{k}_j + \tilde{\mu}_j, \tag{A14.7}$$

where

$$\tilde{\mu}_j \equiv \left(h_j T_0 - \frac{\mu_j n \tilde{\alpha}}{\overline{N}_j} \right) w.$$

Equation (A14.7) is linear in $\overline{y}_j$ and $\overline{k}_j$. It should be noted that R and $\tilde{\mu}_j$ are functions of z. It is straightforward to solve the linear equations. I express the solution in the following form:

$$\overline{y}_j = \sum_{i=1}^{J} g_{ij}(z) \overline{k}_i + g_{0j}(z), \tag{A14.8}$$

where $g_{ij}(z)$ and $g_{0j}(z)$ are functions of z. I don't give expressions of these functions as they are too tedious. From (14.24), I have

$$N_x = \tilde{\alpha} n + \tilde{\beta} n x. \tag{A14.9}$$

From (14.19) and (14.23), it follows:

$$x = \sum_{j=1}^{J} \frac{\chi_j \overline{y}_j \overline{N}_j}{n\tilde{p}}. \tag{A14.10}$$

Insert (A14.10) in (A14.9):

$$N_x = \tilde{\alpha} n + \tilde{\beta} \sum_{j=1}^{J} \frac{\chi_j \overline{N}_j \overline{y}_j}{\tilde{p}}. \tag{A14.11}$$

From (A14.11) and (A14.1), it follows:

$$\frac{\text{zK}}{\overline{\overline{\beta}}} + \tilde{\alpha} n + \tilde{\beta} \sum_{j=1}^{J} \frac{\chi_j \overline{N}_j \overline{y}_j}{\tilde{p}} = \text{N}. \tag{A14.12}$$

Insert (14.33) in (A14.12):

$$\frac{\text{z}}{\overline{\overline{\beta}}} \sum_{j=1}^{J} \overline{k}_j \overline{N}_j + \tilde{\alpha} n + \tilde{\beta} \sum_{j=1}^{J} \frac{\chi_j \overline{N}_j \overline{y}_j}{\tilde{p}} = \text{N}. \tag{A14.13}$$

By (14.1) and $T_j + \overline{T}_j = T_0$, I get:

$$N = \tilde{T}_0 - \sum_{j=1}^{J} h_j \overline{N}_j \overline{T}_j, \tag{A14.14}$$

where

$$\tilde{T}_0 \equiv \sum_{j=1}^{J} h_j T_0 \overline{N}_j.$$

Insert (14.12) in (A14.14):

$$N = \tilde{T}_0 - \frac{1}{w} \sum_{j=1}^{J} \overline{N}_j \sigma_j \overline{y}_j. \tag{A14.15}$$

Insert (A14.15) in (A14.13):

$$\frac{\text{z}}{\overline{\overline{\beta}}} \sum_{j=1}^{J} \overline{k}_j \overline{N}_j + \sum_{j=1}^{J} \overline{N}_{0j} \overline{y}_j = \tilde{T}_0 - \tilde{\alpha} n,$$

where

$$\overline{N}_{0j} \equiv \left(\frac{\chi_j \tilde{\beta}}{\tilde{p}} + \frac{\sigma_j}{w} \right) \overline{N}_j. \tag{A14.16}$$

Insert (A14.8) in (A14.16):

$$\sum_{j=1}^{J} \tilde{g}_j \bar{k}_j = \tilde{T}_0 - \tilde{\alpha} n - g_0, \tag{A14.17}$$

where

$$\tilde{g}_j \equiv \frac{z\overline{N}_j}{\overline{\beta}} + g_j,\ g_j \equiv \sum_{m=1}^{J} \overline{N}_{0m} g_{jm},\ g_0 \equiv \sum_{m=1}^{J} \overline{N}_{0m} g_{0m}.$$

Solve (A14.17) in $\bar{k}_1$:

$$\bar{k}_1\left(z, \left\{\bar{k}_j\right\}\right) = \left(\tilde{T}_0 - \tilde{\alpha} n - g_0 - \sum_{j=2}^{J} \tilde{g}_j \bar{k}_j\right) \frac{1}{\tilde{g}_1}. \tag{A14.18}$$

In summary, it is shown that all the variables can be expressed as functions of z and $\left\{\bar{k}_j\right\}$ by the following procedure: r and w by (A14.3) $\rightarrow \bar{k}_1$ by (A14.18) $\rightarrow \tilde{p}$ by (14.29) $\rightarrow \bar{y}_j$ by (A14.8) $\rightarrow \overline{T}_j, d_j, s_j$ by (14.12) $\rightarrow K$ by (14.31) $\rightarrow \tilde{N}$ by (A14.1) $\rightarrow$ π_j by (A14.6) $\rightarrow x$ by (A14.9) $\rightarrow N_x$ by (A14.9) $\rightarrow N$ by (14.34) $\rightarrow F$ by (A14.2) $\rightarrow \tilde{c}_j$ by (14.19) $\rightarrow p$ by (14.20) $\rightarrow l$ by (14.24) $\rightarrow \varphi$ by (14.21) $\rightarrow \overline{\pi}$ by (14.26) $\rightarrow U_j$ by (14.10).

From the procedure and (14.22), it follows:

$$\dot{\bar{k}}_1(t) = \Phi_0\left(z(t), \left\{\bar{k}_j(t)\right\}\right) \equiv s_1(t) - \bar{k}_1(t), \tag{A14.19}$$

$$\dot{\bar{k}}_j(t) = \Phi_j\left(z(t), \left\{\bar{k}_j(t)\right\}\right) \equiv s_j(t) - \bar{k}_j(t). \tag{A14.20}$$

Take derivatives of (A14.18) with respect to time:

$$\dot{\bar{k}}_1 = \frac{\partial \bar{k}_1}{\partial z} \dot{z} + \sum_{j=2}^{J} \frac{\partial \bar{k}_1}{\partial \bar{k}_j} \dot{\bar{k}}_j. \tag{A14.21}$$

From (A14.18)– (A14.21), it follows:

$$\dot{z} = \Phi_1\left(z(t), \left\{\bar{k}_j(t)\right\}\right) \equiv \left(\Phi_0 - \sum_{j=2}^{J} \frac{\partial \bar{k}_1}{\partial \bar{k}_j} \dot{\bar{k}}_j\right) \left(\frac{\partial \bar{k}_1}{\partial z}\right)^{-1}. \tag{A14.22}$$

Equations (A14.22) and (A14.20) determine the motion of $z(t)$ and $\left\{\bar{k}_j(t)\right\}$. I thus confirmed the lemma.

Chapter 15
Further Issues

> A theory is a good theory if it satisfies two requirements: it must accurately describe a large class of observations on the basis of a model that contains only a few arbitrary elements, and it must make definite predictions about the results of future observations.
>
> Stephen Hawking

The modern world economy is experiencing rapid growth. This book aims to construct a theory that links these changes in a single analytical framework with minimal assumptions. By integrating multiple theories of the modern economy into a comprehensive analytical framework, a dynamic economic growth theory of heterogeneous groups is developed. This book comprises multiple models that highlight the interplay between heterogeneous households and various variables, including economy, technology, institutions, structure, and environment. Each model can be mathematically integrated with other models introduced in this book. It provides a computational simulation procedure that allows anyone to understand the dynamics of the system using a computer.

This book is part of my general economic theory and focuses on the further development of growth theory with heterogeneous households. It addresses the dynamic relationships between demography, human capital, physical capital/wealth accumulation, knowledge growth, technological innovation, gender, institutions, market structure, division of labor and consumption, distribution of income and wealth, and determination of price structure in a single analytical framework. The theory is based on a small number of concepts in a compact framework. It develops a theoretical framework that allows for reasonable generalization from one model structure to another and systematically deepens the understanding of complexity of economic dynamics with heterogeneous households (such as races or classes).

The mainstream of economics is still a collection of diverse ideas and theories. Economists traditionally rely on verbal descriptions or linearized equations with a few variables. Traditional methods cannot describe changes in variables that are linked by complex nonlinear relationships. Dynamic phenomena due to complex nonlinear

W. Zhang, *A Dynamic Economic Theory of Heterogenous Households*,
https://doi.org/10.1007/978-981-95-8918-0_15

relationships are beyond the ability of economists to investigate a few decades ago. Recent developments in mathematics, sciences, and computers, as well as the availability of individual and government data, mean that the theory developed in this book is not only theoretically insightful but also empirically testable, conceptually extendable, and functionally generalizable. It applies to my concept of disposable income and utility functions to explore the complexity of economic development with heterogeneous households. I integrate diverse ideas and theories in economics within an integrated framework.

The analytical framework allows me to analyze many problems. The book is based on many traditional ideas and models. Each traditional theory has a vast literature. My theory is general in that it connects the main economic forces in many theories. It is an "open" general economic theory and can be further generalized by incorporating new findings from sciences, engineering, economics, psychology, political sciences, social sciences, history, etc. Each model in the book can be expanded by generalizing some of its functional forms and associations. The theory can be enriched by applying ideas in different theories, such as cognitive science, modern psychology, industry theory, organization theory, population (birth and death rates) theory, and mathematical biology.

References

Aakvik A, Salvanes KG, Vaage K (2010) Measuring heterogeneity in the returns to education using an education reform. Eur Econ Rev 54:453–500
Abel A, Bernanke BS, Croushore D (2007) Macroeconomics. Prentice Hall, New Jersey
Acconcia A, Simonelli S (2008) Interpreting aggregate fluctuations looking at sectors. J Econ Dyn Control 32:3009–3031
Acemoglu D (2009) Introduction to modern economic growth. Princeton University Press, Princeton
Acemoglu D, Guerrieri V (2008) Capital deepening and nonbalanced economic growth. J Polit Econ 116:467–498
Acs Z, Audretsch D, Feldman M (1992) Real effects of academic research. Am Econ Rev 82:363–367
Adams JD (1990) Fundamental stocks of knowledge and productivity growth. J Polit Econ 98:673–702
Adsera A (2005) Vanishing children: from high unemployment to low fertility in developed countries. Am Econ Rev 95:189–193
Agénor PR (2004) Does globalization hurt the poor? Int Econ Policy 1:21–51
Aghion P, Howitt P (1998) Endogenous growth theory. The MIT Press, Cambridge
Aghion P, Blundell R, Griffith R, Howitt P, Prantl S (2009) The effects of entry on incumbent innovation and productivity. Rev Econ Stat 91:20–32
Aguiar M, Hurst E (2007) Measuring trends in leisure: the allocation of time over five decades. Q J Econ 122:969–1006
Akcigit U, Kerr WR (2018) Growth through heterogeneous innovation. J Polit Econ 126:1374–1443
Akerlof GA (1997) Social distance and social decisions. Econometrica 65:1005–1028
Akinsola FA, Odhiam NM (2017) Inflation and economic growth: a review of the international literature. Comparative Econo Res 20(3):41–56
Albanesi S, Olivetti C (2009) Home production, market production and the gender wage gap: incentives and expectations. Rev Econ Dyn 12:80–107
Alesina A, Ichino A, Karabarbounis L (2011) Gender based taxation and the division of family chores. Am Econ J Econ Policy 3:1–40
Alonso-Carrera J, Freire-Sere MJ (2004) Multiple equilibria, fiscal policy and human capital accumulation. J Econ Dyn Control 28:841–856
Amano M (1980) A neoclassical model of the dual economy with capital accumulation in agriculture. Rev Econ Stud 47:933–944
Andersson F, Forslid R (2003) Tax competition and economic geography. J Pub Econ Theory 5:279–303

W. Zhang, *A Dynamic Economic Theory of Heterogenous Households*,
https://doi.org/10.1007/978-981-95-8918-0

Andreoli F, Casalone G, Sonedda D (2018) Public education provision, private schooling and income redistribution. J Income Inequality 16:553–583
Angelov N, Johansson P, Lindahl E (2016) Parenthood and the gender gap in pay. J Labor Econ 34:545–579
Anselin L, Varga A, Acs Z (1997) Local geographic spillovers between university research and high technology innovations. J Urban Econo 42:422–448
Anselin L, Varga A, Acs Z (2000) Geographic and sectoral characteristics of academic knowledge externalities. Papers Reg Sci 79:435–443
Antecol H (2000) An examination of cross-country differences in the gender gap in labor force participation rates. Labor Econ 7:409–426
Arnold LG (1997) Basic and applied research. Finanzarchiv 54:169–186
Arrow KJ (1962) The economic implications of learning by doing. Rev Econo Stud 29:155–173
Arrow KJ (1974) General economic equilibrium: Purpose, analytic techniques, collective choice. Am Econ Rev 64:253–272
Arrow KJ (1998) What has economics to say about racial discrimination? J Econ Perspect 12:91–100
Arrow KJ, Debreu G (1954) Existence of an equilibrium for a competitive economy. Econometrica 22:265–290
Arrow KJ, Hahn FH (1971) General competitive analysis. Holden-Day Inc., San Francisco
Atkinson AB, Pijketty T, Saez E (2011) Top incomes in the long run of history. J Econ Lit 49:3–71
Attanasio O, Pistaferri L (2014) Consumption inequality over the last half century: some evidence using the new paid consumption measure. Am Econ Rev Papers Proc 104:122–126
Azariadis C (1993) Intertemporal macroeconomics. Blackwell, Oxford
Bachmann R, Frings H (2017) Monopsonistic competition, low-wage labour markets and minimum wages—an empirical analysis. Appl Econ 49:5268–5286
Bacolod M, Blum BS, Rangel MA, Strange WC (2023) Learners in cities: agglomeration and the spatial division of cognition. Regional Sci Urban Econ 98:103838
Bagwell LS, Bernheim DB (1996) Veblen effects in a theory of conspicuous consumption. Am Econ Rev 86:349–373
Baierl G, Nishimura K, Yano M (1998) The role of capital depreciation in multi-sectoral models. J Econ Behavior Organ 33:467–479
Bakshi GS, Chen Z (1996) The spirit of capitalism and stock-market prices. Am Econ Rev 86:133–157
Baldnzi A, Bucci A, Prettner K (2019) Children's health, human capital accumulation, and R&D based economic growth. Macroecon Dyn 48(3):616–627
Balestra C, Dottori D (2012) Aging society, health and the environment. J Popul Econo 25:1045–1076
Baldwin RE, Krugman P (2004) Agglomeration, integration, and tax harmonization. Eur Econ Rev 48:1–23
Bandyopadhyay D, Tang XL (2011) Understanding the economic dynamics behind growth-inequality relationships. J Macroecon 33:14–44
Banerjee N (1999) Can markets alter gender relations? Gender Technol Dev 3:103–122
Banerjee AV (2004) Educational policy and the economics of the family. J Dev Econ 74:3–32
Barkai H (1959) Ricardo on factor prices and income distribution in a growing economy. Economica 26:240–250
Barkai H (1966) Ricardo's second thoughts on rent as a relative share. South Econ J 32:285–350
Barro RJ (2001) Human capital and growth. Am Econ Rev, Papers Proceed 91:12–17
Barro RJ, Becker GS (1989) Fertility choice in a model of economic growth. Econometrica 57:481–501
Barro RJ, Sala-i-Martin X (1995) Economic growth. McGraw-Hill Inc., New York
Basu K (1989) A theory of association: social status, prices and markets. Oxf Econ Pap 41:653–671
Batabyal A, Nijkamp P (2013) A multi-region model of economic growth with human capital and negative externalities in innovation. J Evol Econ 23:909–924
Baxter M (1996) Are consumer durables important for business cycles? Rev Econo Stat 78:147–155

Bayindir-Upmann T, Ziad A (2005) Existence of equilibria in a basic tax competition model. Regional Sci Urban Econ 35:1–22

Becker GS (1957) The economics of discrimination. University of Chicago Press, Chicago

Becker GS (1965) A theory of the allocation of time. Econ J 75:493–517

Becker GS (1974) A theory of social interactions. J Polit Econ 82:1063–1093

Becker GS (1976) The economic approach to human behavior. The University of Chicago Press, Chicago

Becker GS (1981) A treatise on the family. Harvard University Press, Cambridge

Becker GS, Murphy KM, Spenkuch JL (2016) The manipulation of children's preferences, old-age support, and investment in children's human capital. J Labor Econ 34:S3–S30

Beenstock M (2021) Macroeconomics meets regional science: how national economic activity is related to regional economic activity. Int Reg Sci Rev 45(3):321–351

Behrens K, Murata Y (2007) General equilibrium models of monopolistic competition: a new approach. J Econ Theory 136:776–787

Behrens K, Murata Y (2017) City size and the Henry George theorem under monopolistic competition. J Urban Econo 65:228–235

Behrman J, Pollak R, Taubman P (1982) Parental preferences and provision for progeny. J Polit Econ 90:52–73

Ben-David D, Loewy MB (2003) Trade and neoclassical growth model. J Econ Integr 18:1–16

Benabou R (2002) Tax and education policy in a heterogeneous-agent economy: what levels of redistribution maximize growth and efficiency? Econometrica 70:481–517

Benassy JP (1996) Taste for variety and optimum production patterns in monopolistic competition. Econ Lett 52:41–47

Beneria L, Feldman S (ed) (1992) Unequal burden: economic crises, persistent poverty, and women's work. Westview, Boulder

Benhabib J, Perli R (1994) Uniqueness and indeterminacy: on the dynamics of endogenous growth. J Econ Theory 63:113–142

Bergmann B (1971) The effects on white income of discrimination in employment. J Polit Econ 792:294–313

Bertocchi G, Spagat M (2004) The evolution of modern educational systems: technical vs general education, distributional conflict, and growth. J Dev Econ 73:558–582

Bertoletti P, Etro F (2015) Monopolistic competition when income matters. Econ J 127:1217–1243

Bhagwati JN (1991) International trade—selected readings, 2nd edn. The MIT Press, Cambridge

Bhattacharya J, Chakraborty S (2017) Contraception and the demographic transition. Econ J 127:2263–2301

Biagetti M, Sergio S (2009) Inequality in workers' lifelong learning across European countries: evidence from EU-SILC data-set. MPRA Paper, No. 17356

Bick A, Fuchs-Schundeln N (2018) Taxation and labor supply of married couples across countries: a macroeconomic analysis. Rev Econ Stud 85:1543–1557

Bishnu M, Garg S, Garg T, Ray T (2021) Optimal intergenerational transfers: public education and pensions. J Publ Econo 198:104411

Bishnu M, Garg S, Garg T, Ray T (2023) Intergenerational transfers: Public education and pensions with endogenous fertility. J Econ Dyn Control 153:841–856

Blackburn K, Cipriani GP (2002) A model of longevity, fertility and growth. J Econ Dynam Control 26:187–204

Bleakley H, Chin A (2008) What holds back the second generation? The intergenerational transformation of language human capital among immigrants. J Human Resour 43:267–298

Bodie Z (1992) Labor supply flexibility and portfolio choice in a life cycle model. J Econ Dyn Control 16(3–4):427–449

Bodie ZS, Detemple JB, Otruba S, Walter S (2004) Optimal consumption-portfolio choices and retirement planning. J Econ Dyn Contr 28:1115–1148

Boerma J, Karabarbounis L (2020) Labor market trends and the changing value of time. J Econ Dyn Control 115:1–19

Boerma J, Karabarbounis L (2021) Inferring inequality with home production. Econometrica 89:2517–2556
Boldrin M, Christiano L, Fisher J (2001a) Habit persistence, asset returns, and the business cycle. Am Econ Rev 91:149–166
Boldrin M, Nishimura K, Shigoka T, Yano M (2001b) Chaotic equilibrium dynamics in endogenous growth models. J Econ Theory 96:97–132
Bond-Smith S (2021) The unintended consequences of increasing returns to scale in geographical economic. J Econ Geogr 21:631–681
Bond-Smith S (2024) Combining agglomeration economies and endogenous growth without scale effects. Spat Econ Anal 19:287–308
Borck R, Pflüger M (2006) Agglomeration and tax competition. Eur Econ Rev 50:647–668
Bongaarts J, Sobotka T (2012) A demographic explanation for the recent rise in European fertility. Population Dev Rev 38:83–120
Borjas G (1992) Ethnic capital and intergenerational income mobility. Q J Econ 107:123–150
Borjas GJ (1995) Ethnicity, neighborhoods, and human-capital externalities. Am Econ Rev 85:365–390
Borjas GJ (1998) To ghetto or not to ghetto: ethnicity and residential segregation. J Urban Econo 44:228–253
Bosi S, Seegmuller T (2012) Mortality differential and growth: what do we learn from the Barro-Becker model? Math Popul Stud 19:27–50
Boskin M, Sheshinski E (1983) Optimal tax treatment of the family: married couples. J Public Econo 20:281–297
Boucekkine R, de la Croix D, Licandro O (2002) Vintage human capital, demographic trends, and endogenous growth. J Econ Theory 104:340–375
Bourguignon F (1981) Pareto-superiority of unegalitarian equilibria in Stiglitz's model of wealth distribution with convex saving function. Econo 49:1469–1475
Bovenberg AL, Smulders S (1995) Environmental quality and pollution-augmenting technical change in a two-sector endogenous growth model. J Pub Econ 57:369–391
Bovenberg AL, Goulder LH, Jacobsen MR (2008) Cost of alternative environmental policy instruments in the presence of industry compensation requirements. J Polit Econ 92:1236–1253
Brecher RA, Chen ZQ, Choudhri EU (2002) Absolute and comparative advantage reconsidered: the pattern of international trade with optimal saving. Rev Int Econ 10:645–656
Brems H (1970) Ricardo's long run equilibrium. History Polit Econ 2:225–245
Bresnahan TF, Trajtenberg M (1995) General purpose technologies: engines of growth'? J Econo 65:83–108
Bretschger L (2013) Population growth and natural-resource scarcity: Long-run development under seemingful unfavorable conditions. Scand J Econ 115:722–755
Breuer JB, Mcdermott J, Weber WE (2018) Time aggregation and the relationship between inflation and money growth. J Money, Credit, Bank 50:351–375
Bridgman B, Duernecker G, Herrendorf B (2018) Structural transformation, marketization, and household production around the world. J Dev Econ 113:102–126
Buccella D, Fanti L, Gori L (2021) The R&D investment decision game with product differentiation. Working Paper, University of Pisa
Burmeister E, Dobell AR (1970) Mathematical theories of economic growth. Collier Macmillan Publishers, London
Caravale GA, Tosato DA (1980) Ricardo and the theory of value distribution and growth. Routledge & Kegan Paul, London
Cardak BA (2004) Education choice, endogenous growth and income distribution. Economica 71:57–81
Carneiro P, Heckman JJ, Masterov DV (2005) Labor market discrimination and racial differences in premarket factors. J Law Econ 48:1–39
Casarosa C (1985) The new view of the Ricardian theory of distribution and economic growth. In: Caravale GA (ed) The legacy of Ricardo. Basil Blackwell, London

Caselli F, Ventura J (2000) A representative consumer theory of distribution. Am Econ Rev 90:909–926
Castelló-Climent A, Hidalgo-Cabrillana A (2012) The role of educational quality and quantity in the process of economic development. Econ Educ Rev 31:391–409
Caucutt EM (2002) Educational vouchers when there are peer group effects—size matters. Int Econ Rev 43:195–222
Cárdenas-García PJ, Brida JG, Segarra V (2024) Modelling the link between tourism and economic development: evidence from homogeneous panels of countries. Humanit Soc Sci Commun 11:308
Cervellati M, Sunde U (2015) The economic and demographic transition; Mortality, and comparative development. Am Econ J Macroecon 7:189–225
Chakraborty S (2004) Endogenous lifetime and economic growth. J Econ Theory 116:119–137
Chakraborty B, Gupta MR (2009) Human capital, inequality, endogenous growth and education subsidy: a theoretical analysis. Res Econ 63:77–90
Chang WY (2006) Relative wealth, consumption taxation, and economic growth. J Econ 88:103–129
Chang WY, Tsai FH (2003) Money, social status, and capital accumulation in a cash-in-advance model: a comment. J Money, Credit, Bank 33:657–661
Chang WY, Tsai HF, Lai CC (2004) Taxation, growth, and the spirit of capitalism. Eur J Polit Econ 20:1011–1025
Chari VV, Hopenhayn H (1991) Vintage human capital, growth, and the diffusion of new technology. J Polit Econ 99:1142–1165
Charles KK, Guryan J (2008) Prejudice and wages: an empirical assessment of Becker's the economics of discrimination. J Polit Econ 116(5):773–809
Chatterjee S (1994) Transitional dynamics and the distribution of wealth in a neoclassical growth model. J Public Econ 54:97–119
Chatterjee BS, Ravikumar B (1992) A neoclassical model of seasonal fluctuations. J Monet Econ 29:59–86
Chen HJ (2005) Educational systems, growth and income distribution: a quantitative study. J Dev Econ 76:325–353
Chen MK, Chevalier JA (2008) The taste for leisure, career choice, and the returns to education. Econ Lett 99:353–356
Chen HJ, Guo JT (2009) Social status and the growth effect of money. Jpn Econ Rev 60:133–141
Chen HJ, Guo JT (2011) Money, social status and endogenous growth in a generalized cash-in-advance model. Pac Econ Rev 16:267–284
Chen JL, Xie XR, Sun CQ, Lin L, Liu L (2022) Optimal trade policy and welfare in a differentiated duopoly. Manag Decis Econ 43:3019–3043
Cheng IH, French E (2000) The effect of the run-up in the stock market on labor supply. Federal Reserve Bank Chicago Econ Perspect 24:48–65
Chiarella C, Flaschel P (2000) The dynamics of Keynesian monetary growth: Macro foundations. Cambridge University Press, Cambridge
Cho SW (2010) Household wealth accumulation and portfolio choices in Korea. J Hous Econ 19:13–25
Choo E, Siow A (2006) Who marries who and why. J Polit Econ 114:175–201
Chu AC, Cozzi G, Liao CH (2013) Endogenous fertility and human capital in a Schumpeterian growth model. J Popul Econ 26:181–202
Ciarli T, Lorentz A, Savona MMV (2010) The effect of consumption and production structure on growth and distribution: a micro to macro model. Metroeconomica 61:180–218
Cigno A, Komura M, Luporini A (2017) Self-enforcing family rules, marriage and the (non)neutrality of public intervention. J Popul Econ 30:805–834
Cimoli M, Porcile G (2010) Specialization, wage bargaining and technology in a multigoods growth model. Metroeconomica 61:219–238
Clemens C (2004) Status, risk-taking and intertemporal substitution in an endogenous growth model. J Econ 2:103–123

Clemens C, Heinemann M (2015) Endogenous growth and wealth inequality under incomplete markets and idiosyncratic risk. J Macroecon 45:300–317
Cochrane J (1970) The first mathematical Ricardian system. Hist Polit Econ 2:419–431
Coibion O, Gorodnichenko Y, Kueng L, Silvia J (2017) Innocent bystanders? Monetary policy and inequality. J Monet Econ 88:70–89
Cole HL, Mailath GJ, Postlewaite A (1992) Social norms, savings behavior, and growth. J Polit Econ 100:1092–1125
Colombo S, Lambertini L (2023) R&D investments with spillovers and endogenous horizontal differentiation. Reg Sci Urban Econ 98:103861
Combes PP, Mayer T, Thisse JF (2008) Economic geography: the integration of regions and nations. Princeton University Press, Princeton
Comin D, Lashkari D, Mestieri M (2021) Structural change with long-run income and price effects. Econometrica 89:311374
Conde-Ruiz JI, Giménez EL, Pérez-Nievas M (2010) Millian efficiency with endogenous fertility. Rev Econ Stud 77:154–187
Cordoba JC, Liu X, Ripoll M (2016) Fertility, social mobility and long run inequality. J Monet Econ 77:103–124
Corneo G, Jeanne O (1997a) Status, the distribution of wealth, and growth. Discussion paper A-561, University of Bonn
Corneo G, Jeanne O (1997b) On relative wealth effects and the optimality of growth. Econ Lett 54:87–92
Corneo G, Jeanne O (1999) Social organization in an endogenous growth model. Int Econ Rev 40:711–725
Corneo G, Jeanne O (2001) On relative wealth effects and long-run growth. Res Econ 55:349–358
Coronado JL, Perozek M (2003) Wealth effects and the consumption of leisure: Retirement decisions during the stock market boom of the 1990s. Board of Governors of the Federal Reserve System, Finance and Economics Discussion Series No. 2003–20
Could ED, Moav O, Weinberg BA (2001) Precautionary demand for education, inequality, and technological progress. J Econ Growth 6:285–315
Coussey M (2002) Tackling racial equality: International comparisons. Home Office Research, Development and Statistics Directorate, London
Cox D (1987) Motives for private income transfers. J Polit Econ 95:508–546
Cozzi G, Galli S (2009) Science-based R&D in Schumpeterian growth. Scottish J Polit Econ 56:474–491
Cozzi G, Galli S (2011) Privatization of knowledge: did the U.S. get it right? MPRA Paper 29710
Cremers ET (2006) Dynamic efficiency in the two-sector overlapping generalizations model. J Econ Dyn Control 30:1915–1936
Currarini S, Jackson MO, Pin P (2009) An economic model of friendship: Homophily, minorities, segregation. Econometrica 77:1003–1045
Cutler D, Glaeser E (1997) Are ghettos good or bad? Quart J Econ 112:827–893
Dana RA, Florenzano M, Levy D (1989) Production prices and general equilibrium prices: a long-run property of a Leontief economy. J Math Econ 18:263–280
Daruich D, Kozlowski J (2020) Explaining intergenerational mobility: role of fertility and family transfers. Rev Econ Dyn 36:220–245
Davis C, Hashimoto KI (2015) R&D subsidies, international knowledge diffusion, and fully endogenous productivity growth. Macroecon Dyn 19:1816–1838
Day C (2016) Fertility and economic growth: the role of workforce skill composition and childcare prices. Oxf Econ Pap 68:546–565
De Hek PA (2005) On taxation in a two-sector endogenous growth model with endogenous labor supply. J Econ Dyn Control 30:655–685
De la Croix D, Doepke M (2003) Inequality and growth: why differential fertility matters. Am Econ Rev 93:1091–1113
De la Croix D, Licandro O (1999) Life expectancy and endogenous growth. Econ Lett 65:255–263

Debreu G (1959) Theory of value: an axiomatic analysis of equilibrium. Yale University Press, London
Dee TS (2004) Are there civic returns to education? J Public Econ 88:1697–1720
Delgado M, Porter ME, Stern M (2010) Clusters and entrepreneurship. J Econ Geogr 10:495–518
Deming DJ (2017) The growing importance of social skills in the labor market. Q J Econ 132:1593–1640
Desmet K, Rossi-Hansberg E (2012) Innovation in space. J Polit Econ 126:903–983
Desmet K, Nagy DK, Rossi-Hansberg E (2018) The geography of development: On the spatial economic impact of global warning. J Urban Econ 88:16–37
Dessing M (2002) Labor supply, the family and poverty: The s-shaped labor supply curve. J Econ Behav Organ 49:433–458
Diebolt C, Hippe R (2019) The long-run impact of human capital on innovation and economic development in the regions of Europe. Appl Econ 51:542–563
Diewert W (1977) Walras' theory of capital formation and the existence of a temporary equilibrium. In: Schwödiauer G (ed) Equilibrium and disequilibrium in economic theory. Reidel, Dordrecht
DiPasquale D, Wheaton WC (1996) Urban economics and real estate markets. Prentice Hall, Englewood Cliffs
Dixit A, Stiglitz JE (1977) Monopolistic competition and optimum product diversity. Am Econ Rev 67:297–308
Doepke M (2004) Accounting for fertility decline during the transition to growth. J Econ Growth 9:347–383
Drugeon JP, Venditti A (2001) Intersectoral external effects, multiplicities & indeterminacies. J Econ Dyn Control 25:765–787
Duernecker G, Herrendorf B (2018) On the allocation of time—a quantitative analysis of the roles of taxes and productivities. Eur Econ Rev 102:169–187
Duesenberry J (1949) Income, saving, and the theory of consumer behavior. Harvard University Press, Cambridge
Dur R, Glazer A (2008) Subsidizing enjoyable education. Labour Econ 15:1023–1039
Easterlin R (1981) Why isn't the whole world developed? J Econ Hist 41:1–19
Eatwell J (1987) Walras' theory of capital. In: Eatwell J, Milgate M, Newmann P (eds) The new Palgrave dictionary of political economy. Macmillan, London
Echevarria E (1997) Changes in sectoral composition associated with economic growth. Int Econ Rev 38:431–452
Eckstein Z, Lifshitz O (2011) Dynamic female labor supply. Econometrica 79:1675–1726
Eckstein Z, Zilcha I (1994) The effects of compulsory schooling on growth, income distribution and welfare. J Public Econ 54:339–359
Edmonds E, Pavcnik N (2006) International trade and child labor: cross-country evidence. J Int Econ 68:115–140
Ehrlich I, Lui F (1997) The problem of population and growth: a review of the literature from Malthus to contemporary models of endogenous population and endogenous growth. J Econ Dyn Control 21:205–242
Eicher T, Turnovsky SJ (2000) Scale, congestion and growth. Economica 67:325–346
Elsayed A, Degrip A, Fouarge D (2017) Job tasks, computer use, and the decreasing part-time pay penalty for women in the UK. Br J Ind Relat 55:58–82
Epple D, Romano RE (1998) Competition between public and private schools, vouchers and peer-group effects. Am Econ Rev 88:33–62
Erceg C, Guerrieri L, Gust C (2005) Can long-run restrictions identify technology shocks? J Eur Econ Assoc 3:1237–1278
Erosa A, Koreshkova T, Restuccia D (2010) How important is human capital? a quantitative theory assessment of world income inequality. Rev Econ Stud 77:1421–1449
Ethier WJ, Svensson LEO (1986) The theorems of international trade with factor mobility. J Int Econ 20:21–42
Fang H (2001) Social culture and economic performance. Am Econ Rev 91:924–937

Farhi E, Panageas S (2007) Saving and investing for early retirement: a theoretical analysis. J Financ Econ 83:87–121
Feagin JR (2000) Racist America: Roots, current realities, and future reparations. Routledge, New York
Fender J, Wang P (2003) Educational policy in a credit constrained economy with skill heterogeneity. Int Econ Rev 44:939–964
Ferber MA, Green CA (2007) Career of family: what choices do college women have? J Lab Res 24:143–151
Fernandez R, Rogerson R (1998) Public education and income distribution: a dynamic quantitative evaluation of education finance reform. Am Econ Rev 88:813–833
Fershtman C, Weiss Y (1993) Social status, culture and economic performance. Econ J 103:946–959
Fershtman C, Murphy KM, Weiss Y (1996) Social status, education and growth. J Polit Econ 106:108–132
Findlay R (1984) Growth and development in trade models. In: Jones RW, Kenen RB (eds) Handbook of international economics. North-Holland, Amsterdam
Fisher JDM (2006) The dynamic effects of neutral and investment-specific technology shocks. J Polit Econ 114:413–451
Fisher WH, Hof FX (2005) Status seeking in the small open economy. J Macroecon 27:209–232
Flaschel P, Franke R, Semmler W (1997) Dynamic macroeconomics. The MIT Press, Cambridge
Fleisher B, Hu YF, Li HZ, Kim SH (2011) Economic transition, higher education and worker productivity in China. J Dev Econ 94:86–94
Fogli A, Veldkamp L (2011) Nature or nurture? Learning and the geography of female labor force participation. Econometrica 79:1103–1138
Fonseca T, de Faria P, Lima P (2019) Human capital and innovation: The importance of the optimal organizational task structure. Res Policy 48:616–627
Forbes K (2000) A reassessment of the relationship between inequality and growth. Am Econ Rev 90:869–870
Forsythe N, Korzeniewicz RP, Durrant V (2000) Gender inequalities and economic growth: a longitudinal evaluation. Econ Dev Cult Change 48:573–617
Frank R (1985) The demand for non-observable and other non-positional goods. Am Econ Rev 75:101–116
Frank MW (2009) Inequality and growth in the United States: evidence from a new state-level panel of income inequality measures. Econ Inq 47:55–68
Frenkel JA Razin A (1987) Fiscal policy and the world economy. MIT Press, Cambridge
Friedman M (1969) The optimum quantity of money. In: Friedman M (ed) The optimum quality of money and other essays. Aldine, Chicago
Fujita M Thisse JF (2002) Economics of agglomeration. MIT Press, Cambridge
Fukuyama F (1992) The end of history and the last man. Penguin Books, London
Fukuyama F (1996) Trust: The social virtues and the creation of prosperity. Free Press, Boston
Furuoka F (2009) Population growth and economic development: new empirical evidence from Thailand. Economics Bull 29:1–14
Futagami K, Konishi K (2019) Rising longevity, fertility dynamics, and R&D-based growth. J Popul Econ 32:591–620
Gabaix X (2011) The granular origins of aggregate fluctuations. Econometrica 79:733–772
Gabardo FA, Pereima JB, Einloft P (2017) The incorporation of structural change into growth theory: a historical appraisal. Economia 18:392–410
Gabriel PE, Schmitz S (2014) A longitudinal examination of racial differences in occupational distributions among prime-aged males in the United States. Econ Bull 34:106–114
Gale D (1955) The law of supply and demand. Math Scand 3:33–44
Galor O (1992) Two-sector overlapping-generations model: a global characterization of the dynamical system. Econometrica 60:1351–1386
Galor O (2005) From stagnation to growth: Unified growth theory. In Aghion P, Durlauf SN (eds) Handbook of economic growth. North Holland, Amsterdam

Galor O, Moav O (2004) From physical to human capital accumulation: inequality in the process of development. Rev Econ Stud 71:1001–1026
Galor O, Weil DN (1996) The gender gap, fertility, and growth. Am Econ Rev 86:374–387
Galor O, Weil D (1999) From Malthusian stagnation to modern growth. Am Econ Rev 89:150–154
Galor O, Zeira J (1993) Income distribution and macroeconomics. Rev Econ Stud 60:35–52
Gandolfo G (2005) Economic dynamics. Springer, Berlin
Garbinti B, Groupille-Lebret J, Pietty T (2021) Accounting for wealth-inequality dynamics: methods, estimates, and simulations for France. J Eur Econ Assoc 9:620–663
Gedikli A, Erdogan S, Cevik EI, Cevik E, Castanho RA, Couto G (2022) Dynamic relationship between international tourism, economic growth and environmental pollution in the OECD countries: Evidence from panel VAR model. Econ Res 35:5907–5923
Gersbach H, Schneider MT, Schneller O (2013) Basic research, openness, and convergence. J Econ Growth 18:33–68
Ghent AC, Owyang MT (2009) Is housing the business cycle? evidence from U.S. cities. J Urban Econ 67:336–351
Giannola M (2024) Parental investments and intra-household inequality in child human capital: evidence from a survey experiment. Econ J 134:671–727
Giovanni JD, Levchenko A, Mejean I (2014) Firms, destinations, and aggregate fluctuations. Econometrica 82:1303–1340
Glaeser EL, Gottlieb JD (2009) The wealth of cities: agglomeration economies and spatial equilibrium in the United States. J Econ Lit 47:983–1028
Glomm G, Kaganovich M (2008) Social security, public education and the growth-inequality relationship. Eur Econ Rev 52:1009–1034
Gomme P, Kydland FE, Rupert P (2001) Home production meets time to build. J Polit Econ 109(5):1115–1131
Gong L, Zou HF (2001) Money, social status, and capital accumulation in a cash-in-advance model. J Money Credit Banking 33:284–93
Goodfriend M, McDermott J (1995) Early development. Am Econ Rev 85:116–133
Gómez MA (2008) Convergence speed in the AK endogenous growth model with habit formation. Econ Lett 100:16–21
Grembi V, Nannicini T, Troiano U (2016) Do fiscal rules matter? Am Econ J Appl Econ 8:1–30
Grossman GM, Helpman E (1991) Innovation and growth in the global economy. The MIT Press, Cambridge
Grugan J (2004) Desegregation and black dropout rates. Am Econ Rev 94:919–943
Guner N, Kaygusuz R, Ventura G (2012) Taxing women: a macroeconomic analysis. J Monet Econ 59:111–128
Gutierrez M (ed) (2003) Macro-economics: making gender matter. Zed Books, London
Guvenen F, Kiruscu B, Ozkan S (2014) Taxation of human capital and wage inequality: across-country analysis. Rev Econ Stud 81:818–850
Haavelmo T (1954) A study in the theory of economic evolution. North-Holland, Amsterdam
Hall BH (2007) Measuring the returns to R&D: the depreciation problem. NBER Working Paper, No. 13473
Hanushek E, Kimko D (2000) Schooling, labor-force quality and the growth of nations. Am Econ Rev 90:1194–1204
Harrison SG (2003) Returns to scale and externalities in the consumption and investment sectors. Rev Econ Dyn 6:963–976
Hazan M, Zoabi H (2006) Does longevity cause growth? a theoretical critique. J Econ Growth 11:363–376
Heckman JJ (1976) A life-cycle model of earnings, learning, and consumption. J Polit Econ 84:S11-44
Heijdra BJ, Romp WE (2008) A life-cycle overlapping-generations model of the small open economy. Oxf Econ Pap 60:88–121
Henderson JV (2003) Marshall's scale economies. J Urban Econ 53:1–28

Henderson JV, Schalizi Z, Venables AJ (2001) Geography and development. J Econ Geogr 1:81–105
Herrendorf B, Herrington C, Valentinyi A (2015) Sectoral technology change and structural transformation. Am Econ J Macroecon 7:104–133
Herrendorf B, Valentinyi A (2006) On the stability of the two-sector neoclassical growth model with externalities. J Econ Dyn Control 30:1339–1361
Higgs R (1977) Competition and coercion: Blacks in the American economy 1865–1914. Columbia University Press, New York
Hinloopen J, Smrkolj G, Wagener F (2014) From mind to market: a global dynamic analysis of R&D. J Econ Dyn Control 37:2729–2754
Hock H, Weil DN (2012) On the dynamics of the age structure, dependency, and consumption. J Popul Econ 25:1019–1043
Hori T (2011) Wage inequality and structure of consumption demand. J Income Distrib 20:83–103
Iacopetta M (2011) Formal education and public knowledge. J Econ Dyn Control 35:676–693
Ikeda S, Ono Y (1992) Macroeconomic dynamics in a multi-country economy—a dynamic optimization approach. Int Econ Rev 33:629–644
Impicciatore G, Panaccione L, Ruscitti F (2012) Walras's theory of capital formation: an intertemporal equilibrium reformation. J Econ Theory 106:99–118
Ireland NJ (1994) On limiting the market for status signals. J Public Econ 53:91–110
Ireland NJ (1998) Status-seeking, income taxation and efficiency. J Public Econ 70:99–113
Jaffe A (1989) Real effects of academic research. Am Econ Rev 79:957–970
Jaffe A, Trajtenberg M, Henderson R (1993) Geographic localization of knowledge spillovers as evidenced by patent citations. Quart J Econ 63:577–598
Jensen BS (1994) The dynamic systems of basic economic growth models. Kluwer Academic, Dordrecht
Jensen BS (2003) Walrasian general equilibrium allocations and dynamics in two-sector growth models. German Econ Rev 4:53–87
Jensen BS, Larsen ME (2005) General equilibrium dynamics of multi-sector growth models. J Econ 86(S1):17–56
Jensen BS, Wong KY (eds) (1998) Dynamics, economic growth, and international trade. The University of Michigan Press, Ann Arbor
Jensen BS, Richter M, Wang C, Alsholm PK (2001) Saving rates, technology, trade and stochastic dynamics. Rev Dev Econ 5:182–204
Johnson HG (1971) Trade and growth: a geometric exposition. J Int Econ 1:83–101
Jones CI (2019) Paul Romer: Ideas, nonrivalry, and endogenous growth. Scandinavian J Econ 121:859–883
Jones RW, Kenen PB (eds) (1984) Handbook of international economics—International trade. North-Holland, Amsterdam
Jones LE, Manuelli RE (1997) The sources of growth. J Econ Dyn Control 21:75–114
Jones BF Liu X (2022) A framework for economic growth with capital embodied technical change. Working Paper 30459, National Bureau of Economic Research
Jones LE, Manuelli RE, Rossi PE (1993) Optimal taxation in models of endogenous growth. J Polit Econ 101:485–517
Joulfaian H-E, Rosen HS (1993) The Carnegie conjecture: some empirical evidence. Quart J Econ 108:413–435
Judd KL (1998) Numerical methods in economics. MIT Press, Cambridge
Kaganovich M, Zilcha I (1999) Education, social security and growth. J Public Econ 71:289–309
Kaiyama M (1973) On the growth model of a dual economy. Econo Stud Q 24:1–15
Kaldor N (1956) Alternative theories of distribution. Rev Econ Stud 23:83–100
Kaplan G, Violante GL (2018) Microeconomic heterogeneity and macroeconomic shock. J Econ Perspect 32:167–194
Kelly M (1997) The dynamics of Smithian growth. Quart J Econ 112:939–964
Kim KK, Marcouiller DW, Deller SC (2005) Natural amenities and rural development: Understanding spatial and distributional attributes. Growth Chang 36:273–297

Kim WC, Fabozzi FJ, Cheridito P, Fox C (2014) Controlling portfolio skewness and kurtosis without directly optimizing third and fourth moments. Econ Lett 122:154–158
Kirk D (1996) Demographic transition theory. Popul Stud 50:361–387
Kleven H, Landais NC, Søgaard JE (2019) Children and gender inequality: evidence from Denmark. Am Econ J Appl Econ 11:181–209
Kline S, Rosenberg N (1987) An overview of innovation. In: Landau R, Rosen-Berg N (eds) The positive sum strategy. National Academy Press, Washington
Konrad K (1992) Wealth seeking reconsidered. J Econ Behav Organ 18:215–227
Krueger AB, Lindahl M (2001) Education for growth: why and for whom. J Econ Lit 39:1101–1136
Krugman PR (1979) A model of innovation, technology transfer, and the world distribution of income. J Polit Econ 87:253–266
Krugman PR (1980) Scale economies, product differentiation, and the pattern of trade. Am Econ Rev 70:950–959
Krugman P, Venables AJ (1995) Globalization and the inequality. Quart J Econ 110:857–880
Kurz M (1963) A two-sector extension of Swan's model of economic growth: the case of no technical change. Int Econ Rev 4:68–79
Kurz M (1968) Optimal economic growth and wealth effects. Int Econ Rev 9:348–357
Kuwahara S (2019) Multiplicity and stagnation under the Romer model with increasing returns of R&D. Econ Model 79:86–97
Kyle B, Lee SH (2023) Monopolistic competition and efficiency under firm heterogeneity and nonadditive preferences. Am Econ J Macroecon 15:208–267
Lagerlof NP (2003) From Malthus to modern growth: the three regimes revisited. Int Rev Econ 44:755–777
Laitner J (2000) Earnings within education groups and overall productivity growth. J Polit Econ 108:807–832
Lancaster K (1980) Intra-industry trade under perfect monopolistic competition. J Int Econ 10:151–175
Lancia F, Prarolo G (2012) A politico-economic model of aging, technology adoption and growth. J Popul Econ 25:989–1018
Lazear E (1977) Education: consumption or production. J Polit Econ 85:569–597
Leamer EE (2007) Housing is the business cycle. NBER Working Paper No. 13428
Lee LF (2007) Identification and estimation of econometric models with group interactions, contextual factors and fixed factors. J Econ 140:333–374
Lee BC (2023) Wealth inequality and endogenous growth. J Monet Econ 133:132–148
Lee R, Mason A (2010) Fertility, human capital, and economic growth over the demographic transition. Eur J Popul 26:159–182
Lei F, Yang F (2022) Consumption and hours in the United States and Europe. J Econ Dyn Control 144:104540
Leung C (2004) Macroeconomics and housing: a review of the literature. J Hous Econ 13:249–267
Levy G (2005) Politics of public provision of education. Q J Econ 120:1507–1534
Li JL, Lin SL (2008) Existence and uniqueness of steady-state equilibrium in a two-sector overlapping generations model. J Econ Theory 141:255–275
Liao LP, Du MZ, Wang B, Yu YN (2019) The impact of educational investment on sustainable economic growth in Guangdong, China: a cointegration and causality analysis. Sustainability 11(3):1–16
Lorenz HW (1993) Nonlinear dynamic economics and chaotic motion. Springer-Verlag, Berlin
Loury G (1977) A dynamic theory of racial income differences. In Wallace PA Mund AL (eds) Women, minorities, and employment discrimination. Lexington Books, Lexington
Lucas RE (1977) Understanding business cycles. Carn-Roch Conf Ser Public Policy 5:7–29
Lucas RE (1988) On the mechanics of economic development. J Monet Econ 22:3–42
Ludwig A, Schelkle T, Vogel E (2012) Demographic change, human capital and welfare. Rev Econ Dyn 15:94–107
Mailath GJ, Postlewaite A (2006) Social assets. Int Econ Rev 47:1057–1091

Majekodunmi TB, Shaari MS, Abidin NZ (2023) The environmental influence of national savings in D-8 countries: Empirical evidence using an ARDL model. Environ Sci Pollut Res 30:94456–94473

Malchow-Møller N, Nielsen S, Skaksen JR (2011) Taxes, tuition fees, and education for pleasure. J Public Econ Theory 13:189–215

Maliar L, Maliar S (2001) Heterogeneity in capital and skills in a neoclassical stochastic growth model. J Econ Dyn Control 38:635–654

Manasse P, Turrini A (2001) Trade, wages, and 'superstars.' J Int Econ 54:97–117

Mansfield E (1998) Academic research and industrial innovation: an update of empirical findings. Res Policy 26:773–776

Maoz YD, Moav O (1999) Intergenerational mobility and the process of development. Econ J 109:677–697

Marco R, Llano C, Pérez-Balsalobre S (2022) Economic complexity, environmental quality and income equality: a new trilemma for regions? Appl Geogr 139:102646

Marglin SA (1984) Growth, distribution and prices. Harvard University Press, Cambridge

Marino AM (1975) On the neoclassical version of the dual economy. Rev Econ Stud 42:435–443

Martín AR (2010) Endogenous retirement and public pension system reform in Spain. Econ Model 27:336–349

Martin P, Ottaviano G (2001) Growth and agglomeration. Int Econ Rev 42:947–968

Mas-Colell A, Whinston MD, Green JR (1995) Microeconomic theory. Oxford University Press, Oxford

McCann P, Ortega-Argilés R (2015) Smart specification, regional growth and applications to European union cohesion policy. Reg Stud 49:1291–1302

McKenzie LW (1959) On the existence of general equilibrium for a competitive market. Econometrica 27:54–71

Meade JE (1961) A neoclassical theory of economic growth. Allen & Unwin, London

Miles D, Scott A (2005) Macroeconomics—understanding the wealth of nations. Wiley, Chichester

Mincer JA (1974) Schooling, experience, and earnings. National Bureau of Economic Research, Working Paper 0053

Minniti A, Parello CP (2011) Trade integration and regional disparity in a model of scale-invariant growth. Reg Sci Urban Econ 41:20–31

Mino K (1996) Analysis of a two-sector model of endogenous growth with capital income taxation. Int Econ Rev 37:227–251

Montesano A (2008) A restatement of Walras' theory of capitalization and money. Hist Econ Rev 47:86–109

Morimoto T, Tabata K (2020) Higher education subsidy policy and R&D-base growth. Macroecon Dyn 24:2129–2168

Morishima M (1964) Equilibrium, stability and growth. Oxford University Press, Oxford

Morishima M (1977) Walras' economics. Cambridge University Press, Cambridge

Morishima M (1989) Ricardo's economics—a general equilibrium theory of distribution and growth. Cambridge University Press, Cambridge

Mulligan CB, Sala-I-Martin X (1993) Transitional dynamics in two-sector models of endogenous growth. Q J Econ 108:739–773

Munir K, Ameer A (2022) An assessing nonlinear impact of urbanization, economic growth, technology and trade on environment: evidence from African and Asian emerging economies. GeoJournal 87:2195–2208

Munshi K, Myaus J (2006) Social norms and the fertility transition. J Dev Econ 80:1–38

Mutreja P, Ravikumar B, Sposi M (2018) Capital goods trade, relative prices, and economic development. Rev Econ Dyn 27:101122

Nadiri MI, Prucha IR (1993) Estimation of the depreciation rate of physical and R&D capital in the U.S. Total Manufacturing Sector. MBER Working Paper, No. 4591

Naito T, Ornori T (2017) Aging and urban agglomeration under a multi-regional overlapping generations model. Rev Urban Reg Dev Stud 29:135–150

Nakajima T, Nakamura H (2009) The price of education and inequality. Econ Lett 105:183–185
Naz R, Chaudhry A (2017) Comparison of closed form solutions for the Lucas-Uzawa model via the partial Hamiltonian approach and the classical approach. Math Model Anal 22:464–483
Naz R, Chaudhry A (2018) Closed-form solutions of Lucas-Uzawa model with externalities via partial Hamiltonian approach. Comput Appl Math 37:5146–5161
Negishi T (1989) History of economic theory. North-Holland, Amsterdam
Nelson R (2002) Bringing institutions into evolutionary growth theory. J Evol Econ 12:61–74
Nelson R, Winter S (1982) An evolutionary theory of economic change. Cambridge University Press, Cambridge
Ng YK (1987) Diamonds are a government's best friend: burden-free taxes on goods valued for their values. Am Econ Rev 77:186–191
Nikaido H (1956) On the classical multilateral exchange problem. Metroeconomica 8:135–145
Nikaido H (1968) Convex structures and economic theory. Academic Press, New York
Nishimura K, Shimomura K (2002) Trade and indeterminacy in a dynamic general equilibrium model. J Econo Theory 105:244–260
Nocco A (2005) The Rise and fall of regional inequalities with technological differences and knowledge spillovers. Reg Sci Urban Econ 35:542–569
Nocco A, Ottaviano GLP, Salto M (2017) Monopolistic competition and optimum product selection: why and how heterogeneity matters. Res Econ 71:704–717
Obstfeld M, Rogoff K (1998) Foundations of international macroeconomics. MIT Press, Cambridge
Olovsson C (2009) Why do Europeans work so little? Int Econ Rev 50:39–61
Oniki H, Uzawa H (1965) Patterns of trade and investment in a dynamic model of international trade. Rev Econ Stud 32:15–38
Osiobe EU (2019) A literature review of human capital and economic growth. Bus Econ Rev 9:179–196
Ömer Y, Muhammet D, Kerern K (2018) The effects of international tourism receipts on economic theory: evidence from the first 20 highest income earning countries from tourism in the world (1996–2016). Montenegrin J Econ Lab Trans Res 14:55–71
Parenti M, Ushchev P, Thisse JF (2017) Toward a theory of monopolistic competition. J Econ Theory 167:86–115
Park WG (1998) A Theoretical model of government research and growth. J Econ Behav Organ 34:69–85
Pasinetti LL (1960) A mathematical formulation of the Ricardian system. Rev Econ Stud 27:78–98
Pasinetti L (1962) Rate of profit and income distribution in relation to the rate of economic growth. Rev Econ Stud 29:267–279
Pasinetti LL (1974) Growth and income distribution—essays in economic theory. Cambridge University Press, Cambridge
Patinkin D (1965) Money, interest, and prices: an integration of monetary and value theory, 2nd edn. Harper & Row, New York
Patrick B, Nathaniel K, Christopher T (2009) Migration and hedonic valuation: the case of air quality. J Environ Econ Manag 58:1–14
Penalosa CG, Turnovsky SJ (2006) Growth and income inequality: a canonical model. Econ Theor 28:25–49
Peretto PF (2018) Robust endogenous growth. Eur Econ Rev 108:49–77
Persson T, Tabellini GE (1994) Is inequality harmful for growth? theory and evidence. Am Econ Rev 84:600–621
Petrongolo B (2004) Gender segregation in employment contract. J Eur Econ Assoc 2:331–345
Pflüger MP (2004) A simple, analytically solvable Chamberlinian agglomeration model. Reg Sci Urban Econ 34:565–573
Phelps ES (1972) The statistical theory of racism and sexism. Am Econ Rev 62(4):659–661
Piao X, Managi S (2023) Household energy-saving behavior, its consumption, and life satisfaction in 37 countries. Sci Rep 13:1382

Piketty T, Zucman G (2014) Capital is back: Wealth-income ratios in rich countries 1700–2010. Quart J Econ 129:1255–1310
Porter M (1990) The competitive advantage of nations. The Free Press, New York
Porter M (1998) On competition. Harvard Business School Press, Boston
Puu T (2011) Nonlinear economic dynamics. Springer, Berlin
Rauscher M (1997) Conspicuous consumption, economic growth, and taxation. J Econ 66:35–42
Raut LK (1992) Effect of social security on fertility and savings: an overlapping generations model. Indian Econ Rev 27:25–43
Razin A, Ben-Zion U (1975) An intergenerational model of population growth. Am Econ Rev 65:923–933
Reati A (1998) A long-wave pattern for output and employment in Pasinetti's model of structural change. Appl Econ 51:27–75
Rege M (2008) Why do people care about social status? J Econ Behav Organ 66:233–242
Ricardo D (1821) The principles of political economy and taxation, 3rd edn, 1965. Everyman's Library, London
Robinson JA, Srinivasan TN (1997) Long-term consequence of population growth: Technological change, natural resources, and the environment. In Rozenzweig MR, Stark O (eds) Handbook of population and family economics. North-Holland, Amsterdam
Rogerson R, Wallenius J (2016) Retirement, home production and labor supply elasticities. J Monet Econ 78:23–34
Romer PM (1986) Increasing returns and long-run growth. J Polit Econ 94:1002–1037
Romer PM (1990) Endogenous technological change. J Polit Econ 98:S71–S102
Romero JP, Gramkow C (2021) Economic complexity and greenhouse gas emissions. World Dev 139:105317
Saad MB, Brahim M, Schaffar A, Guesmi K, Saad RB (2023) Economic complexity, diversification and economic development: The strategic factors. Res Int Bus Financ 64:101840
Saez E, Zucman G (2016) Wealth inequality in the United States since 1913: Evidence from capitalization income tax data. Quart J Econ 131:518–578
Salvadori N (1991) Post-Keynesian theory of distribution in the long run. In Nell EJ, Semmler W (eds) Nicholas Kaldor and mainstream economics—confrontation or convergence? Macmillan, London
Samuelson PA (1959) A modern treatment of the Ricardian economy: I. The pricing of goods labor and land services. Q J Econ 73:1–35
Sano K, Tomoda Y (2010) Optimal public education policy in a two-sector model. Econ Model 27:991–995
Sasakura K (2022) How Uzawa differs from Lucas. Oxf Econ Pap 74:1214–1227
Scarf HE (1967) The approximation of fixed points of a continuous mapping. J SIAM Appl Math 15:1328–1343
Scarf HE, Hansen T (1973) The computation of economic equilibria. Yale University Press, Yale
Sethi R, Somanathan R (2004) Inequality and segregation. J Polit Econ 112:1296–1321
Shi SY (2006) Wage differentials, discrimination and efficiency. Eur Econ Rev 50:849–875
Shone R (2002) Economic dynamics—phase diagrams and their economic application. Cambridge University Press, Cambridge
Shoven JB, Whalley J (1992) Applying general equilibrium. Cambridge University Press, Cambridge
Sidrauski M (1967) Rational choice and patterns of growth in a monetary economy. Am Econ Rev 57:534–544
Siegel C (2017) Female relative wages, household specialization and fertility. Rev Econ Dyn 24:152–174
Soares RR (2005) Mortality reductions, educational attainment, and fertility choice. Am Econ Rev 95:580–601
Solow R (1956) A contribution to the theory of growth. Quart J Econ 70:65–94
Solow RM (1992) Sustainability: An economist's perspective. Natl Geogr Res Explor 8:10–21

Solow R (2000) Growth theory—an exposition. Oxford University Press, New York
Sorger G (2002) On the multi-country version of the Solow-Swan model. Jpn Econ Rev 54:146–164
Spence M (1976) Product selection, fixed costs and monopolistic competition. Rev Econo Stud 43(2):217–235
Stella A (2015) Firm dynamics and the origins of aggregate fluctuations. J Econ Dyn Control 55:71–88
Stiglitz JE (1967) A two sector two class model of economic growth. Rev Econ Stud 34:227–238
Stockman DR (2009) Chaos and sector-specific externalities. J Econ Dyn Control 33:2030–2046
Stokey NL, Rebelo S (1995) Growth effects of flat-rate taxes. J Polit Econ 103:519–550
Stotsky JG (2006) Gender and its relevance to macroeconomic policy: a survey. IMF Working Paper, WP/06/233
Strulik H (2024) Higher education and the income-fertility nexus. J Popul Econ 37:1–13
Stutzer M (1980) Chaotic dynamics and bifurcation in a macro economics. J Econ Dyn Control 2:253–273
Takayama A (1963) On a two-sector model of economic growth: a comparative statics analysis. Rev Econ Stud 30:95–104
Takayama A (1965) On a two-sector model of economic growth with technological progress: a comparative statics analysis. Rev Econ Stud 32:251–262
Takayama A (1985) Mathematical economics. Cambridge University Press, Cambridge
Tian C (2015) Riskness, endogenous productivity dispersion and business cycles. J Econ Dyn Control 57:227–249
Tilak JBC (1989) Education and its relation to economic growth, poverty and income distribution: Past evidence and future analysis. World Bank, Washington
Tirole J (1988) The theory of industrial organization. MIT Press, Cambridge
Tobin J (1956) The interest-elasticity of transactions demand for cash. Rev Econ Stat 38:241–247
Tobin J (1965) Money and economic growth. Econometrica 33:671–684
Todaro MP (1969) A model of labor migration and urban unemployment in less developed countries. Am Econ Rev 59:138–148
Tournemaine F, Luangaram P (2012) R&D, human capital, fertility, and growth. J Popul Econ 25:923–953
Truong TD (1997) Gender and human development: a feminist perspective. Gend Technol Dev 1:347–370
Tselios V (2008) Income and educational inequalities in the regions of the European union: Geographically spillovers under welfare state restrictions. Pap Reg Sci 87:403–430
Turnovsky SJ, Penalosa CG (2006) Distributional dynamics in a neoclassical growth model: the role of elastic labor supply. J Econ Dyn Control 32:1399–1431
Uzawa H (1961) On a two-sector model of economic growth I. Rev Econ Stud 29:47–70
Uzawa H (1963) On a two-sector model of economic growth II. Rev Econ Stud 30:105–118
Uzawa H (1965) Optimal technical change in an aggregative model of economic growth. Int Econ Rev 6:18–31
Valdés B (1999) Economic growth—theory, empirics and policy. Edward Elgar, Cheltenham
Varvarigos D, Zakaria IZ (2013) Endogenous fertility in a growth model with public and private health expenditures. J Popul Econ 26:67–85
Veblen T (1899) The theory of the leisure class. Modern Library, New York
Veld D, van der Leij M, Hommes C (2020) The formation of a core-periphery structure in heterogenous financial networks. J Econ Dyn Control 119:103972
Vellutini C (2003) Capital mobility and underdevelopment traps. J Dev Econ 71:435–462
Walras L (1874) Elements of pure economics, translated from the French by Jaffé W, 1954. Allen & Unwin, London
Wang WW (2012) Monopolistic competition and product diversity: review and extension. J Econ Surv 26:879–910
Wang P, Yip CK (1992) Examining the long-run effect on economic growth. J Macroecon 14:359–369

Wang P, Yip CK, Scotese CA (1994) Fertility choice and economic growth: theory and evidence. Rev Econ Stat 71:255–266
Waterson M (1984) Economic theory of the industry. Cambridge University Press, Cambridge
Welch F (1967) Labor market discrimination: an interpretation of income differences in the rural South. J Polit Econ 75:225–240
Welch F (1975) Human capital theory: Education, discrimination, and life cycles. Am Econ Rev 65:63–73
Whatley W, Wright G (1994) Race, human capital, and labour markets in American history. In: Grantham G, MacKinnon M (eds) Labour market evolution. Routledge, London and New York
Whelan K (2003) A two-sector approach to modeling U.S. NIPA Data. J Money, Credit, Bank 35:627–656
Wong KY (1995) International trade in goods and factor mobility. MIT Press, Cambridge
Yaman F (2011) Ethnic externalities and 2nd generation immigrants. Working Papers 11/08, Department of Economics, City University London
Yao WJ, Kinugasa T, Hamori S (2013) An empirical analysis of the relationship between economic development and population growth in China. Appl Econ 45:4651–4661
Yazdi SK (2019) Structural breaks, international tourism development and economic growth. Econ Res 32:1765–1776
Yip C, Zhang J (1997) A simple endogenous growth model with endogenous fertility: Indeterminacy and uniqueness. J Popul Econ 10:97–100
Yotov YV, Piermartini R, Monteiro JA, Larch M (2016) Advanced guide to trade policy analysis: The structural gravity model. World Trade Organization, Geneva
You W, Zhang Y, Lee CC (2022) The dynamic impact of economic growth and economic complexity on CO2 emissions: An advanced panel data estimation. Economic Anal Policy 73:112–128
Young AA (1928) Increasing returns and economic progress. Econ J 38:527–542
Zhang WB (1990) Economic dynamics—growth and development. Springer-Verlag, Heidelberg
Zhang WB (1991) Synergetic economics. Springer-Verlag, Heidelberg
Zhang WB (1992) Trade and world economic growth—differences in knowledge utilization and creativity. Econ Lett 39:199–206
Zhang WB (1993a) Woman's labor participation and economic growth—creativity, knowledge utilization and family preference. Econ Lett 42:105–110
Zhang WB (1993b) Government's research policy and economic growth—capital, knowledge and economic structure. Res Policy 22:327–336
Zhang WB (1995) Growth, taste change and sexual division of labor. Seoul J Econ 8:395–411
Zhang WB (1996a) Preference, structure and economic growth. Struct Chang Econ Dyn 7:207–221
Zhang WB (1996b) Knowledge and value—economic structures with time and space. Umeå University, Umeå Economic Studies, Umeå
Zhang WB (1997) Capital, incomes and lifestyles. Seoul J Econo 10:119–133
Zhang WB (1998) Japan versus China in the industrial race. Macmillan, London
Zhang WB (1999a) Capital and knowledge—dynamics of economic structures with non-constant returns. Springer-Verlag, Heidelberg
Zhang WB (1999b) Confucianism and industrialization. Macmillan, London
Zhang WB (2000) A theory of international trade—capital, knowledge and economic structures. Springer, Berlin
Zhang WB (2002a) An economic theory of cities—spatial models with capital, knowledge, and structures. Springer, Berlin
Zhang WB (2002b) Singapore's modernization—westernization and modernizing Confucian manifestations. Nova Science, New York
Zhang WB (2003a) The American civilization portrayed by ancient Confucianism. Algora Publisher, New York
Zhang WB (2003b) Taiwan's modernization. World Scientific, Singapore
Zhang WB (2003c) A theory of interregional dynamics—spatial models with capital, knowledge, and structures. Springer, Berlin

Zhang WB (2005a) Economic growth theory. Ashgate, Hampshire
Zhang WB (2005b) A two-sector growth model with labour supply. Aust J Labor Econ 8:245–260
Zhang WB (2005c) Differential equations, bifurcations, and chaos in economics, in Series on advances in mathematics for applied sciences, vol 68. World Scientific, Singapore
Zhang WB (2006a) Growth with Income and wealth distribution. Macmillan, London
Zhang WB (2006b) Discrete dynamical systems, bifurcations and chaos in economics. Elsevier, Amsterdam
Zhang WB (2006c) Hong Kong - The pearl made of the British mastery and the Chinese docile-diligence. Nova Science, New York
Zhang WB (2007a) New China's long march from servility to freedom. Nova Science, New York
Zhang WB (2007b) Economic growth with learning by producing, learning by education, and learning by consuming. Interdiscip Descr Complex Syst 5:21–38
Zhang WB (2008a) Growth and residential distribution with economic structure and amenity: A synthesis of Solow-Uzawa's growth, Alonso's urban, and Muth's housing models. Pap Reg Sci 87:277–303
Zhang WB (2008b) International trade theory: Capital, knowledge, economic structure, money and prices over time and space. Springer, Berlin
Zhang WB (2009a) Monetary growth theory: Money, interest, prices, capital, knowledge, and economic structure over time and space. Routledge, London
Zhang WB (2009b) A discrete one-sector growth model with endogenous labor supply and heterogeneous groups. Discret Dyn Nat Soc 2009:1–17
Zhang WB (2010) Fukuzawa Yukichi: The pioneer of East Asia's westernization with ancient Confucianism. PublishAmerica, MD, Frederick
Zhang WB (2011) The rise and fall of China's last dynasty: the deepening of the Chinese servility. Nova Science, New York
Zhang WB (2012a) Tourism and economic structure in a small-open growth model. J Environ Manage Tourism 3:76–92
Zhang WB (2012b) Economic growth with heterogeneous households, gender division of labor, and elastic labor supply. J Income Distrib 21:15–37
Zhang WB (2012c) International trade and global growth with capital accumulation, heterogeneous households and elastic labor supply. Int J Soc Syst Sci 4(2):1129–1149
Zhang WB (2013a) Renewable resource dynamics and elastic labor supply in a neoclassical growth model with housing and agriculture. Int J Sustain Econ 5:321–339
Zhang WB (2013b) Income and wealth distribution with physical and human capital accumulation: Extending the Uzawa-Lucas model to a heterogeneous households economy. Latin American J Econ 50:257–287
Zhang WB (2013c) Flexible exchange rate and growth of a small open monetary economy with imported good and externalities. Economic Research Guardian 3:32–52
Zhang WB (2013d) A synthesis of the Uzawa-Lucas model with the Walrasian-general-equilibrium and neoclassical-growth theories. Econ Ann 58:8–38
Zhang WB (2013e) Education, endogenous human capital, and monetary economic growth with MIU approach. Czech Econ Rev 7:100–118
Zhang WB (2013f) A study of the role of government in income and wealth distribution by integrating the Walrasian general equilibrium and neoclassical growth theories. Interdiscip Descr Complex Syst 12:28–45
Zhang WB (2014a) Population change with endogenous birth and mortality rates, wealth accumulation, and renewable resource change. Int J Econ Sci 3:103–129
Zhang WB (2014b) Ethnic human capital externalities and inequality in a general equilibrium growth model. J New Econ Assoc 21(11):33–54
Zhang WB (2014c) Capital and knowledge examined by integrating Arrow's learning-by-doing, the Walrasian equilibrium theory, and neoclassical growth theory. South Asian J Macroecon Public Financ 3:267–293

Zhang WB (2014d) Endogenous population with human and physical capital accumulation. Int Rev Econ 61:231–252

Zhang WB (2014e) Gender discrimination, education and economic growth in a generalized Uzawa-Lucas two-sector model. Timisoara J Econ Bus 7:1–34

Zhang WB (2014f) Land value and rent dynamics in an integrated Walrasian general equilibrium and neoclassical growth theory. Ann Alexandru Ioan Cuza University of Iasi, Econ Sci Section 61(32):235–258

Zhang WB (2014g) A study of the role of government in income and wealth distribution by integrating the Walrasian general equilibrium and neoclassical growth theories. Interdiscip Descr Complex Syst 12:28–45

Zhang WB (2015a) How do the richest 1% own 50% of wealth in an integrated Walrasian equilibrium and neoclassical growth model. Int J Econ Behav 5:59–80

Zhang WB (2015b) Population growth and gender time distribution in a small-open growth model. J Econ Int Finance 7:144–150

Zhang WB (2015c) A synthesis of the Heckscher-Ohlin and Oniki-Uzawa trade models with heterogeneous tastes, different technologies, and endogenous wealth. Scientific Annals of the "Alexandru Ioan Cuza" University of Iasi. Economic Sci 62:391–410

Zhang WB (2015d) National education and global economic growth: A synthesis of the Uzawa-Lucas two-sector model and the Oniki-Uzawa trade model. J Knowl Econ 6:905–928

Zhang WB (2015e) Development, preference change and inequality in an integrated Walrasian-general-equilibrium and neoclassical-growth theory. Int J Sustain Dev World Policy 4:41–55

Zhang WB (2015f) Birth and mortality rates, gender division of labor, and time distribution in the Solow growth model. Revista Galega De Economía 24:121–134

Zhang WB (2016a) Population growth and preference change in a generalized Solow growth model with gender time distributions. Oradea J Bus Econ 1:7–30

Zhang WB (2016b) Gender-differentiated human capital and time distributions in a generalized Heckscher-Ohlin model with endogenous physical capital. Knowl Horiz Econ 8:112–132

Zhang WB (2016c) Endogenous population dynamics and economic growth with free trade between countries. Social Sci Educ Res Rev 3:3–30

Zhang WB (2017a) Job discrimination against women and endogenous population change in a generalized Solow growth model. The USV Ann Econ Pub Admin 17:6–20

Zhang WB (2017b) Economic development and environmental change with endogenous birth and mortality rates. Asian J Econ Model 5:77–97

Zhang WB (2017c) Economic growth and structural change—a synthesis of the Walrasian general equilibrium, Ricardian distribution and neoclassical growth theories. Asian Dev Policy Rev 5:17–36

Zhang WB (2017d) Income and wealth distribution in a neoclassical two-sector heterogeneous-households growth model with elastic labor supply and consumer durable goods. Manage Econ Rev 2:101–117

Zhang WB (2017e) Discrimination and inequality in an integrated Walrasian-general-equilibrium and neoclassical-growth theory. Asian J Econ Model 5:57–76

Zhang WB (2017f) Social status and inequality in an integrated Walrasian-general equilibrium and neoclassical-growth theory. J Econ Dev 42:95–118

Zhang WB (2018a) Growth, research, and free trade with knowledge as global public capital. Econ Stud J 2018:37–66

Zhang WB (2018b) Nonlinear progressive income taxation and inequalities in income and wealth between heterogeneous households. Sci Bull Econ Sci 17:42–53

Zhang WB (2018c) An integration of Solow's growth and Dixit-Stiglitz's monopolistic competition models. SPOUDAI J Econ Bus 64:3–19

Zhang WB (2019a) A simple growth model based on neoclassical growth, monopolistic competition, and Walrasian general equilibrium theories. Int J Acad Res Bus Soc Sci 9:91005–91027

Zhang WB (2019b) Tax competition between regional governments and national and interregional economic growth. Soc Soc Work Rev 3:6–31

Zhang WB (2020a) Money and growth in a MIU-based Walrasian general equilibrium model. Montenegrin J Econ 7:7–20
Zhang WB (2020b) The general economic theory: an integrative approach. Springer International Publishing, Switzerland
Zhang WB (2020c) Monopsony and discrimination in labor market in the Solow-Stiglitz two-group neoclassical growth model. World J Appl Econ 6:1–19
Zhang WB (2020d) Global development, trade, human capital, and business cycles. Oradea J Bus Econ V(Special Issue): 9–29
Zhang WB (2020e) Creativity returns to scale, and growth with Solow, Dixit-Stiglitz, and Romer Integrated. Eastern J Econ Financ 5:1–16
Zhang WB (2020f) Increasing returns and economic geography with Solow, Dixit-Stiglitz, and Krugman unified. Spatial Econo 16:19–38
Zhang WB (2020g) Modelling global development and population dynamics with education. Slovak J Int Relat 18:208–240
Zhang WB (2021a) America the great and its self-destruction: viewing the superpower through the lenses of ancient Confucianism and chaos theory. Algora Publisher, New York
Zhang WB (2021b) A neoclassical growth model with endogenous birth and mortality rates. Economic Annals 66:99–125
Zhang WB (2021c) The butterfly effect in China's economic growth—from socialist penury towards Marx's progressive capitalism. Macmillan, London
Zhang WB (2023) Chaos, complexity, and nonlinear economic theory. World Scientific, Singapore
Zhang WB (2024a) A theory of interregional and international economics -integrating neoclassical growth theory and new economic geography. World Scientific, Singapore
Zhang WB (2024b) Trust and justice: complexity of man, complexity of society, and complexity theory. Lexington Books, Maryland
Zhang WB (2024c) Complexity theory and uncertainties: interdependence between man, society, and the environment. Springer International Publishing, Switzerland
Zhang WB (2024d) Han Feizi's political economic thought and leadership: impact on East Asia. Ethics International Press Limited, Bradford
Zhang WB (2025a) An economic theory of gender and population change—integrating neoclassical and new economic growth theory. Springer International Publishing, Switzerland
Zhang WB (2025b) A nonlinear dynamic theory of economic growth and environment change. World Scientific, Singapore
Zhang WB (2025c) A contemporary reading of Confucius in the light of the Yi Jing and complexity theory. Ethics International Press Limited, Bradford
Zhang WB (2026) A dynamic theory of tourism and economic growth. World Scientific, Singapore
Zhu R (2011) Individual heterogeneity in returns to education in urban China During 1995–2002. Econ Lett 113:84–87
Zidar OM (2019) Tax cuts for whom? Heterogenous effects of income tax changes on growth and employment. J Polit Econ 127:1437–1472
Zou HF (1994) The spirit of capitalism and long-run growth. Eur J Polit Econ 10:279–293
Zou HF (1995) The spirit of capitalism and savings behavior. J Econ Behav Organ 28:131–143

MIX
Papier aus verantwortungsvollen Quellen
Paper from responsible sources
FSC® C105338

If you have any concerns about our products,
you can contact us on
ProductSafety@springernature.com

In case Publisher is established outside the EU,
the EU authorized representative is:
Springer Nature Customer Service Center GmbH
Europaplatz 3, 69115 Heidelberg, Germany

Printed by Libri Plureos GmbH
in Hamburg, Germany